People and Rural Schools of Shelby County, Illinois

"If you find mistakes in this, please consider that they are there for a purpose. I publish something for everyone, and some people are always looking for mistakes!"

Helen Cox Tregillis

HERITAGE BOOKS
2010

HERITAGE BOOKS
AN IMPRINT OF HERITAGE BOOKS, INC.

Books, CDs, and more—Worldwide

For our listing of thousands of titles see our website
at
www.HeritageBooks.com

Published 2010 by
HERITAGE BOOKS, INC.
Publishing Division
100 Railroad Ave. #104
Westminster, Maryland 21157

Copyright © 1984, 2001 Helen Cox Tregillis

Other books by the author:
Ancestors: A Teaching Story Using the Families of Cox, Hayes, Hulse, Range, Worley and Others with Suggested Lessons
Central Illinois Chronicles, Volumes 1-3
Illinois, the 14th Colony: French Period
Indians of Illinois
People and Rural Schools of Shelby County, Illinois
River Roads to Freedom: Fugitive Slave Notices and Sheriff Notices Found in Illinois Sources
The Native Tribes of Ohio

All rights reserved. No part of this book may be reproduced or transmitted in any form or by any means, electronic or mechanical, including photocopying, recording or by any information storage and retrieval system without written permission from the author, except for the inclusion of brief quotations in a review.

International Standard Book Numbers
Paperbound: 978-0-7884-1722-1
Clothbound: 978-0-7884-8304-2

TABLE OF CONTENTS

Chapter One...Shelby County and the State...............1
Chapter Two...Shelby County School Superintendents.....5
              Joseph Oliver, Edward Evey, Samuel Moulton,
              Samuel F. King, Anthony Thornton Hall, Enoch
              McGrew, John Stapleton, Homer S. Mouser,
              William B. Marshutz, Milton B. Barbee, James
              A. Montgomery, Charles M. Fleming, Lee W.
              Frazer, Charles B. Guin, Otto O. Barker, W.
              Frank White, J. Kenneth Roney.
Chapter Three.Early Subscription Schools and Teacher
              Schedules......................................23
Chapter Four..People and Rural Schools of Shelby
              County...30
              Ash Grove......................................30
              Big Spring.....................................42
              Cold Spring and Herrick........................50
              Dry Point and Lakewood.........................64
              Flat Branch....................................75
              Holland and Clarksburg.........................84
              Moweaqua......................................101
              Oconee..105
              Okaw..111
              Penn..118
              Pickaway......................................122
              Prairie.......................................133
              Richland......................................141
              Ridge...148
              Rose..161
              Rural...171
              Shelbyville...................................178
              Todds Point...................................187
              Tower Hill....................................190
              Windsor.......................................199
Chapter Five..Teachers and Miscellaneous..............209
              1876 List of teachers.........................209
              1886 County Institute.........................210
              Rural Music Festival, 1935....................210
              A Big Thank You...............................211
              Late Additions................................212
                  Opal Brownlee, Jessie Landers, Lewis
                  D. Howe
Index

PREFACE

During the winter of 1935-36, an inventory was taken of the Shelby County courthouse and the records contained therein. Such an inventory was taken by the Illinois State Historical Records Survey and their survey included the contents of the superintendent of school's office. They noted, "All of the records of this office are kept in the office of the superintendent of schools on the second floor of the county building."

Their inventory was as follows with the earliest year given: distributive fund, one volume, 1916; state distributive fund, one volume, 1919; check register, one volume, 1935; teachers' receipts, one volume, 1939; non-high school district record, 2 volumes, 1917; record of teacher certificates, 5 volumes, 1894; teachers' permanent records, 3 volumes, 1914; state board certificate approvals, one volume, 1927; lists of Shelby County teachers, 206 pigeon holes, 1939; pupil records, one volume, 1927 to 1935; annual superintendent reports, one volume, 1913; county superintendent examination reports, one volume, 1914; trustees' annual report, one volume, 1916; school directory, one volume, 1939; township treasurers' bonds, two volumes, 1928; map and plat, one map, 1919.

Almost one hundred years of records were not accounted for; hence, the difficult task of gleaning, searching and gathering from other sources. Unfortunately, all of the above noted inventory was not existent in the remaining records presented to the local historical society when the office of the Shelby county superintendent of schools was finally disbanded in the 1960's. The main assortment consisted of pupil records beginning 1939 through the 1960's and a miscellaneous collection of Shelby county school directories 1924 through the 1960's.

Those country schools are the subject of this book. That is, a survey was made, as complete as possible to cover over a hundred years of school history and over 150 of the common schools of Shelby County which existed in operation from 1827 to 1948, when the consolidation of rural schools was finally completed. That is, the year 1948 was used by the author as the cut-off date and teacher of that year was used as "last" for that particular school even though another might have continued after 1948.

SHELBY COUNTY AND THE STATE

Chapter One

As early as 1787, the Northwest Ordinance included a statement on the schools and the means of an education.

In preparation for statehood in 1818, Illinois was to provide "section 16 in every township" for the use of schools. All this was stipulated by Congress before Illinois became a state.

Joseph Duncan, a Kentucky born hero of the War of 1812 and Senator from Jackson County, Illinois, drafted and introduced a bill for free schools and it was signed by Gov. Edward Coles in January, 1825. Section 1 stated: "...be it enacted by the people of the state of Illinois represented in the General Assembly, that there shall be established a common school or common schools in each of the counties of the state." (Ill.FactBk) The common schools which taught the 3 R's were to be open to every class of white citizens between the ages of 5 and 21 years of age. The schools' districts of each county were to be created by the county commissioners court. The commissioners court then would direct that each township was to elect at least three officers later known as township school trustees who were responsible for superintending schools, examining and employing teachers, leasing all land belonging to district, and reporting back to the county commissioners court. The districts were not to have any fewer than 15 families and those residents were in turn subject to a tax levy for the schools. That mandatory tax created problems.

In February, 1827 -- the same year that Shelby County was created -- an amendment was adopted which removed the requirement of mandatory tax -- "that no person should be taxed for school purposes without consent, but the persons residing in the limits of a school district should have the priviledge of subscribing for the establishment of the school and the rents and profits of any school lands within the boundaries of the townships were to be assigned and appropriated for the use of the school under the superintendence of trustees."

Such trustees then were responsible for the Shelby county's known few schools of the time -- the one at the Cold Spring settlement or Wakefield, and the other one near the present day Shelbyville. Moses Storey and Joseph Oliver were those early teachers in the county respectively.

In January, 1829, the legislature created the post of county school commissioner. He had no direct supervision of the county schools but mainly operated as an agent of the sale of school land, especially sections 16 or other school land in the counties. This job Joseph Oliver most certainly did. During the years 1831 to 1842, there were numerous transactions to raise money for Shelby County schools.

For the second Shelby county school commissioner -- Edward Evey --, his duties were increased by an act passed in 1845. Evey in his third year in office had to assume the responsibility of supervising the common schools in the county, examining and certifying teachers. On the state level, the secretary of state was charged with the administration of the various county commissioners from which he received annual reports.

Another change occurred in Evey's tenure. In 1847, the office of county school commissioner became elective for a two year term. Augustus French had become the Illinois governor the year before and one of his most important suggestions concerned the school law.

Illinois' school system was still not efficient or adequate. The Secretary of State did not have time to deal with administrating schools along with all his other duties. Finally a proposal was made and passed that a temporary appointed state school superintendent perform the functions until the next general election of 1855. The appointed superintendent was Ninian Edwards who prepared a bill which became law in 1858. His bill "really made the schools free by providing for a sufficient state and local tax for their support,.."(1881 History,Ill.Hist) "The essential points of this free school law were: (1) a school system based on law (2) a school free of all rates or charges against the children, their parents or guardians, and (3) the defraying of the expense of the free schools by a system of taxation both local and state, augmented by the income from the permanent school fund." (Hist.ofIll.)

Another crux in the Illinois school system was the lack of teacher training. For a number of years, organizations were trying to institute a teachers' normal school. It was not until the spring of 1857 that Judge S.W. Moulton, both state legislator and Shelby county school commissioner, introduced a bill providing for the creation of a normal school. Moulton had been born and schooled in the state of Massachusetts where they had an excellent training program for teachers in normal schools. In October 1857 at Bloomington, Illinois, 19 students, prospective teachers, were the first enrollees. The first class graduated in June, 1860. Thus the first state Normal University was begun.

During the Civil War years, there were no major changes in the school laws. Samuel F. King was the Shelby County school commissioner who presented annual reports to the county board of supervisors, one of which was made in the month of December, 1863. In it he stressed that the county should well be proud of her schools, even though many of the best teachers were called to serve in the war.

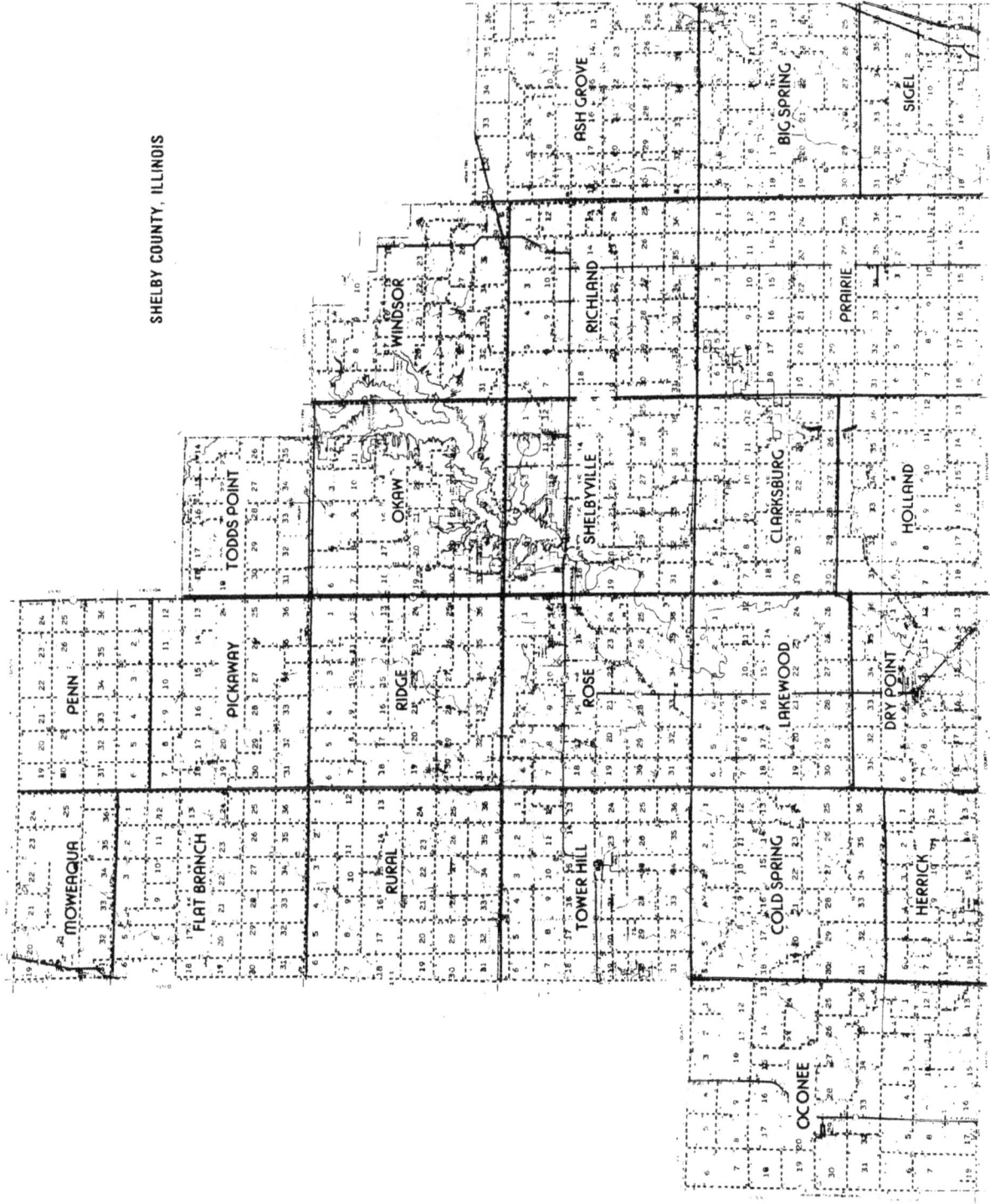

Anthony T. Hall, a young lawyer, became the first Shelby county superintendent of schools to be elected under the new law of 1865. The term was now four years. It was during Hall's years in office that the county board of supervisors fully supported the advancement of schools.

In essence, W. J. Boon who served on the county board of supervisors made the following resolution:

"That we recommend and favor the passage of a law by our State legislature that shall have for its object a system of compulsory education and that shall embody the following points. 1st. That all children between the ages of seven and fourteen years, not laboring under mental or physical disability, shall be compelled to attend a public school at least twelve weeks in each year. 2nd. That the supervisors of the several townships in counties under township organization and the board of county commissioners in counties not so organized may be empowered to furnish necessary books and clothing to indigent children for the purpose of enabling them to attend school. 3rd. That children who are taught in the rudiments of an English education at home or in a private school or who reside more than two miles from a public school shall be exempt from the provision of such law." The motion was tabled until the next meeting.

It was also during Hall's tenure, that the board proposed to support the teacher's normal institute by providing a committee to help the superintendent. Legislation of 1869 provided that the school directors were to allow school teachers to attend the teachers institute in the counties. However, that was not to be until the second successor to Hall, John Stapleton.

Thus, the county superintendent's role was finally established and maintained throughout the next century. More of their roles will be discussed in the next chapter on the county superintendents.

Shelby County townships became fully organized and named in 1860. Each township then had an average of nine school districts, most with four sections. Each district then had at least three elected trustees who were in charge of that particular school district.

Finally in the year 1870, the state of Illinois revised and ratified a new constitution which included ARTICLE VIII: Education. There were only five paragraphs or items required in the article.

"Number 1. The General Assembly shall provide a thorough and efficient system of free schools whereby all children of this State may receive a good common school education.

Number 2. All lands, moneys, or other property donated, granted or received for school, college, seminary or university purposes, and the proceeds thereof shall be faithfully applied to the objects for which such gifts or grants were made.

Number 3. Neither the General Assembly nor any county, city, town, township, school district or other public corporation shall ever make any appropriation, or pay from any public fund, whatever, anything in aid of any church or sectarian purpose, or to help support or sustain any school, academy seminary, college, university or other literary or scientific institution, controlled by any church or sectarian denomination whatever; nor shall any grant or donation of land, money, or other personal property ever be made by the State or any such public corporation to any church or for any sectarian purpose.

Number 4. No teacher, State, county township or district school officer shall be interested in the sale, proceeds or profits of any book, apparatus, or furniture, used or to be used in any school in this State, with which such officer or teacher may be connected, under such penalties as may be provided by the General Assembly.

Number 5. There may be a county superintendent of schools in each county, whose qualifications, powers, duties, compensation and time and manner of election and term of office shall be prescribed by law."

During 1870, there were 112 schools in Shelby County with 173 teachers. Seven thousand seven hundred and three youngsters attended school and the county contained 9,533 children of school age. Thus, 80.8 percent of the school-age children attended school in the county. Anthony T. Hall would have been the county superintendent who had submitted the report to the state.

Another major law which affected the county was the passage of 1905 which provided that any school district could establish a high school. An amendment was added in 1911 and by 1915 there were 7 high schools in Shelby County.

Finally in 1943, the major blow to the Shelby County small rural schools was the passing of the consolidation law. Not only did it effect Shelby County and her more than 160 rural schools, but it also hit the other 9900 one-room schools throughout the state. At the time of consolidation, the average class-room size was ten students.

The act of consolidation to amend sections 84b, 84c, and 84f of school law originally created in 1909 was finally approved July 23, 1943. Laws provided that county superintendents could hold elections for consolidation if at least 20 percent of the people in that area would sign a petition.

"The contigous territory bounded by school district lines, organized into a community consolidated school district, shall be regarded as a school district and the board of education thereof shall be endowed with the same powers and duties as boards of education elected in consequence of the general school law in common school districts having a population of 1,000 or more, and not exceeding 100,000 inhabitants..."84f

SHELBY COUNTY SCHOOL SUPERINTENDENTS FROM 1831 to 1943

Chapter Two

This chapter contains the biographies of the county officers for Shelby county schools from 1831 to 1943; that is, the years of small rural schools until the state law on school consolidation. Even though the county superintendent held office until the 1960's, this chapter, indeed, the book its self, contains only those superintendents who dealt directly or indirectly with the small country schools.

For Shelby County, the chief school officer was the county commissioner from 1831 to 1865, those being Joseph Oliver, Edward Evey, S.W. Moulton, and Samuel F. King, respectively. These commissioners' roles were essentially concerned with the dispensing of land or mortgages for county school funds.

In 1865, the office became changed to county superintendent with an elective term of four years, with a two year variation thrown in. Those county superintendents were Anthony T. Hall, Enoch McGrew, John Stapleton, Homer Mouser, William B. Marshutz, Milton Barbee, James A. Montgomery, Charles M. Fleming, Lee Frazer, Charles B. Guinn, O. O. Barker, W. Frank White and J. Kenneth Roney.

During the 1860's the role of county superintendent became broadened. He was required to visit all the townships in the county and inquire into the condition and manner of conducting their schools, to examine persons proposing to teach, to grant certificates to qualified persons and to report to the county board on all his acts relating to management of school funds.

Even though Shelby County began normal institutes for teachers as early as 1875, it was not required by law by the state until 1889.

Years later by the 1920's, the county superintendent was required to inspect with regard to specifications, plans submitted to him for the heating, ventilation, lighting, etc., of public school rooms and buildings; inspect and report on deficiencies. If the school house met all the requirements, then he would mark it a standard model.

Such notations of "standard" were printed by the schools' names in the county directories.

Thus the superintendent's role became widely expanded until the office was disbanded in the 1960's. For the superintendent, his duties included: selling township fund lands and issuing certificates of purchase; examining the complete accounts of every township treasurer in his county and report irregularities to the township trustees; conducting a teachers' institute, holding quarterly examinations for teacher's certificates and issuing such; holding examinations for normal and university scholarships, visiting the public schools in the county, observing methods of instruction, making recommendations to teachers, and advising school officers; observing sanitary and safety conditions, and notifying trustees and state authorities of unsatisfactory conditions; inspecting plans and specifications, and approving those meeting state regulations.

JOSEPH OLIVER
County Commissioner
1831 to 1843

Joseph Oliver was appointed school commissioner in 1831. He had been born in the state of Virginia in 1794, son of Captain William Oliver, a revolutionary soldier, and one of twelve children. He received a common school education--learned to read, write and cypher.

Oliver married in Fayette County in 1823 to Eliza Barthrick, daughter of Daniel Barthrick. He and Eliza had three children: Mary Jane, Benjamin and Eliza. His wife died in 1834, and Oliver married the second time, Sally Fearman, the next year. Sally and he had three children: William, Margery A. and Joseph.

During the term of office of Oliver, there were approximately ten schools in the county. For these schools, he had the responsibility of raising money and disposing of land for the schools' support. That policy of raising revenue was established in 1829 so that the state in return could also borrow money.

The years of 1835-36 must have been growing years for the county since transactions were plentiful for the school commissioner.

Individuals such as James Stuart, W.F. Thornton, M. M. Basye, Abs. Dollerhide, Baily Phillips, John Waggoner, Peter Miers, John D. Tanner, William M. Todd, John H. Todd, William Hall, Henry Hart, Lucian Minor, and so on, took out mortgages for various support of schools in their residential area.

Such a transaction usually read, "Know all men by these presents, that I, ____, of the county of Shelby and State of Illinois, do assign over and transfer to Joseph Oliver school commissioner and agent for the inhabitants of county of Shelby, for the use of the inhabitants of Township ___ North, Range ___ East, the following described real estate, that is to say, the _____, all in Township ____ North, Range ___ East, containing ___ acres, which real estate I declare to be in mortgages for the payment of ____ dollars, this day loaned to me by the said school commissioner, with 12 percent interest, per annum, thereon

JOSEPH OLIVER.

until paid, according to a certain promisory note, this day by me executed to the said Joseph Oliver, etc..."

The sale of land had to be authorized by the state of Illinois. Again the county commissioner was the county agent for such a transaction.

An example would be one made in October 1837 between Absolom Conner and the county or state. The certain lot of land in(Cold Spring township) T 10 N R 2 E was in section 16. Conner paid $1.25 an acre for 40 acres for the land from the state to raise revenue for schools.

Joseph Oliver lived until October 31, 1884, reaching the age of 90. His obituary appeared in the Shelbyville Democrat, the newspaper's local column.

EDWARD EVEY
County Commissioner
1843 to 1853

Edward Evey served as school commissioner for Shelby county from 1843 to 1853. His role would have been much the same as Joseph Oliver's -- disposing of property and raising mortgages for revenue for the county schools.

Evey came from Hagerstown, Maryland with his parents, Henry and Rebecca Livers Evey. He later married Laura Ann Durkee in 1840 and practiced law for a time before becoming a school commissioner. He married for a second time, Amanda E. Paulk in 1871. He had two daughters, Allis and Drucilla. Both he and his family early moved to California.

During his term of commissioner, he took mortgages from Daniel Downs in 1848, Ichabod Dodson in 1849, Samuel Egbert in 1841, John Morrison in 1845, Benjamin Overton in 1845 and Joseph Smith in 1846.

Again the land sold was authorized by the state of Illinois, usually in section 16 of each township.

William L. Donnel purchased 40 acres in section 16 of Ridge Township in 1849. He also purchased another 40 acres in section 16 in 1847.

In November 1850, J. A. McClanahan of township 9 north range 2 east (Cold Spring Township) submitted to Edward Evey, school commissioner, the biennial report of the two schools during that time period according "With the provisions of the 59th section of the act of the general assembly of the entitled, 'An act to establish and maintain common schools in townships approved February 12, 1849,..'" Both of the school houses were of log. This same area was to be later Herrick Township which was created from Cold Spring township.

SAMUEL MOULTON
County Commissioner
1853 to 1861

Samuel W. Moulton was born in Hamilton, Mass., in 1823, where he attended the common schools of Massachusetts. He left at the age of 20 years and travelled in the south for a number of years, working as a teacher. In 1844 he married Mary H. Affleck in Mississippi.

He came finally to Shelby county in 1850 or a short time before. Before in Coles County, Illinois, he studied law and was admitted to the bar.

In 1853 Moulton was elected to the state legislature and at the same time served as the county school commissioner of Shelby County. Moulton was appointed chairman of the committee on education. In the spring of 1857, he authored the bill and submitted it to the legislature, creating the first normal school for Illinois teachers. He was familiar with the good program of normal schools back in his home state of Massachusetts, and he used such a source for his proposal.

He served in the state legislature till 1858. Of all the records searched in Shelby County, his name appeared in the official capacity of county school commissioner in his suit entered against the estate of William Prentice, deceased. It seems that William Prentice had borrowed money in 1843 to the amount of $366.66 from the county schools then, promising to pay it back in 1845. William Prentice did not pay back the money and his heirs were sued for the money after he died.

In 1864, Moulton was elected to the 39th Congress from the state of Illinois at large, and in 1880, he was elected to the 47th Congress from the 15th Congressional district.

Moulton lived until 1905, and his widow died in 1921.

SAM'L W. MOULTON.

SAMUEL F. KING
County Commissioner
1861 to 1865

Samuel F. King was born in the state of Tennessee sometime around the year 1827. During the year 1850, he was living in Shelby county with James and Margaret Cutler, and his occupation was listed as a school teacher.

In 1856, he married Zenobia Kershner here in Shelby County, Illinois.

King had followed Samuel W. Moulton as county school commissioner. For him, he still had the duties of maintaining and selling real estate to support the schools of the county.

He also had the job of reporting to the county board of supervisors at the end of the year to indicate the state or condition of the school system. He made and wrote such a report on the 3 December 1863. He presented the paper to the county clerk Burrel Roberts for later release to the county board.

He began thus: "Sirs: I herewith present my report of conditions of schools in this county for the year commencing Oct. 1st, 1862 and ending Sept. 30th, 1863.

It is with infinite pleasure that I am able to say that not withstanding the unfortunate and perplexing state of the country, the fearful war in which we are engaged, the number of first class teachers which have been called into the same and the great, the injurious excitement which is a consequence of such a crisis, yet the condition of the schools in your county will compare well with any former period.

It should cheer us all to see with what alacrity the people enter into the labor of erecting and repairing school houses and other duties incident to the education of the young. And if it be true as said by the Hon. J. P. Brookes, Supv., that 'the want of a general diffusion of knowledge among the masses is the CAUSE of the present rebellion' -- how ardently should all patriots and Christians seek to establish good schools in the county.

It may be said that with few exceptions politics and sectionalism have been avoided in the schools of your county; and it is recommended that your Hon. Board pass a resolution (having the same published) requesting Boards of Directors to follow the example of the Board of Education of Chicago, banishing these subjects entirely from the school room. It is confidently believed that such an expression coming from the highest authority of our county, would have a happy influence with school officers.

Patriotism, morality and the eternal truths of the Bible may be taught by a discriminating teacher, but politics, the peculiar doctrine of parties and sects should never be.

Amt. of cash of hand and received from all sources from Oct. 1st, 1862 to Sept. 30, 1863 was $ 7187.39
    Amt. paid to treasurer   6839.58
    Amt. int. 2 percent on 7187.39   143.74
    Amt. per diem 100 days visiting schools   200.00
    Amt. for paper   3.50
    Whole amt. paid out   7186.82
    Amt. on hand   62.50

I certify that I spent in labor under section 20 of the School Law one hundred days.

                             Samuel F. King, Comm.

The above is presented with my great respect to the consideration of the your Hon. Board by
                S. F. King
                School Commissioner
                Shelby County, Illinois

Sworn to and subscribed before me this 3rd day of December 1863. B. Roberts, Clerk"

ANTHONY THORNTON HALL
County School Superintendent
1865 to 1872

Anthony T. Hall was born circa 1840 in Tennessee. He was a nephew to Anthony Thornton, a prominent individual in Illinois state and local government of Shelby county.

Like his uncle, Hall had entered the profession of law. He was only about 18 years of age when he came to Shelby County in 1858.

By 1864, Hall had become widely known among the county, and ran as a candidate for the office of county school superintendent, the first year an election was held for the post. He won.

The first month in office, January 1865, he requested funds from the county board for stationery, revenue stamps and other supplies.

From then on, he submitted his pay request to the county board each month at the pay rate of $3 per day in 1865-66, and $5 per day by 1868, usually a maximum of 90 to 100 workdays a year.

As superintendent, Hall also had the task of placing before the board, any recommended individual who would be a suitable candidate for the Normal School for teachers. Such an individual was Edward A. Campbell whom Hall felt met the qualifications, and the board approved Campbell "as a suitable person to become a pupil in said university, from Shelby County, Ill., the same being a representative district."

In November 1871, Hall submitted his resignation effective the April 1872. He had been re-elected in 1868, and the board had decided then to create a committee to help the superintendent hold teacher institutes for the county. The county board commended him for the manner in which he reacted to their action on the resignation.

Later in a hunting trip that fall of 1872 with George Chafee, Hall became ill and died two to three days later at the age of 32.

ENOCH MCGREW
County School Superintendent
1873 to 1873

Enoch A. McGrew was born circa 1835 in Indiana. He was a lawyer in Shelbyville in partnership with Homer S. Mouser.

When Hall resigned in April 1872, as county superintendent of schools, the board had the task of filling the vacancy until the next election late that year.

Board members submitted the names of McGrew, along with Thomas J. Fritts, Homer S. Mouser, John C. Woods, M.D. Lane, N. Williams and R. T. Holloway.

McGrew was finally declared elected on the fifth ballot, defeating Homer S. Mouser by 5 votes, and Thomas J. Fritts by 9 votes. McGrew acted as superintendent until the election. That was the length of his service as county school superintendent.

Afterward, he continued practicing law until his death in 1878 at the age of 47. He lies buried alone in Glenwood Cemetery.

JOHN STAPLETON
County School Superintendent
1873 to 1877

John Stapleton was born in the state of Indiana circa 1844. He came to Shelby County around 1851 with his wife and son Joseph. By 1870, he had two more children, Nancy and William.

Stapleton was elected county superintendent of schools of Shelby County in the spring election of 1873, after the temporary term of Enoch A. McGrew.

To take office, Stapleton took out a bond of $12 thousand for his office and it was witnessed by N. P. McNutt, Paschal Hinton and William Pope, on the 20th day of November 1873. In that bond, Stapleton agreed to "faithfully discharge all the duties of said office according to the laws which now are or may thereafter be in force, and shall deliver over to his successor in office all money, books, papers, and property in his hands as such county superintendent then this obligation to be void; otherwise to remain in full force and virtue."

In January 1874, the county board was inquiring for office space for the county superintendent, and finally selected a room on Main Street over W. Wesley Hall's shoe store which leased for $40 per year, and Stapleton agreed that such space would be adequate for his use. However, a year later, the board directed Stapleton to move to the seminary building so that Stapleton would have sufficient room to administer examinations for teachers. The contract with Hall was rescinded.

Stapleton made his annual report to the county board ending Sept. 1874. He included general statistics for the county schools:

```
"No. of persons under 21 years of age    16,132
 No. of persons between 6 and 21          10,466
 No. of persons enrolled  males 4008
                          females 3638     7,696
 Grand total of days attendance          550,344
 Average percent of attendance                72
 No. districts having no school                1
 No. districts having libraries                2
```

```
      No. school houses      Frame  123
                             Brick    6
                             Log     15    144
              Financial Statistics
   Treasurers receipts                  $12,749.51
      Balance on hand Oct. 1, 1874       11,240.05
      State funds from county supt.       3,699.22
      Interest on Township funds
      Special district taxes             41,677.63
      Other sources                         760.34
         Total                          $70,126.75
   Total payments                        55,278.71
   Bal in hands of treasurer             70,126.75"
```

Later Stapleton had trouble collecting his salary from the county board, and it was backlogged for over a year. Apparently, the difficulty arose over his number of days on duty which was not set by law by the state or the local board.

The first county institute was held by Stapleton the summer of 1875. The local board under the proposal of Thomas J. Fritts commended Stapleton for "successfully conduct (ing) a 'normal school' in this city with view of bringing a higher standard to the art of teaching." Professors McCormick and DeGarmo of the state Normal school were speakers during that year.

On a petition dated 22 August 1876, all the names of the county teachers were included in a request to the county board stating:

"Whereas it is the duty of the county superintendent to give such directions in the science,.art and methods of teaching as he may deem expedient and necessary; to be the official adviser and constant assistant of the school officers and teachers of his county; to labor in every practicable way to elevate the standard of teaching and improve the condition of the common schools of his county; and if so directed by the county board, visit, at least once in each year, every school in his county, to note the methods of instruction, the branches taught, the textbooks used, and the discipline, government and general condition of the schools, and, (School Law Section 20); Whereas, we believe it to be for the best interest of our schools, Therefore, we the school teachers of Shelby County, do hereby direct our county superintendent to visit, as far as practiceable, the schools of this county, at least once during the ensuing year." One hundred and six teacher signed their names to that petition.

During the early spring of 1877, Stapleton held the teachers examinations in the old seminary building, in eight different sessions beginning at 8:30 a.m. each day. During that same year, the third institute of Stapleton's was held for the county teachers under the direction of Professor Henry McCormick of the state Normal school and Professor E. P. Murdock of Chicago and principle elect of Shelbyville Graded schools. The textbooks used for the institute were: Edward's readers, Harvey's grammar, any good geography, Ray's arithmetic, Anderson's history, Gray's botany, Hooker's phsiology, Tenney's zoology, Cooley's philosophy, and Page's theory and practice for school economy.

HOMER S. MOUSER
County School Superintendent
1877 to 1882

Homer S. Mouser was born circa 1843 in Marion Co., Ohio, and graduated from Ohio Wesleyan University where he received BA and MA degrees.

After he came to Shelby County, he studied law with Henry and Read of Shelbyville. He was admitted to the bar in 1869 and entered partnership with E. A. McGrew.

In the election of 1877, he defeated John Stapleton by 1028 majority votes. Before he was elected, he had lost his first wife, and two children, who are all buried in the Glenwood Cemetery. He married second a sister of Jeff Brewster of Shelbyville.

He served only one term as superintendent of schools and moved with his family to Huron, South Dakota.

Homer Mouser wrote a letter to Jasper Douthit who published the letter in the newspaper of Our Best Words. Written in 1889, the letter contained information about prohibition and the republican convention in South Dakota.

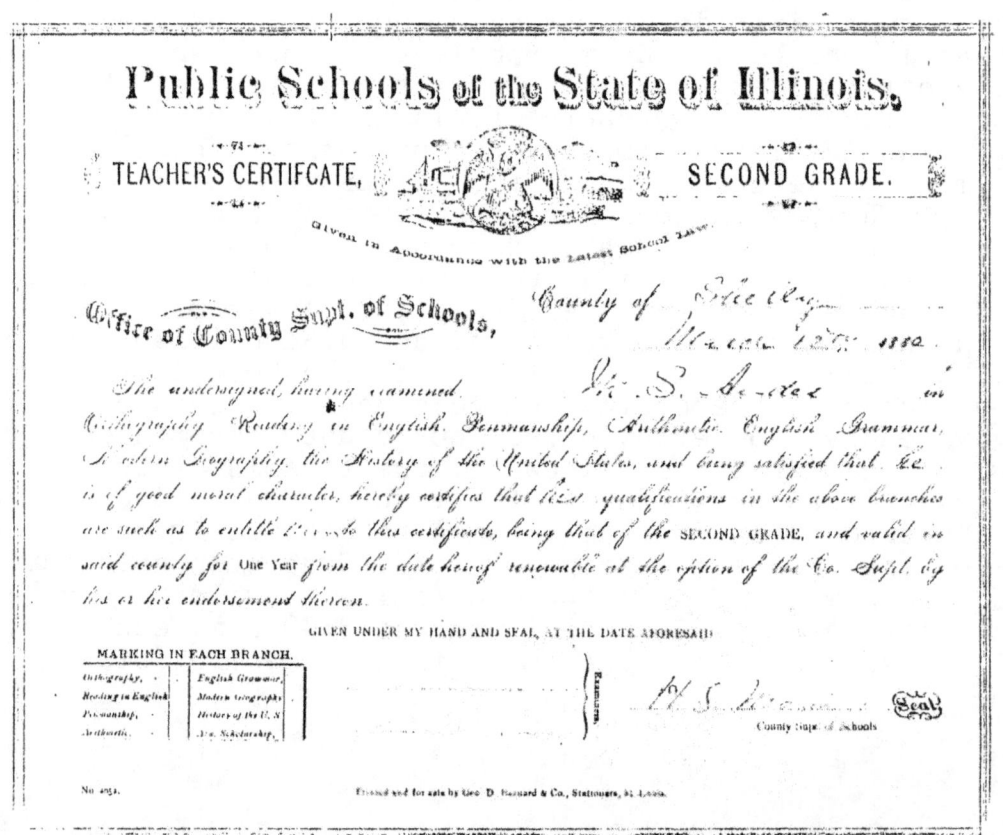

WILLIAM B. MARSHUTZ
County School Superintendent
1882 to 1886

William B. Marshutz was born in Bavaria on the 1 Sept. 1848 and came to the United States in 1862. For a time he worked in Hopkinsville, Kentucky before he came to Shelbyville in 1869.

He worked as a bookkeeper for three years at Kleeman and Goldsteins, a department store, a local editor for the Shelby County Leader, a newspaper for two years, and finally owned a store in partnership with his brother-in-law, James D. Hunter. He had married 28 May 1873 Ella Hunter.

In 1879 he was appointed public administrator by Gov. Collum of Illinois. Later, Marshutz in 1881 was elected as county superintendent of schools. He served in that capacity for one term.

Apparently the law governing the county superintendent's number of days required on duty was not clear to the local authorities for in a letter written by Marshutz to the editor of Our Best Words on 8 November 1890 read: (NOTE: All the preceding county superintendents also had trouble collecting their salaries from the county board.)

"In stating your objections in your paper to the re-election of County Superintendent Barbee, you, as a matter of comparison mentioned my name. Mr. Levi Corley in answering your objections, appears in your columns, as drawing my name into the controversy also, I have expressed to you personally and also to Mr. Corley, my protest against this. Being a private citizen, seeking no political preferment, I maintain that my name should be own private property and not be used in newspapers to advance or to detract the aspiration of any one seeking public office.

But since it has been stated that while I occupied the office of County Superintendent of schools, I made the same claims (and that they were allowed by the board of supervisors) that Mr. Barbee made, and which were rejected, and for which he entered suit against the county, I want to say that this is a misrepresentation as far as it alludes to me.

While I was superintendent, the law binding the present superintendent did not govern me. An examination of the session laws of Illinois 1885 (pages 240 and 241) will disclose to any one the fact, that section 71 of what is commonly known as the school law, (enacted on June 26, 1885,) allowing the superintendent $5 per diem for visiting schools, compelling him to report to the county board, etc., etc., only went into effect upon the election of the future

superintendent, viz. after the election of 1886, after expiration of my term of office. Section 20 of the same law enacted at the same time went into effect at once and it took the power away from the board to limit the number of days that should be allowed to the superintendent and directed said officer to visit schools, etc. When, therefore, anyone asserts that the board allowed me any claim that they refused to allow to my successor in office, or that I ever presented any claim for time not expended in the service of the county as prescribed by law, he simply guessed at something of which he had no knowledge. And may I be permitted to add, Mr. Editor, that any one attempting to instruct the public by publishing statements in newspapers should first inform himself as to facts, so that he may be sure to state the truth.
Very respectively,
Wm. B. Marshutz"

MILTON B. BARBEE
County School Superintendent
1886 to 1894

Milton Barbee was born in Ross County, Ohio circa 1855, son of Hazel and Phoebe Ann Clayton Barbee. He attended early school in Holland township, Shelby County, and later attended Shelbyvile High School.

In 1879-80, he was a medical student and boarded with John Casey in Shelbyville. He studied law in the law firm of Moulton, Chafee and Headen, and was admitted to the bar in 1885.

He married Maria B. Barrickman in 1882, and by 1890, they had two daughters and one son. He only worked as a lawyer for a year when he ran for election in 1886 for the county school superintendent's office. He served in that capacity for three terms.

Barbee submitted his reports to the county board of supervisors, on his visits to the county schools. On his reports dated 15 January 1889 and 8 July 1889, he had visited most the schools in the county and he listed them by name and date of visitation. On the one following year, he merely listed all the schools by district number.

In 1888, he held final examination for pupils at the Shelbyville High School, where pupils were to have an average of 79 or better to write for the test.

Professor A. T. Stone of Du Qoin and T.E. Cleland of Washburn and R.S. Hill of Galena were the guest speakers for the normal institute held by Barbee in 1890.

Barbee held the Shelby County normal for the teachers for four weeks during the year of 1891, which he had done each year of his office.

Also during his term of office, he would have printed lists of teachers and their respective schools issued to the county.

By 1917, Milton and Maria Barbee were still living in Shelbyville, where Milton was an insurance agent.

MILTON BARBEE

JAMES A. MONTGOMERY
County School Superintendent
1894 to 1902

James A. Montgomery was born in Park County, Indiana, the son of Dr. John and Mariah Barbara Allen Montgomery.

He married Georgia A. Carpenter here in Shelby County. He attended Lincoln University, Lincoln, Ill., and Westminister College, Fulton, Mo. He taught for a period of fourteen years, half of that time in Indiana and half in Shelby County.

He taught in 1876-77; taught three years in the Windsor Graded school, two of which he was principal. He also had charge of the schools in Stewardson for two years.

He was elected to the office of county superintendent of schools in 1894 and served two terms.

In 1917, James and Georgia Montgomery were living in Shelbyville, where he was still a teacher and a coroner. He died in 1926 and left surviving his wife, one daughter and three sons.

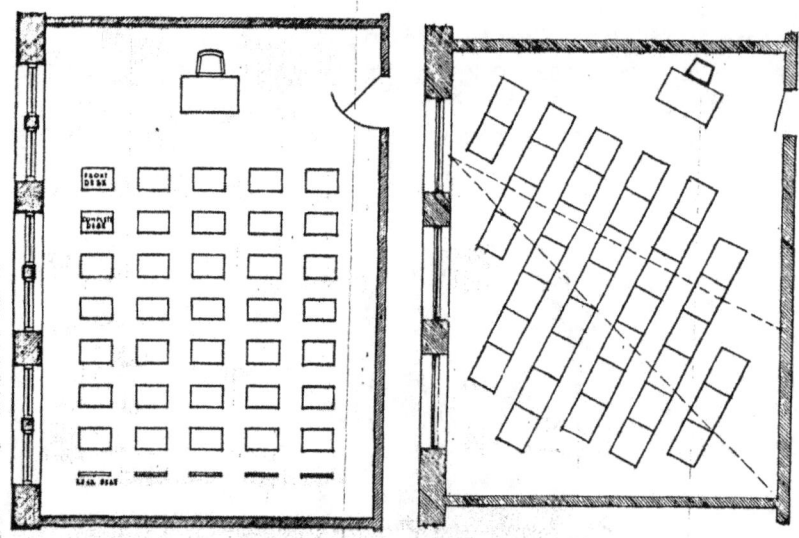

A better arrangement is that shown at the right. The lighting from the left is faultless. The only objection that can be raised is that "it looks strange." The pupils' eyes and ease of labor are of more importance than "looks."   Rural Schools of Illinois-1929.

CHARLES M. FLEMING
County School Superintendent
1902 to 1910

Charles M. Fleming was born in Shelby County, the son of Samuel W. and Mary Jane Fraker Fleming. During his early days, he attended East Salem school southeast of Shelbyville.

After graduate from high school, Mr. Fleming taught school at Sandy Hill in Rose Township, before he entered State Normal School in 1884. He graduated in 1889, and became principal at Cowden Public Schools in 1890. He became ill and had to resign that position.

In 1896 he became principal of Stewardson schools, and before that, he had married in 1885, Miss Anna M. Ruch, daughter of John and Magdalene Vulmer Ruch. They had four children: Roy C., Homer R., Mary J., and Joseph A. who died young.

Fleming became county superintendent of schools in 1902 and served in that capacity for two terms.

Besides visiting schools all over the county, auditing books, and assessing teachers, Fleming issued a monthly Shelby County School News whose purpose was to "keep the teachers and school officers of the county as close in touch with other and with the office of the county superintendent as possible in order that all may work in harmony and to the best interests of all concerned..."

For 1908, Fleming made the following annual report to the State Superintendent: (partial excerpt)

"No. of boys in county under 21   6929
 No. of girls in county under 21   6510
   Total number under 21   13,439
 ...Highest monthly wages paid
     1907-08 $166.66
   Highest monthly wage paid in
     country school $70
   Lowest monthly wages paid in
     village school $30
   Lowest monthly wages paid in
     country school $20
   Average monthly wages for men   57.40
   Average monthly wages for women 42.11"

LEE W. FRAZER
County School Superintendent
1910 to 1918

Lee W. Frazer was born 1863 in Shelby County, the son of Lewis A. and Rebecca Rankin Frazer. His ancestors had long been in Shelby County in the Ash Grove, Windsor area.

Frazer became the superintendent of schools in 1911, succeeding Charles M. Fleming. He continued the tradition of the Shelby County School Bulletin, issued from the superintendent's office.

Earlier Frazer had taught at Grove school in Ash Grove, served as assessor of Windsor and Richland townships, village clerk of Strasburg, teacher of high school in Windsor and principal at Strasburg.

In November 1911, he announced the mid-winter teacher's meeting on the topic of discussion, and the meeting was to be at the new high school building in Shelbyville on Friday, Dec. 1. He urged every teacher in the county to attend and learn more about the art of monitoring discussion in the classroom. The institute was lead by Professors John M. Forsythe, H. D. Sparks, William Harris, A. F. Lyle, O. C. Bailey, and R. H. Butler.

August 14-18 was the week for the county institute in 1911, led by Supt. Frazer. The week was tried rather than a longer period of two weeks as accustomed over the many years previous. During the week, the teachers had a daily schedule of orthography, reading, history of Illinois, music, bookkeeping, arithmetic, agriculture, grammar, etc.

CHARLES B. GUIN
County School Superintendent
1918 to 1922

Charles B. Guin was born in 1875, the son of Ervin J. and Eunice Riggins Guin. He married Ivy E. Rose, daughter of J. R. P. and Clarinda Baker Rose in 1905.

Charles had attended Rose school, Windsor township, as a boy and had T. L. Hilsabeck as a teacher. His younger brother Willie also attended school there.

Guin became a school teacher, teaching in various schools of the county, one of which was Banner school in Windsor township in 1897-98.

In 1918 he was elected to the office of the county superintendent of schools. He served one term till the next election in Nov. 1922, when Otto O. Barker became superintendent.

Guin held the institute in 1919 for June 23 to 27 to be held at the Shelbyville High School building. There was to be a full daily program of lectures by Miss Clara C. Schum of Carlinville, William Harris of Shelbyville, G. P. Randle superintendent of Danville schools, and James M. Matheny, educational lecturer of Indianapolis.

For 1922, Guin reported that there were 260 teachers in the county with an average salary of $899 per year. There were 74 men teachers and 186 women teachers. For the men the average salary was $1135 and for the women, $805.

Guin then served as principal of the high school at Findlay for a number of years. Besides being the principal, he usually taught math or science in the high school there, from 1924 to at least 1935-36.

OTTO O. BARKER
County School Superintendent
1922 to 1927

Otto O. Barker was born in 1869, the son of J. R. and Alice Hart Barker. He was one of six children: Callie, Irma, Jay, Bertha, Ferne and O. O.

Barker served as a teacher for many years and served one term as county superintendent of schools from 1922 to 1927. Previously he had served as assistant county superintendent under Lee Frazer.

For the county's schools, he reported in June 1926 that there were 173 school districts in the county, and 154 of them were rural. Some of those schools he classified as being standard according to state requirements. During that time there were 5014 girls under the age of 21 and 5307 boys under the age of 21 in the county.

Barker taught at West Salem school in Shelbyville township in 1935-36.

He was active in church and civic affairs. He died in 1955 and was buried in Glenwood Cemetery.

W. FRANK WHITE
County School Superintendent
1927 to 1938

W. Frank White was born July 1874, the son of Ulysses and Eliza Ann Tull White. He married in 1902 Lura Mae Williams, and had one daughter Clytheria Glean who died early.

White was a graduate of Austin College in Effingham in 1900. He taught in Shelby County for many years before he became county superintendent in 1927. He served three terms.

When he took office that first fall, his salary for the year was $2600. He likewise made annual reports. For one of the institutes, the guest speakers were Dr. W. P. Dearing, president of Oakland Independent City college and Samuel Grathwell, explorer and scholar.

To the newspaper in the late twenties or early thirties, he reported, "Today Shelby County has 154 rural one-room schools, 13 high schools, 5 parochial schools and 14 city schools.

The average attendance of the rural schools is about 15 pupils. The rural school having the largest attendance is Fancher, 37 pupils, Mrs. Florence E. Allen of Shelbyville; school having smallest attendance is Roley, 3 pupils, Warren C. Williams, Mode, teacher..."

A later check of the school directories indicated that the above report was made in 1934. White also "felt that some day the schools in this county would be consolidated, but expressed his belief that it would not be for a number of years as the present system of roads would render transportation of school buses impossible during months of winter and spring."

White died in 1966 and left his widow Lura surviving.

Co. Supt. of Schools office in courthouse

Left to right: Oscar Storm, Frank White, Opal Banks Perry, and E.P. Chapman

J. KENNETH RONEY
County School Superintendent
1938 to 1950

J. Kenneth Roney was born in Dalton City, the son of John Schoolfield and Josephine Reeder Roney. In 1935 he married Bess Ressler and had no children.

Roney attended college and became an elementary school teacher. He had attended school at the University of Illinois where he obtained both a bachelors and a masters degree in elementary education.

For a time, Roney was principal of the Main Street School, 1934-36, in Shelbyville, before he decided to run for the county superintendent of schools against W. Frank White.

In February 1938, Roney presented a program to the Kiwanis Club on the modern trends of education. He used two of his students to help him with the presentation.

In November of that year was the election, and Roney included his political ad in the local newspapers. In one of his particular ads, he stressed local control of the schools, recognition of the rural schools by the state, public accounting of all money expended by the office, a rural school directors association, and more funds from the state and federal levels for the schools.

Roney served as superintendent of schools for twelve years. He lived until 1977 and was buried in Glenwood Cemetery in Shelbyville.

ELECT

J. Kenneth

RONEY

Democratic Candidate For
COUNTY
SUPERINTENDENT
OF SCHOOLS
OF
SHELBY COUNTY
General Election
Tuesday, November 8, 1938

EARLY SUBSCRIPTION SCHOOLS AND TEACHER SCHEDULES 1841 to 1856
Chapter Three

Among various materials of court records and supervisors records were isolated teacher schedules which were saved for some reason or another. They were few in number, that is, the original copies found that were turned into the county office for record or collection for the subscription fees.

The townships were not fully organized until 1859-1860 when they were finally named and the location boundaries spelled out. Following the location of the schools therein, the name of the present township is given in parentheses.

The entire document found is being quoted so as to preserve the information thereon and make known the method that a teacher reported.

Document No. 1

State of Illinois, Shelby County: We, the undersigned, certify that we are school directors of District 2 in Township 11 Range 5 East (Richland Township) in the county aforesaid, that we have performed the duties of directors, that we have carefully examined the foregoing schedule, and find the same to be correct, that the scholars named therein, were, at the dates of their attendance, residents of district no. 2 in Township 11 Range East and that is due to the said teacher for instructing the scholars therein named at the times therein mentioned, the sum of $11 dollars and 55 cents. We also certify that the said teacher exhibited to us a legal certificate of qualification and good moral character before he was employed to teach said school, and that said school was an English one, in which the English language was the medium of communication. Witness our hands, this 27th day of September 1849.

                      John Renshaw, Abner Poe
                              Directors

Schedule of a common school kept by Michael Ramsey in district 2 Township 11 N R 5 East for the Range 6 East of the third principal meridian in the county of Shelby and state of Illinois.

Names of scholars attending my school, and residing in district 2 in Township 11 Range 6 East of the third principal meridian in Shelby County August 13, 1849 to September 24, 1849.

James Cochran	Calvin Clawson	Hiram C.P. Barker
Jane McKinsey	Daniel Clawson	Daniel W. Barker
Jefferson Cochran	James Clawson	Samuel Parks
Robert Evens	Hiram Storm	William Morgan
Julia Ette Evens	John H. Stradly	George Morgan
Nancy Jane Evens	Malinda Jane Nolen	Levi Clawson
John Clawson	Mary Eveline Nolen	Jessey L.B. Ellis
William Evert Clawson	Elizabeth Barker	Nancy Jane Clawson

Sarah Ann Clawson.

I certify that the foregoing schedule of scholars attending my school as therein named, and residing as specified in said schedule to the best of my knowledge and belief is correct, that it was a school for the purpose of teaching various branches of an English education, and that the common medium of communication in said school was the English language.   Michael Ramsey, teacher

Witnessed Sept. 27, 1849 by
Joseph M. Brown, J.P.

NOTE: Michael Ramsey is not listed in the 1850 Shelby County census. He was either missed by the census taker or already gone from the county. Most of these students lived in the northwest area of Ash Grove Township.

Document No. 2

State of Illinois, Shelby County: We, the undersigned, school trustees of Township Ten Range Two (Cold Spring Township) in the county aforesaid certify that we have examined the foregoing schedule and find the same to be correct and that the school was conducted according to law, there is now due the said S. H. Perryman the sum of thirty four dollars fifty three and one third cents and the said teacher has a certificate of qualification and good moral character. Witness our hands this the 28th day of September 1850.   Charles McKay, Hanson Middleton
school trustees

Schedule of a common school taught by S. H. Perryman in Township 10 Range 2 in the county of Shelby and State of Illinois May the 6th 1850.

Names of scholars attending my school and residing in Town Ten Range Three, May 6th, 1850.   May 6, 1850 to August 2, 1850.

Charles Wakefield	Elizabeth Williams	Andrew Wakefield
Miranda Wakefield	Susan Foster	Allen Wakefield
Sarah Wakefield	Calvin Foster	Mariah Wakefield
Mary Wakefield	John Foster	Rachel Wakefield
James Perryman	James Beck	Silas Perryman
Julia Perryman	Nancy Beck	Pernetta Hall
Charles Ploughman	Thos Beck	Jonathon Hall
Sarah Utterback	William Beck	Mary Hall
James Williams		

I certify that the foregoing schedule of scholars
attending my school as therein named and residing as
therein specified to the best of my knowledge is correct
that it was a school for the purpose of teaching an
English education and that the common medium of communication
in said school was the English language.
                              S. H. Perryman, teacher
NOTE: S. H. Perryman must have been Henry Perryman who
      was 17 in the year 1850. Silas was his younger
      brother.

Document No. 3

State of Illinois, Shelby County: We the undersigned
school directors in district no. 3 in Township 9 Range
3 East in the county aforesaid certify that we have
examined the foregoing schedule and find the same to be
correct and that the school was conducted according to
law. There is now due the said A. V. Perryman, the sum
of $6.51, and that said teacher has a legal certificate
of good moral character and of qualifications to teach
a common school. Witness our hands this 13th day of
July 1850. Samuel Akins, James Sanford, John Fletcher,
                school directors
Schedule of a common school kept by A. V. Perryman
in district 3 Township 9 Range 3 East in the county of
Shelby and state of Illinois (Dry Point Township).
Names of scholars attending my school and residing
Township Ten Range 3 East Shelby County and State of
Illinois   April 10, 1850 to July 5, 1850

Melinda Stripling	Sarah Jones
Fanny Stripling	Samuel Jones
Jackson Stripling	Nathan Jones
Nancy Jones	Bird Hall
Martha Jones	Lemuel Atkins
Richard Jones	Elizabeth Atkins

I certify that the foregoing schedule of scholars
attending my school as therein named and residing as
specified in said schedule to the best of my knowledge
and belief is correct that it was a school for the purpose
of teaching various branches of an English education and
that the common medium of communication in said school
was the English language.   A.V. Perryman, teacher

Document No. 4

I certify the foregoing to be correct schedule of a common
school kept in Township 11 North Range 4 East of the 3rd
principal meridian in which the foregoing scholars attended
from Township 11 North Range 5 East (Richland Township)

of the third principal meridian, said school commencing on the 5th day of April 1841, that each scholar attended the number of days attached to each of these named in the abstract given under my hand and seal this 30th day of June 1841   William O. Kelly, teacher

Jane Balch	John T. Walden
Monroe Balch	Silvester N. Balch
John T. Balch	Louisa Ann Walden
Felix M. Balch	Hugh N. Walden
Benjamin Walden	Alexander Rose

NOTE: No William O. Kelly is listed on the 1850 census of Shelby County.

Document No. 5

State of Illinois, Shelby County: We, as school directors in township 11 range 3 (Rose Township) in the county aforesaid, certify that we have examined the foregoing schedule and find the same to be correct and that the school was conducted according to law. There is now due the said Elias Corley, as per contract, the sum of $17.45 2/3, and that said teacher has a legal certificate of good moral charcacter and of qualifications to teach a common school. Witness our hand this 3rd day of October 1850.
    Briant Corley, school director

Schedule of a common school kept by Elias Corley township 11 North Range 3 east the third principal meridan in the county of Shelby and state of Illinois.

Names of scholars attending my school in Township 11 North Range 3 East   January 1850 and September 1850

Anson Hall	Mary Poteet	Robert Drenen
Wesley Hall	Nancy A. Fisher	Caroline Bowman
Isaac Hall	Mary Miller	Samuel Barrett
James Peek	Mary Peek	William Boldman
Thomas Peek	Margaret Peek	Rebeckah Boldman
L. H. Sutton	John Fisher	John Drenen
Elias Sutton	Caleb Bowman	Leah Barrett
Samantha Sutton	Isem Bowman	Mary R. Barrett
Nicholas Page	Joseph Drenen	Rachel Barrett
Wm. W. Page	James W. Drenen	William Easton
William Fisher	James Fisher	Cyram Drenen
William Drenen	Asbury Hall	Ruhama Boldman
	Luvena Drenen	

I certify that the foregoing schedule of scholars attending my school therein named and residing as specified in said schedule to the best of my knowledge is correct. That it was a school for the purpose of teaching various branches of an English education, and the common medium of communication in said school was the English language.

Elias Corley, teacher

NOTE: According to the 1850 census, Elias Corley was the son of Briant Corley, and was 21 years old at the time.

Document No. 6

Schedule of a common school kept by Walter Herron at Prentiss's school house in Township Eleven North Range Four East of the third principal meridian in the county of Shelby in the state of Illinois.
Names of scholars residing in township 11 north range 4 east (Shelbyville Township). February 16,1845 to March, 1845

Hiram Drenning   Amanda Jane Parish
Robert Drenning   Lucinda Ellen Austin
Alexander Austin   Henry Austin
Adaline Harmon   Caroline Renshaw

I certify that the foregoing schedule of the names of the scholars therein named, residing in township eleven north range four east of the third principal meridian, is correct.
Given under my hand, this 6th day of April in the year of our Lord, one thousand eight hundred and forty six.

Walter Herron

NOTE: Prentice school was either the top floor of the log cabin courthouse or there was a separate building at this early date for school in Shelbyville.

Document No. 7

County of Shelby, State of Illinois: Scholars attending my school and living in township 11 N R 4 E in the county of Shelby and state of Illinois from April 1st to Aug. 2, 1850 (Shelbyville Township).
I do certify that the parents or guardians of the children whose names are on this abstract are debters to me per said children's tuition $37.86 3/4.

Sam'l F. King, teacher

Isabella Beattie   Laura Wagoner   Levi Mathias
Mary J. Beattie   Malinda Bryant   Mary Mathias
Sarah A. Beattie   Lidia Bryant   Narcissus Garner
B. Green   Sarah E. Bryant   Letith Garner
William Green   Jno. Fraser   Fo. Garner
David Henson   Helen Fraser   Jas. Garner
Jno. Henson   Thos. Fraser   Nathan Garner
Sarah Henson   Jane Waymire   Mary Harmon
Julian Henson   Harriet Waymire   William Page
Sarah Wagoner   James Waymire   Christiana Clements
Stephen Wagoner   Belinda Mathias   America Clements

I certify that the foregoing abstract of scholars attending my school, as therein named, and residing as therein specified to the best of my belief is correct; that it was a school for the purpose of teaching various branches in an English education and that the medium of communication in said school was the English language.
      Sam'l F. King, teacher

NOTE: Samuel F. King later served as county superintendent of schools from 1863 to 1865. In 1850 he was 23 years of age.

Document No. 8

Schedule of a common school kept by John Roberts McCartney at the Liberty school house in district number three in Township 11 North Range 4 East (Shelbyville Township) of the third principal meridian in the county of Shelby in the state of Illinois.

Names of scholars attending my school, and residing in district no. 3 in township 11 north range 4 east in Shelby County. 28 July 1856 through Sept. 30, 1856

Francis M. Douthit	George W. Douthit	Eliza J. Reed
William F. Douthit	Mary E. Reed	James Reed
Lavina Reed	William Reed	John O. Reed
Sarah Reed	Elisia Reed	Marion Reed
Andrew I. Reed	William B. Reed	Maoma Griffith
Perry O. Reed	Mahala Griffith	Amos McClain
Joseph Griffith	William McClain	Margaret McClain
Martha J. McClain	Edmund McClain	Joseph McClain
Mary E. Valentine	Rhoda A.E. Patterson	Sarah F. Patterson
James A. Patterson	William Forbes	Thomas Stewardson
John Stewardson	James Stewardson	Lorenxi Miller
Henry Rhap	Eliza J. Rhap	James Arledge
John Arledge	Charles Arledge	William H. Douthit
Rachel Syfert	Leah Syfert	Mary Ann Syfert
	Levi Syfert	

I certify that the foregoing schedule of scholars attending my school as therein named and residing as specified in said schedule to the best of my knowledge and belief is correct and that it was school for one purpose of teaching various branches of an English education.
      John Roberts McCartney, teacher

State of Illinois, Shelby County: We, the undersigned directors of the board of education in township 11 range number 4 in the county aforesaid certify that we have examined this schedule and find the same to be correct and that the school was conducted according to law. That there is now due said John Roberts McCartney, teacher as per contract the sum of sixty one dollars and ten cents and that the said teacher has a legal certificate of good moral character and of qualification to teach a common school.

Witness our hands this 1st day of October A.D. 1856
Directors of the board of education
Allen B. Reed, Thomas Stewardson, Jarvis Valentine

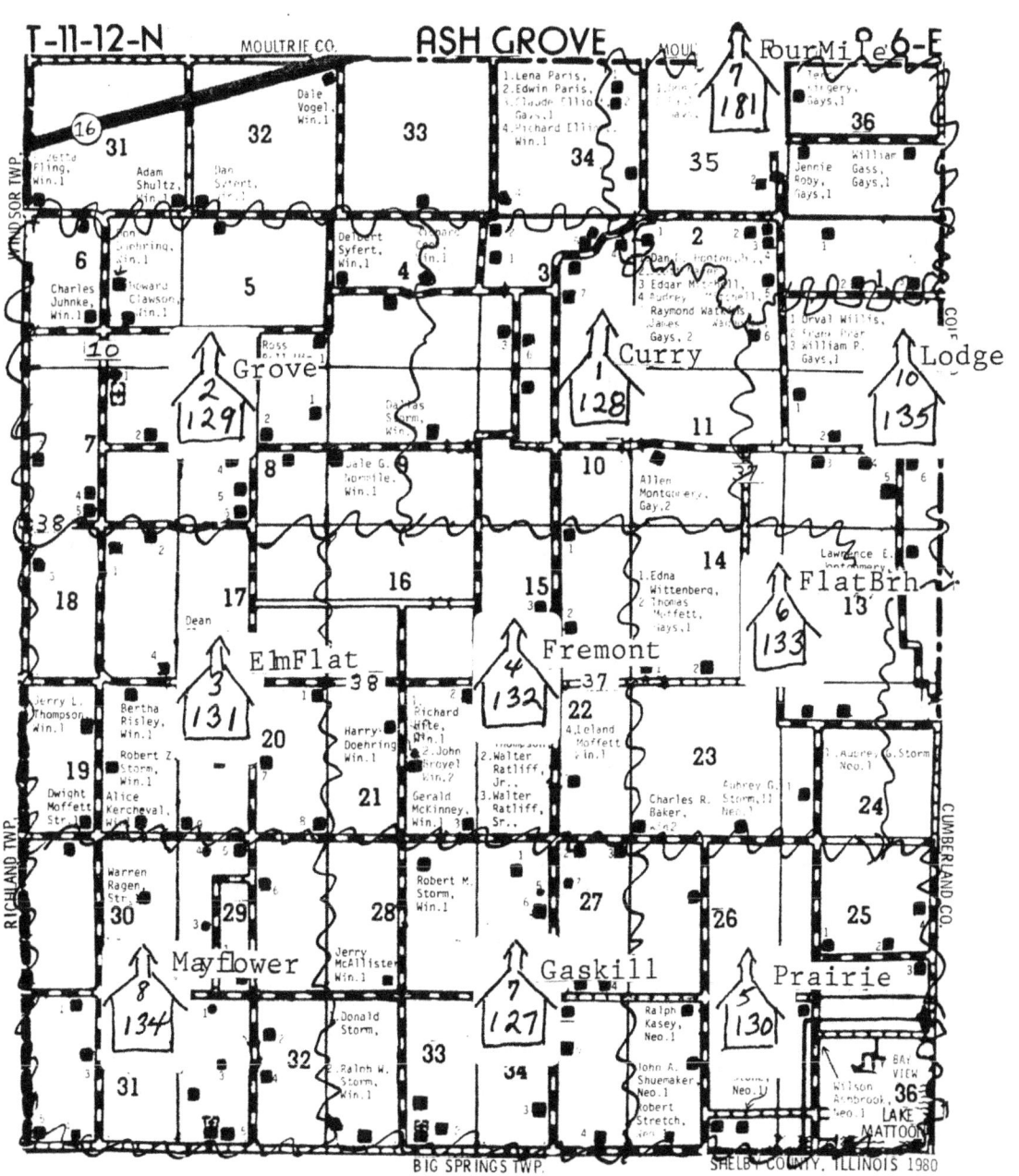

The wavy line indicates school district of 1903.

PEOPLE AND RURAL SCHOOLS OF SHELBY COUNTY
Chapter Four

By the turn of the century, there were twenty-four townships in Shelby County and over 150 rural schools. This chapter is about those schools where students received their early education, played with their many friends, and in many cases retained warm memories of those years.

Townships are given in alphabetical order beginning with Ash Grove first, and so on. Schools within each township are in the order of their district number before 1900. With each school are various teachers' names and their years of teaching, directors' names and their years of office, and different data pertaining to the school itself. In some cases, a photograph of a class or building is included.

During the fall and winter of 1983-84, standardized questionnaires were mailed to prospective individuals who might provide more input on the rural schools of Shelby County.

Enclosed with the questionnaire was a cover letter and a self-addressed, stamped envelope to facilitate a higher rate of return. Also news releases were published in local newspapers to alert individuals to mailings.

Approximately one out of eight questionnaires were completed and returned of the 896 mailed. Most included the humorous antecdotal or memory. A very few indicated "no comment." Their respective responses follow the discussion of their particular school of attendance.

ASH GROVE TOWNSHIP

Ash Grove was settled as early as 1826. John Price settled in section 7 and taught the first school in an empty cabin. The first log schoolhouse built in 1833 stood on the southeast corner of section 4 and Younger Green, a one-armed man, was its first teacher.

L. B. Neighbor, an early settler in Ash Grove who had written an account of the 1860's, was quoted in the 1939 Shelbyville Democrat. In one of the issues, it read, "The principle social center, that decade of the 1860's, was 'old Union', a log schoolhouse on the Big Spring line, 80 rods west of Uncle Neddie Brant's. Here school was conducted for a large district. Here was held famous and largely attended spelling matches. Here there was an occasional singing school, taught by some itinerant knight of the tuning-fork..." In another issue of the newspaper, it read..."The Carruthers and the Betts family both furnished teachers. I have mentioned Miss Hattie Betts as the teacher of Fremont (now Sexson) in 1867. Mrs. William Betts was a teacher of repute at Old Union... John Carruthers taught at the Good School, the Fremont, and Elm Flat, the Prairie School, the Gaskill and Old Union."

CURRY SCHOOL
District 1 or 128

Curry School was located in the northeast quarter of section 10 of Ash Grove township. Its name came from John W. Curry who was a resident in the area. The school was first built there in 1866, with William M. Wilson and John W. Curry as its directors. Three years later, the directors were George W. Templeton, Vincent Storm and E. W. Rouse.

By the 1880s, directors of the school were W. R. Storm, C. R. Ellis, David Watson, J. M. Reed and G.F. Curry. They had the responsibility of maintaining the building, overseeing the teachers conduct and methods and managing the school.

In 1891, Vincent and Lillie Storm sold land to the trustees for a new Curry school in part of the northeast quarter of the northwest quarter of section 10 of Ash Grove township. They renewed the lease in 1899.

Many years later, circa 1940, a reunion was held at the Curry school where Frank Clawson gave a short history of the school. He pointed out that since 1892, eighteen of the teachers who had taught at Curry had attended school there.

When the schools were being sold after consolidation, Clem Boling bought the school building in 1947 from the trustees Elred Venters, Wayne Dewar and Glen Shadows. Nadene Steele had been the last teacher of the school in 1945 and had a school of eleven pupils.

Some of the teachers at Curry were: Charles Colbert, 1874; J. A. Montgomery, 1875; N. C. Robinson, 1876; Samuel W. Robinson, 1877; John R. Womack and C.C. Cash, 1878; W. W. McIntosh and Joseph Brown, 1879; Joseph Brown and Clara Garvin, 1880; J. C. Wallace and James Miner, 1881; James Miner and L. H. Righter, 1882; J. J. Brown, 1883; B. F. Burns, 1884; W. O. Wallace and B.F. Burns, 1885; John Bingamon, 1886; Molly Mc Vay, 1889; Ada Lutz, 1889; W. L. Wallace and Lissa Ellis, 1890; Robert Zimmer, 1891; S. Clawson, 1892; C. H. Ferguson, 1893; Herman Grider, 1901; Burl C. Bennett, 1909; Frank Clawson, Inez Clem, 1922; A.V. Wallace, 1924; Ernest Zimmer, 1926-27; Ruth Libotte, 1934; Thelma Quicksall, 1935; Hazel Storm, 1939-43, Nellie Simmons, 1944 and Nadene Steele, 1945.

RICHARD GANNAWAY

He attended school at Curry and had teachers Mr. Zimmer and Verne Wallace; he also attended Lodge with teacher Thelma

Ross, Banner with teacher Miss Jackson, and Rose with teacher Rose Goddard, during the years 1925 to 1933.

He recalled, "I have many memories of the five schools and seven teachers I had. As to transportation, when the snow got deep my dad took me in a wagon, in a buggy when bad. I walked and had a bicycle in my high school days. I always carried a sack lunch. We traded sandwiches (usually egg, peanut butter) cold biscuits, etc. I remember being corrected by missing recesses, standing on tiptoe with my nose in a chalk ring and having to help with some chores. All plumbing facilities were at the back of the school yard. Was it cold!"

Gannaway was the son of Bess Storm and Russell Gannaway; grandson of Susie Huntington and George Storm, Amanda Mayhew and Sam Gannaway; and great-grandson of Vincent and Lilly Storm and Robertson and Elizabeth Gannaway.

ASH GROVE
District 2 or 129

Ash Grove school was located in the south half of the northwest quarter of section 8 of Ash Grove township. Often the school was called simply Grove. Its name came from that of the township.

Residents in 1866 chose to levy a tax of thirty cents on the hundred dollars to finance the school and directors for that term were J. Henry Price, Perry Sexson, and D. L. Storm. Three years later the levy was 75 cents on the hundred dollars and school directors were James T. Poe, George W. Price and V. Tressler.

During the 1880's, some of the school directors were Perry Sexson, V. Tressler, T. G. Storm and J. H. Cochran. In 1891, Valentine and Catherine Tressler sold land in section 5 to the school trustees.

Some of the teachers at Grove were: J. F. Brown, 1875; W. W. McVay, 1876-77; B. F. Burns and J. O. Chisenhall, 1878; J. A. Hilsabeck, 1879-80; Clara Garvin, 1881; L. W. Frazier, 1882; Clara Garvin, 1883; J. M. Miner and Belle Smith, 1884; Z. B. Smith and H. A. Hilsabeck, 1885; Ella Hubbard, 1885; Lou Oliver, 1886; Z. P. Ferguson, 1887-88; Sylvester Clawson, Isaac Sexson and Lillie A. Ellis, 1889; Z. P. Ferguson and Jennie Swingle, 1890; H. A. Hilsabeck, 1891; Z. P. Ferguson, 1892-93; Jessie M. Wallace, 1894; Bertha Tull, 1901; Anthony V. Wallace, 1909; Daisy Wallace, 1924; Clyde P. Richman, 1926-27; Edna Ferrell, 1934-35; Omer Thomas, 1939-41; Grace Camfield, 1942; Mabel Morgan, 1943; Roscoe Hash, 1944-45; and Harold E. McMillan.

Roscoe Hash was the last teacher with 13 pupils, and directors were William W. Juhnke, Roy Templeton, and

Clarence Doehring. The next year, 1946, the school was Ash Grove consolidated with 63 students and two teachers.

ELM FLAT
District 3 or 131

Elm Flat school was located in the west half of the northwest quarter of section 20 of Ash Grove township. Residents of this area decided to first build in 1866 with a tax levy of $2 on the hundred dollars. Directors for that first term were William B. Bennett and Robert Hopkins. Three years later, the tax levy was 75 cents on the hundred and the directors were Morgan F. Sexson and E. P. Bennett.

Directors for the 1880s were William A. Storm, D.L. Storm, Hiram Storm and Jack L. Clawson. Earlier in 1873 William and Nancy C. Clawson leased land to the trustees located in section 20 for the use of Elm Flat school.

Some of the teachers of Elm Flat school were: George Moore, 1875; George Moore and W. Hartsel, 1876; G. M. Moore and Jacob Wallis, 1877; T. L. Hilsabeck and Albert Gilpin, 1878; George E. Phelps and J.B. Walker, 1879; George M. Moore, 1880; Isaac Storm and W. O. Wallis, 1881; S. B.Patterson and Ellie Roberts, 1882; G. M. Moore and Ella Roberts, 1883; William O. Wallis and Jacob Wallis, 1884; Jacob Wallis and Stephen E. Vanderen, 1885; Nora Hardy Curry, 1886; John Bingamon, 1887-88; C.E. Colbert, 1888; John Ferguson and Jennie Swengel, 1889; Sylvester Clawson, William Packer and Clem Hart, 1890; Nellie Zimmer, 1891; J. B. Ferguson, 1892; Frank Clawson, 1893; Arthur B. Storm, 1894; Alsuma Turner, 1901; Frank Crockett, 1909; Alma Nichols, 1924, standard school; Guy V. Storm, 1926-27, standard school; Fay Clawson, 1934-35; Vernon Hartsell, 1939-41; Inez F. McKinney, 1942; Ellen Roy, 1944-45; and John Carruthers.

Ellen Roy was the last teacher of the school before consolidation with a school of eight pupils. Directors for that last year were Lloyd Elson, Dean Clawson and George Slifer.

ESTHER KULL
She attended Elm Flat for six years and had teachers Pearl Gray, Kit Peters, Frank White, Faye Curtis, Mabel Lockart, W. D. Herron and Sadie Morgan.

"My teacher Mr. Frank White kissed me when I was about 6 or 7 years old. I can still feel my blushing face."

Esther was the daughter of Henry O. and Caroline Ulmer Spannagel; grand daughter of Chris and Eva Streng Spannagel and Matthias and Caroline Schmidt Ulmer; great-grand daughter of Christian and Maria Kull Spannagel and Jacob and Helen Weber Ulmer.

BEATRICE STORM SHEAKS
She attended Elm Flat for eight years, graduating in 1928? She had teachers Sadie Morgan, Fay Clawson, Guy V.

Storm and Alma Nichols.

"Some of my fond recollections are of the pie suppers where there would be standing room only in the building. Also the last day of school celebration picnic dinner at noon, where all parents come. This was the day all the farmers quit work for the hour or so of the picnic and the tables were loaded with the delicious food.

I also remember the long class benches where we went for your studies. Also I was fascinated by the globe of the world that sat on a pedestal in the front of the room. Also I remember the anatomy cabinet. On the walls of the school were the aladin lamps used for lighting. In the front of the school were pictures of Lincoln and Washington, each with a flag draped in each corner. In the middle was the stove.

During the winter in the bitter cold weather, the cloak room where the lunches were kept was so cold the lunches froze. One day the teacher put the frozen lunches on the stove and some of them got too hot so the ones that weren't ruined shared with everyone.

I remember going to school in a sled with a wagon box on top filled with fresh straw. My cousin and I were on the straw and covered with a beautiful lap robe. The sled was pulled by a team of horses."

Beatrice was the daughter of F. Guy and Opal G. Conrad Storm and grand daughter of James Lowery Storm.

FREMONT OR SEXSON
District 4 or 132

Fremont was located in the northeast corner of the northwest quarter of section 22 in Ash Grove township. The earliest document found that specifically names the school was a deed from William W. and Mary J. McDaniel in 1851 to the school trustees for new location of a new Fremont school near the old Fremont school. "...for the purpose of a school house, all the following described land commencing at a wild cherry tree, three poles south east of the Fremont school house, and, thence west nine poles then east nine poles, thence south, to the place of the beginning, one half acre more or less including the Fremont school house and well, thereunto belonging, it being in the northwest quarter of the northwest quarter of section 22." (Deed book 13, page 363).

Residents then in 1866 made a levy of 50 cents per hundred dollars, and directors for that year were Green B. Sexson, Isaac F. Dickson and Barney M. Runnels. Three years later, the tax levy was 75 cents on each hundred dollars and directors were J. H. Brackin and Thomas Bland.

Directors during the 1880s were W. A. Sexson, Thomas Bland, J. T. Blythe, G. R. Thompson and M. C. Noble. During the 1880s, a new school house was built. Andrew Ulmer had leased the land to the trustees in 1884. Just a few years later, H. J. and Jane Storm sold or leased land to the school trustees.

Some of the teachers at Fremont were: D. C. Cannon, and R.B. Howell, 1875; Jacob Wallis, 1875; Jacob Wallis and T. L. Hilsabeck, 1877; Lizzie Garvin, 1878; J. B. Walker, 1879; J. C. Wallace, 1880; G. M. Moore and Jane McAndrew, 1881; Maggie McAndrew and Sarah E. Quinn, 1882; Sarah E. Quinn, 1883; Floy N. Moore and J. C. Wallace, 1884; John Carruthers and Robert Bingamon, 1885; C.E. Colbert, 1886-87; Jacob Zimmer, 1888-90; Will Zimmer, 1891; R. M. Bingamon, 1892; J. F. Clawson, 1894; Nellie Clawson, 1893; Otis Storm, 1901; Robert Zimmer, 1909; Violet Brown, 1922; Hazel Edwards, 1924; Ruth Wilson, 1926-27; Reta Storm, 1934; Mary Tefft, 1935; Edna McKinney, 1940; Dorothy Ellis, 1945, and John Carruthers.

There was no school held at Fremont in the years 1939, 1941, 42, 43 and 44. Dorothy Ellis was the last teacher in 1945 with a class of eight pupils. Directors for that year were Clint Storm, Hal Storm and O.R. Bennett.

Albert and Corabel McGranahan bought the old school property in 1946 from the trustees, which at that time was located in section 21, the northeast quarter of the northeast quarter.

GUY D. PARR
He attended Sexton corner or Fremont school for four years. He recalled teachers Irene Wallace Ferrell and Marie Storm.

Guy was the son of Guy R. and Mary Settles Parr; and grandson of George D. and Eliza Tilley Parr and Jesse and Effie Clark Settles.

PRAIRIE
District 5 or 130

Prairie was located in the northeast corner of the northeast quarter of section 35 of Ash Grove township. Residents of this area levied a one cent tax on the hundred dollars, and directors at that time were Henry Kail, Aaron Gaskill and A. Mowel. Three years later, the levy was $1.25 per hundred, probably for a new building that year. Directors were G. W. Cross, Abraham Mowel and J. M. Vanderen.

In 1871, John and Emma J. Carruthers provided the land of one half acre in the northeast corner of the northeast quarter of section 35. That same agreement was renewed in 1882.

Directors of the 1880s were J. O. Storm, Godrey Doll, John Worley, Nio Shafer, Clem Higgins and Reuben Swingel.

During 1921 in the county spelling contest to be held at the Cowden High School, Wayne and Josye Hutton were the entries from Prairie School.

Some of the teachers at Prairie school were: G. E. Phelps, 1875; John Carruthers, 1876-77; George E. Phelps and Lizzie Garvin, 1878; Lizzie Garvin, 1879; George E. Phelps, 1880; Edward Barry and J. C. Wallace, 1881; J. C. Wallace and Katie Coulter, 1882; Jennie Zimmer, 1883; Jacob Wallis, 1884; Jennie Good, 1885; Jennie Swengel, 1886; Jacob Zimmer, 1887; Carrie Goode, 1888; Jennie Good, 1889; John Bingamon, 1890; Lulu Carruthers, 1890; Nellie Good, 1892; Will Zimmer, 1893; Robert Zimmer, 1894; Cora Montgomery, 1901; Leota Cox, 1917; Ernest Zimmer, 1922-24; Frank Crockett, 1926-27; Ruth Nippe, 1935-41; Inez Riney, 1942; Edna McKinney, 1943-45, and Alma Crockett.

Edna McKinney was the last teacher with a school of ten pupils, and directors for that year were William H. Price, Kenneth Dearman and W. D. White.

FLAT BRANCH
District 6 or 133

Flat Branch was located in the southeast quarter of section 14 of Ash Grove Township. Residents of this area levied a tax of 50 cents on the hundred dollars in 1869, and directors for that year were Calvin Mayhew, J. Ellis, and J.W. Gilpin.

Theodore Stephenson leased land to the trustees in 1897. Earlier the directors in the 1880's had been D.C. Ganaway, J. M. Roy, Albert Hust, George Montgomery, and Henry Figenbaum.

Some of the teachers of Flat Branch school were: Lide Campbell, 1875; Albert Gilpin, 1876; Mary C. Hart and D. C. Ganaway, 1877; Lide Campbell and Lucy M rrison, 1878; Stephen M. Vanderen, 1879; J. C. Ganaway, 1880; John H. Bingamon, 1881; D.C. Ganaway and Sue Phillips, 1882; John H. Bingamon, 1884; J.R. Champion and Ella Roberts, 1885; A. M. Brant, 1886; Lydia McAllister, 1888; J. S. Allison, 1890; Nellie Zimmer, 1892; Emma Blystone, 1894; Minnie Good, 1901; Artie I. Kimbrough, 1922; Flossie Lockart, 1924; Faye Clawson, 1926-27; Mrs. Violet K. Griffith, 1934-35; Flossie Walk, 1939-42; Nellie Simmons, 1943; and Bertha Gray, 1944-45.

Bertha Gray was the last teacher of the school with a class of eight pupils, and directors for that last year were Lester Weber, Lawrence Kull and Albert Grant.

GASKILL
District 7 or 127

Gaskill school was located in section 34. Before 1875, the school was located in section 33. In 1869, the residents levied a two percent tax on hundred dollars for the purpose of building and directors were H. B. Worley, J.B. Daniels and M. Rominger.

During the 1880's the directors were Joseph Z. Butler, M. J. Akers, H. H. Akers, H. W. Neighbor and John Worley.

Some of the teachers at Gaskill were: Alice McVay

and George Phelps, 1875; George F. Bruce, 1876; India Buchanan, 1877-78; J. C. Campbell and Olive Buchanan, 1879; Jennie Curry, 1880; S. D. Gardner and Harry Gardner, 1881; Bell Crume, 1882; William McIntosh and Rose Richardson, 1885; Gertie Carruthers, 1885-88; Ella Lowe, 1888; Hiram Landes, 1889; Lula Carruthers, 1890; R. N. Carruthers, 1891; Josie Hoffman, 1892; Lulu C. Doll, 1893; Nannie Wilhelm, 1894; P. H. McClory, 1901; Ralph Bauer, 1917; Ruth Ferguson, 1922; Inez Clem, 1924; Carl Carruthers, 1926; Mary Smith Veech, 1927; Mrs. Irene Ferrell, 1934-35; Ethel Brown, 1939-40; W. K. Rose, 1942; and Lucille Wilson, 1942-45.

Lucille Wilson was the last teacher with a school of 12 pupils, and directors for that year were Joseph Schwereman, Roy Burrell and Claude Wilson.

MAE L. DUFFY

She attended Gaskill for five years and had teachers Mamie Morgan, Frank Crockett and Leota Cox.

"The pie and box suppers we had in school, the Christmas programs and locking the teacher out until they said treat. Also the programs and basket dinners we had on the last of school.

We always started to school on the first Monday of September and we had a spring term sometimes changing teachers for April and May. My first spring term at Gaskill Stella Carruthers taught."

Mae was the daughter of Alfred and Susan Duffey and grand daughter of James Lapsley.

MAYFLOWER or WILDCAT
District 8 or 134

Mayflower was located in section 31 of the northwest quarter of Ash Grove township. Residents decided to build in 1869 with a tax of $3 on each one hundred dollars, and an additional $1.50 for general school purposes. Directors for that year were John Nantz and Westwood Ferguson.

Directors for the 1880's were James W. Clawson, John L. Clawson, J. T. Blythe, Samuel Rankin, and R. F. Abercrombie. In 1884 Andrew and Sophia Ulmer had sold or leased to the trustees for a new school site in the northeast quarter of the northeast quarter of section 31.

Some of the teachers at Mayflower were: William Hartsel, 1875-77; A. R. Hill, 1878; William Hartsel and Lizzie Ashbrook, 1879; J. O. Chisenhall and J. C. Wallace, 1880; Jesse W. Tull, 1881; John Carruthers, 1882; John Kenney and Joanna Kenney, 1883; John Carruthers and W. O. Wallis, 1884; Z. P. Ferguson, 1885-86; Sylvester Clawson, 1887; Carrie Gharrett and Minnie Ashbrook, 1887; Minnie Ashbrook, G. R. Carruthers, and C. E. Colbert, 1888; C. E. Colbert, 1889; Robert Bingamon, 1889; John B. Ferguson, 1890; Charles E. Colbert, 1891; Robert Zimmer, 1892; Ada Lutz, 1894;

Ella Abercrombie; Marie Storm, 1927; Clyde Richman, 1924; Mabel Rawlings, 1926; M. S. Griffith, 1934; Omer Thomas, 1935; Marie Baker, 1939-41; Robert Gill, 1942; Leota Bridges, 1943-44; and Ethel Dietz, 1945.

Ethel Dietz was the last teacher of the school with a class of eight pupils, and directors for that year were Nelson Zimmer, William Giesler, and Roy Bridges.

A large reunion was held for the school in September 1940. A potluck dinner was followed by a program of readings of former students and teachers. There was also an orchestra composed of Bart Storm, J. T. Walker, Deloris Gaddis, and Ona Rankin. People attending voted to have the affair an annual event.

LODGE or WORLEY
District 10 or 135

Lodge school was located in the section 12 of the northeast quarter of Ash Grove township. E. W. Rouse had sold an acre in section 11 to the trustees in 1867. In 1875 H. B. and Amanda T. Worley sold an acre for a two story building; school to be in the lower floor and Masonic Hall Lodge No. 595 in the upper floor, in section 12.

Directors during the 1880's were D. W. Chamberlin, J. H. Gray, Phillip Zimmer, John Swengel and William Kennedy.

Some of the teachers at Lodge were: Georgia Sawyer, 1875; Charles Coulter, 1876; Jennie McAndrew and John Carruthers, 1877; John Swengel, 1878; John Carruthers, 1879-81; George E. Phelps, 1882; John Carruthers and Jennie Zimmer, 1883; Stephen E. Vanderen and Lillie McAllister, 1884; John Bingamon, 1885; John Barrett, 1886; John B. Ferguson and Maggie McVay, 1887; James Baxter, 1888; Jennie Goode, 1889; Ada J. Lutz, 1890; John Crockett, 1894; Nellie Good, 1891-93; Dora Shoemaker, 1901; Ruth Bolen, 1924; Thelma Ross, 1926-27; Nel Strader, 1934; Inez M. Farr, 1939-41; Helen Bridges, 1942-43; Bernice Abercrombie, 1944; Violet Griffith and Lucille Wright.

Bernice Abercrombie was the last teacher in 1944 with two pupils, and directors for that year were Ernest Chamberlain, George Anderson, and Kenneth Winings.

MILDRED BODEN

She attended Lodge School for eight years and had teachers, Thelma Ross, Noel Strader, Margaret Thenor, Violet Kerchival Griffith and Lucille Wright.

Both her parents and all her brothers and sisters attended Lodge School.

FOUR MILE or UNION
District 7 or 181

Four Mile school was located in the northeast quarter of section 35 of the extreme northeast corner of Ash Grove township. Residents of this area levied 3/4 percent on one hundred dollars and directors for that year of 1866 were Samuel L. Bitner, Jehu Gray, and William S. Colson. Three years later, the levy was 2 percent on the one hundred dollars and directors were T. J. Reynolds, Jehu Gray and I. J. Curry. J. M. Casstevens had sold land to the trustees in 1860 which was located in the northeast quarter of section 35 of the extreme corner of Ash Grove township.

Class of 1926-27: Standing, Victor Maxedon, Velma Mitchell, Marjorie Akers, Margaret Phipps, John Ferre, Berry Akers, Dwight Akers, and Robert Ferree with dog. Seated, Obeta Quinn, Martha Ferree, Adelaide Maxedon, Vernon Mitchell and Donald Akers.
Photo courtesy of Marjorie Easton

Gertrude Bjurstrom, Teacher Four Mile school 1926-27.

Photo courtesy of Marjorie Easton

Some of the teachers at Four Mile were: Georgia McIntosh, 1877; Clara Garvin, 1878; Sue Phillips, 1879; H. Gardner, 1882; S. D. Gardner, 1883; Jerry Reynolds, 1889; T. L. Hilsabeck, 1891; E. F. Wilson, 1892; Charles Colbert, 1893-94; Nannie Wilhelm, 1894; Stephen A. Cross, 1901; Ed. Marvell; Morris Winings, 1922-24, standard school; Gertrude Bjurstrom, 1926; Ada E. Kirk, 1927; Ruth W. Gammill, 1934; Helen Kern, 1935; Mescal J. Lovelass, 1939-40; Margarie Lyon, 1942; Lois Jane Bartley, 1943-44; Inez Jarvis, 1945; and George R. White, 1946.

Directors during the 1880's were E. N. Casstevens, Michael Smith, William L. Curry, R. J. Fosley and T. J. Casstevens.

George R. White was the last teacher of the school in 1946-47 with a school of twelve pupils, and directors were Raymond Watkins, Harry Roby, and Robert Angell.

Hugh Nelms purchased the building from the trustees in 1948 for $1250.

MARJORIE LOUISE EASTON

She attended Four Mile school from 1924-27 and had teachers Maurice Winings and Gertrude Bjurstrom.

She was the daughter of Joshua B. and Nellie Major Akers; grand daughter of Thornton and Dora Horsley Akers, and Seneca and Mary Diehl Major; and great-grand daughter of Joshua and Mary Akers and Berry M. and Dora M. Horsley.

DEAN STORM

He attended Four Mile school for four years and had teachers Minnie Bohlen, Ed Marvel and Ralph Roby.

"I remember that my brother, Truman, and I had to walk 1½ miles to school. The youngsters argued 'politics' to and from school. Jeff Farley, Mrs. George Bell's father, owned the farm just north of the school. One day some of us went to his house. He showed us an eagle, which he had killed in South Dakota. He shot and crippled it and it attacked him. He told us that it would have killed him, had he not been wearing a sheep-skin coat. This story made a deep impression on me! I can remember many of those who attended school with me. Burl, Grace, Dean, and Dale Beldon; Lesa Parsons, Della Rentfro, Everett, Stella and Raymond Webb; Ora, Oscar, Edgar and Stella Mitchell; Ed, Walter, and Lois Curry; Ralph, Edna, Rachel and Ethel Drake; Russell and Elsie Purkiser; Julia Casstevens, Truman and Dean Storm.

I remember attending school, for a very short time at Curry School. Perhaps in the spring with my brother."

Dean was the son of Zach and Florence Ferguson Storm; grandson of Anderson and Penelope Sears Ferguson, and David Frank and Sarah E. Bennett Storm; great-grandson of John H. and Isabel Dickson Storm, Zachariah and Mary Crenshaw Ferguson, William Bell and Lavina Curry Bennett, and Pleasant D. and Nancy M. Pearson Sears.

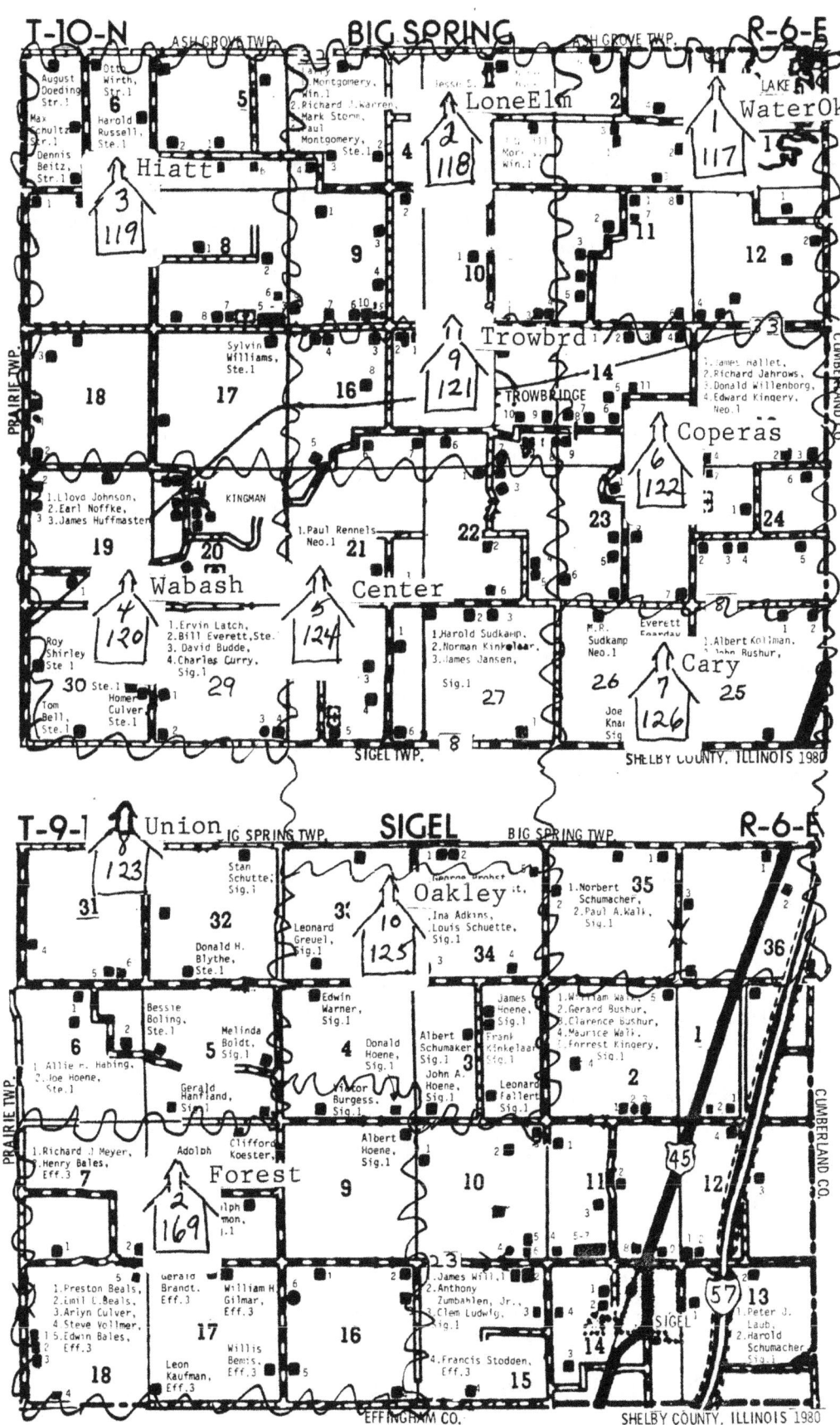

The wavy line indicates the 1903 school district.

BIG SPRING AND SIGEL TOWNSHIPS

Originally Big Spring was much larger than it is today. It and other townships in town ten north were reduced in size by 1895. Several streams—Copperas, Drake, Bills, Brush, Hog, Rattlesnake, and Clear including the Little Wabash—ran through the township much as they do now.

The earliest school known here was taught in a cabin belonging to John Spain in section 20. The school was probably not distant from the mill settlement established by Samuel Weatherspoon in 1832.

Thomas Bell was one of the first teachers. Another early teacher was Evan Baker who himself had attended the township schools.

In 1861 there were four school districts and by 1870 there were 12 districts. By 1895 the newly formed Sigel township had two of those 12 school districts, its main one being at Sigel.

BAKER SCHOOL

Baker school was located a half mile of Joe Schabbing's home on the corner of section 11 of T 9 N R 6 E, later Sigel township. The school was located there in the 1850's and 1860's. Teachers during that time were Jim Walker, Mr. Vonderheide and Herschel Brown.

WATER OAK
District 1 or 117

Wateroak school was located in section 1 of Big Spring township in the southwest corner of the southwest quarter. Residents assessed themselves at $1.25 per hundred dollars for building purposes in 1869. Directors for that year were G. W. Cross, Abraham Mowel, and J. M. Vanderen.

Directors during the 1880's were Anderson Blystone, James H. Cross, John Daughtery, and H. P. Soliday.

Some of the teachers of Water Oak were: Lulu Carruthers, 1889; Mollie Mc Vay, 1891; Charles Colbert, 1892; William Packer, 1893-94; Maurice Leffler, 1901; Mildred Latimer, 1909; Claude H. Beck, 1917; Frank Crockett, 1924; Mary A. Smith, 1926; Carl Carruthers, 1927; Harry Ewing, 1929; Clara Watson, 1934-35; John F. Clawson, 1939-40; Edna McKinney, 1941-42; Regis McClory, 1943; Margie Wakeland, 1944, and Shirley Doll, 1945.

Shirley Doll was the last teacher of the school with four pupils. Directors for that year were Clyde Lane, Raymond Laurence and Clint Huffman.

Trustees sold the property of Water Oak school in 1949 to Belva Dodds Dugan. Lorenzo and Mary E. Roberts had leased the property to the trustees in 1883.

Water Oak School 1929. Front row, Edith Antrim Giesler, Dwight Ferguson, Warren Ferguson, Ruby Gentry, Bill Antrim, Maxine Gentry. 2nd row, Page Soliday, Foster Soliday, Hope Bauer Doll, Virginia Shewmaker, Orville Antrim, Burl Bauer, James Antrim. 3rd row, Henry Woolrey, Anna Mae Hall, Raymond Antrim, Harry Ewing, teacher, Virginia Antrim, Pete Young, George Hall, Ruby Gentry, Harold Gentry, Irene Ferguson.
Photo courtesy of

LONE ELM
District 2 or 118

Lone Elm School was located in the southwest section 3 of Big Spring township. Directors during the 1880's were W. H. Sims, A. Y. Lambert, S. F. Worland, George Y. Keck, and D. T. Kennedy.

Some of the teachers at Lone Elm were: Frank Kennedy, 1901; Ernest Zimmer, 1909; Mamie Morgan, 1917; Lenora Lockart, 1922; Mabel Huff, 1924; Helen Huff, 1926; Albert Leonard Anderson, 1927; Lucille Wilson, 1934; Carl Carruthers, 1935; Mary Veech, 1939; Lucille Wilson, 1940-41; Henry Wiersum, 1942-44; Doloris Daughtery, 1945-46.

Doloris Daughtery was the last teacher with a class of nine pupils. Directors for that year were Dean Hellman, Orval Latch, and George Daughtery.

HYATT
District 3 or 119

Hyatt school was located in the southeast corner of the northeast quarter of section 7 of Big Spring township. Residents of this area in 1866 assessed five cents on the hundred dollars, and directors were Alfred Blythe, Fielden Figgins and George W. Hiatt. Three years later, the taxes were $1 on the hundred dollars, probably for building purposes, and the directors were Ewing Houchin, F. C. Turner, and Minor Quicksall.

Directors for the 1880's were John Figgins, George Shafer, C. O. Johnson, C. Jenson and G. W. Blyth.

Some of the teachers at Hyatt school were: E. F. Wilson, 1888; John Barrett, 1889; Frank Clawson, 1891; Edna Sexson, 1892; C.W. Jolly, 1894; L.W. Frazer, 1901; Guy V. Storm, 1917; Ezra Blythe, 1909; R. H. Zimmer, 1899; Agnes Huff, 1924; Sadie M. Laver, 1926-27; Owen Scott, 1934-35; Thelma G. Quicksall Mueller, 1939; Fred Hash, 1940-41; Flora Shallenbarger, 1942; Cora Hollaway, 1943; and Nina Haverstock, 1944-46.

During the month of December, 1900, R. H. Zimmer, teacher reported that for the month of November, he had enrolled students Edgar Storm, Grover Storm, Grover Jensen, Seth Blythe, Re Storm, Harry Storm, Oscar Storm, Clark Hiatt, Lyman Hiatt, Francis Blythe, Grace Storm, Blanche Jensen, Hettie Blythe, Alice Jensen, Donnie Storm, and Bessie Storm who had perfect attendance.

Nina Haverstock was the last teacher of the school with seventeen pupils. Directors for that year were Glen Hiatt, William Widdersheim and Lester Storm.

VIOLET CROSS

She attended Hiatt school for eight years, and had teachers Agnes Huff, Helen Huff, Guy V. Storm, and Irl L. Schyler.

"There were only two of us in first grade when I started to school; our teacher was Miss Agnes Huff and we both loved her. After we got our lessons, she would let us sit on edge of stage and play as long as we didn't get too noisy. Later in the school years we were advanced to the next grade higher, rather than go through the eight grades with only two students. When we graduated, Irl L. Schyler was our teacher.

There were seven of us graduated from 8th grade together. The year must have been 1929 when graduating."

Violet was the daughter of Grover B. and Nellie Storm Storm; grand daughter of William B. and Antoni Renner Storm; Johnnie J. Storm and Hannah Hiatt Storm; great-grand daughter of James and Emilie Rankin Storm, Wilson and Margaret Storm Renner, William and Elizabeth Rankin Storm, and George and Elizabeth Pierson Storm Hiatt.

WABASH
District 4 or 120

Wabash School was located in section 30, northeast corner of northeast quarter. Directors of the 1880's were James E. Wade, Minor Quicksall, T. L. Elam, J. H. Quicksall and Arnold Becker.

Some of the teachers of Wabash School in Big Spring township were: Sylvester Clawson, 1888; E.F. Wilson, 1890; Sylvester Clawson, 1891; W. B. Stine, 1892; Sylena Quinn, 1893; Sylvester Clawson, 1894; R. H. Zimmer, 1899; John Quinn, 1901; Maude McAllister, 1909; Guy V. Storm, 1922-24; Grace Klarman, 1926; Henry R. Riney, 1927; Glen W. Giesler, 1934-35; Ruth Anderson Manhart, 1939; Glen Giesler, 1940-41; Lucille Boyce, 1942; Catherine Anderson, 1943-45; Celestine Peifer, 1946; Beulah E. Fritz, 1917.

Celestine Peifer was the last teacher with fourteen pupils. Directors for that year were Fred Haverstock, L.D. Elam, and Walter Tabbertt.

FARABA GENEVA ANDERSON SHIRLEY

She attend Wabash school for eight years and had teachers Guy Storm, Henry Riney, Agnes Huff, Grace Klarman Schultz.

"The school was down in the Little Wabash Valley, half mile from the river with hills and woods on three sides. In winter, we had hour noons so could slide on the hills. In the spring, we all went wild flower picking, bluebells, violets, boy britches. We filled the water trough at the well full and took bouquets home in the evening. Average number was 30 and 40 children, one teacher, usually six grades."

Faraba was the daughter of Fred E. Ora Beals Anderson; grand daughter of Mathias and Johanna Munson Anderson, and Archibald and Faraba Baker Beals; great-grand daughter of Hans Christian Anderson and John and Eliza Beals. She noted that grandpa Anderson was from Sweden and marched with Sherman to the sea.

CENTER
District 5 or 124

Center School was located in the west side of section 28 of Big Spring township. Residents of this area in 1866 assessed themselves at $1 per $100 and directors were Nathan Arnold and William Teater. Three years later, the assessment was set at 75 cents per 100 and directors were William Teater, John Donahue, and A. J. Hanks.

Directors of the 1880's were Giles M. Lugar, Charles V. Chapplear, Jacob Coons, and Isaac Carey.

Some of the teachers at Center were: Robert Binagmon, 1888-89; W.T. Colbert, 1891; Ed J. Quinn, 1892; Maud Beals, 1893; R. M. Bingamon, 1894; Mamie Cross, 1901; Ora Quicksall, 1909; Alva W. Thompson, 1917; Mary A. Smith, 1924; Velma

Johnson, 1926-27; Agnes Huff, 1934; Mrs. Dorothy L. McMillan, 1935; Helen Bridges, 1939; Carl Carruthers, 1940; Mary Veech, 1941; Lola Chapplear, 1942-45; and Shirley Doll, 1946.

Shirley Doll was the last teacher of Center with a school of six pupils. Directors for that year were Clem Sheehan, Benjamin Mills, and Charles Chapplear.

Center School was sold in 1949 to Oscar Gentry and others for $250.

COPPERAS
District 6 or 122

Copperas school was located in the northeast quarter of section 23 of Big Spring township. Residents of this area assessed themselves at $1 per $100 in 1866 and directors for that time were Samuel Young, Thomas Moran, and Hugh Smith. Three years later, the assessment was 50 cents per $100 and directors were Samuel Young and John W. McKay.

Directors of the 1880's were O. C. Jimmason, Richard Downey, W. C. Bayne, P. S. Kennedy, Jasper Swanson and John Hunk.

Some of the teachers at Copperas were: John Barrett, 1888; Francis Hoffman, 1889; Carrie Goode, 1890; Josie Huffman, 1891; Selena Quinn, 1892; Rinaldo Baker, 1894; O.W. Blomquist, 1901; Hugh Worland, 1909; Edna Wilson, 1917; Charles A. Price, 1924; Regis E. McClory, 1926-27; Dorothy E. Lindley, 1934; Agnes Huff, 1935-46.

Agnes Huff was the last teacher of Copperas with a school of 18 pupils; diretors for that last year were Linden Parker, Joseph W. McClory, and Walter Mehl.

School trustees sold the school property in 1949 to Ray Fromme for $300.

CARY or QUAKER
District 7 or 126

Cary School was located in the southeast quarter of section 26 of Big Spring township. Residents of this area assessed themselves in the year 1866 at one per cent per $100. Directors for that year were Jacob Coons, and John J. Cary. Three years later, the tax was one and half percent on the 100 dollars. Directors were W. W. Mills and Jesse B. Mills.

Earlier in 1863 Martin A. and Augusta Simonson had sold one acre in the northeast corner of the east half of the southwest quarter of section 26 of Big Spring township. Directors for the 1880's were George Moran, J. H. Carey, and Charles H. Baker.

Some of the teachers of Cary were: Flora Goode, 1889-1891; Mollie Fenton, 1893; Selena Quinn, 1894; Jennie Hastings, 1901; Regina Keck, 1909; Emma Moran, 1924;

Harriett Figenbaum, 1926; Mary V. Hunk, 1927; Mabel Huff, 1934; Helen V. Bridges, 1939, and Ellen Roy, 1939-42.

In 1926 a new model for the school was erected at the cost of $4500. Ellen Roy was the last teacher of the school of five pupils, and directors for that last year were Edward Duvall, Ben J. Sudkamp, Jr., and John Hofman.

The trustees sold the building in 1947 to Clarence Walk for $2000. Another teacher was R. E. McClory in 1917.

UNION
District 8 or 123

Union school was located in the northeast corner of section 31 of Big Spring township.

Some of the teachers at Union school were: W. B. Stine, 1891; C.W. Wilson, 1892; W. B. Stine, 1893; Fanny E. Lugar, 1894; Rose Harmon, 1901; Ruby Beals, 1909; Iola Williams, 1917; Ward Dappert, 1922; Emma Harmon, 1924; Ora Fritz, 1926-27; Marie Baker, 1934-35; Robert Gill, 1939-40; Nina Haverstock, 1941-43; Dorothy Dautenhahn, 1944; Marie Kackley, 1945, and Henry Widdersheim, 1946.

Henry Widdersheim was the last teacher with ten pupils and directors were Elza Storm, Samuel Baker, and Alva Patterson.

School trustees sold the property in 1949 to Oscar Gentral for $250.

TROWBRIDGE
District 9 or 121

Trowbridge school was located in the southeast quarter of section 9 of Big Spring Township.

Some of the teachers at Trowbridge were: Anna Keck, 1891; R. M. Bingamon, 1893; Nellie Fitzgerald, 1892; Nellie Good, 1894; Emma Rice, 1901; Pearl Gray, 1909; Guy McClory, 1917-22; Dorothy Ray, 1924; Margaret Quinn, 1926-27; Sadie Price, 1934; Lucille M. Wilson, 1935-39; Earl French, 1940; John Clawson, 1941; Glen Giesler, 1942; Rose Will, 1943-44; Sadie Laver, 1945, and Edna McKinney, 1946.

Edna McKinney was the last teacher with 22 pupils, and directors for that year were Joseph Keck, Earl Barrett, and Ben Patterson. Before 1891, the school was in section 9 and called Daughtery with teachers Edward Cross, and John L. Henderson.

OAKLEY
District 10 or 125

Oakley school was located in the southeast corner of section 33 of Big Spring township.

Some of the teachers at Oakley were: Hettie Ensey, 1891; Bessie Chapman, 1893; Della E. Warren, 1894; Otto Dappert, 1901; E. Della Mattox, 1909; Nina Baugher, 1917; Charles E. Chapplear, 1922-26; J. Russel Peters, 1927; Thelma Noyes, 1934-35; Darrell E. Cruthis, 1939; Margaret McGrath, 1940 and Mary McClory, 1941-42.

Mary McClory was the last teacher of the school of 9 pupils, and directors were Joe Shumaker, Wiley Warner, and Alphone Hoene.

FOREST
District 2 or 169

Forest school was located in the southwest quarter of section 8 of Big Spring later Sigel township. In 1875 the school was on the property of J. Moser; and by 1914 it was still much in the same location.

Some of the teachers at Forest were: Maggie McVey, 1888; John B. Goode, 1891; Charles E. Storm, 1892; J. A. Quicksall, 1893; Ed J. Quinn, 1894; J.M. Quicksall, 1901; Rose Harmon, 1909; Emma E. Harmon, 1922; Melinda Rincker, 1924-standard school; Minnie Martin, 1926-standard school; Otis Dappert, 1927; Dwight Dappert, 1934-35; Frieda Christman, 1939-40; Amy Webb, 1941-42; Rita Anderson, 1943; Rita Meek, 1944; Lena Duever, 1945; and Mrs. J.R. Gibbons, 1946.

Mrs. J. R. Gibbons was the last teacher of the school with 7 pupils, and directors for that year were Adolph Harmon, Otto Dappert and Victor Burgess.

Students who attended Forest in the year 1939-40 were: William Bartimus, Erma Hatke, Rose Harmon, Donald Culver, Frieda Schultz, George Bartimus, James Boldt, Grace Bartimus, Mary Harmon, Ray Boldt, Delores Hatke, James Bemis, Charles Harmon, Joyce Culver, Faith Schultz, and Kathleen Culver.

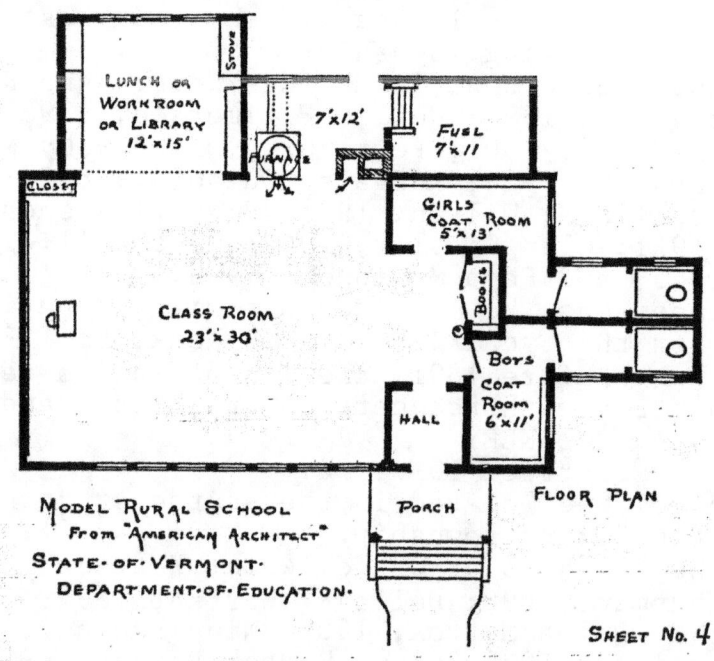

This is an excellent plan. If a basement is desired, the fuel room should be used for an entrance from outside and inside. The chimney should then be in the back of the room in the place of "Books". The heater room can then be used for a work room for the little children.

Rural Schools of Illinois, 1929.

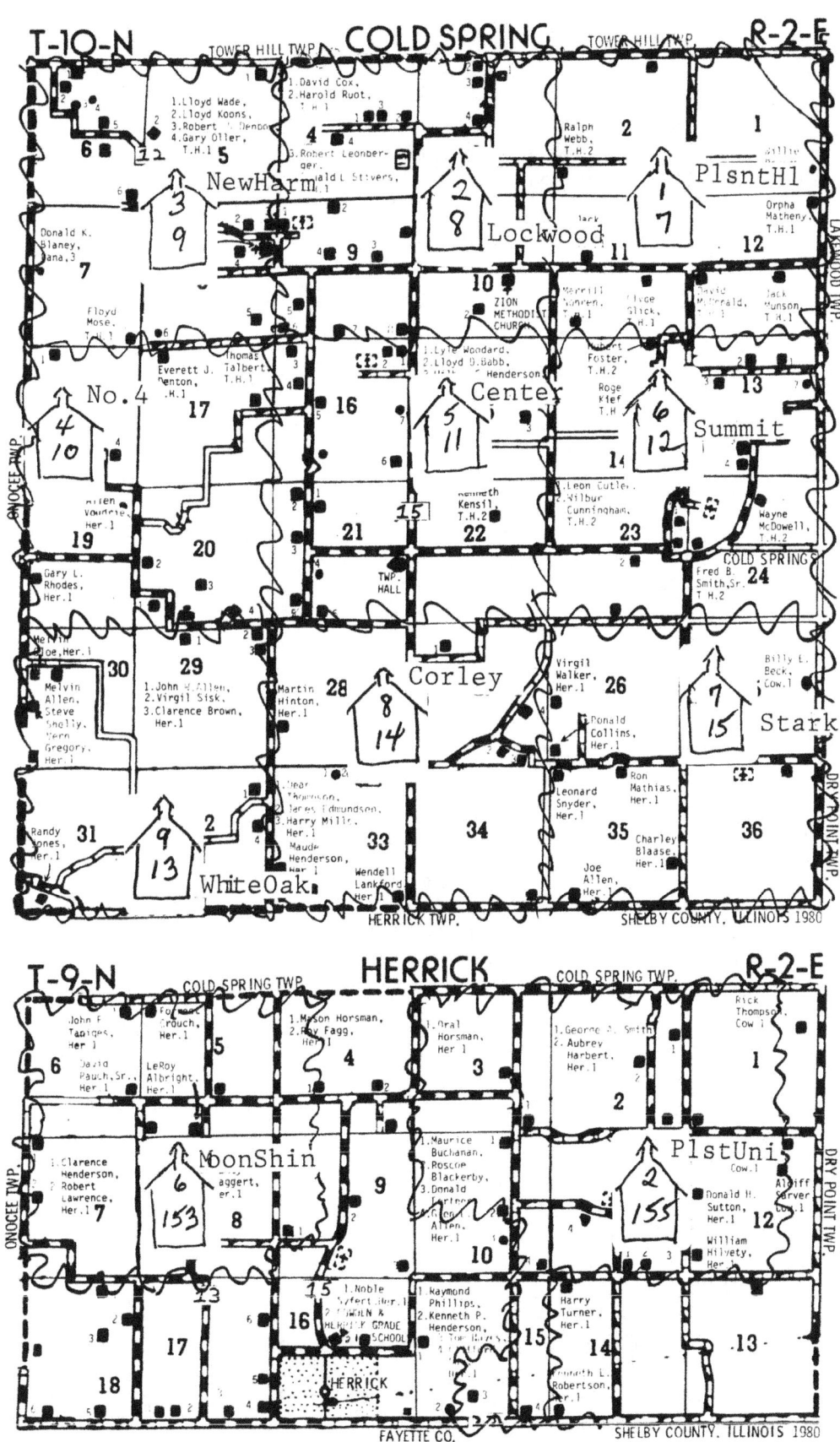

The wavy line indicates the 1903 school district.

COLD SPRING AND
HERRICK TOWNSHIPS

As early as 1821 school was taught in the settlement of Cold Spring by Moses Storey who continued teaching for some 40 years. As more people came, two local men decided to plat a town and named it Williamsburg after Dr. Baylis Williams.

The early township books did not include those schools for Town 9 N R 2 E which later became Herrick township. Those schools were combined with boundard schools in Fayette County, and records kept there accordingly.

Beginning in the 1860's the township was divided into seven school districts. In October 1866 an order was made for 4 districts but one year only, the entire township of town 10-2 was formed into one school district with Debbie Gilford, Frank E. Shepherd, Annie Swallow, C.S. Milliken, and Nannie Listen as the teachers for 1866.

A census was taken for the four districts in Oct. 1867, and it went as follows: district 1-163, district 2-91, district 3-141, district 4-215, making a total of 610 students under 21 years of age but over 6 years of age. Earlier in 1866, there were 293 boys, 297 girls, a total of 191 under the 6 years and colored numbered 19.

In April 1867 the People Spring school house sold for $125 and money was divided between districts 3 and 4. In that same month, the Hornbeck school sold for $10 to Claris Hornbeck.

A petition was taken by residents of Cold Spring in April 1884, requesting that the township be redistricted. Nine school districts were created for the following school year, and remained so till the 1940's.

In many cases, the students of a particular school had many teachers in one school year, as they were only hired for a short period of time. Also, a different teacher would be hired for the summer term, ususally a female.

PLEASANT HILL
District 1 or 7

Pleasant Hill school was located in the northeast corner of section 11 of Cold Spring township. In 1866 taxes were a half percent on the $100, and directors were S. Thompson and W. W. Newkirk. Three years later, the taxes were 35 cents per $100, and directors were William Creekmur, Edmund Glick, and Mathew Jackson.

Directors of the 1880's were H. R. Fairchild, W.C. Foor, J. W. Hall, Ed Glick, Thomas McKittrick, and Naries Swander.

In 1884 Allen and Pernetta B. Wakefield sold one acre in the northeast corner of section 11.

Some of the teachers at Pleasant Hill were: J.S. Tilley, 1862; Michael Stevenson and Harriett Correll, 1864; James S.Tilley and Annie Franklin, 1865; Henry Doner, 1866; Henry Doner and C.S. Milliken, 1867; Henry Doner, William Price and Lizzie Milliken, 1868; Henry Doner and M.E. Milliken, 1869; Henry Doner, 1870; Ella Corley and Henry Doner, 1871; J. H. Addington and T.C. Eiler, 1872; H. Doner and Lizz Fry, 1873; Samuel McKittrick, G.T. Wolfley, M.E. Myers, and H.W. Fellers,1874; Mary E. Myers and Isaac G. Holt, 1875; H.C. McTaggart, S.F. Corley, and B. F. Buckingham, 1877; Annie R. Huffer, Jennie Roland, and D.C. Corley, 1878; D.C. Corley and Charles E. Reeves, 1879; J. W. Creekmur and W. M. Fellers, 1880; W. M. Fellers and J. W. Creekmur, 1881; James A. Patton and Anna R. Miller, 1882; Anna R.Huffer, A. H. Perryman and F. L. Smart, 1883; (school now located in section 11) Liza Hall, 1884; Mattie Rhodes, Ollie Brown, 1885-86; A. H. Perryman, 1886; W. M. Fellers and Homer L. Fairchild, 1888; May O. Ferrell, 1887; W. M. Fellers, 1889; J. N. Fluckey and Albert Johnson, 1890; Nettie Miller, 1891; C. T. Bowman, 1892; Jesse Price, 1893; Pearl Cox, 1901; Effie Robertson, 1905; J. L. Moore, 1906-07; Bruce Curry, 1909; Omer Peek, 1911; Nellie Gatons, 1912; Maud Wakefield, 1913; Vivien Fletcher, 1916; James Moore, 1918; Norris Newkirk, 1922; Nita Tucker, 1934; Beulah Munson, 1926-27; Lourene M. Johnston, 1934; Arlene Parr, 1935.

Arlene Parr was the last teacher with 12 pupils, and directors were Lloyd Wakefield, W. F. Wortman and C. M. Glick.

The trustees sold the Pleasant Hill school in 1950 to Harry R. Morgan for $800.

LOCKWOOD
District 2 or 8

Lockwood school was located in the northwest quarter of section 10 of Cold Spring township. The first school must have been built around 1869 since the taxes were 75 cents on the $100, and directors were W. W. Newkirk and Peter Hoodlet.

Directors of the 1880's were Jacob Johnston, Daniel Lockwood, Alfred Simpson, Alex Foster, and A. N. Morrison.

Some of the teachers at Lockwood were: A. J. Morrison, 1862; Thomas B. Wamsley, 1863-64; Harriett E. Kirkpatrick, 1865; William O. Robertson, 1867; Harriet Correll, 1868; John M. Roberts, George T. Wolfely, and Frank J. Bain, 1869; George T. Wolfely and C. C. Perryman, 1870; C. C. Perryman, 1871; George T. Wolfely and Florence Young, 1872; B. B. Corley and Mary E. Kelley, 1873; T. B. Wamsley and T. J. Holt, 1874; B. B. Corley and Spencer Moon, 1875; Spencer

Moon and S.F. Corley, 1876; S. F. Corley and D. C. Corley, 1877; D.C. Corley and Frank Baines, 1878; Frank Baines and Jesse Mount, 1879; Hattie J. Myers and Lucy D. Brown, 1880; T. P. Miller, Connie Vincent and W. M. Fellers, 1881; W. M. Fellers, 1882-83; (school now located in the northwest quarter of section 10) Chattie Morrison, 1884; Nora Brandon, 1885; Nora Brandon and W. M. Fellers, 1886; G. W. Leighty, 1887; G. W. Leighty and William Foster, 1888; W. N. Foster and Mary Leighty, 1889; Maud L. Richardson and W. M. Fellers, 1890; Alex Foster and W. M. Fellers, 1891; W. M. Fellers, 1892; M. Turner, 1893; Pearl Cox, 1901; Nellie Eckert, 1905; Rosella Bechtel, 1906-07; Eva Bodine, 1909; Maude Archey, 1911; Lela Lohr and Vivian Fletcher, 1912; Guy Henderson, 1913-14; Golda McCain and Guy Henderson, 1915; Eva Davis, 1916; Guy Henderson,1917; Leela Darst, 1918; Ruth Rhodes, 1924; Lucille Bartow, 1926; Alva W. Thompson, 1927; Floy Foster, 1934-35; Norma G. Jones, 1939-41; Betty Roberts, 1942; Rhoda Cain,1943-44; Lois Caskey, 1945; Anetta Jones, 1946; and Nona L. Murray, 1948.

    Nona L. Murray was the last teacher with 19 pupils, and directors were John Pease, Orville Jones and John Glick.

WILLIAM G. FELLERS

    He lives in Lancaster, California and is a grandson of William Monroe Fellers who taught school in Cold Spring township for many years.

    A questionnaire was sent to him in 1982 but it was not returned.

NEW HARMONY
District 3 or 9

    New Harmony school was located in the northwest quarter of section 8 of Cold Spring township. Earlier in the 1860's district 3 was located in section 29 of Cold Spring township. John and Polly Brown had sold one acre in the northwest corner of section 29 for the school in 1868. The taxes of 1869 were a half percent per $100 and directors were J.Pee, J. W. Henderson, and R. H. Price.

    By 1884, the school was located in section 8 when A. J. Morrison sold a half acre to the school trustees. Some directors of the 1880's were J. Buller, F. M. Spurgin, J. W. Sphar and O. H. Prentice.

    Some of the teachers of New Harmony or district 3 were: O.H.T. Rosenburg, 1862 with 35 pupils; B.B. Corley and Frank E. Roberts, 1866; John C. Gregory and Nancy L. Henderson, 1867 (school then called Felix Bunch house); B.B. Corley and Elias Kost, 1868; Spence Iveson and Mattie Blackwell, 1869; Samuel W. Buckhanan and Mattie Blackwell, 1870; Willis F. Corley and Edward Blackwell, 1871; W. F. Corley and Samuel W. Buckhanan, 1872; M. E. Myers, 1873; M.E. Myers and Spencer Moon, 1874; Jasper Craig, 1875;

Spencer Moon, Jasper Craig and Jennie Fry, 1876; I. G. Holt, C. J. Brown and J. R. Thompson, 1877; Joseph R. Thompson, D. C. Corley and Mary E. Myers, 1878; A. B. Frazier, Daniel K. Torrence and MaryE.Myers, 1879; Mary E.Myers, 1880; T. P. Miller and Jesse Mount, 1882; James E. McDermith and Etta Roudybush, 1883; (school now located in the northwest quarter of section 80; J. D. Mount and Etta Roudybush, 1884; H. Agnes Prescott and Jennie Gower, 1885; Allis Gower, 1887; Ella Thomas, 1888; Mary Leighty and Ella Johnson, 1889; Rose Humphrey, 1890-92; Henry Newkirk and Rose Humphrey, 1893; W. N. Babb, 1901; Ethel Barrett, 1905; O.H. Stilgebour, 1906-07; Lucy Warnick, 1909; Hazel Gladman, 1912-13; Jessie Gatons and Georgia Clark, 1913; Clemie Warnick, 1914; Pearl Seiber, 1915-18; Lucille Bartow, 1924; Helen Mills, 1926; Raymond Bales, 1927; Josephine Jenkins, 1927-35; Floy Foster, 1939-40; Grace Hall, 1941-42; Josephine Jenkins, 1943; Lucille Koons, 1944.

Lucille Koons was the last teacher with a school of 5 pupils, and directors were Albert King, Lee Koons and Harry Dickey.

The trustees sold the New Harmony school in 1950 to Eston and Rhea Eads for $750.

NUMBER FOUR or BLACK OAK
District 4 or 10

Number Four was first located in the southwest quarter of section 23 and land for it was given by Claris and Mary Hornbeck in 1862. By 1888, Frank and Elizabeth Johnson sold one square acre for district 4 or Number 4 in the southwest quarter section 18 of Cold Spring township.

Taxes in 1869 were 75 cents per $100, and directors were Sheldon Thompson, Ephraim A. McCrackin. Directors of the 1880's were James H. Tressler, John Davis, Benjamin Larrimore, A. J. Corley, Nelson King and P. W. Young.

Some of the teachers of Number Four were: William T. Reese and Mary A. Myers, 1862; J. D. Walton and D. H. May, 1864; John A. Brumfield, 1865; J. S. Burris, 1866; B.B. Corley and C. J. Horsman, 1867; B. J. Young, Elvina Corley and Sadie E. Fraught, 1868; John C. Gregory, C.S. Milliken and George Corley, 1869; J. B. Perryman and D. Patton, 1870; S.Severns, J. M. Spurgeon and Henry Doner, 1871; James W. McNutt and J. B. Perryman, 1872; S. W. Buckhanan and B.B. Corley, 1873; M. D. Hornbeck, John Frizzell, Jennie Fry and Emma Oliver, 1874; Samuel Buckhanan, John Frizzell, B.B. Corley and Jennie Fry, 1875; Samuel Buckhanan, Jennie Fry, and Mary E. Myers, 1876; Hattie J. Myers, Alonzo Roberts, and Mary E. Myers, 1877; S. W. Buckhanan, and E. A. McCracken, 1878; Mary E. Myers and Hattie J. Myers, 1879; Lucy D. Brown, Jennie Worley, J.W.

Creekmur and I. G. Holt, 1881; R. M. Herron, W. L. Myers, 1882; R. M. Herron, J. E. McDermith, and Ettie Roudybush, 1883; (school now located in section 18) Nora Brandon, 1884; Elizabeth Clark, 1885; Isabella Fisher, 1886; Maggie Elwell, 1887; Thomas Inman, 1888; Mary Dow and J.A. Beckett, 1889; C. A. Price, 1890; David Ash, 1891; Frona Bumgardner, 1892-93; W. M. Fellers, 1901; Foy Morse, 1905-06; Ella Finley, 1906-07; Susie Lockart, 1909 (school now called Black Oak); Clem Warnick and I. R. Holt, 1911; Eva Price, 1912; Bessie Smart and Imogene Price, 1913; Stella Hamilton, 1914; H. L. Culberson, 1915; Gertrude Welch, 1916; Nellie Crouch, 1917; James Hand, 1918; Charles F. Rhodes, 1924; Beulah Hoke, 1926; Vincent E. Cashin, 1927; Elmer E. Smith, 1934; John J. Strain, 1935; Nona L. Murray, 1939; 1940; 1941; W. D. Williams, 1942; Nona Murray, 1943; Ruth Gatons, 1944-45; Pauline D. Sanders, 1946.

Pauline D. Sanders was the last teacher with a class of 13 pupils, and directors were Victor Glick, Clarence Wafford and George Gatons.

CENTER or JOHNSTON
District 5 or 11

Center school was located in the southwest quarter of section 15 of Cold Spring township. In the 1860's the school district covered sections 15, 16 and 22.

A new school was built in 1884 when Jacob Johnston deeded land to the trustees S. Thompson, W. W. Newkirk, and Henry Doner. The school was called Johnston for a number of years until 1901. Other directors of the 1880's were J.W. Morrison and T. H. Babb.

Some of the teachers of Center were: Martha Graham, 1862 with a class of 20 pupils; Jonathon Pea and B.W. McMahan, 1863; J.S. Tilley and Permelia A. King, 1864; Benjamin B. Corley, 1865; James M. Spurgeon, 1866; A. L. Leighty, 1885; Ella Leighty, 1886; H. Agnes Prescott, 1887; J.T. Kelly, and Salla E. Richards, 1888; Fanny Brooker, 1890; Anna Hall and Joseph Kelly, 1891; Rose Humphrey, 1892; Cynthia McKittrick, 1901; Foy Morse, 1905-06; Mollie Dobbs, 1909; T. Morrison, 1906-07; J.W. Archey, 1911; Amiee Fry, 1912-13; Nellie Gatons, and Guy Henderson, 1914; Ethel Silknitter, 1915; Guy Henderson and Alice Rhodes, 1916; Irvil Nance, 1917-18; Maxine Jenkins, 1924; Elmer E. Smith, 1926; Florence Stockdale, 1927; Charlotte B. Kirk, 1934; J. Wilson Johnston, 1935; (school once again called Johnston) Verla Lynch, 1939; 1940; Floy Foster, 1941-42; Hattie Glick, 1943; Anna Maude Foster, 1944-46.

Anna Maude Foster was the last teacher with a school of 16 pupils, and directors were Russell Simpson, W. N. Babb, and Felix Hinton.

Johnson school was sold in 1951 to Lyle and Elouise Woodard for $530 which at that time was located in the northwest corner of the southwest quarter of the southwest quarter of section 15.

SUMMITT
District 6 or 12

Summitt school was located in the southeast quarter of section 14 of Cold Spring township. During the 1860's the district covered sections 14,15,23, and 24.

A frame school house was built in 1872 and a new one was built in 1884. Directors of the 1880's were George W. Bechtel and James F. Dunaway.

Some teachers of Summitt school were: Jacob Brown, 1862 with a class of 23 pupils; J.F. Campbell and J. P. Williams, 1863; John McMahan, 1864; S.Severns, 1865; Joseph T. Kelly, 1885; H. Agnes Prescott, 1885; W. M. Fellers and H. Agnes Prescott, 1886; Francis Hoffman, 1887; Francis Hoffman and Ella Leighty, 1888; E.C. Graybill, 1889; H. Agnes Prescott, 1890; F. J. Snapp, 1891; Orson Hall, 1892; Charles Price, 1893; Mollie Robertson, 1901; Jessie Johnson, 1905-06; J. Spracklin, 1907; Anetta Eckart, 1909; Jeanne Brown and Rosetta Bechtel, 1911; May Montooth, 1912; John G.Duncan, 1913-15; Victoria Pfeiffer, 1916; Leroy Hunter, 1917-18; Florence Hall, 1922; Elmer E. Smith, 1924-standard school; Lillian Tressler, 1926-27; Leroy Hunter, 1934; Charlotte B. Kirk, 1935; Helen McDonald, 1939; Elmer Smith, 1940-42; Celestine Woolard, 1943; Ferne Boone, 1944; Celestine Woolard, 1945; Mary Hampton, 1948.

Mary Hampton was the last teacher with 13 pupils, and directors were Fred B. Smith, Merrell Nohren and Bennie Landers.

Trustees sold Summitt school in 1951 to Dale Walters for $450.

LLOYD L. SMITH

He attended Summitt school where his first teacher was Leroy Hunter, and others were Ned Guthrie and Guy Henderson. He also noted that Elmer Smith was a teacher at Lockwood School.

FLORENCE MONROE

She attended Summitt school and had teachers Glenna Allen, Florence Hall and Elmer Smith. She attended three years for the sixth, seventh and eighth grades.

"I remember one thing that was a high light to all of us because we got a free pass to go the Shelby County Fair for one day."

Florence was the daughter of Theodore and Ethel Nohren. Other teachers were Noel Nance, Martha Parr Jackson, Harold Miller and Rosette Bechtel.

STARK
District 7 or 15

Stark school was first located in the northeast quarter of section 26 in 1867 when Samuel and Mary Tressler sold a half acre to the school trustees. The district then covered sections 25,26,35 and 36. Later in 1886, Morgan and Urana Bryant deeded one acre in the southwest quarter of section 25, to school trustees Sheldon Thompson, W. W. Newkirk and Henry Doner in the year 1886.

Some teachers of the Stark school were: L. P. Williams, 1862-class of 22 pupils; Pemelia A. King and L. P. Neal, 1863; B. W. McMahan, C.A. Wakefield, and Margaret L. Perryman, 1864; Orville Robertson and P. A. King, 1865; S. W. Buchanan, 1871; Mary and Hattie Myers; Ida Marks, 1884; Chattie Morrison, 1885; W. L. Myers, 1886; Hattie Myers, 1887; Albert Johnson, 1888; Mollie Rice, Lucy Southern and Albert Johnson, 1889; Al Johnson and Nora Brandon, 1890; Ella Leighty, 1891; M.C. Corley, 1892-93; Thornton Sellers, 1901; Ella Finley, 1904; Nellie Smith, 1906-07; Rosetta Bechtel, 1909; Earl Crowder and Addie Askins, 1911; Hesse E. Nance, 1912; Orthel Smart, 1913; Jessie Roberts and Bessie Smart, 1914; J. G. Duncan and Bessie Smart, 1915; Aleoa Nance and Celesta Smart, 1916; Elmer Smith, 1917-18; Myra Dowell, 1924-standard school; Mabel R. Moore, 1926-improved and decorated, 1927; Charles O. Danneberger, 1934; Harold Miller, 1935; Grace Hall, 1939-40; Hattie Wakefield, 1941; Hazel Cothern, 1942; Juanita Henderson, 1943-44; John Strain, 1945-46.

John Strain was the last teacher with 16 pupils, and directors were Clyde Frost, George Caskey, and Pearl Hudson.

Some of the directors of the 1880's were Newton Reed and J. F. Culp.

BARBARA MINERVA CHERRY BUMGARDNER

She attended Stark from 1924 to 1932 and had teachers Myra Dowell, Dona Price, Mabel R. Moore, J. Harrison Cherry, Jr. (her brother), and George W. Weaver.

"Grandfather George Cherry bought this place in the early 1890's. Sarah and Lillie attended Stark. All of my brothers and sisters finished their grade school there. My sisters were Marie and Pearl, brothers, George, J. Harrison and Charles N. Charles went to school the same eight years that your mother (the author's) Lena Stoneburner did. In the first years that I attended there were several students so we could play different games as Andy Over Over the school house, hide and seek, behind the coal house, or the shed for horses or the out houses for boys and girls. Sometimes we would hide on top of the coal house. Some years we would play two base baseball; the little kids could fan out then get on a base then a big kid would really hit a long ball and everyone would run to the second base and back to the first one. Anyone who was tagged out had to go to opposing team. We played stink base, sometimes fox and goose in the snow. If the weather was bad, we played hide the thimble, hunt cities or countries on a map. When my brother J. Harrison taught, there were only four students most of the winter so we played marbles on the floor by using chalk to make three small holes and a large granny hole. He also put up a basketball hoop and we shot baskets on nice days. The three sided barn was for the teacher to use for their horse if they used a horse for transportation. The building I went to school in, burned but a new building was built, but there is no building now. George Cherry, my grandfather, lived on farms south of this one so that my father Jim Cherry and older brother Dr. T. E. Cherry attended Dog Prairie. George's daughters finished their grades at Stark. I was in the seventh grade when Charles started. There was Donald Smart (deceased), Wendell Salmons, Lena Stoneburner, and Charles Cherry. Franklin Stoneburner has farmed the Cherry farm since 1946."

Barbara was the daughter of James Harrison and Clara Frances Simpson Cherry, Sr., grand daughter of George W. and Minerva Cox Cherry and James Spencer and Barbara Jones Simpson; great-grand daughter of Andrew and Sarah Miller Cherry, James and Ann Ivison Simpson.

CLARA ELIZABETH MANUEL FROST

She attended Stark school from 1918 to 1920, and had teachers Ray Hudson and Helen Moore.

"Our teacher would let us go outside to watch a horseless carriage go by or a dirgable fly over. One cold winter morning two boys came to school after catching a skunk. After a little while, the teacher sent them home.

I also attended Number 6 school in Dry Point township, two schools near Tower Hill, one southwest called Sheep Shanks. Teachers there were Lena Cly, Pearl Garrett and Cora Warren.

The school north and south of Tower Hill was called Frog Pond. The teacher there was Pauline Miller. My last country school was Boiling Springs; it is near the River north and east of Cowden. It is still standing and has been made into a house and someone lives there. The teachers there were Ray Hudson and Mrs. Etta Culp. The teacher at Number 6 had the last name of Nance but I can't remember his first name. It was either Orville or Maurice but am not sure which they were, brothers and both were teachers.

Stark school circa 1925 with Pearl Seeley sitting on the steps.
Photo courtesy of Barbara Bumgardner

Stark school 8th grade graduates in 1938. Pictured are Donald Smart, Lena Stoneburner (author's mother), and Charles Cherry.
Photo in author's collection

I graduated from Boiling Springs in 1926 and entered Cowden High School that September."

Clara was the daughter of William Fred and Lamora Deal Manual; granddaughter of Joseph and Elizabeth Spring Manual, and John and Clara Jane Bell Deal; great-granddaughter of George and Maria Bell, Washington and Lucinda Deal, Frederick and Rachel Spring, and George and Sarah Manual.

JOSEPHINE D. MURPHY
    "Back about 1910, 11, and 12, we lived in Cold Spring township. Our post office was Herrick. I went to country school. Stark was its name. I've been back; it is now long gone. Kids I knew then were the Cherry three, Pearl, Marie and George, the Wakefields, Robertsons, Hawyer, Horsman, Faulkner and Seely. Teachers I remember were Hesse Nance, Addie Askins, and Orthel Smart."

PEARL NEVA CHERRY SEELY
    She attended school from 1903 to 1913, and had teachers Ethel Barrett, Addie Askins, Jessie Roberts, Isaac Robertson, Sally Eckert, Hessie Nance, Orthel Smart, Bessie Smart, Rosetta Bechtel, and Art Davlin.
    Pearl was the daughter of James Harrison Cherry and Clara Frances Simpson Cherry; granddaughter of George W. and Minerva Cox Cherry, and James Spencer and Barbara Jones Simpson; great-granddaughter of Andrew and Sarah Miller Cherry, James and Ann Ivison Simpson.

Corley school of 1932 with teacher Paul V. Wakefield. Front, l to r, Billy Corley, Jean Corley, Dorothy Stoneburner, Velma Davis, Herman Sphar and Jimmy Corley. Back, l to r, Lloyd Hinton, George Henry Henderson, teacher, and Dorothy Sphar.

CORLEY
District 8 or 14

Corley school was located in the southeast corner of the southeast quarter of section 28 of Cold Spring township. In 1884 Owen D. Corley and his wife deeded one acre to the trustees for Corley school. The grounds and school house were also repaired in that year.

Directors of 1889 were C. Corley, J. W. Henderson, and J. B. Price.

Some of the teachers at Corley school were: W. M. Fellers, 1884; H. B. Price, 1885; Mary E. Dow and Ella Leighty, 1886; Ella Leighty, 1887; William N. Foster and Mary E. Dow, 1888; Frank Turner, 1889; John H. McNutt, 1890; C. M. Davis and Captolia Evey, 1891; W. M. Fellers and Ruth E. Huber, 1892; M. Turner, 1893; Etta Corley, 1901; Ethel Barrett and Rosah Bechtel, 1904; Rosetal Bechtel, 1905-06; W. M. Fellers, 1906-07; T. E. Morrison, 1909; Ina Askins and Amy Fry, 1911; Guy Henderson and Maud Wakefield, 1912; Vivien Fletcher, 1913-16; Fay McVay and Lillian Tressler, 1917; Guy Henderson and Lenora Watson, 1918; Nona Linn, 1924-26; Elmer Smith, 1927; Paul Wakefield, 1932-34; Virginia F. Strain, 1935; Alice N. McCoy, 1939; Nellie Hamilton, 1940-41; Anetta Jones, 1942; Elmer Smith, 1943; Hattie Glick, 1944; Ruth Farrier, 1945.

There was still school in 1948 but no teacher was listed in the directory. There were ten pupils that year with directors George Salee, Martin Hinton, and Frank Corley.

During the month of May 1892 Ruth E. Huber had the following students at Corley with perfect attendance: Grace Roudybush, Effie Rhodes, Maggie Henderson, Ezra Henderson, Emery Henderson, Tony Henderson and Willie Bennett.

The trustees sold Corley school to Lloyd and Lowell Spurgeon of Marion County, Illinois in 1953 for $850.

SYLVIA SNYDER

She attended Corley school and had teachers Etta Culp and Nona Murray. She went there eight years.

Sylvia was the daughter of Linzie and Ella Miller Stoneburner; granddaughter of John and Maggie Mohler Stoneburner, and Benedict and Lucie Spockwell Miller.

WHITE OAK
District 9 or 13

White Oak school was located in the northwest corner of the northwest quarter of the southwest quarter of section 32 of Cold Spring township. W. T. and Eva Linn deeded one acre to the school trustees in 1892.

Directors in 1889 were Austin Bland, W. T. Linn and G.W. Pinney.

Some of the teachers at White Oak school were:

Mattie Robertson, teacher at Corley school circa 1910. Photo given to author's grandfather Lawrence Stoneburner.

Typical grade card during administration of Lee W. Frazer. On back was note to parents explaining the scoring method, and a place for their signatures.

BI-MONTHLY REPORT CARD
Shelby County Common Schools
SUPERINTENDENT'S EXAMINATION

Report of Lawrence Stoneburner a pupil in Fourth year
District No. 14 Shelby County, Illinois.

	Oct. 191_	Dec. 1915	Feb. 1916	April 191_	Term Average
Days Tardy		4	1		
Days Absent		8	5		
Deportment		95	100		
Attention		95	99		
Reading		81	96		
Spelling-Orthography		95	100		
Writing					
Language					
Arithmetic		100	88		
Geography		94	96		
Grammar		65	78		
U. S. History		88	95		
Physiology		93	100		
Civics					
Drawing					
Botany - Agriculture					

Elmer E. Smith, Teacher.

Jeanie Gower, 1884; Anna Gower and Mattie Rhodes, 1885; William Corley and Anna Gower, 1886; H. B. Price and Anna Gower, 1887; H. B. Price and Elizabeth Clark, 1888; Elizabeth Clark and Lucy Miller, 1889; Lucy Miller, 1890; Marion Turner, 1891-93; H. W. Buckner, 1893; Lizzie Morrison, 1901; A.R. Moon, 1905-07; Roy C. Rhodes, 1909; Ava Morgan and Lenora Price, 1911; Roy Rhodes, 1912; Mattie Smart and Bessie Smart, 1913; Thomas Dobbs, 1914; Thomas Dobbs and Alice Rhodes, 1915; Alice Rhodes and Henrietta Neece, 1916; Alice Rhodes, 1917-18; Hazel Linn, 1924-26; John Strain, 1927; George W. Weaver, 1934; Clark Jenkins, 1935; Clarence M. Coleman, 1939-40; Robert Gill, 1941; John Strain, 1942-43; Celestine Woolard, 1944; Minnie Strain, 1945; Forrest Crouch, 1946.

Forrest Crouch was the last teacher with 5 pupils, and directors were Thomas Allen, Violet Allen and Helen Sanders.

HERRICK
District 1 or 154

Peter Myers deeded land in 1856 to the school trustees in section 9 Township 9 N R 2 E, for school, church and burying grounds, north where the present town of Herrick is today.

In 1850, this school and one other early one were the only two schools--both log cabins in this township range. In 1866, a special tax of 25 cents per 100 dollars was assessed for the use of the school and directors were A. T. Smart and J.S. Burris. Three years later, the tax was 75 cents per 100 dollars, and directors were W. T. Hadley, H.C. Whittington and J. B. Moon.

Directors in 1881 were F. F. Moon and J. W. McNutt. By 1894, citizens of this area petitioned to the Shelby County board for a new township to created from Cold Spring. Supervisor Fellers entered the petition which read,

"To the Honorable County Board of Supervisors of the County of Shelby, State of Ill. The undersigned legal voters of the town of Cold Spring in said county do petition your honorable board to divide said town as follows: Beginning on the east side of town 10 ten and nine range two east of 3rd P.M. on the section line between said towns thence west on said section line to west side of range two east of the 3rd P.M. That the territory with the following boundaries are to coincide with the boundaries of the congressional boundaries of town ten range two east of 3rd P.M. shall contine to form and exist as the said town of Cold Spring and that part of the territory of said town nine range two east of 3rd P.M. to the county line of Fayette and Shelby Co. shall form a new town to be named _____ . That the each of said towns will not be less than seventeen square miles and your petitioner will ever pray."

A special election was to be held in the new township of Herrick then on the first Thursday of April 1894 with 3 judges from each township. From Herrick, Willie Corley, Jesse Moon and John McNutt. From Cold Spring, William Fellers, Jacob Johnson and James Brown.

PLEASANT UNION
District 2 or 155

Pleasant Union school was located in section 11 of Herrick township. The school was also known as Dog Prairie. John E. Sarver provided land for the school in 1860. In 1866, taxes of 25 cents per 100 dollars was assessed for the school, and directors for that year were John T. Simpson, John Sarver and John Palmer.

For a couple of years, the trustees had a school located on a new plot furnished by Richard A. Snow in the same section but different spot. In 1878 John and Harriet Sanner sold a plot to the trustees in the northwest corner of the same section.

Directors for the 1880's were Noah Miller, Richard Snow, John Jones, William Bryant and Thomas R. Snow.

Some of the teachers at Pleasant Union were: C. M. Davis, 1889; Ed Smith, 1890; U. G. Fletcher, 1892-94; Isaac Robertson, 1901; Estella Robertson, 1909; Hal Guthrie, 1922; W. D. Williams, 1924; Ed Brown, 1926; Wade Murray, 1934; Silver Bumgardner, 1939; Silver B. Horsman, 1940-43; W. D. Williams, 1944-45; Nellie Hamilton, 1946; Lois Caskey, 1946-48.

Lois Caskey was the last teacher in 1950 with 15 students; directors in 1948 were Elmer Corley, William A. Blackerby, and H. Seeley.

HELEN BLACKERBY

"The small, well-kept cemetery still remains today, but the school was closed in the early 1950's. The main building was torn down and the lumber used for a machine shed on the William A. Blackerby farm. The cloak rooms were taken off and moved to and are presently part of the Roscoe Blackerby home 3/4 mile west of the school location.

Some of the teachers were W. D. Williams, Burl Moon, Grace Lankford, Nona Murry, Silver Horsman and Lois Caskey."

JAMES R. BRYANT

He attended Pleasant Union from 1922 to 1930, and had teachers Hal Guthrie, Wade Murry, W. D. Williams, Albert Wall, J. Burl Moon and Grace Lankford.

James was the son of Edgar and Luella Corley Bryant; grandson of James Richard and Addie Belle Corley Bryant, and

Orven Douglas and Missouri Frances Mckinney Corley; great-grandson of William Charles and Louisa Frances Dodson Bryant, Caniel and Unity Jane McKee Corley, and Daniel and Jane Henderson Corley, and Levi and Catherine Mattox Corley.

MOONSHINE
District 6 or 153

Moonshine school was first located in section 8 in the southwest quarter. Land for it was given by James B. and Margaret A. Moon in 1885.

By 1914 it was moved to section 5 where it remained until it burned in 1936. Henry Inman had built a new school in the same location for 1937.

Some of the teachers at Moonshine were: Frank Turner, 1890; John McNutt, 1891; Thomas Sarver, 1892; M. L. Turner, 1894; Otto Lockart, 1901; Bettie Roberts, 1909; Zelpha Chamberlain, 1917; Edith Carroll, 1924; Ruth Rhodes, 1926; Maude Sallee, 1927; Elma E. Taniges, 1934-35; Hazel Lee Cothern, 1939; Betty Roberts, 1940; Virginia Strain, 1941; Nona L. Murray, 1942; Betty Roberts, 1943; Virginia Strain, 1944; Elma Taniges, 1945-46; and Virginia Strain, 1948.

Virginia Strain was the last teacher with 16 pupils; directors for that year were Ivel Collins, M. R. Potts and Allen Smart.

The school was sold by the trustees in 1953 to the American Legion for $1340, which was one acre in the southwest corner of the NW¼ SE¼ of section 5 of Herrick township.

Properly adjusted, note position of feet, thighs, elbows and shoulders.

Rural Schools of Illinois, 1929.

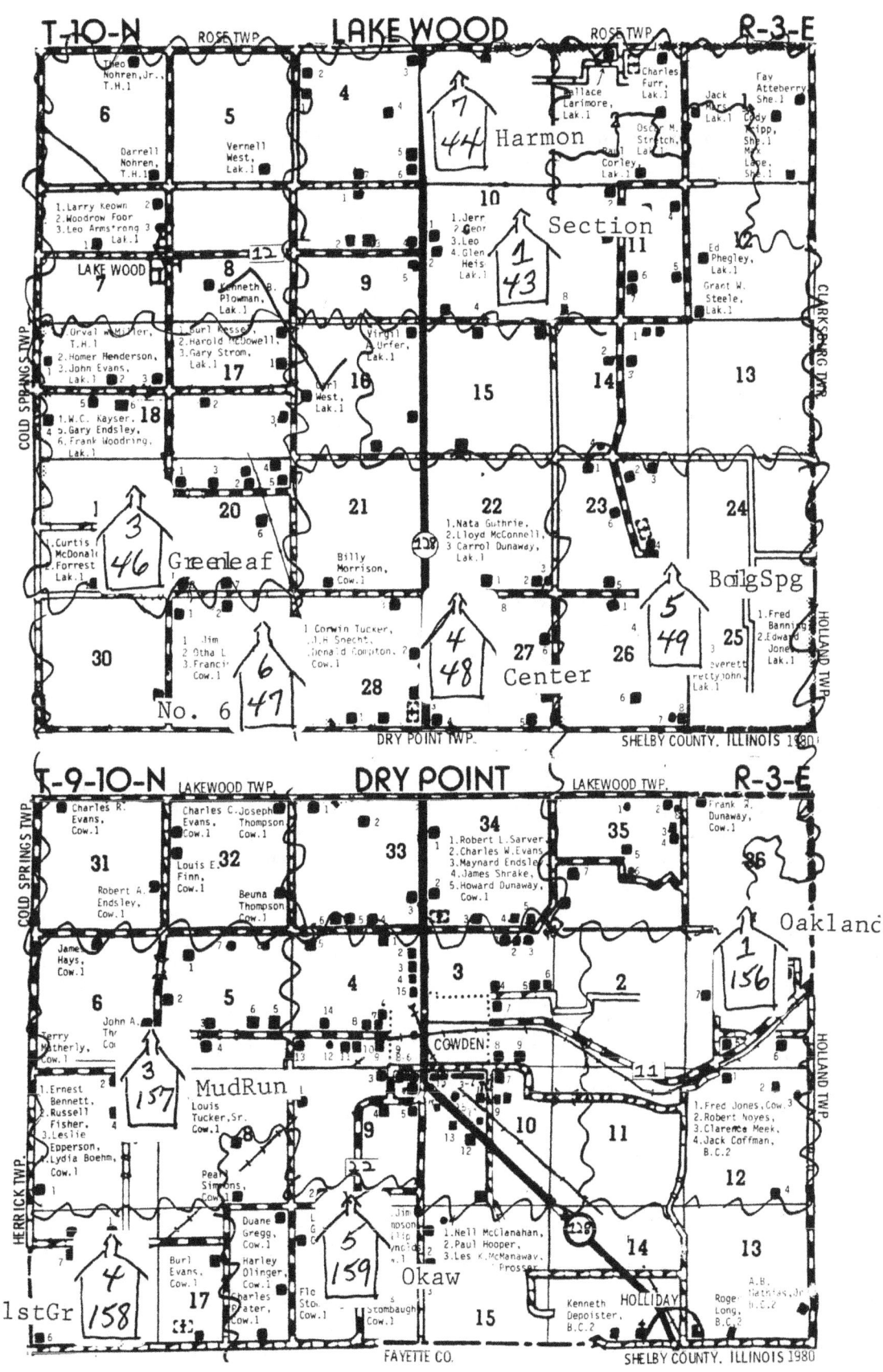

The wavy line indicates the 1903 school district.

DRYPOINT AND LAKEWOOD TOWNSHIPS

Dry Point originally was one of the larger townships bordering the south county line. It's most populous areas were Lakewood and Cowden.

In 1860, there were three school districts in town 10 north range 2 east. District 1 was probably in the area of section 10, later location of Section school, district 2 in location of present-day Lakewood, and district 4 in area of section 27 later Center school. The southern part of Dry Point had two districts in 1860, district 2 and 4. District 2 at later Cowden and district 4 in section 18. By 1870, there were 10 school districts.

Children of the early times attended a school several miles distant in the neighboring township of Cold Spring. By 1834 Elias Bissen taught in the area of later Thompson Mill on the river a short distance from later day Cowden.

SECTION
District 1 or 43

Section school was located in the southeast quarter of section 10 of Dry Point, later Lakewood township. Taxes in 1866 were 40 cents on the 100 dollars, and directors were Gideon Walker, Silas Whitfield and Reuben Askins. Three years later, they build a school with assessments of $1.60 per hundred dollars, and directors were Reuben T. Askins, David Barton and William Barton.

Directors of the 1880's were J. Middlesworth, William Barton, M. C. Jones, James Askins, George A. Moore, and Ebenezer Barden.

Some of the teachers at Section school were: James Barton, 1888; Silas Wakefield, 1891; Lizzie Askins, 1892; C.F. Evey, 1893; Aura Valentine, 1894; Lizzie Barton, 1901; Jean Veisure, 1906; Clyde Howe, 1909; Josephine Jenkins, 1922; Gladys Fluckey, 1924; Juanita Moore, 1926; Lena Thomas, 1927; W.D. Williams, 1934; Lonnie F. Parr, Jr., 1935; Lyle Specht, 1939-42; Ruby Gilmore, 1943-44; Forrest Fowler, 1945; Perry E. Pritts, 1946; Pearl Lockart, 1948.

Pearl Lockart was the last teacher with 16 pupils; directors were Frank Carnes, Joe Klepzig, and Edward Phegley.

GREENLEAF
District 3 or 46

Greenleaf school was located in the southeast quarter of section 19 of Dry Point, later Lakewood township. Taxes were seven percent per $100, and directors were S. Severns, J.D. Huffer and T. N. Hall. Three years later the taxes were 40 cents per $100, and directors were John M. Roberts, and Simeon Dowell.

Section school in 1910. Back row, l to r, Harley Baldwin, Arthur Finks, Addie Askins Bowman, Ocla Trout Phegley, Issac Finks, teacher Cleve Askins, Lloyd Steele, Harley Barton. 2 row, l to r, Blanche Russell, Edith Neil Corley, Lester Barton, Agnes Courtesy, Helen Dowell, Onie Russell Askins, Beulah Askins Kirk, Myra Dowell, Ruby Askins, Onie Curlin, Nelly Hodson. Front, l to r, Clarence Curlin, Cleo Finks, Arnold Baldwin, James Hodson, Charley Barton, Lonnie Finks, Levi Duckett.   Photo courtesy of Edith Corley

---

Additional teachers at Section school were: John Gregg, 1862; John R. Moore, 1863; Annie Finkbine and J. K. Burdick, 1864; Samuel Patton, 1865; Colmady P. Roberts, 1868-69; Ann Finkbine, 1869; Friese E. Perryman, 1870; C. P. Roberts and Laura A. Patton, 1871; F.C. Torrence, 1872; J.T. Harrol, 1873; S.W. Buchanan, 1874; D. McLaughlin and A. Perryman, 1875; James Barton, 1876; Mary Cobb, 1877; J.G. Hott and W. A. Carlisle, 1878; James Barton, 1879; William J. Eddy, 1880; J.A. Hilsabeck, 1881; B. J. Young, 1882; Lizzie Hall, 1882; James Barton and Lizzie Hall, 1883; Anthony Middleton and Emma Wortman, 1884; Mary Leathers, 1885; James Barton and Carrie Vanderpool, 1886; Minnie Vanderpool and C.S. Bowman, 1887; Lizzie Dush and W.R. Tom, 1888; Carrie Peek and William Inman, 1889; Alice Smith and Maggie Cleary, 1890; Eva Barrett, 1895-96; Jennie Middleton, 1896; Aura Valentine and H. Fairchild, 1897; Minnie Lovell, 1902; Edgar Fry, 1903; Vernon Steel, 1903; Eva Barrett, 1904-05; William Steel, 1906; and Clev. A. Askins, 1910.

Directors for the 1880's were Thomas Banning, Charles Wakefield, Simeon Dowell, J.L.M. Askins, and Joseph Bucher.

Some of the teachers of Greenleaf school were: C.T. Bowman, 1888; Ed W. Smith, 1889; J.E. Price, 1890; Jeanie Middleton, 1891; Walter Askins, 1892; H. M. Newkirk, 1893; R. M. Carruthers, 1894; Hugh Davis, 1901; Theresa Hyland, 1903; Golda Tressler, 1904; Agnes Hall, 1909; John G. Duncan, 1917; I. R. Holt, 1912; Leroy Hunter, 1924-27; Gertie M. James, 1934; Leroy Hunter, 1935; Juanita Moore, 1939; Juanita Moore Henderson, 1940; Mattie Dugan, 1941-43; Sadie Gregg, 1944; Josephine Jenkins, 1945-46.

Josephine Jenkins was the last teacher with 17 pupils; directors were Perry Price, Eileen Walter and J. P. Lee.

The trustees sold the property in 1950 to the Full Gospel Church of Lakewood, a half acre for $100.

PAUL V. WAKEFIELD

He attended Greenleaf school for eight years and had teachers Delbert W. Jones, Martha Parr Jackson, Elmer E. Smith, Roy Wakefield, and Leroy Hunter.

"A field trip in the woods, an egg roast. Eggs were not cooked enough. One boy tried to break egg on his head and white and yellow of the egg streamed down his hair and face.

There were many fine field trips that included study of birds, flowers, plants, and trees during the teaching of Leroy Hunter. Hunter wore overalls to school--was a very outstanding teacher. He knew more than the average college instructor."

Paul was the son of John W. and Gertie Sherwood Wakefield; grandson of David Wakefield and James and Lura Sherwood.

NOEL M. BANNING

He attended Greenleaf school from 1924 to 1924, and had teachers Leroy Hunter, Elmer Smith and Roy Wakefield.

"I can think of no incident worthy of relating. Some other teachers of the 20's and 30's were Delbert Jones, Harold O. Wakefield, U. L. Evans, Mattie Dugan, Gertie Moore, James and Jaunita Moore.

My father also attended the school and I have a memento of the 1898-99 school year which names the students (35 of them) and the teacher was a Miss Viola Barrett. Another teacher of that era I have heard of was Vesta Carlisle of Cowden who rode to and from school on the B & O train which made a special stop for her at the nearest crossing."

Noel was the son of Clark Vilas and Mabel Corley Banning; grandson of Thomas M. and Adaline Spracklin Banning, and William and Nora Hatten Corley; great-grandson of Laranza and Susannah Banning, George and Arloa Turner Minor Spracklin, William and Elizabeth Corley, and John William and Delilah Hatten.

CENTER
District 4 or 48

Center school was located in the west half of section 27 of Dry Point, later Lakewood township. In 1866 taxes were 50 cents per 100, and directors were Aaron Morehouse, Benjamin Reynolds and J. C. Neel. Three years later, a new school was built with the taxes being $1.75 per 100, and one of the directors was John Fowler.

Some of the teachers at Center school were: ___Mitchell, 1888; Albert Johnson, 1890; Rose Wonus, 1892; Iva Hall, 1893; Clara Fogle, 1894; C.W. Middleton, 1901; Clemie Warnick, 1909; Irvil Nance, 1917; Nellie McConnell, 1922; Bertha O. Baird, 1924; Nellie Morrow, 1926-27; Elbert Askins, 1934-35; Doy Hogge, 1939-42; Letta Richards, 1943; A.W. Thompson, 1944-45; Letta Richards, 1946; Joyce Krietemeier, 1948.

Joyce Krietemeier was the last teacher with 9 pupils; directors that year were John O'Kelley, Maynard Endsley, and Gerald Reid.

BOILING SPRINGS
District 5 or 49

Boiling Springs school was located in the east half of section 26 of Dry Point, later Lakewood township.

Directors of the 1880's were J. J. Askins, John M. Phillips and P. L. Barrow.

Some of the teachers at Boiling Springs were: S.A.D. Howe, 1888; Maggie Cleary, 1890; W.R. Thom, 1891; Ida Christy, 1892; Ida Walker, 1893; Jennie Middleton, 1894; M. L. Banning, 1901; Lillian Tressler, 1909; Helen Howe, 1917; Ray H. Hudson, 1924; Myra Dowell, 1926; Myra D. Taylor, 1927; Melvin A. Steele, 1934; Harold O. Wakefield, 1935; Alleva N. Dill, 1939-40; Kelsey W. McMillen, 1941-43; Grace Hall, 1944-45; A. H. Thompson, 1946; Grace Middlesworth, 1948.

Grace Middlesworth was the last teacher with 9 pupils; directors were Leverett Pettyjohn, George Ridlen and Curtis Pettyjohn.

In January 1894, Ida Walker had 51 pupils enrolled with average daily attendance of 39. For the month of December-January, she reported the following with perfect attendance: David Pettyjohn, Austin Hobbs, Henson Hobbs, Eddie Banning, Simon Mulverhill, Jesse Shell, Christ Middleton, James Barrow, Harry Shell, Jacob Shell, Mary Hobbs, Lola Hobbs, Allie Wade, Ettie Sherburn and Grace Wade.

RAYBURN BANNING

He attended Boiling Springs school for two weeks and had teacher Nellie McConnell Morrow.

"I only went to school two weeks, then my folks moved to Cowden. I finished school in Cowden. I graduated in two weeks there I guess. After graduating in Cowden, I moved back to my grandparents house and farmed. I could tell you a lot of history on Stringtown, that is what they call this area of country."

Rayburn was the son of Fred L. and Myrtle Banning Banning; grandson of John M. and Angie Banning and Charles N. and Arwilda Banning; great-grandson of Joseph and Charlotte Banning and William and Rachel Himes, and Henry and Martha Himes Oller and Alexander and Jane Murray Banning.

He also noted other teachers at Boiling Springs as being: Vesta Carlisle, Burl Askins, Mary Phillips, Nettie Pettyjohn, Charles Middleton, Bessie Cihak, Jerry Reynolds, Maurice Nance, Hal Guthrie, Ruby Phillips Smith, Juanita Moore Henderson, and Joan Beaumont Holmes.

CLARA M. COMPTON

She attended school at Boiling Springs, Mud Run and Sylvan, and had teachers Ethel Van Reed, Isaac Wortman, Delbert Jones, Florence Hickman, Niles Hickman, Marinda Howe and Opal Summers.

"In the year 1910 there was an outbreak of smallpox. One pupil, Clarence Patterson, died with the disease. The school was closed and all the pupils had to be vaccinated against small pox before they could come back to school. This was at Sylvan school."

Clara was the foster daughter of Mr. and Mrs. George Compton, daughter of William and Jennie Middleton Oller; granddaughter of Henry and Martha Himes Oller, Robert Middleton and Clara Goodrich Middleton; great-granddaughter of Russel and Margaret Denton Middleton and M. William and Eliza Jane Oller.

NUMBER SIX
District 6 or 47

Number Six school was located in the southeast quarter of section 29 of Dry Point later Lakewood township. At one time the school also had the names of Black Log and Champion.

Directors of the 1880's were George W. Sullivan, E. Hartwick, Joseph Hall, Jacob Wonus, C.H. McClanahan, Milford McGee and John W. Bryant.

Some of the teachers at Number Six were: J. G. McDermith, 1888; H. M. Hagan, 1889; Clara Auld, 1890; Maggie Moran, 1891; James L. Moore, 1892-93; Elijah Jones, 1894; Bertha Baird, 1901; Sallie Eckert, 1909-school called Champion; Verlea Moore, 1922; Lillian Tressler, 1924;

Fern L. Hoffman, 1926; George L. Cherry, 1927; Lonnie F. Parr, Jr., 1934; Wayne Sherwood, 1935; Leroy Hunter, 1939-40; Forrest Fowler, 1941-44; and Carolyn Lockart, 1945-48.

Carolyn Lockart was the last teacher with 17 pupils; directors were Thebe James, Walter Riefsteck, and Ed McClanahan.

Green Leaf School
DISTRICT NO. 46
Lakewood, Shelby Co., Illinois

Presented By
I. R. HOLT.
Teacher

December 25, 1912

Lee W. Frazer   Co. Supt.
School Officers
Logan Askins   President
W. W. Wakefield   Clerk
J. F. Blakemore

DELBERT JONES

He also taught at Number Six or Champion. He also noted other schools he "served during (his) 33 years." He began at a period when schools were beginning to change from five months winter and 2 months spring. Therefore some of his are 7 months and then 2 months at another school, making a nine month year. Those schools were East Center, Champion-district 65, Lakewood, Greenleaf, Clarksburg, Sylvan, Holland, Fancher, Mt. Tabor, Washington, Hiatt, Keystone, Mud Run, Pleasant Grove, Valley, Pleasant Union, Victor and Herrick.

HARMON OR HARMONY
District 7 or 44

Harmon school was located in the southwest quarter of section 3 of Dry Point later Lakewood township. It was started by the turn of the century in the Harmon cemetery area.

Some of the teachers at Harmon school were: Clyde Askins, 1901; Myrtle Hubbard, 1909; Mevil Arnel Harmon,

1911; Pearl A. Warren, 1917-school called New Harmony; Ray Wakefield, 1922; Nyle Funk, 1924; Josephine Jenkins, 1926-27; Grace Hall, 1934-35; Floy Foster, 1938.
   Floy Foster was the last teacher with a salary of $66.25, and the directors or 1935-36 were C. L. Russell, Orrie Wade and Andrew Fultz.

   Harmon school circa 1911. This is the way Harmon school in Drypoint township. The students shown include, front row from left: Gerald Bowman, Glen Bowman, Maxine Jenkins, and ? Olehy. Back row, from left, Mevil Arnel Harmon, the teacher, ? , Clem Archey, John Harmon and Virgil Archey.
Photo courtesy of Walmsley Harmon

OAKLAND
District 1 or 156

Oakland school was located in the north half of section 1 of Dry Point township. Directors of the 1880's were George Smallsreed, Joseph Long, John Hedrick, F.O. Denton, W. H. Peifer, and W.F. Binion.

Some of the teachers at Oakland were: J. D. Peifer, 1889; Ella Clary and J. D. Peifer, 1890; Ella Clary and J. D. Peifer, 1891; J. D. Peifer and Jennie Middleton, 1892; Jennie Middleton, 1893; R. W. Thorn, 1894; Eva Barrett, 1895; Eva Barrett and R. W. Thorn, 1896; R. W. Thorn and Mollie Robertson, 1897; Mollie Robertson and Elden Sayler, 1898; Elden Sayler and C.W. Middleton, 1899; C.W. Middleton and Charles Lewis, 1900; Charles Lewis, 1901; Edna M. Casstevens and C.W. Middleton, 1902; Clara Thompson, and C.W. Middleton, 1903; C.P. Middleton and Hardin Middlesworth, 1904; Hardin Middlesworth and Walter Beals, 1905; Willie Dush and John Baird, 1906; Henry Clausen and Bertha Baird, 1907; John Baird and Jessie Riggs, 1908; Jessie Riggs and Grace Scovil, 1909; Burt Lewis and Cloyd Wright, 1910; W. D. Williams and H. O. Clausen, 1911; Edgar Peifer, 1912-13; H. D. Banning, 1922; Estella Robertson, 1924; Ray Hudson, 1926; Perry E. Pritts, 1927; John L. Stockdale, 1934-35; Forrest G. Fowler, 1939-40; and Alleva N. Dill, 1941-48.

Alleva N. Dill was the last teacher with 19 pupils. Directors were Ralph Lape, J. D. Casstevens and Everett Polley.

MUD RUN
District 3 or 157

Mud Run school was located in the southeast quarter of section 7, then located later in section 6. In 1866 there was a special school tax and directors were John H. Akins and William Austin. Three years later, the tax was 2½% per $100 and directors were William W. Nance and Franklin A. Cosart.

Directors of the 1880's were R. R. Jones, George F. Wade, William Taylor, G. W. Moore and William H. Akins.

Some of the teachers at Mud Run were: Cora B. McGrail, 1888; Lizzie Dush, 1889; Ella Johnson, 1890; Emma Perryman, 1891; Mary S. Leighty and Ella J. Cosart, 1892; Mary S. Leighty and Luella Moore, 1893; Luella Moore, 1894; James L. Moore and Luella Moore, 1895; A.L. Lane and Mary Simpson, 1896; James L. Moore, 1897; Henry Cosart, 1898; Henry Cosart and Edith Leighty, 1899; Edith Leighty and T.C. Torrence, 1900; Grant Johnson and C.W. Johnson, 1901; Mattie Hall and Lillie Tressler, 1902; Lillie Tressler, 1903; Emma Hubbart and Myra E. Howe, 1904; Myra E. Howe and John Baird, 1905; John Baird and

Stella Spracklin, 1906; Stella Spracklin Jones and Sallie Eckert, 1907; Charlie Dush and Vesta Carlisle, 1908; Vesta Carlisle and H.B. Daughtery, 1909; H. B. Daughtery and Jetty Tressler, 1910; Jettie Tressler, 1911; Roy C. Rhodes and Gertie Moore, 1912; Gertie Moore, 1913; Alleva Nance, 1922; Alleva N. Dill, 1924; Lorene Lankford, 1926; Bernice Ellis, 1927; Delbert W. Jones, 1934-35; Hal Guthrie, 1939-48.

Hal Guthrie was the last teacher with 17 pupils; directors were Glenn Boehm, Hesse E. Nance, and Gordon Prater.

GREENLEAF
PUBLIC SCHOOL
NUMBER 46.

Dry Point Twp., Shelby Co., Ill.

Presented by
GOLDA TRESSLER, Teacher.
C. M. Fleming, Co. Supt.

School Officers.
Wm. Wonus.   Webster Smith.
Chas. Wakefield.

Greenleaf School,
District No. 46,
Drypoint Twp.,
Shelby County, Illinois

1903-1904

..PRESENTED BY..
THERESA HYLAND, Teacher

Chas. M. Fleming, County Supt.

PLEASANT GROVE
District 4 or 158

Pleasant Grove school was located in the southeast quarter of section 18 of Dry Point township. Taxes in 1866 were 60 cents per 100, and directors were N. T. Pinkley and H. D. Petty. For building purposes, the taxes three years later were $1 per 100, and directors were William Sickels and David H. Devor.

Directors of the 1880's were H. G. Lorton, Samuel Kessler and John Fletcher.

Some of the teachers at Pleasant Grove were: Mattie Brandon, 1888; R. W. Thorn, 1889; R.W. Thorn and Mattie Brandon, 1890; M. G. Fletcher and Mattie Brandon, 1891;

M. J. Fletcher and U.G. Fletcher, 1892; Emily L. Lemhan, 1893; Mary Graybill, 1894; Mary Graybill and A.D. Barber, 1895; Thomas Graybill, Sarah D. Rogers, 1896; M. G. Fletcher, 1897; Harry O. Kesler and U. G. Fletcher, 1898; U.G. Fletcher and F.H. Rose, 1899; F. H. Rose and T.P. Torrence, 1900; Glenna Lockart, 1901; Glenna Lockart and Jessie Riggs, 1902; Lucy Lorton and Bertha Baird, 1903; Bertha Baird and Lucy Lorton, 1904; Lucy Lorton and Bessie Lockart, 1905; Bessie Lockart and Lucy Lorton, 1906; Roe Middlesworth, 1908; Roe Middlesworth and Meda Newberry, 1909; Meda Newberry and Elsie Viseur, 1910; Bertha Baird and Miles Nance, 1911; Miles Nance and Lucy Lorton, 1912; Ruby O. Fletcher, 1917; Hal Guthrie, 1924; Helen Perkins, 1926; Bertha Baird, 1927; Kelsey Wakefield, 1934; L.D. Williams, 1935; Grace F. Bender, 1939-42; Doy Hogge, 1943; Nona Murray, 1944; Norma White, 1945, and Forrest Fowler, 1946-48.

Forrest Fowler was the last teacher with 21 pupils and directors were Burl Evans, Hadley Tucker, and Harley Olinger.

In 1894 during the month of February - March, the following students had perfect attendance: Logan Lockart, Lois Kesler, Bob Butler, Sarah Ethridge, Perry Simmons, Elsie Butler, Mamie Lockart, Glennie Lockart, Eber Simmons, Bessie Lockart, Jennie Lockart, Quincy Lockart, Otto Lockart, Harley Lockart, Lunly Simmons, Lucy Lorton, Mamie Lorton, Moody Kesler, Steve Simmons, Harry Lockart, Thomas Lorton, Myrtle Aldridge and Edward Ethridge.

MARY MINERVA DUNAWAY ANDERSON

She attended Pleasant Grove school from 1922-25 and Oakland school from 1928-30, and had teachers Harry McDermith and Perry Pritts.

"One time on our last day of school which was the first day of May (this was while I was going to Oakland school. I do not remember the exact year.), my brothers were always anxious to go barefooted as soon as my mother would allow them to. It was warm enough that day that she let them go to school barefooted. During the day it started getting colder and the next thing we knew it was snowing, and my brothers had to walk home in the snow barefooted."

Mary was the daughter of Carl and Mary Gertrude Simmons Dunaway; granddaughter of William Marion and Minerva Ann Taylor Simmons, and Richard Allen and Mary Ellen McMillen Dunaway; great-granddaughter of James and Serepta Matthews Simmons, and James Richard and Sarah Jane Massey Dunaway.

OKAW
District 5 or 159

Okaw school was located in the southwest quarter of section 16, near the town of Holiday.

Directors in the 1880's were J. J. Askins, John M. Phillips, E. J. Holman, Charles Kesler and James M. Christy.

Some of the teachers at Okaw school were: Ivy Hall, 1890; Musa Ayers, 1891; Ida Christy, 1892; Thomas Owing, 1893; Clara Fogle and Thomas Owing, 1894; Mayetta Stewart and Ella Peters, 1895; Ella Peters and Jennie Middleton, 1896; Viola Barrett, 1897-98; H. O. Kesler and Lillian Tressler, 1899; Lillian Tressler and Ethel Torrence, 1900; Daisy Hunter and Agnes Barrett, 1901; Daisy Hunter, 1902; Emma Hubbart and Minnie Steagall, 1903; Minnie Steagall, 1904-05; Vera Frye and Charlie Dush, 1906; Charlie Dush and Lura Lockart, 1907; Lura Lockart and Winnie Nance, 1908; Winnie Nance and Ruby Hornbeck, 1909; Ruby Hornbeck and Sallie Eckert, 1910; Elsie Viseur and Delbert Banning, 1911; Delbert Banning and Bessie Banning, 1912; Bessie Banning, 1913.

Okaw school was dissolved sometime before 1924, and then students began going to Cowden.

In December 1899 at the school, the following students were in a literary program: Grace Riley, Fred Nehil, Susie Osborn, Edgar Goad, Clyde Taylor, Jessie Riggs, Orville Musser, Mattie Richards, Grace Ruby, Ella Musser, Josie Musser, Ethel Omstead, Harry Riley, Willie Angel and Clarence Holliday.

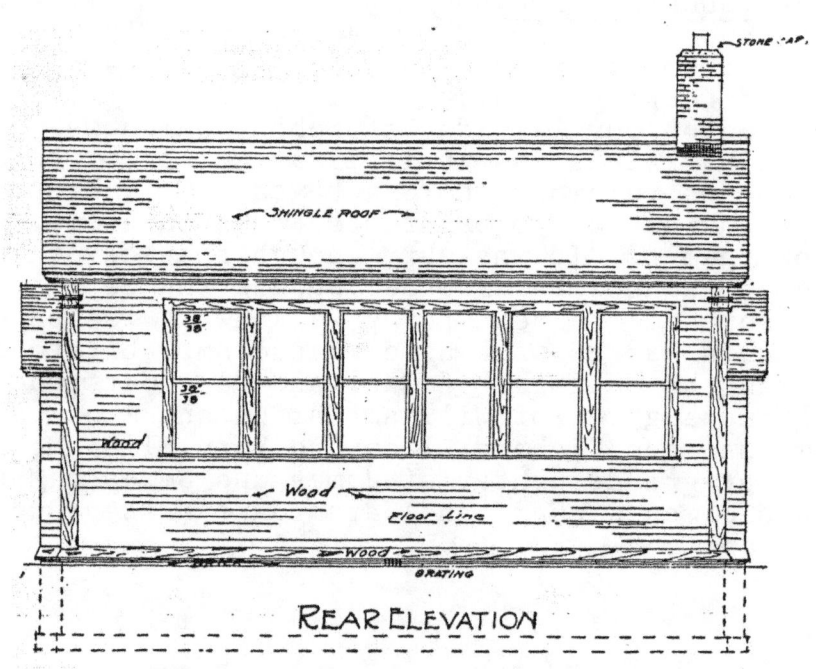

This side should be north, east or west if possible.

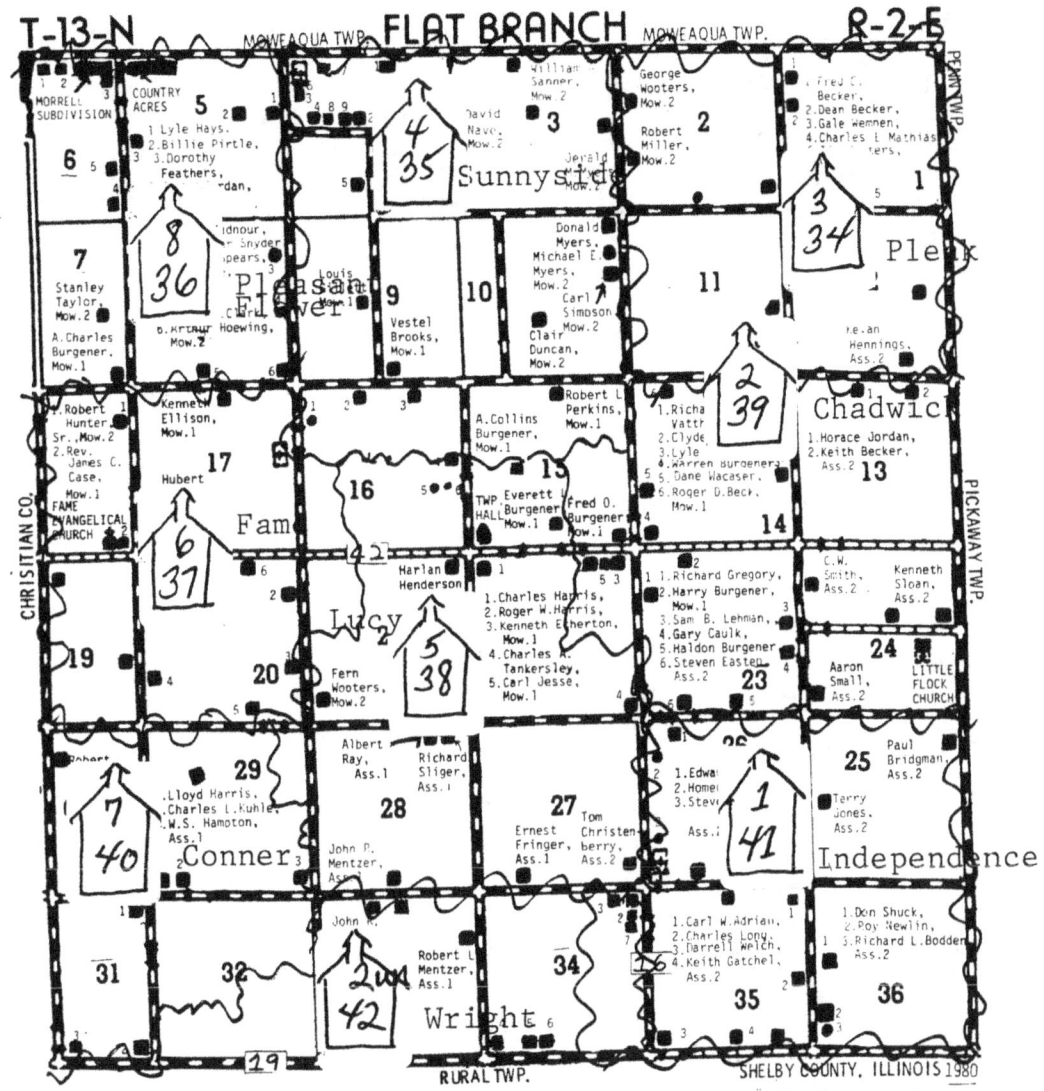

The wavy line indicates the 1903 school district.

FLAT BRANCH TOWNSHIP

According to a newspaper article written in 1881 by Prof. C. L. Howard, "the first school house erected in the northwestern part of the county was built in 1833, near the center of section 12 in Flat Branch township. David Simon was the first teacher, and James Rodman, the second. This school was very popular, and on account of its location was attended by pupils from surrounding townships."

INDEPENDANCE
District 1 or 41

Independance school was located in the southeast quarter of section 26 of Flat Branch township. Taxes in 1866 were 40 cents per 100, and directors were W. C. Cochran and Calvin Thomas. Three years later for building purposes, taxes were $1.75 per 100 directors were A. G. Pierce and James F. Pound.

Directors of the 1880's were J.W. Reed, George Story,

F. M. Thomas and M. Spence. In 1892 Robert C. and Agnes Cochran sold a half acre in the southeast corner of section 26 for Independence school.

Some of the teachers at Independance school were: Lena M. Klein, 1892-94; Myrtle Jackson, 1901; Alice Hill, 1909; Leonore W. Price, 1924; Hal Guthrie, 1926-27; Florence Stockdale, 1934; Dede Ann Shull, 1935.

Dede Ann Shull was the last teacher with 6 pupils; directors were: A.W. Spence, A.A. Story, and George Tolly.

During the month of November-December of 1900, Lillie Stegmeyer, teacher, reported the following pupils with perfect attendance: Albert McKittrick, Ray McKittrick, Emery McKittrick, Ada McKittrick, Willie Henderson, Earl Higgenbotham, Charles Higgenbotham, Virgil Higgenbotham, Frank Matlock, Willie Beckett, Jessie Beckett, Tressia Beckett, Pearlie Beckett, Georgia Cochran, Juna Cochran, Arthur Spence, Edna Spence, Leslie Pierce and Mattie Miller.

WRIGHT
District union 2 or 42

Wright school was located in the southwest quarter of section 33 in Flat Branch township. James B. and Sarah L. Wright sold land to the school trustees in 1868 with the provision the school be fenced and in good repair, at least 40 shade trees be in good growing order inside the fence, etc. Directors that year were Jacob Long and George W. Taylor.

Directors of the 1880's were Louis Oaks, A. Middleton, and Edward Ransford.

Some of the teachers at Wright school were: M. Foor, 1892; Carrie Harper, 1893; Mont G. Lockard, 1901; Blanche Jensen, 1909; Cordia Thomas, 1912; Flora Moore, 1913; Margaret S. Hennon, 1915-18; Nellie E. Mounts, 1918; Zelma J. Salmons, 1920-21; Ralph Wempen, 1922; Hal Guthrie, 1925; Vida Bass, 1924; Rose Wempen, 1926-28; Lola Knoop, 1929-30; Gertrude Miller, 1931-39; Dorothy Mowry, 1940.

Dorothy Mowry was the last teacher with 7 pupils; directors were Wayne Middleton, Mrs. Mildred Wempen and William Mounts.

In June 1893 at Wright school, the following students presented the final program for the year: Edna Hunter, Darvin Domas, Cora Oakes, Carl Wright, Roy Hunter, Lula Ransford, Roy Padgett, Otto Rose, Eula Oakes, Lucy Robinson, Jim Wright, Floy Foor, Jessie Foor, Maud Piper, Minnie Stitt, Daisy Robinson, Katie Middleton and Ada Hunter.

CHADWICK
District 2 or 39

Chadwick school was located in the northeast corner of section 14 in Flat Branch township. The trustees in 1868 had bought from William Chadwick the one acre for the school. Earlier in 1866, taxes were 20 cents per 100 for the school and directors were James Thomas, S.A. Bryson and John E. Gross. Three years later the taxes were one and a half percent per 100 and directors were S. Denton, S. A. Bryson and A. Jenkins.

Directors of the 1880's were A. Jenkins, James Thomas, J. H. McGrath, Chris Burgener.

Some of the teachers at Chadwick school were: Charles Connor, 1890; Frank South, 1892; J. M. Reynolds, 1894; A. J. Steidley, 1901; Amy Burgener, 1909; Elsie M. Hill, 1917; Mary H. Beery, 1924; Ruth Harrell, 1926; Opal Knearem, 1927-29; Lela Wright, 1930; Mary Wooters, 1931; Dorothy James, 1932-33; Alta Bohlen, 1934-35; Mary Wooters, 1936; Effie Osborn, 1937; Mary Wooters, 1938-42; Doris Smith, 1943; and Helen Shaffer, 1944-45.

Helen Shaffer was the last teacher with ten pupils; directors were Carl L. Wooters, Clyde Jesse, and Horace Jordan.

During the month of September 1900, W. F. Herron, teacher, reported the students with perfect attendance: Parentha Mayhill, Louisa Hill, Myrtle Hill, Oscar Hill, David Hill, Leon Hill, Fay Breeding, Charles Breeding, Fred Burgner, Eddie Jordan and Fern Townsend. Absent one day were Minnie Getz, John Getz, Edyth Jordan, Jennie Jones, Geneva Bridgman and Guy Bridgman.

ALFRED COLLINS BURGENER

He attended Chadwick school for eight years and had teachers Amy Burgener, Howard Neil and Lelah Henton.

"Walked a mile back and forth to school everyday in all sorts of weather. The one room school house was heated with coal in a pot belly stove. Kids were all well behaved then too. Lunch was carried to school each day, no hot lunches. Oh! A large hedge whip hung above the black board to keep everyone in line. It was used very few times, however."

Alfred was the son of Alfred M. and Chloe M. Wolf Burgener; grandson of Christopher and Fannie Baker Burgener, and Michael and Laura Howse Wolf.

PLEAK
District 3 or 34

Pleak school was first located in section 11 of Flat Branch in 1867 when Israel and Susan Beery sold a parcel to the school trustees. It then was moved to the northwest of section 12. Taxes the year before were 2% per 100 and directors were John Housh, Elisha McQueen and Israel Beery.

Directors of the 1880's were: Franklin Ward, R. A. Richart, P.B. Housh, A. Gordon, Jr., and William H. Snell.

Some of the teachers at Pleak school were: S.M. Wallace, 1892; W. G. Colbert, 1893; Rosa Trainor, 1894; A. F. Pinkston, 1901; George Hoewing, 1909; Helen Mills, 1924; Albert E. Wall., 1926; Aileen Jordan, 1927; Doris Trulock, 1934; Mae Maloney, 1935; Jemima L. Campbell, 1939-45.

Jemima L. Campbell was the last teacher with 8 pupils; directors were Glen Wooters, Harley Eversole and Fred Becker.

ELSIE JANE BECKER DICKMAN

She attended Pleak in 1925 and had teacher Onita Smock, and from 1926-33, she attended Sunnyside and had Miss Hall for a teacher.

"The girls wore cotton stockings that never staid up with elastic garters. The dresses were all cotton which were starched and ironed with heavy flat irons heated on the coal and cob cook stove.

The teacher always looked crisp and clean even though she had to start and keep the round iron stove, with a tin jacket around it, burning in the cold winter days. The coal and cob house was built on the back of the one room school house.

The front of the room had a stage on which we gave our programs for our parents to come and see. I remember my first week at Pleak school as my desk was next to the furnace and one of the eighth grade boys was starting a fire early in the morning. He threw a wash basin of kerosene in on some hot coals. The flames leaped out burning all his hair off plus other burns. He ran out the door as his folks lived across the road. They owned and operated the country store called, "Pleak Store and Hall'' as the large hall above the store was used for community gatherings such as box socials, talent contest, plays, medicine shows, etc.

Then we moved three miles west, where we drove a horse and storm buggy to Sunnyside school which was a mile and a half from our farm. Sometimes we walked across the field then it was only a mile. I can still see that team of horses lunging forward to pull the buggy loaded with six children and my father as he was the only one to drive a team on real muddy roads.

We all carried our lunch in a tin dinner bucket; ours was a double decker with a wooden handle. The girls cloak room was on one side of the furnace and the boys cloak room was on the other by the main door.

It was a great honor to ring the big bell for school to start at 8 a.m. Then at recess, we rang a brass hand bell.

Our teacher lived in Moweaqua which was four and a half miles from the school. She drove a model A Ford car as I recall.

We played baseball using a flat board with a handle whittled on it as a bat. I think dare base was just as popular a game in the summer, and fox and goose in the winter snow. It wasn't very comfortable sitting all day with wet socks and cotton underwear on. We would throw our wet mittens up on the wire grate on top of the furnace to smell and dry.

As I look back today, our world was very, very small when we compare it to our schools in 1984. Those were the days before electricity. We did have newspapers and a few magazines. Our main references were the World Books, all 12 volumes, and the large Webster dictionary. Oh, yes, we did have large wall maps and picture of the human body. I still see the picture of the ned nosed alcoholic with a wort on the end of his nose.

I would sure hate to go back in time and relive those days."

Elsie was the daughter of Fred and Nellie Wetzel Becker; granddaughter of Omer and Grace Mansfield Becker, and Rheem and Pearl Adams Wetzel; great-granddaughter of William and Mary Johnson Becker, and Benjamin Franklin and Sara Hartwell Wetzel.

SUNNYSIDE
District 4 or 35

Sunnyside school was located in the southeast corner of section 4 of Flat Branch township. In 1866 the taxes were 40 cents per 100 and directors were Nathan T. Campbell and Charles H. Wychoff. Three years later the taxes were one and half percent per 100, and directors were John Virden, and Willis Virden.

Directors of the 1880's were R. H. Groom, James V. Casey, F.W. Ney, Chris Fieker and L.D. Evans. In 1890 Joseph and Susanne Duncan sold a parcel in that township for Sunnyside school.

Some of the teacher at Sunnyside were: W. G. Colbert, 1892; J. E. Longenbaugh, 1893-94; W. B. Foltz, 1901; Stanley McGilligan, 1909; Alice M. Feery, 1917; Ruth Humphrey, 1924-26; Oneta Smock, 1927; Golda Hoffman; and Mollie Moss, 1939-45.

Mollie Moss was the last teacher with 19 pupils; directors were Harold Federman, Clair Duncan and Sylvia Rutherford.

WANDA BAIRD

She attended Sunnyside school and had teachers Edna Barton, Vera Moss, M. Nance, Onita Smock and Ruth Humphrey Hays.

Wanda was the daughter of Jacob and Corda Lockart; the granddaughter of Mr. and Mrs. Leo Lockart and Tom Christie.

EDNA FICKES FISHER
She attended Sunnyside school for the first three grades and had teachers George Hoewing, Standley McGilligan, and Helen Fraker.

Edna was the daughter of Don and Bertha Gonterman Fickes.

LUCY
District 5 or 38

Lucy school was located in the southeast quarter of section 21 of Flat Branch township. Charles M. and Eliza F. Lucy had sold one acre to the trustees in 1867 for the school. The year before the taxes were 70 cents per 100, and the directors were E. Bickner, A. L. Osborn and W. H. Snell. The next year, 1869, the taxes were $4\frac{1}{2}$% per 100, and directors were F. P. Snell, Frederick Ney and John B. Certin.

Directors of the 1880's were C. H. Demoss, F. Hartman, J. F. Williams and Jacob M. Gingery.

Some of the teachers at Lucy school were: W. Shelby, 1888; L. D. Evans, 1892; Molly Foor, 1893; Mollie Wallace, 1894; William Bickner, 1896; Ella Cronin and Marie Shempf, 1897; William McGinley, 1898; William Harris, 1899-1900; Florence Higgenbotham, 1901-02; Grace Harris, 1903; R. C. Fleming, 1909; Rosana Whipple, 1910; Nora Malhoit, 1911-12; Margaret E. Hines, 1913-14; Pearl Seibert, 1915-24; Nellie Erisman, 1926-27; Mildred Pontius, 1934-39; Ruby M. Kelly, 1940; Delores Mowry, 1941; Joyce Winings, 1942-43; Cleta Grubb, 1944; and Lois McClure, 1945.

Lois McClure was the last teacher with 13 pupils; the directors were W. F. Wooters, Clarence Matlock and Wayne Hays.

FAME
District 6 or 37

Fame school was located in the northeast corner of the northwest quarter of section 20. A. Lanson and his wife Sarah E. had deeded a plot to the school trustees in 1869 for the use of a school.

Directors of the 1880's were T.T. Watson, Charles M. Mausey, Just Wright, John Evans and J. T. Haverfield.

Some of the teachers at Fame school were: E. A. Gregge, 1889; W. H. Sands, 1890; Lulu M. Snyder, 1891; Alice O'Brien, 1892-94; Otto Ludwig, 1901; Alta M. Reynolds, 1909; Grace Hoffman, 1912; Edith Brown, 1913; Cleo Gehm, 1914-15; Beatrice B. Morgan, 1916-17; Mary J. Burnett, 1918; Wayne Tolson, 1924; Lelah Wilhelm, 1926; Pauline Bassler, 1927; Grace M. Potter, 1934-37; Irene C. Sherwood, 1938-40; Effie Osborn, 1941-45.

Effie Osborn was the last teacher with 13 pupils; the directors were Blanchette Snyder, Kenneth Ellison and Ralph Wheatley.

CONNOR
District 7 or 40

Connor school was located in the southeast corner of section 30 of Flat Branch township. James A. and Alice S. Osborn had sold land to the trustees in 1883 for the school.

Directors of the 1880's were W. Campbell, F. Herman Kuhle, J. W. Watson, and James A. Osborn.

Some of the teachers at Connor school were: A.D. Sittler, 1890; William Shelby, 1891; Ada Tilley, 1892; C.W. Wallace, 1893-94; Bessie Smith, 1901; Alta M. Reynolds, 1909; Rossie Seitz, 1905; Pauline Bassler, 1922-24; Mildred Moss, 1926; Carl H. Tankersley, 1927; Irene Miller, 1934-35; Enid Elizabeth McKinley, 1935-39.

Enid Elizabeth McKinley was the last teacher with 6 pupils; directors were John Van Syckel, Warren Tankersley and Lewis Kuhle.

In May of 1905, the following pupils had perfect attendance at Connor school: Myrtle Munson, Eva Osborn, Gladys Brule, Carrie Blanchard, Ruth Jacobs, Jessie Munson, Orville Fleming, Wayne Jacobs, Harry Jacobs, and Norbert Brule.

PLEASANT FLOWER
OR
CORRINGTON
District 8 or 36

Pleasant Flower was first located in section 6 after it was moved from Christian County in the 1860's. It was known then as Corrington as it was located on their land. It was later moved to section 8.

Directors of the 1880's were T. G. Hutchison, Henry Nirkam. W. J. Snyder, L. G. Calvin, Charles Stiner and P. G. Ludwig.

Some of the teachers at Pleasant Flower were: L. D. Evans, 1889; Mary O'Brien, 1881; S. M. Wallace, 1890; (school name changed to Pleasant Flower from Corrington) Carrie Harper, 1892; Emma Baumgarten, 1894; Ebner McGinley, 1901; Grace Synder, 1909; Beatrice Beldon, 1922-24; Bessie Brookshier, 1926; Selma D. Funk, 1927; Agnes Pontius, 1934; Jane Housh, 1935; Effie Osborn, 1938-39; Lucille Bartels, 1940; Bernice Stombaugh, 1941; Lucile Thompson, 1942; Lucille Boyce, 1943; Lyla Smith, 1944-45.

Lyla Smith was the last teacher with 13 pupils; the directors were Karl Stiner, Virgil Younker and Robert Manley.

J. WILL WORKMAN

The following story was written by Mr. Workman in February 1941:

"In the late sixties old school district no. 8 was located just across the line in Prairieton township Christian

Co. on the Andy Hays' land and was called the Hays school. It was built of logs and in the middle seventies it was voted to move the school farther east and a frame building 24 x 30 was built on section 6 Flat Branch township, Shelby Co.

The building was used as a schoolhouse and Free Methodist church and the name was changed to Corrington school was it was located on Corrington land.

I started to school there in 1881 at four years of age.

The school was located just across the road from where Chester Dean now lives. The benches were home-made and usually accomodated three pupils varying in age from four to twenty-three years.

My first teacher was Mary O'Brien who was Irish and it required a great deal of diplomacy and that Irish spunk to manage some of those twenty-three year old boys but she did it.

In the summer of 1889 it was voted to move the building ½ mile south of its present location and an eight foot addition was builton and the name changed to Pleasant Flower in the spring of 1890 by a vote of the pupils and the teacher, S. M. Wallace.

New desks were also added that year. In 1903 the number of the district was changed from no. 8 to 36. A new building replaced the old one in the year 1918, Mr. Heitmeyer buying the old one which is now used as a garage."

MARY EVELYN DILLON
She attended Pleasant Flower for six or seven years and had teachers Beatrice Beldon and Bessie Brookshire.

Mary was the daughter of Cecil and Minnie Getz Boley; granddaughter of Peter and Elizabeth Bowman Getz, and John and Laura Cochran Boley.

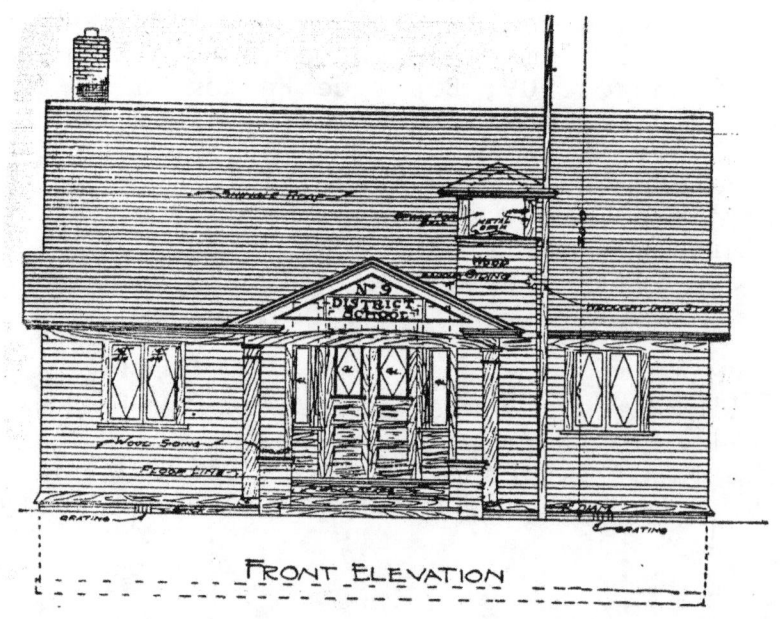

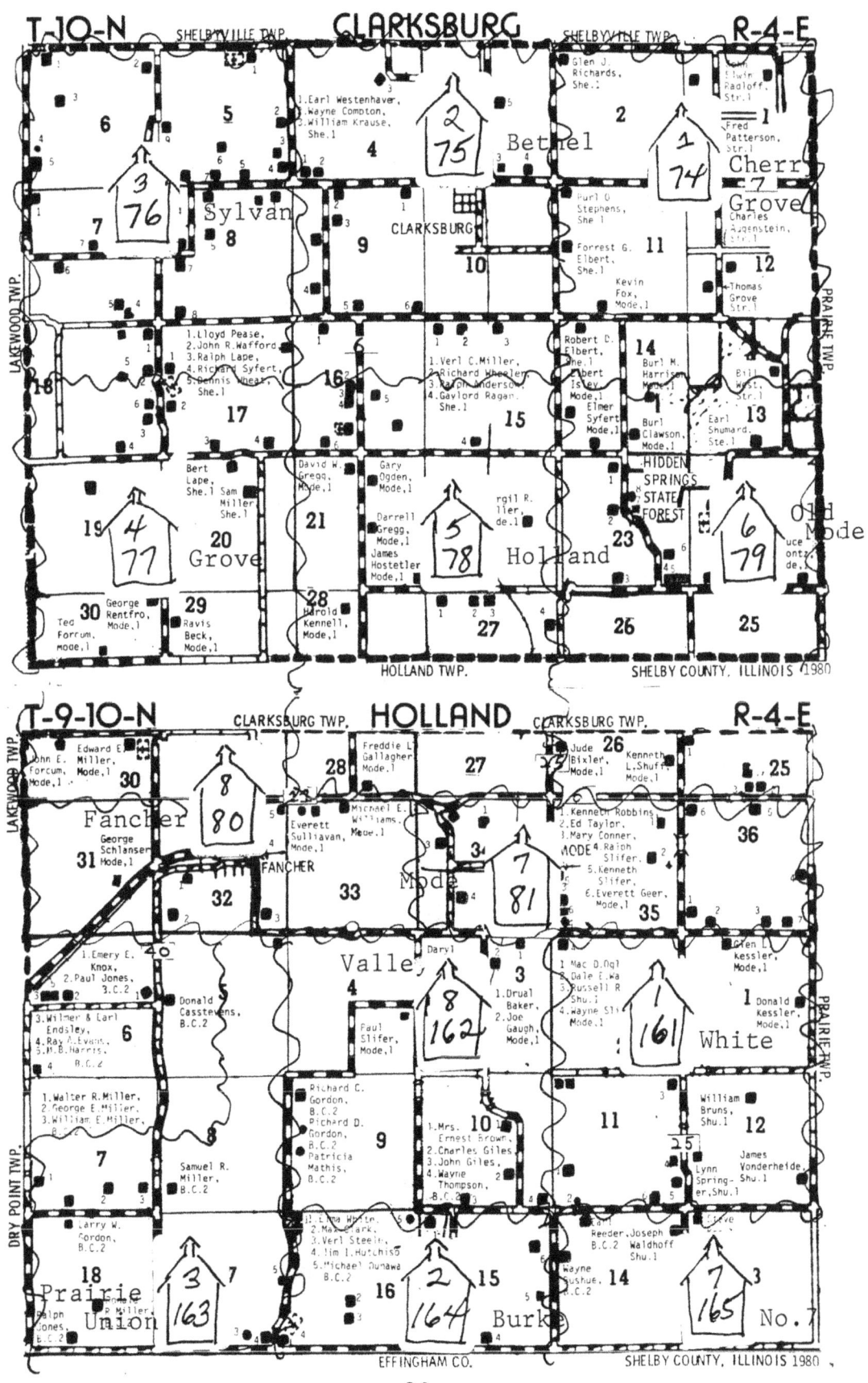

The wavy line indicates the 1903 school district.

HOLLAND and
CLARKSBURG TOWNSHIPS

This is the most complete township listing of school teachers since names for them were found from 1867 until the time of consolidation.

Holland township was much larger than today since Clarksburg township was formed in its northern half during the latter part of last century.

The first school, a small log building, was built in section 29 near the Daniel Gallagher place about 1845. S.R. Davis and John Fleming taught in the township in 1837-38. William Howe was also an early teacher.

CHERRY GROVE
District 1 or 74

Cherry Grove school was located in southeast corner of section 12 of Holland later Clarksburg township. Taxes in 1866 were 50 cents per $100, and directors were J. W. Hogeland and John B. Leathers. Three years later, the taxes were two and half percent for building purposes, and directors were A. Gallagher and John H. Hawbacker. Hiram Graybill was paid $343.67 for building the schoolhouse, and Owen B. Williams provided the land for the site.

The directors of the 1880's were James F. Brown, G.W. Williams, W.D. Wright and William Elliott.

Some of the teachers at Cherry Grove school were: John H. Hagan, Laura Lambing, and Louisa E. Abbott, 1867; Thomas J. Graybill and Anna M. Wilson, 1868; Luther Jacobs and Lizzie Gregory, 1869; John H. Hagan, 1870; Thomas J. Graybill, 1871; Norman P. Smith, 1872; R. C. Thornton and W. A. Miller, 1873; B. F. Wilson, 1874; Levi C. Mechlen, 1875; A. M. Durand, 1876; Milton Barbee and Curney Lindley, 1877; John Knox and Charles Miner, 1878; Charles Miner and Jack Higgens, 1879; Emma Fleming and Effie L. Wright, 1880; John Knox and Jesse Tull, 1881; Jesse Tull, 1882; Jesse Tull, and Grace Powers, 1883; Grace Powers and Mary Anderson, 1884; Mary Anderson and John H. Hagan, 1885; S. M.Williams and Charles York, 1886; Lulu Miller and John H. Hull, 1887; S.D. Thomas and G.W. Chisenhall, 1888; Ella Clara and Carrie Fleming, 1889; Hiram Kensil and Ed Terry, 1890; Sopha Smith and Stella Henry, 1891; G.W. Chisenhall and Fannie Rice, 1892; Fannie Rice, 1893; Homer Peters, 1894; W. F. Ellis, 1895; W.F. Ellis, 1895; M.M. Howe, 1896; Rose Hancock and Mella E. Ellis, 1897; Emma Rice and Rose Warner, 1898; F. A. Voils and Edith Ponsler, 1899; William Adrian Storm, 1901; Edna E. Boise and Robert Huber, 1902; Robert Huber, 1903; Wanita E. Hickman and Effa Beck, 1904; Mils McKittrick and L. D. Williams, 1905; L. D. Williams, 1906-07; Stanley Pontius and Pearl Williams, 1908; J. T. Barr and Clara Mars, 1909; Margaret McKittrick and Edith Ponsler, 1909-10; J. T. Barr, 1911; George Bodine, 1912; W. D. Williams, 1913; Alta E.

Hickman, 1917; Mary Ponsler, 1924; Vesta Schafer, 1926; Ervin Strohl, 1927; Helen B. Stephens, 1934-35; L.D. Williams, 1939-43; Vera Kite, 1944; and Gladys Williams, 1945-46.

Gladys Williams was the last teacher with 6 pupils; directors were Stanley Wheat, Floyd Hurst and Max Elbert.

In March 1900 Frank Voiles the teacher directed the following students in a school program: Deby Wallace, Goldie Watts, Francis Welton, Margaret Wheat, Della Patrick, Grace Houser, Mabel Watts, Verna Cross, Charley Warner, Everett Cross, Charley Wheat, Daisy Hawbecker, Walter Welton, Lawrence Hoffman, Sylvester Faust, Maude Houser, Ralph Hayward, Nettie Hayward, Otta Hawbecker, Wesley Warner and Ella Smith.

BETHEL
District 2 or 75

Bethel school was located in the southwest quarter of section 3 of Holland later Clarksburg township. In 1871 Milton Moore was paid $95 for moving school house.

Directors of the 1880's were John J. Gollogher, S. Arganbright, James Williams, H.R. Travis and T. R. Geer. Bethel became the lower grades for Clarksburg during the latter 1880's or early 1900's. The school then became a two-room school house.

Some of the teachers at Bethel school were: Minerva Gallagher, 1867; A. M. Perryman, 1868; D.V. Brown, 1869; Minerva Gallagher and David V. Brown, 1869; Eelia A. Diehl and Thomas J. Graybill, 1870; Harry C. Graybill, 1871; Norman P. Smith, 1872; Thomas J. Wilson, 1873; Anna M. Perryman and Isaac M. Turner, 1874; Isaac M. Turner, 1875; Frank Wilson, 1876; Josie McCloskey and James Knox, 1877; Mary Patton and Brigam Young, 1878; Alva Travis and S.W. Reeves, 1879; Alva Travis and Thomas Miner, 1880; Emma Fleming and William Ragan, 1881; Lulu Miller and Minnie Wilson, 1882; Emma Spears and Minnie Wilson, 1883; Lulu Miller and Albin Z. Glick, 1884; Emma Wortman and Thomas Wortman, 1885; Louis Thomas and Thomas Wortman, 1886; H. M. Hagan and Silas Green, 1887; Silas Green and James P. Clay, 1888; Byron Travis and Calvin Green, 1889; Calvin Green, 1890; Sopha Smith, 1891; Leslie Stairwalt; G. M. Barbee, 1892; Leslie Stairwalt, 1893; G. M. Barbee, 1894; Edward Terry and Cora Carnes, 1895; Charles Lewis and E. Terry, 1896; C. E. Lewis, Amanda Green and Kittie Fox, 1897; May E. Wilson, 1898; George M. Hannaman and William Huffer, 1899; Warren Green and Charles Lewis, 1900; J. P. Clay and W.R. Shuff, 1901; Ida Warren and William D. Huffer, 1902; Sylvester Arganbright and H. Middlesworth, 1903; Ray Baker and S. Arganbright, 1904; Stevanna Tanner, 1905; Clyde Whitacre and Nettie Eckert, 1906; Clara Mars and J.T. Barr, 1907; Clara Mars, 1908; W.A. Storm and Pearl Williams, 1909; W. A. Storm and Pearl Williams, 1910; W. A. Storm, 1911;

Prudence Ponsler and W.A. Storm, 1912; and Margaret McKittrick, 1913.

In 1892, there were 45 pupils enrolled at Bethel school, and during the last month of school under the direction of Eugene Markland, teacher, these students had perfect attendance: Anna and Albert Geer, Neda and Mab Hickman, Sarah Thompson, Elmer and Delia Hahn, Forest Fisher, Willie Syfert and Cora Arganbright.

In 1900, teacher W. C. Green had 49 pupils enrolled at Bethel school with an average daily attendance of 32.

DORIS R. BRITTON

Doris attended Bethel school for eight years, and had teachers Prudence Ponsler, Clara Fox, Florence Hickman Wortman, Vida Morgan Stine, Arthur Danelin, Carl Mattox, Gertie Kingery Birdsell and Fred Baxter.

She was the daughter of John Wiley and Delia Gallaher Shutt; granddaughter of Preston Ballard and Cynthia Fowler Shutt, and Simon Tracy and Martha Van Hise Gallaher.

PAULINE HUBBARTT

She attended Bethel school for eight years and had teachers Noah B. Strohl, L. D. Williams, Dwayne Ripley and Viola Brandson.

Pauline was the daughter of Tom and Mell Compton Westenhaver; granddaughter of Ezra and Catherine Teegardin Westenhaver; and great-granddaughter of Joseph and Elizabeth Barnett Westenhaver, and Abraham and Elizabeth Crumb Teegardin, Jeddiah and Mary Hege Allen, and Jonathon and Elizabeth Brinker Compton.

SYLVAN
District 3 or 76

Sylvan school was located in the northeast quarter of section 7 of Holland later Clarksburg township. Taxes in 1866 were $1 for building purposes, and directors were H.H. Allen and Jedediah Allen. Three years later the taxes were 50 cents per 100 and directors were Henry H. Allen and Jedediah Allen.

Directors of the 1880's were W. B. Lantz, H.C. Gallagher, J. W. Flowers.

Some of the teachers at Sylvan school were: David V. Brown, 1867; Eliza Gallagher and S. W. Wilson, 1868; N. P. Smith, 1869; Norman P. Smith, Levi Mechlin and B.W.E. Graybill, 1870; N. P. Smith, 1871; Josepine McCloskey and John E. Jones, 1872; Louisa Reynolds, 1873; E. A. Fritter and William H. Ragan, 1874; Enoch A. Fritter, 1875; Charles Miner, 1876; William Wallace, 1877; Nettie Busby and William Ragan, 1878; Ida Hogeland and William Ragan, 1879; Mary Hannamon, 1880; Silas Ragan, 1881; Ida Wilson and John Tull,

Bethel school in 1934 with teacher Dwane Ripley. Shown are front row, Paul Wheeler, Lowell Hickman, Elwin Smith, Leon Pierce, Charles Lines, Morris Summers, Milton Graden. 2nd row, Geneva Dildine, Arthur Glen Shuff, Rosalee Selock, Maureen Smith, Maureen Summers, Emogene Wheat, Edna Fleming, Jean Westenhaver, Jean Fleming, Frances Pierce. 3rd row, Juanita Smith, Letha Fulte, Freda Ragan, Georgia Summers, Fern Ellen Wheat, Dorothy Ragan, Alberta Ragan, Doris Pierce, Pauline Gregg, Kenneth Wheat. 4th row, Gleason Ragan, Ralph Gottman, Pauline Westenhaver, Virginia Shutt, Geraldine McGlennen, Wayne Arganbright, Leon Gregg, Everett Wheat.

Photo courtesy of Pauline Hubbartt

1882; Minnie Wilson and C. Wallace, 1883; John Tull and Minnie Wilson, 1884; Dova Levering and James McDermith, 1885; Lizzie Daisey and Minnie Wilson, 1886; Silas Green, and Mollie Rice, 1887; Mollie Rice, 1888; Mamie Middlesworth and Clara Graybill, 1889; Clara Graybill and Jennie Middleton, 1890; Jennie Middleton and Emma Gerhard, 1891; Eugene Marklin and Emma Gerhard, 1892; Frank South, 1893; Maud Turner, 1894; Frank South, Ida Walker and Henry Clawson, 1895; Ida Walker and R.E. Huber, 1896; R. E. Huber, Emma Rice and Calvin Green, 1897; W. B. Lewis and C. P. Middleton, 1898; Bertha Thomas and T. P. Graybill, 1899; C. P. Middleton and F. May Rice, 1900; M. M. Howe, 1901; Verne Steele and Robert Huber, 1902; Robert Huber, 1903; Charles R. Flenner and Lysta Mars, 1904; Charles Flenner and Clara Mars, 1905; Clara Mars and Emma Hodson, 1906; Emma Hodson and Frances Welton, 1907; William Steele, 1908; Emma Hodson and Ruth Williams, 1909; Vernon Williams and William Steele, 1910; Isaac Wortman and Delbert Banning,

1911; Isaac Wortman and Delbert Banning, 1912; Clover Wortman, 1924; Irene Smith, 1926; Fern Hoffman, 1927; Ervin R. Strohl, 1934-42; Opal Huber, 1943-44; Marjorie Musson, 1945; and Martha Hillyard, 1946.

Martha Hillyard was the last teacher with 22 pupils; directors were Noah Strohl, Paul Lane and E.C. Ragan.

WINTRESS HUBER HARLOW

She attended Sylvan school from 1912 to 1922, and had teachers Isaac Wortman, Marinda Howe, Delbert Jones, Florence and Nile Hickman, Opal Summers and Ruby Meyers.

"In those days our dresses were homemade by our mothers and I remember a girl was playing "drop the handkerchief" and another girl grabbed her by the arm and a sleeve that was just basted in came out of the armhole; her mother had failed to stitch it.

We carried our lunch and we were eating one day at the noon hour when a girl put her spoon in her mouth and flipped the handle and it sailed across the room and hit a boy. Was he mad!"

Wintress was the daughter of Henry and Lydia Huber; granddaughter of Amanda and Marion Daniels, and David and Elizabeth Huber.

EDITH A. HOWE

She attended Sylvan school from first through eighth grades, and had teachers Marinda Howe, Opal Summers Huber, Florence Hickman Wortman, Nile Hickman and Ruby Meyers Cox.

"One of my funny incidents that happened at school was when we all had a 'pickle shower' on our teacher, celebrating her birthday. Our teacher was a lovely young lady. As the story goes, if you like pickles, you must be in love and we all thought she was in love. Just imagine! All 35 pupils, half dozen pickles each, the amount that would be! We had sweet pickles, sour pickles, dill pickles, all sizes and etc. We placed them all in a big box and wrapped the box beautifully and placed it on the teacher's desk. Was she ever surprised when she opened the package! She had a good sense of humor. I don't recall no one having to stay in at recess or after school. I have always wondered what she did with so many pickles and if she still likes pickles today.

Our heart-warming episode was one that usually happened every year. We all looked forward to the last day of school when all the parents planned to arrive at the noon hour with well-filled baskets of food of all kinds. Now this was supposed to be a big surprise on the teacher but think the surprise would have been if they hadn't come! Someone let the secret out of the bag. Some of the parents would bring long and wide pieces of lumber that would fit well on top of teh seats and desks and in a flash our school room would be turned into a huge dining room. Sometimes we would have a nice program of drills, dialogues, songs, speeches in the afternoon. Some of the parents would add a touch of merriment too, by reciting some poetry that they had memorized when they were boys and girls in school. We often had spelling bees. It all was exciting and great fun and left us all with lots of sweet memories of days gone by."

Edith was the daughter of J. Calvin and Otie Severe Howe; granddaughter of Jesse and Martha Severe and Tom and Mary Howe; great-granddaughter of Gilbert and Arlena Severe, and Eliakim and Hannah Munn Howe.

In 1983, 91 people attended the Sylvan school reunion at Shelbyville. Five former teachers gave their remarks and Noah Strohl gave a short history of the school and Marvin Huber gave one on the church.

Sylvan school in 1906, teacher Clara Mars. Some of the pupils are Cemia Severe, Grace Summers, Opal Miller, Gladys Smith, Ruth Huber; Charley McCarty, Wendell Howe, Opal Summers, Ollie Severe, Bell Severe; Ruby Miller, Ruby Summers, Stella Severe, Freeman Summers, Edna Severe, Harold Huber, Vern Severe, Bona Smith, Harlan Davis, and Roy Howe.

Photo courtesy of E. Howe

Sylvan school of 1914 with teacher Marinda Howe. Front row, l to r, Carl Hannaman, Herman Wortman, Harry Davis, Everett Pease, Carl Howe, Norton Patterson, Glen Pease, Clifford Barbee, Glen Miller, Earl Smith, Clarence Smith, Lois Barbee. 2nd row, Homer Tripp, Rose Severe, Louise Howe, Blanche Barbee, Pearl Patterson, Nellie Davis, Clover Wortman, Clara Oller, Marie Summers, Jemima Lewis, Marie Pease, Wintress Huber, Helen Huber, Bernadine Summers, Edith Howe. Back row, Orlan Severe, Paul Pease, Freeman Summers, Bona Smith, Harold Huber, Marinda Howe, Cora Severe, Grace Pease, Ralph Huber, Hobart Pease, Henry Wortman, Edna Severe, Nita Severe and Iva Severe.
Photo courtesy of Wintress Harlow

In 1914 of December, the Sylvan school burned to the ground and a new school was built in 1915. Other teachers at Sylvan school were Joe Barr, Bertha Baird, Irene Smith, Florence Smith Allen, Jemima Lewis Campbell, Velma Rentfrow, Arloa Knight Field, and Ervin Strohl.

GROVE
District 4 or 77

Grove school was located in the west half of section 19 of Holland later Clarksburg township. In 1866 the taxes were one cent on the dollar, and directors were Eli Wildermuth and David McClosky. For building in 1869, the taxes were $1.50 per 100, and directors were William H. Yakey and Jacob Durst.

Directors of the 1880's were S.C. Campbell, E. Harrison, Victor Elbert, and J. A. Walters.

Some of the teachers at Grove school were: Thomas J. Graybill, 1867; H. C. Graybill and Isaac Patton, 1868; Thomas J. Graybill and Isaac Patton, 1869; B. J. Young, 1870; James P. Groves and Thomas J. Wilson, 1871; Samuel Percy, 1872; H. B. Smith, 1874; C.E. Compton, 1875-76; S. T. Knox, 1876-77; Alva Travis and S.T. Knox, 1878; John Knox, 1879-1880; M. Barnhart, 1881; Kit Hogeland and Frank Wilson, 1882; Carrie Snyder and Ellen Huffer, 1883; Mary Flugar and S. S. Jones, 1884; T. H. Righter, 1885; Alie Smith and Mamie Leathers, 1886; Mollie and Mamie Leathers, 1887; Mamie Leathers, 1888; Mollie Rice and G.W. Chisenhall, 1889; G.W. Chisenhall and Ida Hagan, 1890; Bell Elliott, 1891; Ella Perryman and Ann Torrence, 1892; Anna Torrence, 1893; Minnie Moore, 1894; Charles Middleton, 1895-97; Minnie Wireck and C. P. Middleton, 1898; W. B. Lewis, Alma Hasler and William Ray Shuff, 1899; William Ray Shuff and Julia Lantz, 1900; Robert Pugh, 1901; Julia Lantz and Clyde Smith, 1902; Clyde Smith and Alice Severe, 1903; Clyde Smith and Sam C. Strohl, 1904; Verna Steele and C. P. Middleton, 1905; Clara Mars, 1906-07; C.P. Middleton and Elmer Brown, 1908; Mary Phillips and Rollin Davis, 1909; Rollin Davis and Mark McKittrick, 1910; Marinda Howe, 1911; W.D. Williams and Florence Hickman, 1912; Morris Williams and Ruth Huber, 1913; Florence Gallagher, 1922; Ada Klump, 1924; Noah B. Strohl, 1926-34; Frances M. Howe, 1935-40; Frances M. Howe Klauser, 1941; Opal Huber, 1942; Ervin Strohl, 1943-46.

Ervin Strohl was the last teacher with 8 pupils; directors that year were Delbert Lape, Mark M. Howe, and H. P. Ragan.

MARY LEWIS FUHRMAN

She attended Grove school and had teacher Florence Gallogher Elbert; she also attended Fancher where she had teachers Garnet Rand, Robert Gill and Ervin Strohl.

Mary was the daughter of W. B. and Lucretia Gallagher Lewis; granddaughter of Simon T. and Martha VanHise Gallagher, and Frank L. and Jemima Stine Lewis; great-granddaughter of Daniel and Mary Middlesworth Gallagher.

In December 1893 at Grove school, the following students had perfect attendance: Harvey Lantz, Bessie Lantz, Millie Lucas, Roy Lucas, Guy Gallagher, Ersel Gallagher, Adolph Peters, Henry Hacker, Anna Hacker, Ray Summers, Johnnie Lape, Harvey Smith, Clyde Smith, and Amadell Welch.

HOLLAND
District 5 or 78

Holland school was located in the southwest quarter of section 22 of Holland township. The school was a union school and in 1876, the old school house sold for $10.04. Originally the district 5 was number 7 in union with Rose township. For building purposes in 1866, the taxes were $2 per 100 value and directors were George H. Karch and Jacob Emrich. Three years later the taxes were $1.25 per 100 and directors were M. Wortman and John Wade.

In the 1880's the directors were George Mummel, E. M. Howe, John Baber, P.T. Miller and C. H. McCurdy.

Some of the teachers at Holland Union were: Aaron Rider, 1867; James Grove, 1868; Aaron Rider, 1869; Isaac Patton and Mary L. Humphrey, 1870-71; F. H. Keys, 1872; Lucie E. Perryman, 1873; L. C. Mechlin, 1874; Jenny Rolland, 1876; James Tull and Jenny Rolland, 1877; James R. Diehl and G.F. Miner, 1878; Alfred Perryman and Ed Silvers, 1879; Alfred Perryman, 1880; Belle Allen, 1881; Emma Wortman, 1882; Silas Ragan, 1882; Emma Wortman, 1883; Thomas Righter, 1884; Anna Reed and Amanda Huffer, 1885; Anna Reed, 1886; Minnie Fleming and Silas Ragan, 1887; Emma Wilson, 1888; Alice Smith and C.P. Middleton, 1889; Emma Gerhard and Edward Smith, 1890; Emma Gerhard, 1891; Emma GErhard and Silas Ragan, 1892; Silas Ragan, 1893; Effie Stiarwalt and Enola Miller, 1894; Maud Turner and Ada Burk, 1895; Ada Burk and Andrew Warner, 1896; Andrew Warner and Thomas Graybill, 1897; Nettie Burke, 1898; Ada Burk, 1899-1900; T. L. Cook, 1901; T.L. Cook and Effie Stairwalt, 1902; T. L. Cook and Charles Lewis, W. A. Storm, 1903; L. D. Williams and Rosa Gruenwald, 1904; Dista Mars and Charles R. Flenner, 1905; Myrtle Hubbartt and Thomas Baker, 1906; Thomas Baker, Clara Mars and Vernon Williams, 1907; Vern Williams, 1908; J. M. Reynolds, 1909; Morris Williams, 1910-12; L. D. Williams and Grace Summers, 1913; Clarence Ponsler, 1917; Hazel Spring, 1924; Delbert W. Jones, 1926-27; Nile Hickman, 1934-35; Mildred Pontius, 1939-40; Ruby Mae Carter, 1941; Perry Fletcher, 1942; Mable Gorden, 1943; and Ethel Patterson, 1944.

Ethel Patterson was the last teacher with 11 pupils; directors were Carl Rittgers, Leverett Compton and F. M. Miller.

FRONT VIEW

The height of the seat and the character of the back of the chair make it difficult for the 12 year old girl to maintain the correct posture here shown. Note the pressure of the edge of the seat on the thigh causes discomfort by interference with the circulation of the blood and function of the nerves. The feet "go to sleep".

Rural Schools of Illinois

ROSEMARY COMPTON DAVIS
    She attended Holland school for 9 years, and had teachers Nile Hickman, Arloa Knight Fields, Fred Grabb, Reatha Bullington, Hazel Springs, Delbert Jones, Warren Williams and L. Dow Williams.
    "As I recalled my school days at Holland, 1921-30, many pleasant memories come to mind. My father used to take me to school riding horseback, especially when the dirt roads were really muddy. It was a two mile track to school. It wasn't long until my cousin Elva Compton joined me...then came her sister June and my sister Verda Ruth. Soon Elva's brother Royce and Frances and Norma Ragan, also cousins. Then we had a crowd. In the fall, we often stopped by a big orchard belonging to Mr. and Mrs. Jake Gallagher, and ate apples as we trudged along and sometimes getting a stomachache. In the one room school, we listened to all the classes reading and reciting out loud and often laughed at the faltering ones. (A very unkind thing to do.) I remember on one occasion that our teacher was reprimanding me (teacher one of discipline) and just as my sister

Verda thought the teacher was about to reach for the stick she stood up, stomped her foot and said, 'Don't you touch my sister.' I don't remember the outcome of this episode.

On bad weather days some of us arrived at school with wet feet and clothes so the teacher would let us sit around the big stove to try to dry us out. Sometimes I think we waded in the water on purpose. One day I was wearing a pair of my mother's shoes, very pointed toes and laced across the ankle. One of the boys (Joe Allen) began teasing me, and I began chasing him up and down the aisles and out the side door. He was swifter than my kick. Most of the boys and girls in school were my cousins but the Allen family was not. One spring, Richard Allen walked home with me to see if my parents would buy some garden seeds that he was selling. I think my mother did. Anyway, from then on it was in my mind that Richard was my boyfriend.

The Allen boys would hitch up a little goat to a cart and it pulled their sister, Ruth, to school. She had been stricken with infantile paralysis. They had sisters, Kathryn, Jean and Mary in school too. We gathered round to pet this little goat but had to watch that didn't butt us.

The singing times were fun. My cousin Vivien Miller nearly always chose Old Suzanna and did we sing!

The last day of school, we had a picnic and sometimes our parents came with a basket of food. It was kind of sad too as it was the end of the school year. In the spring of 1930, my friend Ruth Allen died. We girls of Holland school were flower girls for her funeral. This was sad. Then I graduatead from the eighth grade in May 1930.

At this writing two of my teachers, Mrs. Arloa (Knight) Fields and Mr. Delbert Jones are still living and among my memories that "stick", I would say THANK YOU big and loud."

OLD MODE
District 6 or 79

Old Mode school was located in the southeast quarter of section 23 of Holland later Clarksburg township. In 1869, the taxes were 50 cents per 100, and directors were John Fancher, John Graybill and J.D. Cross. Also that year district 6 was added to district 4, and district 7 changed to district 6. In 1871, Samuel Beal was paid $300 for building a school house by John Fancher.

Directors of the 1880's were C. J. Middlesworth, W. W. Conner, John Lankford and Mary D. Gallagher.

Some of the teachers at Old Mode were: James A. Johnston and N. P. Smith, 1867; Norman P. Smith, 1868; Mattie Gallagher, 1869; Emma Rolland, 1870; Mrs. N.E. Powel and G.E.

Loar, 1871; Celia A. Diehl, 1872; George E. Loar, 1873; Annie Rolland and T.C. Byland, 1874; Amanda Gallagher, 1875; Amelia G. Robertson, 1875; Amanda Gallagher, 1876-77; Louis Leighty and Ida Hogeland, 1878; Berlin Wallace, 1879; E.B. Allen and H. L. Wallace, 1880; Mary Gallagher and S.E. McDermith, 1881; Minnie Wilson, 1882; F. B. Wendling, 1883; Ralph Wolf, 1884; Louis Thomas and Hiram Kensil, 1885; Silas Green, 1886; S.D. Peifer, 1887; Austin Sittler, 1888; M.L. Herron and Mamie Middlesworth, 1889; Thomas Inman and Isaac Wortman, 1890; Lettie McDonald, 1891; Isaac Wortman, 1892; Alverda Dayhuff, 1893; Charles Wilson, J.W. Bailey and E.E. Herron, 1894; J. W. Bailie, J. Knox and J.M. Williams, 1895; Lyda Bais and Charles Lewis, 1896; Charles Lewis, 1897; J. M. Williams and W.R. Shuff, 1898; Noah Smith, W.B. Lewis, Burt Graybill and John Tripp, 1899; Clara Mars, 1900; Clara Mars and C. Middleton, 1901; Roy Shuff and L. Mae Rice, 1902; W.R. Shuff, Clara C. Wilson and M. M. Barnhart, 1903; C.P. Middleton, 1904; Hugh R. Hilsabeck and Sam Strohl, 1905; C. P. Middleton, 1906; L. D. Williams, 1907-09; (Old school house was sold and a new one was built.) W.R. Shuff and L. D. Williams, 1910; Clarence Ponsler, 1911; Roy Strohl and Clarence Ponsler, 1912; Miles Nance and W.D. Williams, 1913; J.F. Barr, 1917; Warren Williams, 1924; Charlotte Timperley, 1926; Warren Williams, 1927; Jemima L. Campbell, 1934-35; Nile W. Hickman, 1939-40; W. D. Williams, 1941; Thelma Gannaway, 1942-43; and L. D. Williams, 1944-46.

   L. D. Williams was the last teacher with 19 pupils; directors were Aubrey Grove, Cloren Isley, and Elmer Syfert.

   In June 1909, Edna Campbell, a student at the Old Mode school, took first place in the final examination held at the Court House in Shelbyville, with a score or average of 91.1 in a class of 83 other competitors.

MODE
District 7 or 81

Mode school was located southeast quarter of section 34 of Holland later Clarksburg township. George W. and Sophia M. Voris deeded land in the town of New Mode for the school in 1897.

   Some of the teachers at Mode school were: George W. Brown, 1867; Mattie Gallagher and Thomas J. Wilson, 1868; John Stevenson, 1869; Mary L. Humphrey, 1872; Louis Thomas, 1885; John Barrett, 1886; R. D. Miner, 1887; M. L. Herron, 1888; T. R. Sarver, 1889; Thomas Inman and Silas Ragan, 1890; Edward Smith, 1891; W.B. Lewis, 1901; Mr. and Mrs. C.W. Wallace, 1909; Mrs. R. A. Graves, 1917; Zelpha L. Chamberlain, 1924; Leroy Baker and Mary York, 1926; (New additions made to building for the purpose of standardizing the school.)

ANNABELL GALLAGHER KELLER TUCKER

She attended MOde and Fancher schools, and had Mary Ponsler, Paul Christman, Ralph Cox, and Frank Roberts at Mode and Ervin Strohl, Ruby Phillips, Nile Hickman, and Regis McClory at Fancher.

"Oh, my, how I remember the old school days before buses. How we waded snow crotch deep and temperatures so cold, and we walked about one and a fourth mile to get there. It was back before ballpoint pens and we would put our bottles of ink back by the big old furnace stove to thaw out, and one morning we were thawing them and suddenly there was a loud popping noise and the corks blew out and everybody was turning around to see what was happening, which made the teacher mad, and he told us maybe we would like to stay turned around in our seats. We had good times though with spelling bees, and ciphering, and we always put on nice Christmas programs."

Annabell was the daughter of Ray M. and Gertrude Middleton Gallagher; granddaughter of Newton and Letta Allen Gallagher, and Charles and Anna Rogers Middleton; great-granddaughter of Jacob and Sarah Middlesworth Gallagher, Jedediah and Mary Hege Allen and Robert and Sarah Goodrich Middleton.

HOWARD ALLEN DAVIS

He attended Mode school for eight years and had teachers Retha Knight Bullington, Hazel Davis Jones, Ida Leighty Graves, Zelpha Chamberlain, H.R. Reichel, Thomas Anderson, Mona Anderson, Robert Gill, Warren Williams, Mr. and Mrs. Harry R. Sparks, Kelsey Wakefield, Dee Williams, Dow Williams, and Dick Williams.

Howard was the son of Charles Edward and Sarah Alice Gallagher Davis; grandson of Stephen A. Douglas and Sarah Emma Allen Gallagher, and Charles E. and Casamira Emalina Suprunowski; and great-grandson of Jedadiah and Mary Hege Allen, Jacob and Sarah Middlesworth Middlesworth, George Gregory and Margaret Elizabeth Rogers Suprunowski, and William Richard and Sophia Burrel Davis.

Howard married Rosemary Compton, whose story is related on page 93 and 94. Rosemary was the daughter of Russell Gay and Alice Louise Niles Compton; granddaughter of Charles Edward and Mary Alice Merrick Compton; great-granddaughter of Charles and Louisa Swope Compton, Isaac and Margaret Kinder Merrick, Carl and Maria Neihls, and Daniel Webster Bush.

MILDRED J. GALLAGHER BROWN

She attended Fancher school which was a two-room, district number 80 in Holland township, and had teachers Samuel Davis, Garnet Rau Moore, Hazel Howe, Henry Clawson, W.D. Williams, Dell Banning, Robert Gill and Ervin Strohl.

"First I want to say that my grandfather Charles P. Middleton ran for superintendent of schools at Shelby County in 1908. He taught several schools in Shelby County. All of his brothers and sisters were school teachers at one time in Shelby County long ago. Ervin Strohl, my favorite school teacher now for my education, the greatest teacher fthat taught me and the class. Complete state course of study and we also had extra textbooks called Mamie G. textbooks bought form the state which increased our knowledge to almost college courses. Extras like civil government, trees, stars and birds, soils and crops, animal husbandry, geography learning all states, capitals, largest and commmercial cities, draw Illinois from memory putting in all important cities, learnd the different continents and countries and capitols, rivers, mountains, etc. Plants, too. American history from beginning to end. Health and physiology, orthography, dividing words and meaning. I could go on and on. No one thinks I'm not a college graduate.

Mr. Strohl was very strict but he played out on playground with us all, softball, double batter, roundtown, handy over, rabbit and many other games. He lived near Clarksburg and drove a sulky because most of the time, it was so muddy he couldn't have got through any other way. He gave me a ride lots of times as I lived out of town and it was bad walking.

One of the times I can remember was the day all the parents and his brother Noah Strohl and wife came with kettles and everything to eat imaginable. No one suspected teacher and all the pupils were surprised when they begin pouring in. The last year of school we had to finish up in the United Brethren Church at Fancher as our sold school house burned down. The men of community went in, grabbed most of the desks and books and saved them. I came to the Shelby County courthouse and walked with the others to First Christian Church on Broadway and got my diploma, June 1926, from the state of Illinois. Two promotional exams for 7th grade, 2 promotional exams for the 8th grade."

Mildred was the daughter of Ray and Gertrude Middleton Gallagher; granddaughter of Charles P. and Anna Rogers Middleton, and Newton and Meletta Allen Gallagher; great-granddaughter of Robert B. and Clarissa Goodrich Middleton, and Jacob and Sarah Middlesworth Gallagher.

NEVAD MARSH WILLIAMS

She attended Fancher school and had teachers Henry Clausen and Roy Shuff.

Nevad was the daughter of William and Sara Prosser Marsh.

WHITE
District 1 or 161

White school was located in the southeast quarter of section 2 of Holland township. The school was named for

James H. and Mildred A. White who deed a half acre to the school trustees in 1885 with the provision that the trustees would maintain such with a good and sufficient fence.

Other directors of the 1880's were Solon B. Jackson, Calvin Rice, J. H. Hubbartt, H. Bullerman and A. F. White.

Some of the teachers at White school were: Samuel Curry, 1891; Ella Cleary, 1890; Ada Burke, 1892-94; Jake Koontz, 1901; Melvin Steele, 1909; Electa Mabel Largent, 1917; Arloa Knight, 1922-24; H.D. Brady, 1926-27; Fern A. Matson, 1934; Warren K. Jackson, 1935; Clarence Ponsler, 1939-40; Warren Jackson, 1941; Margaret Bruns, 1941-45; and Prudence Ponsler, 1946.

Prudence Ponsler was the last teacher with 8 pupils; directors were William Mietzner, Warde Roberts and Titus Vogel.

A reunion was held at White school in August 1940 with 140 present for the basket dinner and program.

MARGARET ROBERTS BRUNS

She attended White school for seven years and had teachers Marie Fluckey, Harry Meyers and Arloa Knight Field.

"There are many many fond memories of life in the country schools of Shelby County., and it's difficult to list only a part of them, coming to school early on a cold frosty morning, having waded snow and being allowed a special privilege to sit circling the big stove in the corner to warm toes, even after the bell! The same big heater on many occasions, after being fed huge buckets of dusty coal, belched black smoke, and showered the room. White school, district 161, had a wooded area just across the road and at noon, a special treat was a fox and goose game. Two greedy foxes remained in the schoolhouse while the geese all ran to the woods to hide. In a few short minutes, the foxes rushed to find each goose. That game was 100% excitement!

If the creek down the hill was frozen, we'd skate, sans skates always! Good heavy overshoes were fine. Always in nice weather, there were ball games, only two bases, and a light, bouncy homemade ball made good use of as the runner was thrown out when a speedy throw hit him. Everyone participated.

When Arloa Knight Field became teacher, wehad the greatest treat of all--hot lunches. Pupils brought milk and peeled potatoes, and sometimes it was hot mashed potatoes, hot potato soup or hot cocoa. No food ever tasted so good as those first hot lunches at White school. A little kerosene stove was used and each day it was a priviledge to be chosen helper, either help cook or wash dishes, and clean the big granite kettle.

When I was ready for the fourth grade, the teacher decided the fifth grade would be taught. As a result, we completed the eight years in seven. After four years high school plus one year attending Charleston Teachers College, called Eastern Illinois now, I received a certificate enabling me to teach in Illinois. I returned to White, district 161 and taught some of the pupils I had been with there just five years earlier. I spent three years there at that time.

Then during World War II, I again returned to White school and taught some of the children of my former pupils."

Margaret was the daughter of George Everett and Florence Bell Warren Roberts; the granddaughter of John W. and Margaret Fuller Roberts and Sarah Miner Warren; great-granddaughter of Samuel and Malinda Harris Warren, and Daniel and Harriet Miner.

BURK OR
HOLLAND Dist. 2 or 164

Burke school was located in the northeast quarter of section 7, and the trustees bought a half acre from John A. Bartlett in 1870. The trustees then were Amaziah Sparks, W. A. Jones and E. K. Parkhurst.

Earlier in 1866, the taxes were 50 cents per 100, and directors were Jacob Zeigler and Wenzel Bartscht. Three years later the taxes were a half percent on the hundred and the directors were Ira C. Hubbartt and Wenzel Bartscht.

Directors of the 1880's were I.C. Hubbartt, R. J. Supernowski, B.S. Olinger, A. L. Hubbart and N.W. Clagett.

Some of the teachers at Burke school were: Nettie Anderson, 1888; Sara Bartscht, 1891; Ella Bumgardner, 1892; Maude Turner, 1893; C.E. Hart, 1894; Bertie Turner, 1901; Bertha Baird, 1909-now called Holland school; Clarence Ponsler, 1917; Ruth Florey, 1922; Gladys Mattix, 1924; John Stockdale, 1926; Florence Biedert, 1927; W. A. Bruns, 1934; William A. Bruns, 1935; Agnes Willey, 1939-40; Florien Lively, 1941; Irene King, 1942; and Pearl Lockart, 1943-46.

Pearl Lockart was the last teacher with 12 pupils; the directors were Milton Syfert, Roy Slifer and Alvin Musson.

PRAIRIE UNION
OR LITTLE GREASY
District 3 or 163

Prairie Union school was located in the southwest corner of section 17 of Holland township. Taxes in 1869 were one and a half percent per 100, and directors were Thomas Dunaway, William T. Miller and Hart Spare.

Trustees Charles Whately, John Wills and Jesse Dunlap bought from William L. and Louisa M. Haydon and Thomas J. and Laura E. Graybill in 1883, a half acre in section 17.

Other directors of the 1880's were W. T. Miller, J. P. Graybill, C.W. Hubbartt and J. J. Alsop.

Some of the teachers at Prairie Union or Little Greasy were: Mary Leighty, 1888; Jerry Reynolds, 1889; Jennie Middleton, 1890; Ella Bird Vail, 1892; Marion

Culumber, 1893; Montie Markland, 1894; Lola E. Torrence, 1901; Mary Phillips, 1909; Mary E. Sickles, 1917; Neva Henderson, 1922; Ethel Hunter, 1924; Ethel I. Alsop, 1926; Beth Harper, 1927; Ethel C. Allsop, 1934-35; Kathyrn Cook Musser, 1939-41; Mary E. Kessler, 1942-43; Alma E. Light, 1944-45; and Mabel Laue, 1946.

Mabel Laue was the last teacher with 11 pupils; the directors were L. H. Phillips, G. H. Hunt and Sam Miller.

M. A. Randall bought the school property in 1949 for $325 from the school trustees.

NUMBER SEVEN
OR PLEASANT PLAINS
District 7 or 165

Number Seven school was located in the west half of section 13 of Holland township. Directors of the 1880's were Calvin Henderson, F. M. Hubbartt, T.R. Dutton and William Dumont.

Some of the teachers at Number Seven were: Nellie Smith, 1888; Thomas Sarver, 1891; Lillie F. Ellis, 1892; Jo Stanfield, 1893; J.W. Bailey, 1894; Emma Hubbartt, 1901; Mary Lorton, 1909-school now called Pleasant Plains; Mary Davis, 1922; Ruth Scott, 1924; Juanita Brady, 1926; Marie Williams Gowan, 1927; I.E. Grove, 1934-35; Carolyn Specht, 1940-41; Pearl M. Lockart, 1942; Willis Rawlings, 1943; and Mary Kessler, 1944-45.

Mary Kessler was the last teacher with five pupils; directors were Fred Syfert, Elmer Kessler, and Lloyd Kessler.

In 1949 John Kessler bought the old school house for $600 which was a half acre of the southwest corner of the west half of the southwest quarter of the section 13.

VALLEY OR
HUGAWAY
District 8 or 162

Valley school was located in the southwest quarter of section 3 of Holland township. In 1889, the directors were Prestley Whitan, Jesse Courtright, and W.S.Giles.

Some of the teachers at Valley school were: Montie Markland, 1893; Mabel Turner, 1894; Edith Ponsler, 1901; Morris Williams, 1909; Minnie E. Muchow, 1917; Nora Brandon Keller, 1924-27; Clarence Ponsler, 1934-35; Ruby Mae Carter, 1939-40; Jesse Gill, 1941; Mary Ponsler, 1942; Ethel Patterson, 1943, and Mary Ponsler, 1944.

Mary Ponsler was the last teacher with four pupils; the directors were George Syfert, E.F. Dove, and Frank Arnold.

In 1949 E.F.Dove bought the old school house for $505 which was located in the section 3.

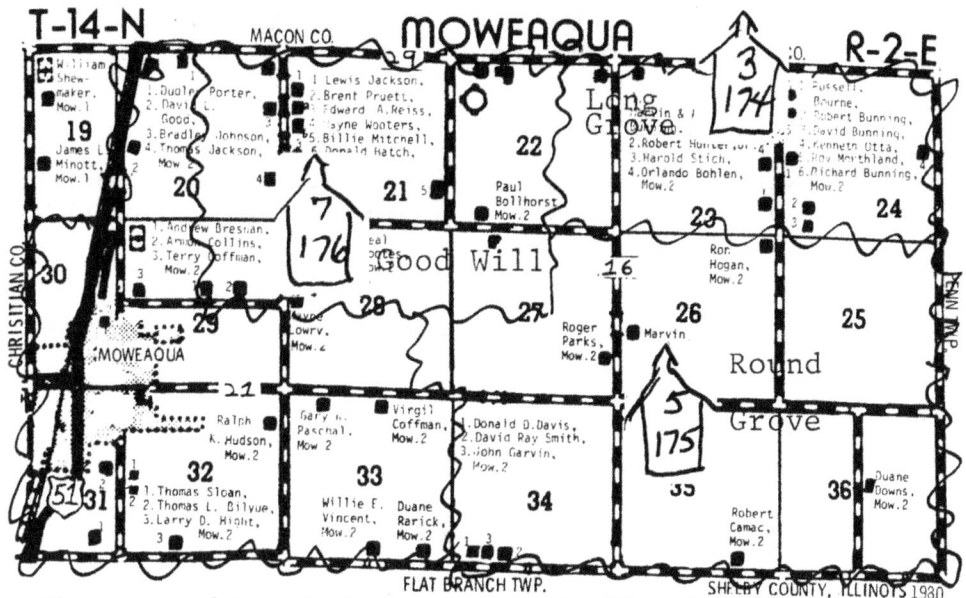

The wavy line indicates the 1903 school district.

MOWEAQUA TOWNSHIP

The earliest school in this northern township was only about a quarter of a mile north of the present town of Moweaqua. The school of 1836 was a log cabin and kept only 3 months each year as children had to walk up to 6 miles each way to attend.

LONG GROVE
District 3 or 174

Long Grove was located in the northwest corner of the northeast quarter of section 23 of Moweaqua township. In 1865 James and Sinia Renfro deeded land to the trustees William Armstrong and John M. Fridley for the school. The directors for the school a year later were W.O.D. Lamb, Edward Culver, and Robert Hight. In 1869, the directors were W. O.D. Lamb, J.C. Thompson, and W.W. Hight.

In 1875 at a meeting of the taxpayers of this district, it was decided to collect only half the school tax that appeared on the books, since the taxbooks showed a requisition of double the amount they required. Oliver Gibson and Ephraim Adamson were the directors for that year.

Directors of the 1880's were Oliver Gibson, Edward Culver, Peter H. Bohlen, John W. Lamb and A. Otta.

Some of the teachers at Long Grove school were: J.E. Wallace, 1888; Justin Love, 1889; S.J. Pritchard, 1890; Charles Conner, 1891-92; Sara Bartscht, 1893; Lillie F. Ellis, 1894; J. M. Reynolds, 1901; Roscoe Carroll, 1909; Helen Hamblen, 1922; Aileen Jordan, 1924-26; Mildred Moss, 1927; Margaret McGrath, 1934-39; Aldyth Gregory, 1940-41; Kathyrn Wright, 1942-43; Gertrude Hemer, 1944; Adith Poole, 1945; and Lyla Smith, 1946.

Lyla Smith was the last teacher with a school of 14

pupils; the directors were Thomas Hemer, Joe Clipston and Henry Hemer. The school is no longer standing today.

ROUND GROVE
District 5 or 175

Round Grove school was located in the northeast corner of the northwest quarter of section 35 of Moweaqua township. John M. and Julia F. Friedley deeded land for the school in 1870. Earlier in 1866, the taxes were two percent per 100, and directors were J. H. Donnel, W. J. Adams, and J.T. Vert. Three years later, the tax was one and half percent per 100, and the directors were James Freeman and W. J. Adams.

The directors of the 1880's were Walter Humphrey, B. F. Doyle, James B. Riley and James S. Stewart.

Some of the teachers at Round Grove school were: Lemuel Buck, 1890; Charles W. Lane, 1889; Sara Bartscht, 1893; Charles Colbert, 1901; Mayme Hines, 1909; Agnes Hamblen, 1922; Helen Keelen, 1924; Naomi Kellar, 1926; Margaret McGrath, 1927; Erma G. Johnson, 1934-35; Lucille Bartels, 1939; Robert Hendricks, 1940; Dora Lee Myers, 1941-42; Sybil Garrison, 1943-44.

Sybil Garrison was the last teacher with 16 pupils; the directors were William Bohlen, M. Wayne Stewart, and William Camac.

BERYL BRIDGWATER RARICK

She attended Round Grove school from 1916 to 1923 and had teacher Frances Harper, and Maple Grove from 1914 to 1915 and had teacher Daisy Wiggins.

"I remember the last day of the school program and the potluck dinners. I can almost taste that fruit salad. The box suppers, Christmas programs. I lived two miles east of Moweaqua, and drove a pony hitched to a buggy to town to bring the teacher out to school. As I was going home one evening in late fall, a train went through town and the whistle scared my pony. She ran and I couldn't hold her so we got home in a hurry that evening."

Beryl was the daughter of Albert and Nellie Barber Bridgwater; granddaughter of Charles and Hanna Cole Barber, and Levi Jack and Sarah Noaks Bridgwater; and great-granddaughter of Christian C. and Margaret Miller Bridgwater.

GOODWILL
District 7 or 176

Goodwill school was located in the northeast corner of the northwest quarter of section 28 of the Moweaqua township. Christopher and Caroline Schroll deeded land to the school trustees in 1871.

Directors of the 1880's were Mark Tolson, Lemuel Parker, George Russell, V. F. Hilvety, Chris Schroll and E.W. Harper.

Some of the teachers at Goodwill school were: Carrie

Stump, 1891; Ruth E. Huber, 1892; W.W. Griffith, 1893; L.C. Whitehead, 1894; Rebecca Rose, 1901; Grace Scovil, 1909; Deborah Gregory, 1917; Ina C. Wyckoff, 1922; Frances Freeman, 1924-stand school; no school 1926-27; Jane Housh, 1934.

Jane Housh was the last teacher with 6 pupils, and the directors were E.G. Russell, J.C. Shepherd, and Richard Tolson.

In August 1937, a memorial service was held at the Goodwill school for seven individuals who had died since March 1 that year. They were Charles Parker, George Shroll, Lynn Stombaugh, Charles Hipes, James Freeman, Samuel Miller, and Mrs. Edna M. Barber. J. T. Haslam, a former teacher of the school, presided at the meeting, and Mrs. Lydia Bullock, a former pupil, acted as secretary. Other former teachers present were Gladys Harper, Mrs. W.T. Durham, and Naomi Keller.

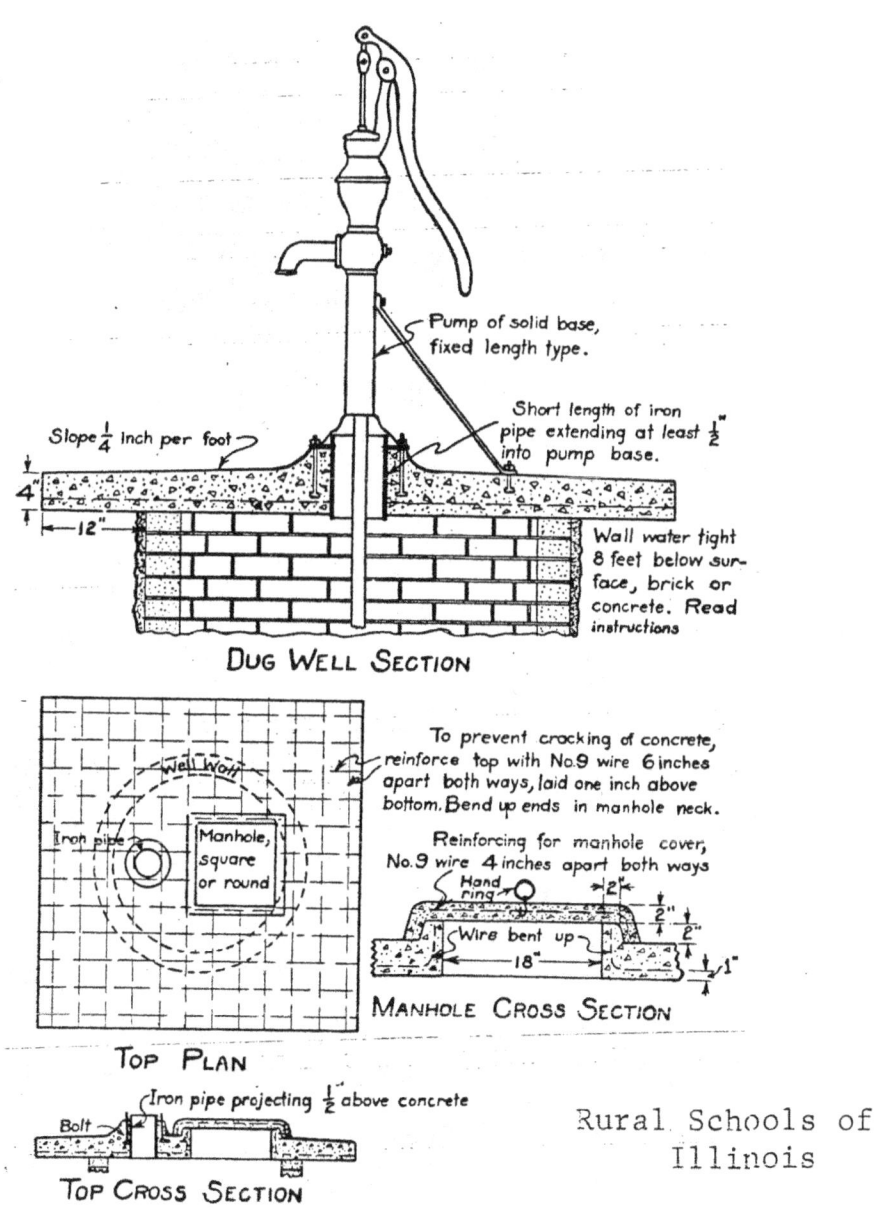

Rural Schools of Illinois

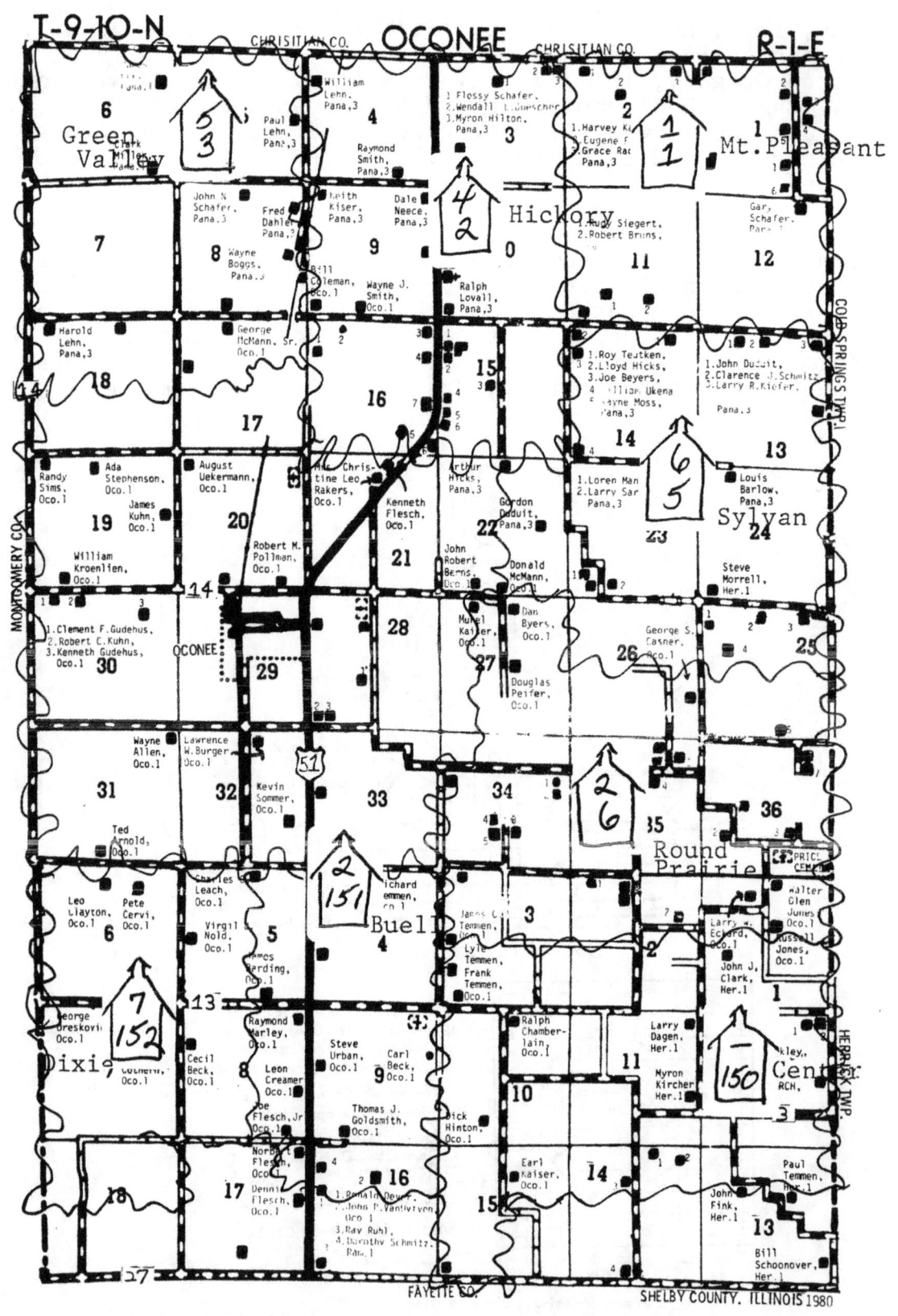

OCONEE TOWNSHIP

On the southeast corner of Shelby County lies Oconee township which is crossed by Opossum Creek. Settlers came here early from Fayette County which lies immediately south of Oconee.

A report made to the county superintendent of schools showed the following in November 1849. No. of schools taught by males, 2; highest number of children taught, 80; average number who have attended school, 40; no. of white persons under twenty-one years, 147; average no. of months in which schools have been taught, 9; average monthly salary of male teachers, $12; highest rate of pay to teachers, $13; lowest rate of pay to teachers, $8; amount of public money paid for teacher's wages, $110; amount annually expended for schools, $160; no.of organized districts, 2; no. of school houses, 2; no. of log school houses, 2. This was a yearly report in accordance with "an act to establish and maintain common schools" aproved February 12, 1849.

Mt. Pleasant
District 1 or 1

Mt. Pleasant school was located in the southeast corner of the southeast quarter of the southeast quarter of section 2 of Oconee township. Residents of this area assessed a half percent per 100 in 1866, and directors were Jonathon Lee, Rozin Perry, and A. M. Hunter. Three years later, the residents built a new school house and paid a tax of 3 percent and 1 percent per 100. Directors were B.J. Pritchett, W. Hamilton and Rezin Perry.

Directors of the 1880's were W. Hamilton, Joshua Carney, George Sisk, Jasper Fry and John Emery.

Mathias and Anne Mount leased land to the trustees in 1874.

Some teachers of the Mt. Pleasant school were: Ella Johnson, 1888; Clara Morgan, 1892; Ella Bumgardner, 1893; Frona Bumgardner, 1894; Wade McNutt, 1901; Earl Crowder, 1909; Pearl Warren Garrett, 1924; Hazel P. Bond, 1926; Oneita Mills, 1927; Vashti Howell, 1934; Daisy S. Rittgers, 1935.

Daisy Rittgers was the last teacher with 6 pupils; directors were Merle E. Potts, N.R. Wilhelm and C.W. Fry.

The trustees sold the building in 1949 to Bess H. Preihs.

Round Prairie
District 2 or 6

Round Prairie school was located in section 35 of Oconee township. Directors of the 1880's were N. P. McNutt, N.C.Price, P.B. Helton and J.W. Cowan.

Thomas and Mary C. Hendricks leased land to the trustees in 1885.

Some of the teachers at Round Prairie school were: C.A. Price, 1892; O.P. Simpson, 1893-94; A. Nelson Corneil, 1901; Fannie Price, 1909; Earla Donaldson Eaglin, 1917; Rhoda G. Cain, 1922-24; Ocla Hamilton, 1926; Sarah Nichols, 1927; Jesse E. Smith, 1934; Nona F. Linn, 1935; Lucy M. Allen Price, 1939-40; Ella E. Morrison, 1941; Mary Morrison, 1942-44; Nona Eckard, 1945; Betty Roberts, 1946.

Betty Roberts was the last teacher with six pupils, and directors were Wilbur J. Hendricks, Merle McNutt, and Francis Blythe.

The trustees sold the property in 1949 to A. C. McTaggart.

Hickory
District 4 or 2

Hickory school was located in section 10 of Oconee township. Residents of this area assessed themselves at 80 cents per 100 in 1866, and directors were S. Wimberly and John Hobson. In 1869, they taxed to build a new school at $2 per 100 and those directors were David Andrew, John Hobson and Frederick Garber.

Directors of the 1880's were C.A. Doyle, Charles Morefield, R.S. Drain and David Andrew.

Some of the teachers at Hickory school were: John Cheney, 1888; J.W. Patterson, 1890; Charles H. Allen, 1891; E.S. DeBaun, 1893-94; Alice Row, 1901; Ethel Hinton, 1909; Mrs. Bertha Hellman, 1922; Louise Allen, 1924; Lucretia Halbrook, 1926; Mrs. Pearl Garrett, 1927; Lucy Allen, 1934; 1935; E.D. Schull, 1939; Ruth Evelyn Thompson, 1940-41; Bertha I. Howell, 1942; Margaret Lape, 1943-45; Lorene H. Lockwood, 1946.

Lorene H. Lockwood was the last teacher at Hickory with a class of 12 pupils; directors were George Vits, William Suey, and Dale Neece.

In 1894 during the month of January, there were 31 pupils enrolled with an average attendance of 26. Those having perfect attendance during that time were: Lulu Andrew, Carrie Wade, Jesse McConnell, Clarence Pope, Charley Andrew, May Drain, Bertie Hitchcock, Charlie Hitchcock, Albert Combest, and Anna Combest.

GREEN VALLEY
District 5 or 3

Green Valley school was located in the southwest corner of the southwest quarter of the southwest quarter of section 5 of Oconee township. Residents of this area assessed taxes at $1.75 per 100 in 1866 for building, and directors were Moses Smith, Mathias Hettiger, and Thomas Whitnerhouse. Three years later, the taxes were one percent per 100, and directors were J.C. Brown, William Guthrie, and George Crosby.

Directors of the 1880's were William Walker, S.R. Weaver,

Newton Porter, and J.C. Brown.

Some of the teachers at Green Valley school were: C.W. Jolly, 1888-90; Ella Row, 1891; C.A. Quackenbush, 1892; C.W. Lane, 1893; Gladys Turner, 1894; Flora Moore, 1901; Emma Roth, 1908-09; Charles Welch, 1913; Charles Nichols, 1924; Basil D. Green, 1926-27; Lois Jean Diefenthaler, 1934; Earl E. Petty, 1935; Marilyn Schwarm, 1939-40; George Crawford, 1941; Emma Bennett, 1942; Clara E. Frankenfield, 1943-44; Alvin Kelly, 1945; and R.A. Kelley, 1946.

R.A. Kelley was the last teacher with a school of 13 pupils; directors were Harold Batton, John Swiney, and John Bruns.

The trustees sold the school property in 1949 to John Rochkes for $180--one acre in the southwest corner of the southwest quarter of section 5.

Green Valley school in 1913 or 1914. Back row, l or r, Myrtle Weaver, Cornelia Olshakie, Mildred Weaver, Hazel Weaver, Lola Porter, Catherine Garber, Charles Welch, teacher, Vienna Hackle; 2nd row, Grace Weaver, Hazel Porter, Elmer Cutler, Ferdinand Garber, Clarabel Woods, Esther Porter, ? , Terra Miles, Belle Garber, Luther Farrar Miles, Henry Garber, ? , Herbert Porter. Bill Garber behind Clarabell.
Photo courtesy of Alma Garber

SYLVAN
OR NUMBER 6 District 6 or 5

Sylvan school was located in the northeast corner of the northeast quarter of section 23 of Oconee township.

Directors of the 1880's were C.A. Doyle, and Elgel Beckett.

Some of the teachers at Sylvan school were: John A. Beckett, 1889-90; J.T. Staley, 1891; James W. Morgan, 1894; M.L. Turner, 1901; Ethel Roberts, 1909; Roy Ireland, 1917; Lenora Watson, 1922; Bernadine Keirn, 1924; Louetta E. Harwood, 1926; Mildred Duduit, 1927; Forrest Moore, 1934; George W. Weaver, 1935; Claude Dunlap, 1939-40; Clarence Coleman, 1941; Charles Wade, 1942; Alma Turrentine, 1943-45; and Evelyn Dodson, 1946.

The last teacher was Evelyn Dodson with a school of 8 pupils; directors were Joe Carnes, John Barlow and Louie Barlow.

The trustees sold the school in 1949 to Eugene Ruot.

During June 1893 in the school with Ruth Huber as teacher, the following students participated in the end of the year program: Stella McCurdy, Robert Huber, Laura Daniel, Otie Severe, Lillie Syfert, Walter Banning, Bessie Huber, Eddie Barbee, Effie Tripp, Hattie Syfert, Maria Banning, May Compton, Chester Smith, Ona Miller, Maud Houser, John McCurdy, Mary Cleason, Eddy Barbee, Nettie Triece, Jo McNeese, Jessie Fisher, Edna Miller and Florence Stone.

JOHN T. BARLOW, SR.

He attended Syvlan school from 1916 to 1924 in Oconee township.

"About the most exciting event I can think of when I attended Sylvan District No. 5 was when the teacher's brother, Mr. Watson, loaded all us kids up in his cattle truck and took us to the Shelbyville park for the day."

John was the son of John F. and Josephine McIntyre Barlow; and grandson of Albert and Cena Gray McIntyre.

"Names of the school teachers at Sylvan as I got all my education at the one school. We only lived about ¼ mile from the school. Roy Ireland, Eula Pope Culberson, Lenora Watson, Clara Huffmaster, Bernadine Keirn, Helen Perkins, Lucille Phipps. Think there should have been another one, but can't recall her name. I suppose most of them are deceased by now. I notice on one of my old attendance certificates that O. O. Barker was county superintendent of schools in 1924. I have two snapshots of the pupils. One in 1924 and the other before that."

CENTER
District 1 or 150

Center school was located first as a log cabin in section 11 of Oconee township. It was later moved to section 12.

Residents taxed at $2.25 per 100 for building purposes in 1866, and directors that year were D. J. Kauffman, and Joel Wollard. Three years later, the assessment was 70 cents per 100, and directors were D. J. Kaufman and John Ingle.

Directors of the 1880's were B. McCoy, George C. Aichele, A.R. Beckett, John Kay, and A.L. Chamberlain.

Some of the teachers at Center school were: Morrill Pattengale, 1889; Elizabeth Clark, 1890; George W. Beck, 1892; Elizabeth Clark, 1893; Sam Beckett,1894; Lottie Gale,1901; Edward Stevens, 1905-09; Lela Hinton, 1917; Blanche Clucas, 1922; Jurella O'Kelley, 1924; Grace Lankford, 1926-27; Glenda Fink, 1934; Bernice Woolard, 1935; Orthel S. Tate, 1939-42; Elma Taniges, 1943; John Strain, 1944; Flo Rittgers, 1945-46; Betty Roberts, 1948.

The last teacher was Betty Roberts with a class of 6 pupils; directors were Wilmer Chamberlain, Wayne Smart, and John Kaiser.

The trustees sold the building in 1953 as a community club. At that time it was located in the northwest corner of the northwest quarter of section 12.

Students who attended Center school in May 1905 were: Oran Woolard, Pete Chamberlain, Corwin Price, Lura Smart Johnson, Agnes Smart, Celestine Smart Woolard, Edna Walker McManmie, May Smith, Velma Boaz Kay, Ross Chamberlain, Orthel Smart Tate, Walter Ebler, Bessie Smart Smith, Audrey Evans, Mary Price, Lem Taniges, Dolly Chamberlain Christman, C. Egbert Chamberlain, Claude Kay, Znobia Smart Wright, Jessie Roberts Rumer, Betty Roberts, Lola Chamberlain Buchanan, Mattie Smart Cope, Fanny Price, Pearl Price, and Gladys Chamberlain Morgan.

GLENDA BERNADINE FINK TOWELL

She attended Center school and had teachers Lois Hinton, Phyllis Price, Illian Tressler, "Dutch" Stephens, and Lois Grider. She attended from 1918 to 1923.

Glenda was the daughter of John and Osia Clark Fink; granddaughter of Ben and Elizabeth Tangiges Fink, and George W. and Mattie Runyon Clark; great-granddaughter of John F. and Mary Taniges, and William and Rachel Clark and James and Catherine Runyon.

BUELL
District 2 or 151

Buell school district was located in the northwest corner of section 4 of Oconee township. Residents paid 50¢ per 100 dollars tax in 1866 and directors were Edward Lees, John Roberts, and George Neel.

Directors of the 1880's were Winand Smith, John Voorhees, Samuel Rogers, Jacob Gaskill and James Lees.

Some of the teachers at Buell school were: Mattie Morgan,

1888-89; Jessie Garretson, 1890; Rosa D. Bowser, 1891; Tilda Simpson, 1892; Louisa M. March, 1893; Tilda Simpson, 1894; Zora Yates, 1901; Mary Smart, 1909; Ruth Osborn, 1924; Clara Watson, 1926; Evelyn Janes, 1927; Melvin R. McCaleb, 1934; John Paczak, 1935; Paul A. Morrison, 1939-40; Olivia Fischer, 1941-42; Nona Eckard, 1943; Barbara Chamberlain, 1944; Norma J. Whittington, 1945-46.

Norma J. Whittington was the last teacher with a class of 8 pupils; directors were Fred Schmitz, Frank Temman, and Dwight Shaff.

DIXIE
OR TENNESSEE
District 7 or 152

Dixie school was located in the southeast corner of the northeast quarter of section 7 of Oconee township. The residents in 1866 had a tax of one percent on the 100, and directors were W.T. Slater and William Manley. Three years later, the tax was the same and the directors were William T. Slater and Joseph E. Rogers.

Directors of the 1880's were F.P. Vest, A.S. Reed, and Sydney Slater.

Some of the teachers at Dixie were: Ida Bowser, 1889; Anna Wilmer, 1890; Ida Bowser, 1891; Roma Bowser, 1892; Docia Sloan, 1894; Paul Welsh, 1901; Thomas Stevens, 1909; Elsie Hamblen, 1917; Basil Green, 1924; Sarah B. M. Diefenthaler, 1926; Florence Nichols, 1927; Kathryn Duduit, 1934; Lois Jean Diefenthaler, 1935; Paul A. Morrison, 1939; Ruth A. Osborn, 1940-44.

Ruth Osborn was the last teacher with seven pupils; the directors were Benton Beck, L. F. Diefenthaler and Loren Manuel.

OPAL WATSON

She attended schools in Oconee township and Cold Spring township.

"I went to school at Pleasant Grove on county line between Cowden and Herrick. I had three teachers in all 8 grades, Lucy Lorton, Meda Newberry, and Roe Middlesworth. Also Round Prairie, Oconee township, Gorden Young.

As to the Corley school, my sister Lenora Watson Porter taught there, and also at Sylvan school in Oconee township. My sister Clara Watson Shull taught at Tennessee school in Oconee township."

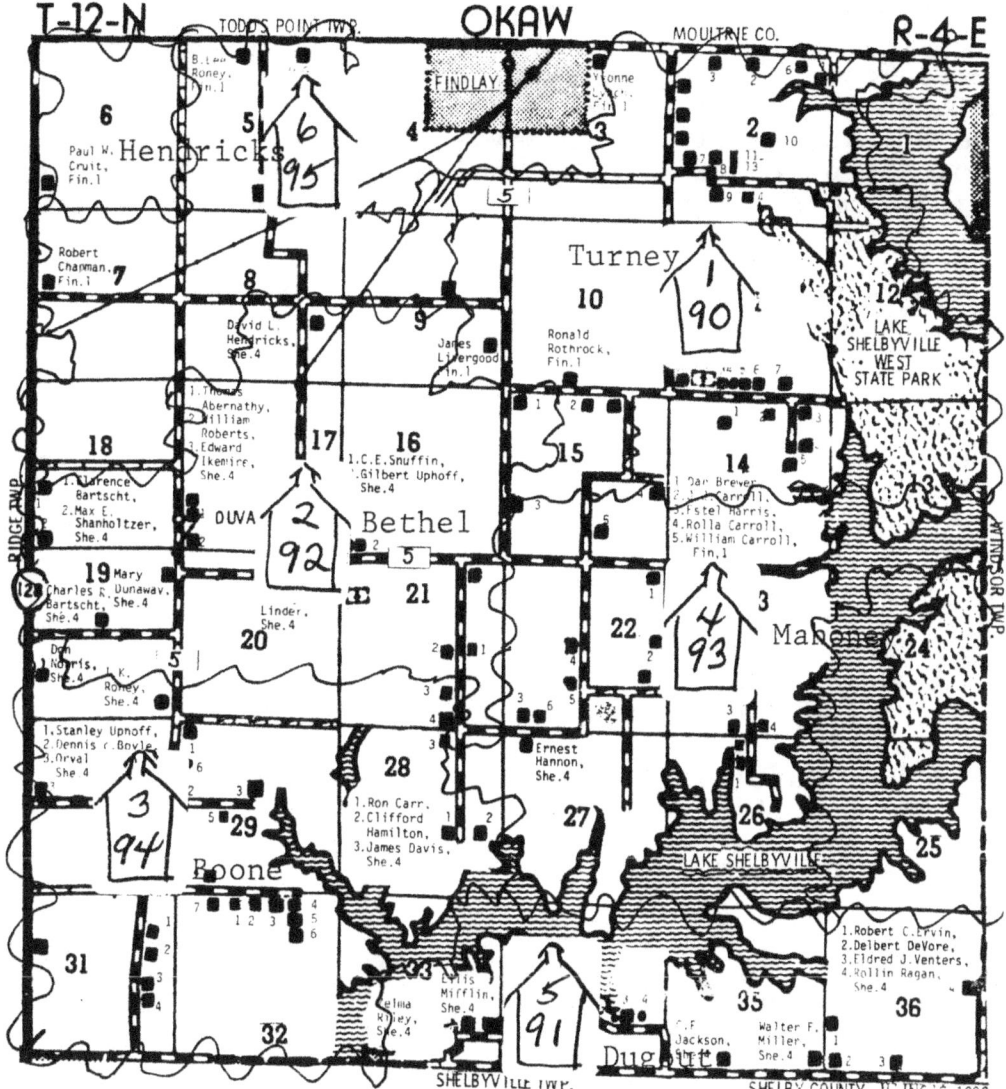

The wavy line indicates the 1903 school district.

OKAW TOWNSHIP

Today Lake Shelbyville covers a large area of the township known as Okaw. Okaw was the name originally of the tributaries of the Kaskaskia. The earliest school, a log cabin, must have been in the area of the later Bethel school in section 21. In 1827, there were already 25 charter members of an early church--Okaw of the Regular Presestinarians which included the familes of Abbott, Tipsword, Jordan, Odem and Harris. Bushrod Henry was the first teacher in 1832.

TURNEY
OR UPPER LAKEY BEND
District 1 or 90

Turney school was located in the northwest quarter of section 11 of Okaw Township. The school also at times was called Upper Lakey Bend. Residents in 1855 taxed themselves at the rate of one percent for building a schoolhouse and two mills for teaching salaries, etc. There were 33 taxpayers in the district: David Truit, Nathan J. Clarage, Tobias Miller, Joseph Carter, William Clarage, Joseph Dickson, James Rose, William J. Walters, John Walters, Zimary Hendricks, William R. Dazey, William T. Dazey, Eli Francisco, Allen Francisco, Joseph Dazey, Colonel Matheney, James Dazey, James Wright, James Brightman, ? White, Felix G. Turney, James Scott, John Hale, D. L. Furguson, John Willit, Philemon Spicer, Alfred Francisco, Izari Francisco, James A. Wortman, Elisha Niles, James Earp, Ichabod Dodson, Ali Person. Directors that year were William Clarage, James W. Scott and Philemon Spicer.

In 1866, the district had a special tax of 25 cents per 100 and directors were James W. Wright and Howard Francisco. Three years later, the tax was 50 cents per 100, and directors were Howard Francisco and Rob Knox.

Directors of the 1880's were Peter Francisco, Akillis Spicer, Philemon Spicer, George Dixon and D. J. Dawdy.

Some of the teachers at Turney school were: S. Robison, 1876; W.B. Stine, 1888; M. L. Herron, 1890; Jennie Dazey, 1891; J.L. Henderson, 1892; C. P. Clay, 1893; Lizzie Dazey, 1894-01; Maude Spicer, 1909; Ruth Turney, 1917; Bart L. Herron, 1922; Earl St. Pierre, 1924; Valette U. Barr, 1926-27; Ralph E. Cuttill, 1934; A.W. Thompson, 1935; Mona C. Anderson, 1939; Harold McMillan, 1940; Laveda Dawdy, 1941-42; Maude Herron, 1943-46.

Maude Herron was the last teacher with 13 pupils; directors were Cyrus Yantis, Bart L. Herron and Elgar Allen.

OPAL E. MILLER

She attended Turney school from 1921 to 1924, and had teachers Bart Herron and Charles Farmer.

"This happened at Turney school when Bart Herron was the teacher. I was just a small girl in first or second grade. One cold winter day, a little boy came to school with his older brothers. There was snow on and he was crying. He had walked to school barefooted. His feet were almost frozen. Mr. Herron brought in a pan of snow and worked with his feet trying to get them warm and to stop the hurting. Finally he got them warm and wrapped them in a sweater. He told the little boy to stay home until he go some shoes to wear. Some people were so poor in those days. Children would come to school with ragged shoes and boots or maybe have their feet wrapped in rags on cold days. Most children had to walk to school. Transportation was by horse and buggy or in wagons. I remember the incident and think how fortunate the children are today. No one has to walk to school barefoot in the snow. Warm buses transport well-dressed children or their parents take them in fast cars to modern, well equipped schools."

Opal was the daughter of Roy and Nonia Adams Miller; granddaughter of John W. and Anna Riebold Miller, and Thomas and Margaret Herndon Adams; great-granddaughter of Joseph and Ellen Miller, and John and Mary Wackley Riebold.

BETHEL
District 2 or 92

Bethel school was located in the northeast corner of section 20 of Okaw township. Residents in 1866 assessed the taxes at 30 cents per 100, and directors were Whitfield Turney, W.G. Parker and Michael Freyburger. Three years later, the taxes were the same and so were the directors.

In 1873, the residents of Okaw township presented a petition to the county board requesting that another voting place be created in the township. Apparently, Bethel school had been the only poll until that time. They proposed the other poll to be at Foster's school house.

Directors of the 1880's were W.S. Robertson, D.F. Turney, J.A. Fearman and James Wilson.

Some of the teachers at Bethel were: Charles Herron, 1888; Grant Ashbrook, 1889; Lizzy Dazey, 1891; F. P. Herron, 1892; H.W. Wright, 1893; Ella Baxter, 1894; William Barr, 1901; Frank Fought, 1909; Essie M. Banks, 1917; T.E. Anderson, 1922; LaVerne Ward, 1924-standard school; Ethel M. Ford, 1926-standard school; Anna Hazel Lee, 1927; Melvin R. Yantis, 1934-35; T.E. Anderson, 1939; Greta Howse, 1940-41; T.E. Anderson, 1942-44; and D. M. Mathis, 1945.

D. M. Mathis was the last teacher with 13 pupils, and the directors were Glen Scott, William Roberts and A. J. Ulrich.

Bethel school in early 1900's. Photo courtesy of Zelma Bryson

Mahoney school in 1910-11 with teacher Ed Chapman. Pictured front are: Mary Birkey, Lola Graven, teacher, Delbert Olmstead, Ben Donnel. Back row, Pearl Patient, Fern Graven, Earl Morse, Marie Herron, and Fay Hyland. One fellow in back not identified.

Photo courtesy of Zelma Bryson

BOONE
District 3 or 94

Boone school was located in the southeast quarter of section 30 of Okaw township. Residents in 1866 assessed taxes at 75 cents per 100, and directors were Hiram Blackstone and Alexander Boys. Three years later, for a new school, taxes were $2 per 100 and directors were Hiram Blackstone, Samuel Hendricks and J.Wagoner.

Directors of the 1880's were E. M. Shumaker, Samuel Hendricks, J.E. Eby, and J. M. Lemen.

Some of the teachers at Boone school were: Palmira Richardson, 1888; Jerry Reynolds, 1890; Minnie Fleming, 1891; Lucy Duvall, 1892; Ella Baxter, 1893; R.J. Herron, 1894; Elza Smith, 1901; John Baird, 1909; Verna Banks, 1922; Doris Shutt, 1924-standard school; Lucille Morris, 1926-standard school; Faye Olmstead, 1934-35; Maxine Barbee, 1939; Ruth Boys, 1940-41.

Ruth Boys was the last teacher with 9 pupils, and directors were Louie Biehler, Gayle Lichtenwalter, and Arch Hostetler.

Trustees sold the school in 1950 to Raymond G. Workman for $2400.

MAHONEY
District 4 or 93

Mahoney school was located in the northwest quarter of section 23 of Okaw township. Before the Civil War, it was located a short way south. Residents in 1866 assessed a tax at 75 cents per 100, and directors were H. B. Morse, S.R. Chapman and Lewis Mahoney. Three years later, the taxes were 40 cents per 100, and directors were David Truitt and H.B. Morse.

Directors of the 1880's were John M. Herron, W. S. Baxter, John Hendricks, and H. B. Morse.

Some of the teachers at Mahoney school were: George S. Terry, Will F. Hilsabeck, Parson Brown, Mr. Perryman, Mr. Shanks, Kizie Richman, Sam Kitch, Charles L. Herron, Mr. Allen, Henry B. Morse, Ulysees S. White, 1874; William Ragan,1875; Charles Miner, 1876; E.A. Richardson, 1877; Sam Robison, 1878-80; A. H. Perryman, 1881; W. Berlin Wallace, 1882-83; Clara Graybill, 1884; Robert M. Herron, 1885; John M. Tull, 1886; Mart L. Herron, 1887; James H.Baxter, 1888; Robert D. Miner, 1889; James H. Baxter, 1890; Robert D. Miner, 1891; Edward N. Herron, 1892-93; Trua Rose and E.P. Chapman, 1895; Edward N. Herron, 1896; W. Edward Hendricks, 1897-98; Scott Miner, 1899; William Barr, 1900; Ollie Herron, 1901; R. J. Herron, 1902-03; Scott Miner, 1904; Edna Renner, 1905; Norma James, 1906; Newton A. Baxter, 1907-09; E.P. Chapman, 1910; R. J. Herron, 1911; Jacob Warner, 1912; Roy Strohl, 1913; Crawford F. Hickey, 1914; Regis Mc-

Mahoney school
Photo courtesy of
Zelma Bryson

Boon school — Thirteen pupils and their teacher were part of the Boon school in 1893, they included, back row — Wilbur Skidmore, Walter Hendricks, John Gabhart, John Eby; Middle row — Roy Skidmore, Ella Baxter (teacher), Sally Eby, Mort Gebhart; front row — Walter Worthmon, Tracy Moyer, Anna Moyer, Pearl Gabhart, Maud Gabhart and Roy Moyer, in center front.

Clory, 1916; Cecil E. Francisco, 1917; Ned Guthrie, 1918; George Tresler, 1919; Louis F. Christman, 1921; Lora E. Morse, 1922; Lora E. Morse Braden, 1923; Doris M. Finley, 1924-25; Lillian Pritts Goddard, 1926; Mary Ponsler, 1926; Ethel M. Ford, 1927; Bart L. Herron, 1928-31; Ruth Merryman, 1932; Juanita Stevens Graven, 1933-34; Opal Knearem Runkel, 1935; Florence Biedert, 1936; Ellis Simmons, 1939; Darrell Cruthis, 1940; Ada S. Gould, 1941; Ruth Davis, 1942-44; Loy E. Herron, 1945-46.

Loy E. Herron was the last teacher with 10 pupils; directors were Earl Morse, Lester M. Herron and Zelma Bryson.

In 1929 for the month of September, the following students had perfect attendance: Shelley Berkley, Coleen Heiland, Dan Herron, Claire Herron, Carolee Herron, Cleo Herron, Raymond Chapman, Earl Chapman, Maurine Graven, Cecil Graven, Kenneth Morse, Frank Morse, Maxine Morse, James Hill, Robert Agney and Louis Hubbs.

FRED N. BAXTER

He attended Mahoney school from 1905 to 1911, and had teachers Edna REnner, Norma James, Newton A. Baxter, and Edward P. Chapman.

"When I try to remember events of my early school days, the first one that comes to mind is that on my first day in school I did not know where my lunch pail had been put by the teacher on my arrival. I am sure that was cause for plenty of tears.

In looking back, I think I was very lucky to have my father, Newton A. Baxter, as my teacher for three school years. He insisted that I excel. He became assistant county superintendent of schools; he then became county superintendent of highways. We moved to Shelbyville; I entered 5th grade under Nelle Edgar as teacher. There followed Ella Willard, Beatrice Graybill, and Frances Davis as my grade school teachers. They were all great!"

Fred was the son of Newton A. and Sallie Eby Baxter; grandsonof Jacob E. and Katherine Seltzer Eby, and William Sidney and Phoebe Quigley Baxter.

DUGOUT
District 5 or 91

Dugout school was located in the southwest quarter of section 34 of Okaw township. Residents in 1866 assessed a tax at 75 cents per 100, and directors were W.D. Bryson and William D. Sexson. Three years later for building purposes, the tax was 90 cents per 100, and directors were W.G. Steele, P.R. Bryson and James Bryson.

Directors of the 1880's were Joseph Mackrell and John William Bryson.

Some of the teachers at Dugout school were: M. M. Barnhart, 1889; James H. Baxter, 1890; J. L. Henderson, 1891;

T.P. Miner, 1892-93; Maude Reynolds, 1894; F.D. Herron, 1901; Bart L. Herron, 1909; Jesse Gill, 1917; Lillian Pritts, 1924; Helen Winson, 1926; Jesse Gill, 1927; Ruth Davis, 1934; Paul Christman, 1935; Gloyd E. Archey, 1939; T.E. Anderson, 1940-41; W. K. Jackson, 1942; Perry E. Pritts, 1943-45, and Alta Lee, 1946.

Alta Lee was the last teacher with 27 pupils, and directors were E. F. Clay, L.E. Mears and Ralph Woods.

GOLDIE BRYSON

She attended Dugout school for 8 years and had teachers Tom Anderson, Robert and Jessie Gill, Ruth Morris, Olive Hampton, Lillian Pritts, and Ray Kingston.

"The school was located across the road from a farm house, and it was in September, and the weather was very warm, so the door was open. A rooster came in and was picking up crumbs arund the dinner pails so he took a notion to crow. All the children thought that was the funniest thing that ever was, to have a chicken in school."

Goldie was the daughter of Ben and Nellie Bryson Gordon; and granddaughter of George Gordon.

MILDRED HILL MCGILLIGAN

She attended Dugout school for 4 years, and had teachers Ruth Davis, Paul Christman and Gloyd Archey.

"When Gloyd Archey was teacher, he told us to bring a sled the next day to school and he would take us all a sled ride by hooking our sled on his car. My parents thought it wuld be great fun so I had permission, but some of the children's parents thought it very dangerous. I was on the sled (all homemade) with Garnet Hudson and Gloyd pulled us as far as the crossroads."

Mildred was the daughter of James Samuel Ralph and Cora May Huffman Hill; granddaughter of Andrew B. and Martha Hill Hill, and John and Hannah Beeson Huffman; great-granddaughter of William and Martha Ward Hill, and William and Cynthia Scribner Hill, and Henry and Mary Beaman Beeson.

HENDRICKS
or EUREKA
District 6 or 95

Hendricks school was located in the southeast quarter of section 5 of Okaw township. Residents taxed at 3% per 100 in 1866, and directors were Charles C. Doser, John Carder, and Stewart Sapperfield. Three years later, taxes were 3 mills per 100, and directors were Levi M. Wright, Stewart Sapperfield, and Henry Evalt.

Directors of the 1880's were William Cherry, Henry Crowl and James M. Pogue.

Some teachers of Hendricks school were: J. H. Baxter,

Dugout school circa 1895. Teacher Florence Bell Warren stands in the middle of the back row. That same year she married George E. Roberts.

Photo courtesy of Margaret Bruns

1891; Theodore Baylers, 1892; C. H. Robinson, 1894; J.F. Williams, 1901; Alta Spicer, 1909; Lillian B. Pritts, 1922- school now called Eureka; Pauline Jackson, 1924-standard school, 1927; Opal Knearem, 1934; Lena Bible, 1935; Warren K. Jackson, 1939; Ethel M. Wilson, 1940-45.

Ethel M. Wilson was the last teacher with 8 pupils, and directors were Bert Bible, Luther Hendricks, and John Graven.

Correct size.

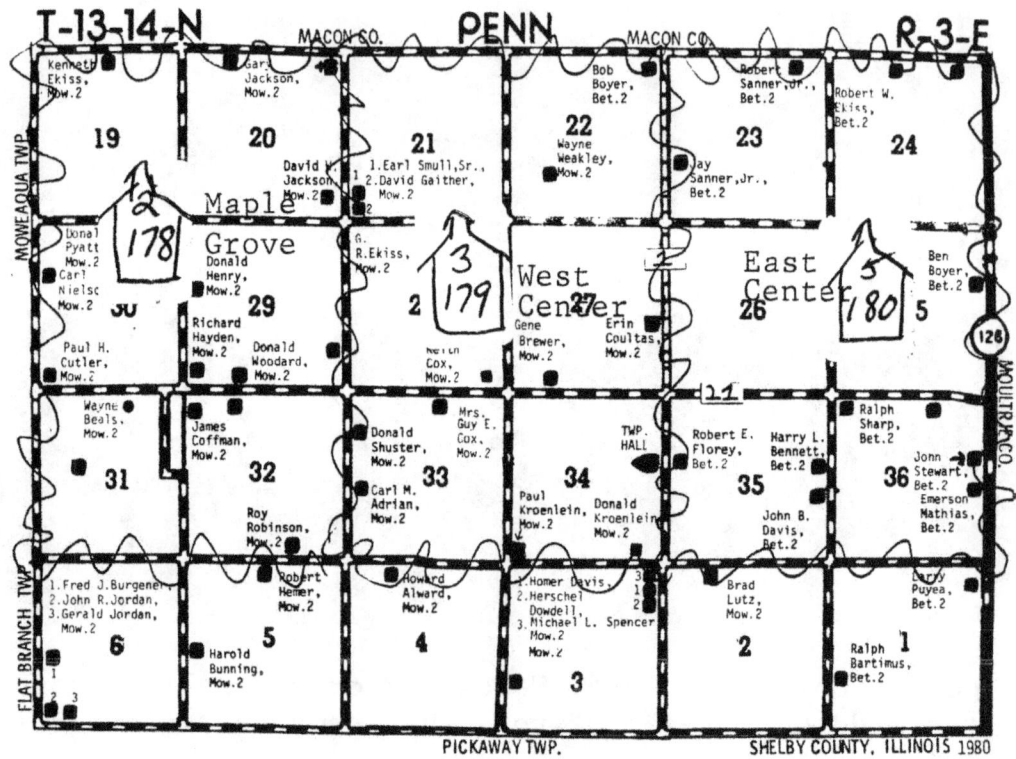

The wavy line indicates the 1903 school district.

PENN TOWNSHIP

Penn township lies in the northern part of Shelby County bordering Macon County. For many years, there were three schools, Maple Grove, West Center or East Center.

The township comprises an area of 24 square miles of rich farm land. Early records indicate that John Armstrong settled there in 1825.

The earliest single tax-based school was built circa 1864. By 1867, Penn township had two schools. The three school districts were finally created by 1875.

MAPLE GROVE
District 2 or 178

Maple Grove school was located in the northeast part of the township in section 30. In 1869, the taxes for the school were 40 cents per 100, and directors were Beverly Armstrong and J. P. Nutter.

In 1871, Thomas and Mary A. Shepherd, Jr. deeded one square acre of land in the southeast corner of the northeast quarter of section 30 of Penn township.

Directors of the 1880's were Samuel Stewart, George Goodwin, W. Parks and F. M. Sanders.

Some of the teachers at Maple Grove were: W.L. Wallace, 1889; S. J. Pritchard, 1891; J. M. Reynolds, 1892; Rose Humphrey, 1893; G. H. Smith, 1900-01; J. V. Williford, 1909; Bart L. Herron, 1917; Mary J. Heitmeyer, 1922-24; Pearl Seiber, 1926-27; Pearl Settle, 1934; Naomi E. Ingram, 1935; Mary Hedges, 1939-40. Margaret McGrath, 1941-44.

Margaret McGrath was the last teacher with 8 pupils, directors were Noble Elmers, Paul Shaddock and Clarence Sanner.

In 1900, there were 21 pupils enrolled at school with an average daily attendance of 20. For the months of Oct., Nov., and Dec., the following students had perfect attendance: Grace Palmer, Ray Palmer, Harry Palmer, Fannie Crain, Betty Crain, James Schneider, Frank Carroll, Roy Wyatt, Paul Hines, Mamie Hines, Roscoe Carroll, Naomi Sanner and Margaret Hines.

WEST CENTER
District 3 or 179

West Center school was located in the east half of section 28 of Penn township.

Directors of the 1880's were James S. Travis, Joseph Beck, J. B. Hyde, George Baker, Henry Small, and W. M. Beck.

Some of the teachers of West Center school were: Honoria Austin, 1889; H. M. Hagan, 1890; Holly Price, 1893; H. H. Price, 1894; W.W. Sheffler, 1900-01; Katharine Hinton, 1909; Ruth Bryant, 1917; Clara Marshall, 1922; Ruby I. Cox, 1924; Clara M. Mahan, 1926-27; Clarence Lambain, 1934; Ruth Alverson, 1935; Margery E. Taylor, 1939-40; Forrest Moore, 1941; Ethel Marie Moore, 1942; Pearl Cole, 1943, and Ruby Cox, 1944.

Ruby Cox was the last teacher with 5 pupils, and directors were Clark Pierce, Reginald Adams, and Floyd Cox.

OPAL B. ATKINSON

She attended West Center and Friendship schools, and had teachers Ruth Payne, Clara Marshall, Ora Culberson, Ruby Cox, Mary Ponsler, and Elsie Kopp.

"Just one room schools. About 25 or 30 children. We walked to school, two mile every day there and back. Me and my two brothers drove a horse in winter hitched to a storm buggy. We took a cold lunch to school and we traded things in our lunch bucket to other school mates. We all played lots of games outside, dare base, blackman, etc. Every Friday one half hour before closing time which was 4 o'clock, we all straightened our desks inside and then we all played inside games. On the last day of school we got to all go to the woods and had a picnic and then sometimes we had a picnic at school with our parents present. The children of the school put on a program."

Opal was the daughter of Simon and Barbara Primmer.

EAST CENTER
District 5 or 180

East Center school was located in the west half of section 25 of Penn township.

Directors of the 1880's were Solomon Wise, Ezekiel Braden, Fred Orris, David G. Sanner, John E. Garman, and J.A. Stewart.

Remodeling etc. done on the school house in 1875,

and new desks were bought that year. Just 10 years later, the school house was repaired again and a new well was dug. During February, 1889, school was closed temporarily since an outbreak of scarlet fever hit.

Some of the teachers at East Center were: Jeff D. Spitler, 1875; Miss Freeland, 1876; Jennie Foster and J.W. Walker, 1878; Jennie Foster and Frank Lindley, 1879; Lizzie Jolly and C.J. Minor, 1880; Ettie Laughlin and Thomas Minor, 1881; Etta Laughlin, 1882-83; John L. Henderson, 1883; Sadie Black, 1884-85; James W.Perryman, 1885; Fannie B. Edmiston, and Charles W. Lane, 1887; Cahrles W. Lane and Maude Gibson, 1888; Honoria Austin and C.A. Fought, 1889; Allie Fleming and James P. Clay, 1890; James P. Clay, 1891; Justin Love and Ralph E. Walker, 1892; M. M. Walker and J. Louie Hart, 1893; James P. Clay, 1894; Effie Douthit and E.A. Crowl, 1895; George Braden, 1896; Mella C. Ellis, William Sheffler, and Cora Ekiss, 1897; William Sheffler and Myrtle Sheffler, 1899; Isaac P. Baker, 1900; Elizabeth Alkire and Lawrence Smith, 1901; Lawrence Smith and Mary Sauks, 1902; Charles Tym, 1903-04; John N. Matthew, 1905; Alta M. Farmer and De Forest Baird, 1906; Maude G.Tyler and Rose Harris, 1907; Alice Hill and Fay L. Grayhill; Goldie O. Tressler, 1909; Elsie Purkiser and Claire Baird, 1910; Lella M. Reed, 1917; Ruth Payne, 1924-26; Mary Davis, 1926-27; Delbert Jones, 1928; Ottis Redfern, 1929-30; Laurence Gray, 1937-39; Margery Taylor, 1940-41; Lois Jane Bland, 1942; Bertha Dalton, 1943-45.

Bertha Dalton was the last teacher with 12 pupils; directors were DeForest E.Baird, George Burrows and G.K. Boyer. The school building sold in a few years for $272.50.

Not properly adjusted.
Both seat and desk too high.

East Center school in 1898 with teacher William W. Sheffler. Front row, l or r, Martha Sanner, Belle Mayberry, Ed Mayberry, Two Lofland boys, Claude Protsman, William W. Sheffler, Mary Protsman and Ira Sanner. 2nd row, Leavitt Taylor, Guy Cox, Ira Mayberry, Bob Sanner, Ross Macklin, Anna Macklin, Floyd Cox, Mary A. Gorman, Lech Wise, Grace E. Gorman, Nellie Sanner, Belle Stewart, Mary Baird, and May Taylor. 3rd row, Etta Sanner, Nell Coulter, Edith Stewart, Laura Protsman, Emma Garman, Dora Lofland, Lawrence Sanner and Manford Mayberry.

Photo courtesy of Robert Sanner

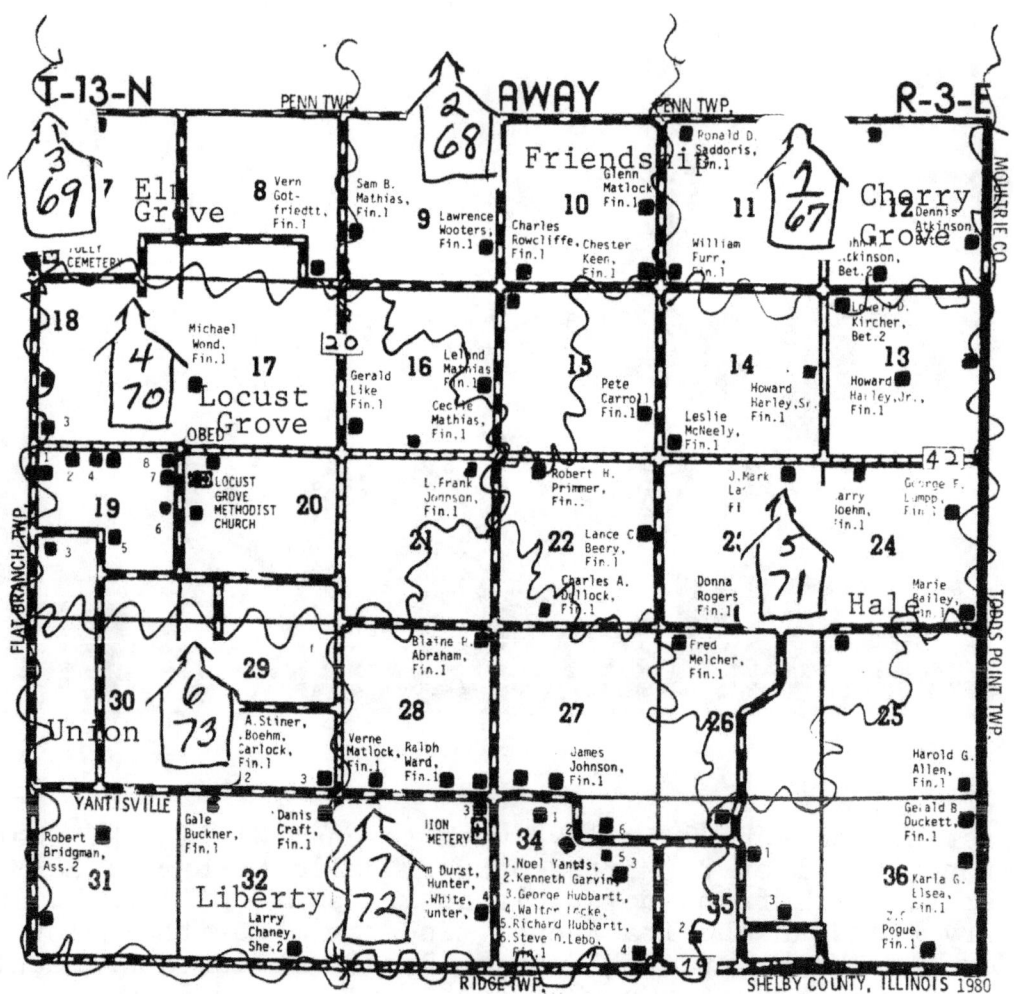

The wavy line indicates the 1903 school district.

PICKAWAY TOWNSHIP

Settlers arrived here in the late 1820's. The first school house was of logs built on section 7 in the edge of the timber, probably near the Tolly Cemetery.

The other early school was called the Yantis school in the 1860's and it was located northwest of later Yantisville. E.A. Moll had built the frame school in 1861 for $475, and nearly all the members of the school were members of the Yantis family. Nathaniel Ernest and his wife Sarah Ann had donated the land to the school trustees, George C. Hott and H. H. Hardy.

Teachers at the Yantis school were: Charles H. Hillard, B.A. Longenbach, Daniel Funk, Mary A. Piatt, Enoch A. McGrew, James Mercer, DAniel Hoy, T.W.B. Mead, William C. Spence, Dianna Freshwater, Mary Warner, Lizzie Durkee, Diana Stokes, T.H.B. Reed, B.F. Pontius, Carrie M. DeGarmo, O.A. Hott, Mollie Robertson, B.H. Gain, Ann Wolfe, A.C. Truitt, S.J. Longenbach, and S. G. Neil.

CHERRY GROVE
District 1 or 67

Cherry Grove school was located in the southwest corner

of the southwest quarter of section 11 of Pickaway township. Students of Penn township also had access to this school as it was on the township line. Residents in 1866 taxed at 50 cents per 100 for the school, and directors were James L. Neil and John Foster. Three years later, the taxes were 85 cents per 100 and directors were G. M. Thompson, James L. Neil and James Laughlin.

The directors of the 1880's were H. B. Thompson, George Wright, James C. Noon, Joseph Roller and P.P. Laughlin.

Students of the school in 1894 gave a program, and they were: Eva Fry, Jannie Milliken, Eva McCarty, Bell Fry, Victor McCarty, Carrie Fry, Grace Robinson, Jim Milliken, Lillie Paisley, Bessie Milliken, May Milliken, Willie Patton, and Etta Milliken.

Some of the teachers at Cherry Grove school were: Onie McCracken, 1891; Lena Wright, 1892; Ruth E. Huber, 1893-94; J. H. Matthews, 1901; Goldie Tressler, 1909; Lillian Tressler, 1922; Verna Banks, 1924-standard school; Freda Boyer, 1926-standard school; Freda Boyer Beitz, 1927; Vivian Pasley, 1934-35; Joyce Winings, 1939-40; Ruby Horn, 1941; Marilyn Schwarm, 1942; Marilyn Bantner, 1943, and Pauline Allen, 1944.

Pauline Allen was the last teacher with a school of 5 pupils; directors were Clifford Bartimus, Allen Saddoris, and Jesse Pearson.

The trustees sold the building in 1948 to Guy E. and Ruth D. Cox.

JOHN M. ATKINSON

He attended Cherry Grove school from 1922 to 1930, and had teachers Lillian Tressler, Raymond Lockmiller, Irene Lash and Bertha Martin.

John was the son of Thomas and Nettie Marshall Atkinson, and grandson of William and Fannie Fear Atkinson.

ELMER MARSHALL

He attended Cherry Grove school, and Center school near Bethany, Illinois. During those years, he had teachers Camellia Bone, M.Loyd Rector, Mary Zanders, and Verna Banks.

"Elmer started to school at Center, Marrowbone Twp., Moultrie county. Camellia Bone was his first teacher, then Mrs. Loyd Rector. All eight grades were taught by one teacher.

Mary Getz was his first girlfriend. She was older and took very good care of him. His family then moved to Henton, Illinois, in Shelby County where he went to Victory school. Mary Zanders was his teacher and was very good. They then had a Catholic teacher (name unknown). She made them make a cross on their face every morning. His dinner bucket was a molasses bucket. He usually had bacon and fried eggs on homemade bread. The teacher told them not to write notes but he did anyway and got caught. She gave him a good whipping. His sister and a friend Lorraine Runkel waited for him at the foot log. They had to cross the branch, and he begged them not to tell his folks; he knew he would get another whipping so they didn't tell.

When he was 13, his folks moved to the Silas McClellan farm east of Prairie Home in Penn township, Shelby County, where they lived until his father died in 1952. They milked cows, raised hogs, chickens, ducks, geese, and did about everything there was to do on a farm at that time. All the farming was done with horses until they got their first tractor in the 20's. There was never an idle moment, except Sunday when the relatives gathered together. They played ball, horseshoes and had big dinners.

He worked one summer for an uncle as a hired hand for $20 per month. They worked from 4 o'clock in the morning till 8 at night or dark. They used a walking plow with a team of horses to break the ground and get it ready to plant. Then used a walking cultivator pulled by horses to cultivate. Then there was the thrashing ring made up of all the neighbors to thrash the wheat and oats and then bale the straw.

Elmer worked for Illinois Power and Light Company in Decatur for 4 years besides helping on the farm. He then worked for Warren Patton, road commissioner and learned to do the job well. Mr. Patton was a rough boss but it paid off. He then worked for Frank Roby who was very good but expected a job well done. They did everything by hand with a pick, ax or shovel. Then Jeff Davis took over as commissioner. He worked for all of them when he wasn't busy on the farm.

He married Mary Clark in 1940. They moved to the John Tolly farm near Obed, Pickaway township, Shelby County in 1944. Their children, 2 boys and a girl, went by bus to the Moweaqua school. They moved to the Simpson farm in the 1960's, west of Moweaqua in Christian County, Prairieton twp. where he served as road commissioner and farmed until 1980 when they retired. They now live in Moweaqua, Illinois."

Elmer was the son of James and Bessie Scribner Marshall; grandson of James Lynn and Rachel Younger Marshall and Seripta Atteberry; great-grandson of James G. and Sarah Roane Marshall, and Abraham and Nancy Bilyeu Lawrence; and great-great-grandson of William and Marie Williams Marshall, and George and Elizabeth Workman Bilyeu. His maternal grandparents were Clem and Hannah Lawrence Scribner.

GOLDIE CONLEY SARVER

She attended Cherry Grove school for all grades, and had teachers Jettie Tressler, Oma Ralston, and Helen Howe.

"I remember one time when airplanes were quite rare. We heard a plane coming so the teacher let us all out to see it. When the pilot saw all of us come outside, he turned and dived toward us! Needless to say we scattered in a hurry--I imagine he got a great kick out of the episode."

Goldie was the daughter of Roy and Dessie Macklin Conley; and granddaughter of D.S. and Jennie Conley and Clara and Joseph Macklin. Mother's side of family were named Marshall, and father's side of family were named Kilpatrick.

FRIENDSHIP
District 2 or 68

Friendship school was located in section 9 of Pickaway township, close to the township line. Residents in this district had taxes of 60 cents per 100, and directors were Christy Andrick, and Jonathon Tolly in 1866. Three years later, the taxes were 40 cents per 100, and directors were Samuel Tolly and Edward Gregory.

Directors of the 1880's were James E. Gregory, C.E. Cole, Cornelius Tolly, S. Premmer, W.J. Palmer and J.G. Thompson.

Some of the teachers of Friendship school were: Frank Snapp, 1888; Lydia Corley, 1892; Eugene Markland, 1893; Lena Wright, 1894; Nellie Scroggins, 1901; Charles M. Farmer, 1909; Ora B. Culberson, 1924-standard school; Ora B. Keller, 1926-standard school; Daisy Wiggins, 1927; Pearl Seiber, 1934; Irma E. Schlobohm, 1935; Lucile Thomason, 1939-41; Clara Jane Heriot, 1942, and Porta Yantis, 1943-44.

Porta Yantis was the last teacher with 12 pupils, and directors were M. H. Primmer, Don Puyear and Lawrence Wooters.

NOMA ETHEL ABRAHAM

She attended Friendship school in Pickaway township, and was the daughter of Simon P. and Barbara Ann Primmer.

CHARLES EDWARD MATHIAS

He attended Frienship school, and had teachers Clemie Warnick, Elsie Kopp, Lewis Taylor, Prudence Ponsler, and Lillie Tressler. He attended for all 8 years.

"March the 12, 1916, my brother and sister (twins) were born in the early morning hours and I walked to school myself that morning with my shoes on the wrong feet, the string tied in knots. And as I soon as I saw my schoolmates, I shouted and shouted, 'There's two of 'em, 2 of 'em.' And when caressed and asked, 'What do you mean, little calves, kittens, puppies or something,'..I said mild and proud like, 'Mommie's home in bed layin' between them!'"

Charles was the son of Samuel B. and Leta Stump Mathias; grandson of ____Hoy and Eliad Longenbach Mathias.

MILDRED COX NEWCOMB

She attended Friendship school in Pickaway township for 8 years, and had teachers Miss Cooper, Freda Parr Noland, and Irma Schlobaum.

"One morning while Bill Puyear and I were walking to school, we found several live hens tied in a gunny sack in a ditch. We were excited and rushed home and told our parents. Apparently someone stolen them during the night, and planed on coming back to get them. I don't remember now what our parents did about the hens."

Mildred was the daughter of Walter and Adeline Thompson Cox; granddaughter of Isiah and Alice Waddell Cox, and Howard and Emma Carlyle Thompson.

ELM GROVE
District 3 or 69

Elm Grove school was located in section 7 in Pickaway township, on the township line. Residents in 1866 had a tax of 40cents per 100, and directors were Daniel Yantis, J.R. Pound and George W. Longenbach. Three years later, the taxes were the same and directors were Charles H. Hillard and Jacob S. Stump.

Directors of the 1880's were John Barbee, William Hill, Frank Gregory, and W. H. Pontius.

Some of the teachers at Elm Grove school were: Charles Conner, 1889; D.E. Yantis, 1894; Walter Gregory, 1901; Carl Gregory, 1924; Stanley Pontius, 1909; Onita Smock, 1926; Leona May Thomas, 1927; Greta Syfert, 1934; Greta S. Howse, 1935; No school, 1939; Grace Lansden, 1940; Grace Paine, 1941; No school, 1942; and C. H. Alverson, 1943-44.

C. H. Alverson was the last teacher with 7 pupils, and directors were Emerson Mathias, Carl Hemer and William Barbee.

In December 1899, A. J. Steidley was the teacher and reported these students with perfect attendance for November. They were: Glen Gregory, Charley Tolly, Roy Tolly, Lannie Mathias, Brinton Mathias, Alta Gregory, May Smith, Ollie Mathias, Jessie Wagner, Myrtle Barbee, Dessa Mathias, Nellie Marshall, Louise Mathias, and Winnie Mathias. For the month of January, those having perfect attendance were Jesse Pinkston, Benjamin Dow, Estel Sims, Charley Tolly, Lannie Mathias, Harley Pinkston, Brinton Mathias, Stanley Pontius, Sam Mathias, Jessie Wagner, Myrtle Barbee, Odessa Mathias, Mary Barbee, Mora Cox, Ethel Cox, Louisa Mathias and Laura Craven for the year 1900.

HOWARD ALWARD

He attended Elm Grove school and recalled teachers Lenore Andies, Glenn C. Smith, Beulah Workman, Tracey Rawlings, Bessie Miller, Lucile Morris, Vivian Sims, Lucile Jordan and Carl Gregory.

LOCUST GROVE
District 4 or 70

Locust Grove school was located in section 18 of Pickaway township. Residents in 1866 had a tax of 75 cents per 100, and directors were G.R. Durkee, Samuel Groves, and E.S. French. Three years later, taxes were 70 cents per 100 and directors were G.A. Durkee and E.S. French.

Directors of the 1880's were E.S. French, James Ward, Hiram Pogue, Adam Brinker, Daniel Moll and George W. Longenbaugh.

Some of the teachers at Locust Grove school were: J.E. Longenbagh, 1892-93; Dollie M. Hobson, 1894; Ed Hart, 1901; Alta M. Farmer, 1909; Charles N. Farmer, 1924-standard school; Earl St. Pierre, 1926-standard school; Herman McDonald, 1927; Opal Nichols, 1934; Maxine Culberson, 1935; Essie M. Mowry, 1939-40; Helen Bridges, 1941; Alta Lee, 1942-45, and Helen Shaffer, 1946.

Helen Shaffer was the last teacher with 10 pupils, and directors were Don Atkinson, Ed Cole, and Glen Stump.

The trustees sold the school in 1950 to Leland H. Henderson.

During June 1894, a program was held at the school, and students participating that year under teacher Sallie Longenbaugh were: Charley Sloan, George Cole, Dessie Swartz, Cora Shride, Ellie Longenbaugh, Bessie Weakley, Roy Swartz, Ross Jordan, Lloyd Jordan, Leta Stump, Bertha Sloan, Pearl Standly, Rolla Stump, Zadie Moll and Maud Standley. Other students who attended school that year were: May Cole, Lola Abraham, Ollie Mathias, Ross Abraham, Harley Abraham, Earl Standley, and Sammy Cole.

HALE
District 5 or 71

Hale school was located in the southeast quarter of section 23 of Pickaway township. Directors of the 1880's were Daniel Terrell, P.P. Laughlin, L. K, Ashbrook, William C. Cullumber and George Wright.

Some of the teachers at Hale school were: Ethel Moon, 1888-89; Lena Wright, 1890; Will F. Miner, 1891; George E. Braden, 1893-94; Mary A. Perry, 1901; A. O. Miner, 1903; Charles M. Quicksall, 1909; Neil Gilbert, 1922; Alta Farmer, 1924-standard school; Donna Rogers, 1926-standard school; 1927; Maxine Culberson, 1934; Elizabeth E. Harbert, 1935; Helen B. Stephens, 1939-40; Essie Mowry, 1941-42; Sadie Price, 1943; Mabel E. Smith, 1944-45.

Mabel E. Smith was the last teacher with 6 pupils, and directors were Carl Harley, Theodore Lofland, and Harry Stewardson.

For the month ending April 2, 1903, A. O. Miner reported the following students as having perfect attendance. They were:

Roy Carroll, Noah Shride, Jesse Batty, Homer Batty, Mary Protsman, Lydia Hill, Mora Shride, Alice Hill, Leda Swartz, Ruth Hill. Absent one day, Laura Protsman, Minnie Batty, and Myrl Batty. Teacher A.O. Miner had an enrollment of 28 students, 13 boys, and 15 girls.

UNION
District 6 or 73

Union school was located in section 29, one mile east of Yantisville in Pickaway township. The school was built in 1882 on land from Robert Hunter.

Some directors of the 1880's were Solomon Yantis, C. J. Rawlings and Levi Corley.

Some teachers at Union school were: Mary Robertson, 1883; L. M. Rawlings, 1888; Ed Mc. Rawlings, 1889-90; Anna Hall, 1891; Sallie Longenbaugh, 1892; G. E. Headen, 1893; E. O. Corley, 1901; Mabel E. Goode, 1909; Lucille Morris, 1924; Lois Barbee, 1926; Thelma I. Cooper, 1927; Francis Hoke, 1934-35; Mabel Stockdale, 1939-40; Opal Knearem, 1941-42; D. M. Mathias, 1943-44; Hazel Cole, 1945-46; Maude Batty, Clara Uhl, John Spracklin, Norton Waggoner, Mamie Braden Pogue, C. P. Middleton, Lucille Corley, Edith Churchhill, Alma Nichols, Portia Yantis, Anna Hall, Edith Noon and Hattie Ayers.

Hazel Cole was the last teacher with a school of 13 pupils; directors were Ralph Yantis, Ronald Cole, and Lloyd Rodman.

Union school was sold in 1949 to Alva W. Bass for $610.

During the month of October, 1892, the following students of Sallie Longenbaugh had perfect attendance: Grace Milton, Harley Yantis, Leroy Yantis, Altie Weakley, Emra Weakley, Adrian Rawlings, and Leroy Macklin. She had an average dailed attendance of 21 with 28 pupils enrolled.

During the months of April, May, 1893, G.E. Headen reported that he had students--Edith Corley, Sylvia Middlesworth, Elma Middlesworth, Cora Weir, Ella Weir, Enos Weir, Maude Smith, Myrtie Smith, Edith Smith, Roy Macklin and Homer Reed--with perfect attendance.

FLORENCE SIMS SHEPHERD

She attended Union school for two years in the early 1920's, and had teachers Edith Corley and Edith Churchill.

Florence was the daughter of Millard and Zena Elizabeth Cotrel Sims; granddaughter of Thomas and Victoria Tull Cotrel, and Beverly and _____ Baldwin Sims; great-granddaughter of Nathan and Victoria Tull, and John Sims.

Union school with teacher Lucile Corley. Front row, l or r, Elda, Eula, Ferne, Edith, Florence, Arther; 2nd row, Geneva, Marie, Gretta, Howard; 3rd row, James Hunter, Earl Woodrow, Ralph, Clyde, Loren; 4th row, Edward, Verne; 5th row, Geneva Jacobs, Helen, Ruby, Dorothy, Mary.
Photo courtesy of Florence Shepherd

LIBERTY
District 7 or 72

Liberty school before cloakrooms
Photo courtesy of Laura Woodward

Liberty school in its last days   Photo courtesy of Willie Askins

Union school with teacher Edith Churchill. Back row, Russell Jacobs, Noble Cordray, Howard Weakley, Marie Sims. 2nd row, Martha Hart, Alta Himes, Gretta Rawlings, Elda Macklin, Opal Bateman, Ethel Reed, Ferne Bushar. 3rd row, Edward Sims, Woodrow Cordray, Lloyd Rodman, Ralph Sims, Arthur Rawlings, Loren Macklin, Clyde Sims. Front row, Dorothy Cordray, Helen Pogue, Mary Sims, Verne Rawlings, ?.

Photo courtesy of Florence Shepherd

Liberty school was located in section 33 one mile west of Yantisville, in Pickaway township. The trustees bought one acre of land in 1883 from John Rawlings for $60.35, and George Jenkins built the school.

Some of the teachers at Liberty school were: Clara Ahl, Carrie Stump, 1890; Vesta Carlisle, 1901; Elson Corley, Minnie parks, Ed Longenbach, David Earl Yantis, Melba Carr, Minnie Gladfelter, Nora Syfert Smith, Blanche Syfert, Oneta Rawlings Lyon, 1909; Opal Olive McKinley Potter, 1935; Mary Mathias, Dorothy Mowry Taylor, 1941; Mrs. Paine, 1942; Mrs. Swanker, 1943, and Dorothy Huffer Ramsey, 1944.

Portia Yantis was the last teacher who taught at Liberty. Sidney E. Rodman bought the Liberty school in 1949 from the trustees for $1500.

Other teachers at Liberty were: Stella Spencer, 1888; Grace Carr, 1891; Purrella Read, 1893; Ellis McKittrick, 1894; Vivian Sims, 1924; Raymond Lockmiller, 1926; Hazel Wortman, 1927;Mary A. Furr, 1934.

JOHN W. SYFERT

He attended Liberty school in Pickaway township from 1917 to 1919, and 1926-27, and recalled teacher Raymond Lockmiller.

John was the son of Raymond and Laura Protsman Syfert; grandson of William and Winnie Yantis Syfert, and John W. and Mary Elizabeth Huff Protsman. The Protsmans came from Spencer County, Indiana in 1874, and the Syferts came from Lancaster Co., Pa.

LAURA MCDONALD WOODWARD

She attended Liberty school for 7 years, and had teachers Ervil Pierce, Ethel Bryant, Agnes Sudbrink, Vivian Sims, Kate Shippy, Helen Seaman Shaffer, and Ruth Humphrey Hayes.

"Liberty was a one room school and one teacher taught all 8 grades. At one time, there were 43 children in school. The building was heated with a coal stove in one corner of the room. Teacher came early and built the fire and did all janitor work with the help of older children, carrying coal from an outside shed, etc.

Each child carried their own lunch in a dinner bucket, and they were all set on a bench until noon hour. Coats were hung on nails over the bench and boots were put under the bench. You were lucky to find your own boots when time to go home.

Around 1919 or 1920, two rooms were added to the front of the building for coatrooms, one for boys and one for girls, with an entryway between them from the outside. Restrooms were outside at the back of the yard.

Our recreation, included playing ball, drop the handkerchief for outside when the weather was nice, hide and seek, playing jack stones--often getting splinters under your finger nails from the old wooden floor boards--guessing games. Certainly, different from recreation today in schools.

We would sometimes have a neighborhood meeting and some entertainment, once a year box and pie social, Halloween party, and the last day of school, have a basket dinner at the school for the teacher. All parents coming and bringing the food at the noon hour.

The old school building was made into a residence and a family lived there after there was no more school. Now it has just gone by the way, just as most small country schools have. It is just nice to have memories of our good old school days and the children that went there with us. Today there are 8 or 9 living that I went to school with and only 2 of the teachers."

Laura was the daughter of Charles H. and Mary Jane Corley McDonald; granddaughter of John H. and Elizabeth Donnel McDonald, and Levi and Catherine Mattox Corley; and great-granddaughter of Thomas J. and Anna Dunkel McDonald, and Nathaniel and Chloe Casey Corley.

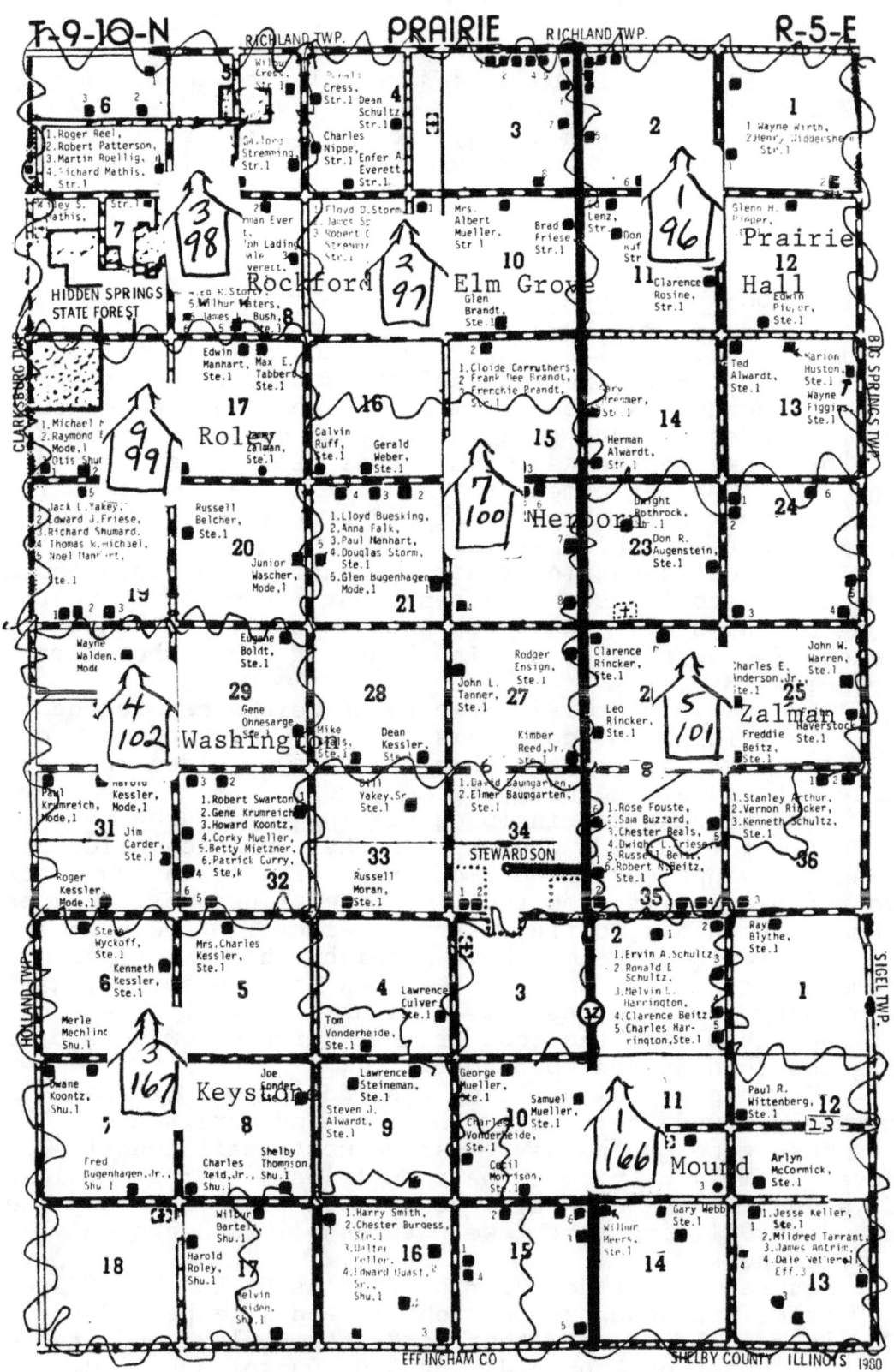

The wavy line indicates the 1903 school district.

PRAIRIE TOWNSHIP

In 1845, the Prairie township was still very sparse in population. The earliest landowner of this area was David Keller in 1835 in section 9 of the southern part of Prairie township. Most them lived in areas near the creeks for the water until the land was cleared for farming.

PRAIRIE HALL
District 1 or 96

Prairie Hall school was located in the northeast quarter of section 11 of Prairie township. The school was later built on land donated by Albert Vogel. It was of different design from others since it had a hall extending across the front for the cloakroom.

Residents taxed at $1.50 per 100 for a new schoolhouse in 1866, and directors were Charles Haze, G. Bolds, and William Wangelin.

Directors of the 1880's were Cho Brehmer, August Bredow, William F. Nehring, H. J. Brehmer, and William Doyld.

Some of the teachers at Prairie Hall were: Jennie Swengel, 1888; F. L. Laughlin, 1891; Ada Lutz, 1892-93; S.B. Storm, 1901; Florence Richards, 1909; Beulah Fritts Tabbert, 1922; Marie Williams, 1924-26; Fern E. Pinkard, 1927; Agnes Stewardson, 1934; Blanche Hankins, 1935; Catherine Anderson, 1939-40; George White, 1941; Ruby Gilmore, 1942; Dorothy Dautenhahn, 1943; Rita Anderson, 1944-46; Thomas Graybill, Claude Beck, Paul Christman, Ezra Blythe, Florence Staehle, Effie Beck, Robert Zimmer, and Fannie Hancock.

Rita Anderson was the last teacher with a class of 8 pupils; directors were Dewey Wirth, Orta Baumgarten, and William Von Behren.

Gaylord Figgins bought the building, moved it, and used it for a machine shed.

ELM GROVE
District 2 or 97

Elm Grove school was locted in the southeast quarter of section 9 of Prairie township. Most of the residents of this area were German, and Chris Altag had donated land at one time for the school.

Residents in 1869 had a tax of 30 cents per 100, and directors were M.B. Williams and Erasmus Blue.

Directors of the 1880's were: Chris Altag, F.W. Hallman, P. Doding, Haman Altag and John J. Klump.

Some of the teachers of Elm Grove school were: W. H. Weber, 1888; Belle Elliott, 1891; Ada J.Lutz, 1892; Sofa Smith, 1894; Mae Rice, 1901; Hazel Gladman, 1909; Charles Stiene, 1922; Fayette Ferguson, 1924; Agnes Shaffer, 1926-27; Omer Thomas, 1934; Agnes Anderson, 1935; Warren C. Williams, 1939-41; Ruth Nippe, 1942-43; Ruth Roellig, 1944; Vera

Everett, 1945; Joe Barr, Nellie Zimmer, Amanda Green, and Mayme Green.

Vera Everett was the last teacher with a school of ten pupils; directors were Albert Mueller, Walter Friese, and Joe Nippe.

The school was sold at auction and torn down.

ROCKFORD
District 3 or 98

Rockford school was located in the northwest quarter of section 8 of Prairie township. It was four miles north and three miles west of Stewardson.

Residents of the area first built in 1866 with a tax of $1.25 per 100, and directors were Carl Shrader and Mathew Miller. Three years later, the directors were George Weber and Lewis C. Baumgarten.

Directors of the 1880's were Iven Homer, Herman H. Ruwe, Andrew Wade, John Welton, Fred Nippe, E. Blue and Samuel Roley.

Some of the teachers at Rockford school were: J. H. Hagan, 1888; John M. Hull, 1889; J. M. Williams, 1890; J.A. Quicksall, 1891; Silas Ragan, 1893; Daisy Wiggins, 1901; Edith Jones, 1909; Noah B. Strohl, 1922-24; Nile Hickman, 1926; Laura A. Barnes, 1927; Roscoe A. Hahn, 1934; Elverna Koontz, 1935; Wilma C. Shaw, 1939; W. K. Rose, 1940; Nile Hickman, 1941; Myrtle Tressler, Vernon Williams, Frances Welton, Clara Fox, Sylvia Prosser, Joe Barr, W.D. Williams, Clay Smith, and Charles Wheat.

The last teacher was Nile W. Hickman with a class of ten pupils; directors were A. W. Kearney, G.A. Roellig, and Paul Roellig.

Gilbert and Alice Ulmer bought the building in 1949 for $410, and used it for livestock.

CLEO M. JONES MORAN

She attended Rockford school for 5½ years, and had teachers Laura Barnes, Vesta Schaffer Harris and Roscoe A. Hash.

Cleo was the daughter of Charles Elwood and Tonia Maude Daniels Jones; granddaughter of Nelson D. and Martha Vandament Jones, and Nathan and Nancy Renner Daniels; and great-granddaughter of Wilson and Margaret Storm Renner, Thomas and Elizabeth Baker Daniels, Joseph and Ruth Nicewanger Jones, and John and Fanny Chapman Vandament.

HARRY Z. NEWLAN

He attended Rockford school in 1923, and was the son of Marion O. and Edna Mae Yarbrough Newlan; grandson of Jack and Hanna Magdalene Goff Yarbrough, and Jacob and Minerva Wright Newlan; great-grandson of Mark and Mary Funk Newlan.

WASHINGTON
District 4 or 102

Washington school was located in the northeast quarter of section 30 in Prairie township. In early days it was both church and school. Residents in 1866 had a tax of 25 cents per 100, and directors were Josiah Huffer, Isaac Friese, and J. Byron Leathers. Three years later, the taxes were 50¢ per 100, and directors were Nelson Duddleston, Josiah Huffer, and Isaac Triece.

Directors of the 1880's were J.W. Carr, John W. Homrighouse, J.E. Johnson, Fred Ruff, and A.L. Blauvelt.

By 1917, the old school had to be replaced by a new one. It was completed for the 1917-18 school year but was struck by lightning during its construction.

Some of the teachers at Washington school were: Lurie Harris, 1890; John M. Tull, 1891; Oliver Stevens, 1893; J. M. Williams, 1895; J.T. Barr, 1901; Willis Cihak, 1909; Warren Williams, 1922; Charles Chappelear, 1924; Clarence Ponsler, 1926; Opal Jackson Cox, 1927; Bertha Miles, 1934-35; Cora Pontius, 1939-40; Catherine Anderson, 1941-42; Glen Giesler, 1943; Harry Joachim, 1944; Roselle Kessler, 1945; Monroe Williams, Dow Williams, Adolph Peters, John Quicksall, Roy Shuff, Vernon Williams, Alma Williams, John Cihak, Jon Blythe, Ethel Knapp, Nona Shumard and Delbert Jones.

Roselle Kessler was the last teacher with 18 pupils; directors were Harold Kessler, Irvin Kessler and Guy Jones.

Ernest Kruger bought the school when it sold, moved it, and remodeled it into a house near Shumway.

WINNOGEAN COHEA WITTENBERG

She attended Washington school for five years, and had teachers Adie Laver and Bertha Miles Beasley.

"Mrs. Miles used to have each family bring ingredients for vegetable soup, meat bone, potatoes, carrots, onions, etc., and would cook it in a big pot on the stove. We had a hot lunch and enjoyed the smell of soup cooking.

Mrs. Miles was a musical teacher, and her pupils loved her."

Winnogean was the daughter of Orval R. and Lena Grupe Cohea; granddaughter of Frank and Ellen Rentfrow Cohea, and Charles and Martha Hankins Grupe.

ZALMAN
District 5 or 101

Zalman school was located in the southeast quarter of section 26 of Prairie township. It was built on land from Henry Zalman, northeast of the present village of Stewardson.

Residents of the area had a tax of 60 cents per 100 in 1866, and directors were A.L. Cline and J. J. Elam. A new school was built in 1869 with taxes of $1.50 per 100, and directors were A. L. Cline and Joel P. Elam.

Directors of the 1880's were Conrad Bartholmey, August

Klitzke, John Manhart, Thomas A. Rincker, S.B. Manhart and John J. Falk.

After the turn of the century, the old schoolhouse was sold to Fred Gruntman, and a new one was built on the old site.

Some of the teachers at Zalman school were: Anna Quinn, 1889-90; Selena Quinn, 1891; William Adams, 1893; M. H. York, 1894; Bertha Hoese, 1901; Ora Beals, 1909; Lorna Stephens, 1922; Leon Lugar, 1924; Frances Opal Quigle, 1926-27; Grace Quicksall, 1934-35; Glen W. Giesler, 1939; Agnes Anderson, 1940-41; Jessie Wolverton, 1942; Ales Beck, Ethel Barker, Nellie Walker and R. A. Peters.

Frank Anderson bought the building when it sold, and Charles Anderson later bought it from him.

NELLIE HAVERSTOCK MIXON

She attended Zalman school for 8 years and had teachers Zepha Hagerman, Beulah Fritz, Electa Largent, Clarissa Flenniken, Lorna Stephens, Leroy Baker and Leon Lugar.

"I think maybe we were in the third grade. Raymond Augenstine and I did write notes to each other. When passing them to each other, our teacher Lorna Stephens called us to the front and put us under her desk, each sitting on a book. Since her dinner bucket containing an apple and some sandwiches were there, and we were very bored. So the only thing to do was to eat her sandwiches and apple. Was this funny? It was to us."

Nellie was the daughter of John and Dora Alice Elam Haverstock; granddaughter of John and Mary Lutz Haverstock, and Robert and Matilda Quicksall Elam; great-granddaughter of Joel and Minerva Austin Elam and John Haverstock.

HERBORN
District 7 or 100

Herborn school was located in the northwest quarter of section 22 of Prairie township. Michael Weber donated land in 1878 for the school known as District 7.

Directors of the 1880's were C.T. Faucett, M. B. Williams, M. Weber, C.F. Rincker and J. D. Williams.

Some of the teachers at Herborn were: Amanda Huffer, 1888; Frank Clawson, 1889-90; J.A. Quicksall, 1891; A.W. Bailey, 1894; Oliver Reeder, 1901; Clara Kull, 1909; Mildred Kuster, 1924; Ward Dappert, 1926; Lulu Young, 1927; Ruth Anderson, 1934-35; Ruther Culver, 1939; Ora Kellett, 1940-41; W. K. Rose, 1942-43; Ada Lutz, Monroe Williams, Henry Pfingsten, Ed Burchfield, Nanna Boise, Arlyn Williams, and Rose Bingamon.

W. K. Rose was the last teacher with 11 pupils and directors were Irvin Friese, J.E. Falk, and Orval Bauer.

Ernest and Chris Kruger bought the building when it sold

in the late 1940's. It was later bought from them, and moved to Beecher City for a house.

MOUND
District 1 or 166

Mound school was located in the southwest quarter of section 11 in the south part of Prairie township. As early as 1856, trustees received land from William Colston for the school site. Taxes in 1869 were 50 cents per 100, and directors were Henry Timperley and Uriah Baldwin.

Directors of the 1880's were William M. Miller, W. P. Wright, Fred Bruns, A.E. Harrington, E. Deal and C.F. Besing.

Enrollment became so large by 1926, that a two story brick school house was built south of the old one for a cost of $7500. The old schoolhouse was bought by Clinton McCormick.

Some of the teachers at Mound school were: Charles E. York, 1888; Laura York, 1889; J. M. Williams, 1891; Jo Stansfield, 1892; Ed J. Quinn, 1893; W. E. Hendricks, 1894; Nellie Walker, 1901; J.T. Barr, 1903; Rose Harmon, 1904; Fanny E. Lugar and Laura Wilson, 1898; Florence Quicksall, 1905; Mollie Harmon, 1906-08; Ada Brown, 1909-10; Regina Keck, 1911-12; Goldys Beals, 1913; Leroy Baker, 1924-standard school; Eleanor Devore, 1934; Earl French, 1939; Vera Grove, 1940-41; Vera Grove Kite, 1942; Amy Webb, 1943-46; W. P. Walters, Mary Pfluger, J. T. Knox, T. L. Hilsabeck, Ed Quinn, Maude Beals, Emma Klarman, Jacob Yakey, Daniel Augenstein, and Ed Herron.

Amy Webb was the last teacher with 16 pupils; directors were Jesse Keller, Samuel Mueller, and Ferdinand McCormick.

The school was sold in the late 1940's and later remodeled to a house.

ELNORA BULLERMAN MEERS

She attended Mound school in Prairie township for seven years and had teachers Lola Kessler Chappelear, Francis Hoehe Dappert and Eleanor Devore.

"My father Edward J. Bullerman was a member of the school board when Mound school was built at the southern end of the county during the depression, and was built mostly with volunteer help. It was the first and possibly only two-room brick school in the county. He also acted as auctioneer at a pie supper held there. A well was switched for the lcoation and produced a very good well. The building was sold after consolidation and converted to a home. At that time, eighth graders took a county-wide test before entering the high school located in the village of Stewardson."

Elnora was the daughter of Edward J. and Eda Mietzner Bullerman; granddaughter of William C. and Elizabeth Danhke

Mietzner, and George and Margaret Feltringer Nolfke Bullerman.

EDWARD A. WITTENBERG

He attended Mound school in Prairie township for 9 years, and had teachers Minnie Muchow, Dorothy Klarman, Leroy Baker, Ward Dappert, Wilma Klarman, and Aurola Knight.

"The program and the family style dinner at the close of each school year."

Edward was the son of Henry and Carolena Koester Wittenberg, and grandson of Albert Wittenberg and William Koester.

KEYSTONE or BAILEY
District 3 or 167

Keystone school was located in the northeast quarter of section 7 on a lot provided by Edward M. Pritchard in 1876. In 1869, taxes were one and a half percent per 100, and directors were Henry Shaffer, Samuel Bailey, and Henry Barnes.

Directors of the 1880's were Samuel Bailey, C.C. Adams, Jacob Dappert, Carl Heideman, and J. Byron Leathers.

Some of the teachers at Keystone were: Minnie Fleming, 1889; Mary Pfluger, 1890; Ada Tull, 1891; Anna Scheef, 1894; Mary Pfingsten, 1898; Mollie Fenton, 1899; Effie Beck, 1900; Ethel Knapp, 1901; Olive Reeder, 1903; Lora Hilsabeck and Margaret Lowell, 1904; Edith Ponsler, 1905; Rose Harmon, 1906; Rena Walker, 1907; Edith Ponsler, 1908; Edith Jones, 1909; Stella Williams, 1910; A.W. Pfingsten, 1911; Hazel Gladman, 1912 and Nella Johnson; Estella Niswonger, 1913; Wilma Klarman, 1922; Clarence Ponsler, 1924; Margaret E. Robinson, 1926; Ralph Cox, 1934; Claude Dunlap, 1935; Helen Kern, 1939; Hazel Schrath, 1940-41; Nellie E. Simmons, 1942; Mary Anderson, 1943; Glenna Dildine, 1944-46; Ada Burke, Roxana Beck, Walter Dunlap and Florence Elliott.

Glenna Dildine was the last teacher with 8 pupils; the directors were Oscar Kessler, Noah Mietzner, and Harold Roley.

Late in the 1940's, the building was sold to the Allied Gun and Rod Club.

ROLEY
District 9 or 99

Roley school was located in the southeast quarter of section 18 of Prairie township on land donated by Samuel Roley.

Roley was of the style with a platform in front for the teacher's desk.

Some of the teachers at Roley school were: C.W. Wilson, 1894; Edna Bolen, 1901; Charles Wheat, 1909; Fern Swank, 1922; Mabel E. Hall, 1924; Fred W. Grabb, 1926-27; Warren C. Williams, 1934-35; Elverna Koontz, 1939-40; Elverna Koontz Von Behren, 1941-42; Vera Everett, 1943-45; Ella Green, Laura

Wilson, Lydia and Nanna Boles, and Emma Harmon.

Vera Everett was the last teacher with 11 pupils; the directors were Otto Garrett, Clarence Brandt, and Clarence Grove.

The school was torn down after it was sold in the 1940's. Elza Grove used the lumber in building a house.

Roley school about 1925-26. Teacher Fred Grabb, Thomas Grove, Helen Williams, Aubrey Grove, Wilma Roley. Middle row, Dean Roley, Danny Washer, Marie Andrews, Alice Grove, Lucille Andrews. Front row, Elza Grove, Nathan Washer, Durward Grove, Earl Shumard, Ervin Washer, Grace Andrews and Vera Grove.
Photo courtesy of Vera Kite

VERA MAY GROVE KITE

She attended Roley school from 1924 to 1932, and had teachers Mabel Hall, Fred Grabb, and Ruth Anderson Manhart. Her father Edwin Grove had also attended the school.

"Of the many memories of Roley school, one which seems

more unusual was the night programs during the early days of the twenties before I started school. The men of the neighborhood had debates or mock trials. One night, my father was sued for having a squeaky windmill. Being very young, I thought it was for real and became very upset. During the middle of the testimony of a neighbor, I screamed out--'That's not true. My daddy is a good man and he oils our wind mill!' They had a hard time explaining to me it was all in fun and my dad wouldn't have to go to jail. The house was always full at these events. Like all of the other rural schools at that time we had the annual pie or box suppers to make money for the library books. We also had the annual egg roast on Saturday night before Easter."

Vera was the daughter of Edwin C. and Oka Ann Hagan Grove; granddaughter of Thomas and Catherine Whitmer Grove, and William and Martha Wallace Hagan; great-granddaughter of Henry and Mary Whitmer, and Abraham and Barbara Wear Grove.

Roley school about 1930. Teacher Ruth Anderson Manhart.
Back row, Erwin Washer, Vera Grove Kite, Alice Grove Thomas, June Prosser squatting, Nathan Washer, ready to catch, Elza Grove, at bat Durward Semour Grove.
                              Photo courtesy of Vera Kite

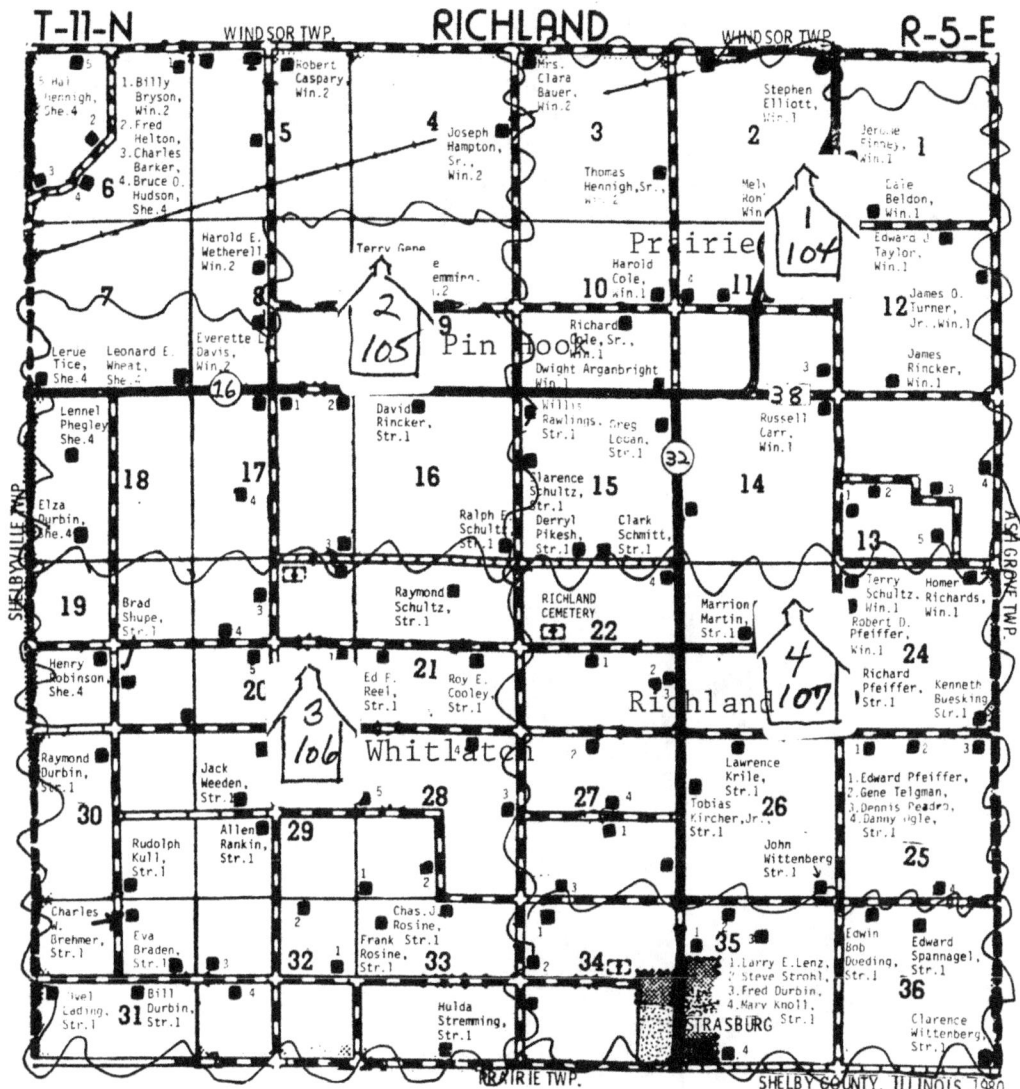

The wavy line indicates the 1903 school district.

RICHLAND TOWNSHIP

This township was settled as early as 1825, especially on the Richland Creek. The second school house--hickory logs--of the county was built in the Richland Creek settlement in section 20. William Robinson and James Rouse were the first teachers.

PRAIRIE OR JACKSON
District 1 or 104

Prairie school was located in the northeast quarter of section 11 of Richland township. Taxes in 1866 were 50¢ per 100, and directors were J.L.B. Turner and Michael Hawk. Three years later the taxes were the same, and directors were J.L.B. Turner, William Hawk and J.F. Poe.

Directors of the 1880's were William Hawk, C.M. Sargent, and Philip Kauf. Wilson and Louise Koontz deeded land to the trustees in 1883 for the use of the school.

Some teachers at Prairie school were: Travis Hilsabeck, 1888; John Bingamon, 1890; Thomas Baker, 1891; Carrie Douthit, 1892; Z.P. Ferguson, 1894; Ethel M. Swain, 1901; T.L. Griffith, 1903; O.O. Barker, 1909; Roy Strohl, 1922; W.D. Herron, 1924-standard school; A.V. Wallace, 1926-standard school-27; Ellen Cole, 1934; Ellen C. Camic, 1939-40; Margaret Robison, 1941-46.

Margaret Robison was the last teacher with 12 pupils; directors were Ray Taylor, Dale Beldon, and Abe Young.

Floyd C. Bauer bought the building in 1947 from the trustees.

Souvenir cover of T.L. Griffith's for Prairie school of 1903-04. For that year, he had 49 pupils composed of the following families: 4 Allens, 1 Andrews, 1 Barker, 2 Broomfields, 3 Chambers, 3 Coles, 4 Deitzes, 4 Flings, 2 Hylands, 3 Hancocks, 3 Rankins, 4 Rubles, 2 Rows, 4 Shewmakes, 1 Sargent, 6 Turners, 1 Webb and 1 Williamson.

PIN HOOK
District 2 or 105

Pin Hook school was located in the southwest quarter of section 9. A school was built in 1869 with a tax of $1.25 per 100, and directors were Edward Collins, Z.B. Ellis, and J.L. Lenox. Three years later, the taxes were 50¢ per 100, and directors were H. Cook, J. N. Lenox, and E. Moberly.

Directors of the 1880's were T. M. Spears, W. H. Shaw, A. E. Walker, Cliff Wilson, J. N. Lenox and James F. Kull.

Some of the teachers at Pin Hook school were: Lilly Ellis, 1888; Carrie Douthit, 1890-91; J. M. Tull, 1892; Lillie F. Ellis, 1893; Bertha M. Douthit, 1894; Mr. Ruff, 1900; Dora Douthit, 1901; Nina Reed, 1909; Oscar F. Storm, 1924-standard school; W. Frank White, 1926-standard school; Juanita McNeely, 1927; Ursula Prater, 1934; Lois Warner, 1935; Elmer R. Williamson, 1939; Wayne Sherwood, 1940; Mildred Pontius, 1941; Nadine Rankin, 1942-43; Nita Vogel, 1944; Willis Rawlings, 1945, and Dorothy Ellis, 1946.

Dorothy Ellis was the last teacher with 16 pupils; directors were LaRue Tice, Morris Rentfrow and Harland Dickinson.

In March 1900, in a program at Pin Hook, Liller Hiler won first prize, and Ruth Thomas, second.

On September 11, 1938, the first reunion of students and teachers, past and present, was held at the school. One hundred and twelve attended, and Flora Kearney of Strasburg and D.A. Richmond of Windsor were the oldest pupils present having attended in 1874 and 1875.

A public sale was held of the school in January 1949, and sale included site, school building, outbuildings, garage, coal shed, and all personal property within building.

WHITLATCH
District 3 or 106

Whitlatch school was located in the northeast quarter of section 29 of Richland township. Taxes in 1866 were 50¢ per 100 and directors were H.C. Shallenberger and Harvey Lowery. Three years later, the taxes were 80 cents per 100, and directors were Amos Shanholtzer, J. J. Christenbery, and B.F. Mose.

Directors in 1874 were William Richards, Joshua Whitlatch and J. Martin. Later directors of the 1880's were W. M. Richard, W. W. Whitlatch, William Stewardson, Albert Kessel, and Samuel N. Curry. Joshua and Nancy Whitlatch leased a parcel of land to the school trustees in 1882. A new school house was built then but it burned in 1910.

Some of the teachers at Whitlatch school were: Andrew C. Ensminger, 1869; Thomas Robison, 1874; Emma McAllister, 1888; Francis Hoffman, 1889; J.E. Wallace, 1891; Phidellia McCulley, 1893; Lee W. Frazier, 1894; Thomas Baker, 1901; C. P. Middleton, 1909; Charles O. Throckmorton, 1917; Paul Christman, 1924-27, standard school; Elmer R. Williamson, 1934; Roscoe A. Hash, 1935; Mabel B. Smith, 1939-42; Elizabeth Stilabower, 1943-46.

Elizabeth Stilabower was the last teacher with 12 pupils; directors were Ralph Ulmer, Ed Reel and Ervin Reel.

Whitlatch school with its outbuildings and personal property was sold at public sale in May, 1949.

CARL BUESKING
He attended Whitlatch school for two years, from 1920 to 1922, and had teachers Otto Throckmorton and W. K. Rose.

"The teacher's transportation to and from school was by horse and buggy.

One day some boys from the upper classes removed the nuts from the buggy's axle, allowing the wheels to come off on the trip home. What wasn't funny was the whipping they received as punishment when the teacher found out who the culprits were."

Carl was the son of Henry F. and Clara Kull Buesking; grandson of Henry, Sr. and Sophia Altag Buesking, and Adam and Hannah Kneller Kull.

GENEVIEVE COLLINS
She attended Whitlatch school from 1923 to 1931, and had teachers Ott Throckmorton, Paul Christman, and Bertha Miles.

Genevieve was the daughter of Virgil and Edna Allen Collins; granddaughter of Daniel and Mary Pikesh Collins, and John and Carrie Cook Allen; great-granddaughter of Edward and Eveline Kocher Collins, and Jedediah and Mary Hege Allen.

CURTIS C. BUESKING
He attended Whitlatch school for two years and had teacher Paul Christman.

Curtis was brother to Carl Buesking, and husband to Genevieve Collins. Carl and Curtis' great-grandmother was Dorothea Brockmeier on the Buesking side.

BERTE B. HUDSON
She attended Whitlatch school for one year and had teacher Oscar Storm.

"I'm sorry but this is about all I know. My father came from Texas and married my mother in Indiana. I went to school in Indiana until 1910. I went to two schools northeast of Decatur but I don't remember the names. One teacher was Mr. Simmen and another was Edwin Pilchard. When I started to Whitlatch school, they were all strangers to me and I wrote a letter to my friend where I moved from and wrote what I thought. While I was at the outhouse, three of the girls read my letter. I think they wished they hadn't, but they told me about it and we were friends afterward. One of them is still living here in town, and we have always been friends."

Berte was the daughter of Thomas and Anna Anion Black; and granddaughter of Robert and Matilda Gunterman Black.

WILLIAM BRYAN RENSHAW

He attended Whitlatch school from 1910 to 1919, and had teachers John Baird, Oscar Storm, Ada McVey, Mamie Kelly, and Otto Throckmorton.

"When I was in the sixth grade some of the pupils drove a horse and buggy to school. The fathers of these pupils had built stables on the schoolyard for the horses. That caused a necessity for feed and hay to be stored in the barn and that attracted mice.

During the noon hour and at recess while the boys were playing in the schoolyard, some of the girls would sew our coat sleeves shut. That gave us an idea to catch a mouse and put in one of the girl's desk. She jumped out of her seat with a scream. That was the end of all pranks."

William was the son of Charles and Elizabeth Shanholtzer Renshaw; grandson of James and Jane Frizzell Renshaw, and Jefferson and Anna Fisher Shanholtzer; great-grandson of John Renshaw.

RICHLAND
District 4 or 107

Richland school was located in the southeast quarter of section 23 of Richland township. Taxes of 1866 were 50¢ per

Whitlatch school in 1918. Front, Everett Richards, Everett Renshaw, Chester Stilabower. Standing, Maurine Richards Kull, Grace Luce, Hester Stilabower, Fern Renshaw Bartley, Otto Throckmorton, tchr, Bryan Renshaw, Opal Kull Keller, Edna Richards, Nelle Richards Ulmer, Ruby Small Smith.
Photo courtesy of William Renshaw

100 and directors were W.A. Brown, John Shay and Jacob ?. Three years later, taxes were 80 cents per 100, and directors were N.C. Turner and James Griffin.

Directors of the 1880's were Christian Bauer, Jesse Caskey, Benjamin Harves, and John L. Willhelm. Jesse B. Caskey had leased an acre for the school in 1884.

Some of the teachers at Richland school were: Lilly Knapp, 1888; Grant Ashbrook, 1890; Charles E. Storm, 1891; Ethel M. Swain, 1894; E.A. Peber, 1901; Faye Curtis,1909; Flossie Schroth, 1917; Vera Hamilton, 1922; Iva M. Robb, 1924-26, standard school; Florence Kircher,1927; Mildred York, 1935; Mildred Y. Hash, 1935-39; Ruby Hash, 1940-41; Marie Baker, 1942; Ruth Roellig, 1943; Ruth Nippe, 1944; Joyce Krietemier, 1945-46.

Joyce Krietemier was the last teacher with 11 pupils; the directors were Elmer Richards, Elmer Doehring, and Leonard Thompson.

Richland school was sold in January 1949 at public sale.

OTTO M. BAUER

He attended Richland school in 1897, and had teachers Cecilia Beck, Andrew Neber, Frank White, Ethel Barker.

"I started school when I was five and a half years old. I had to walk one and a half miles in the winter months through mud and snow. The first school I attended was Richland. The school set by the Wabash railroad.

My main studies were writing, spelling, arithmetic, geography, and drawing. I left Richland when I was eight or nine years old and went to St. Paul Lutheran in Strasburg.

There was one school room at St. Paul, with one teacher who taught 100 or more students at the same time. I was confirmed when I was 13 years old (1905), then I went back to Richland and graduated from the fifth grade when I was 17 years old.

When I was at Richland, I received a certificate for not being tardy for one full school year.

One particular event that I remember during my school days was an episode with a silver dollar.

My father made brooms and sold a half a dozen to one of his customers for $1.50, and one of the boys would have to bring the money home. One day, like boys do, we went out on the playground to play, and I decided we would take a silver dollar and throw it up in the air to see who could throw it the highest. The ground was soft, and we ended up losing the silver dollar. It is probably still there. As luck would have it, I had a few silver dollars so I took one of them and paid my father back for the brooms." Told to Robin Nance his great-granddaughter.

Otto was the son of John and Rachel Baumgarten Bauer; and grandson of Lewis and Conea Baumgarten.

HARRY OTIS JONES

He attended Richland school in 1913, and had teacher Oscar Storm. He also attended Little Brick from 1914 to 1922, and had teachers Nelson Corley, Florence Mose, Ethel Roessler, and Florence Smith Allen.

Harry was the son of Forrest W. and Edith Gertrude Crowder Jones: grandson of William Howe and Hannah Poe Jones, and John and Emily Kennedy Crowder.

CELIA SCHULTZ

She attended Richland school for 8 years, and had teachers Mamie Kelly, Frieda Engel, Bessie Rowe, Nell Hancock, Oscar Storm, and Louise Chatham.

Celia was the daughter of William F. and Anna L. Scheef Kull; granddaughter of Adam F. and Hannah Kneller Kull, and John H. and Elizabeth Falk Scheef; great-granddaughter of Christopher Frederick and Johanna Marie Weidner Kull.

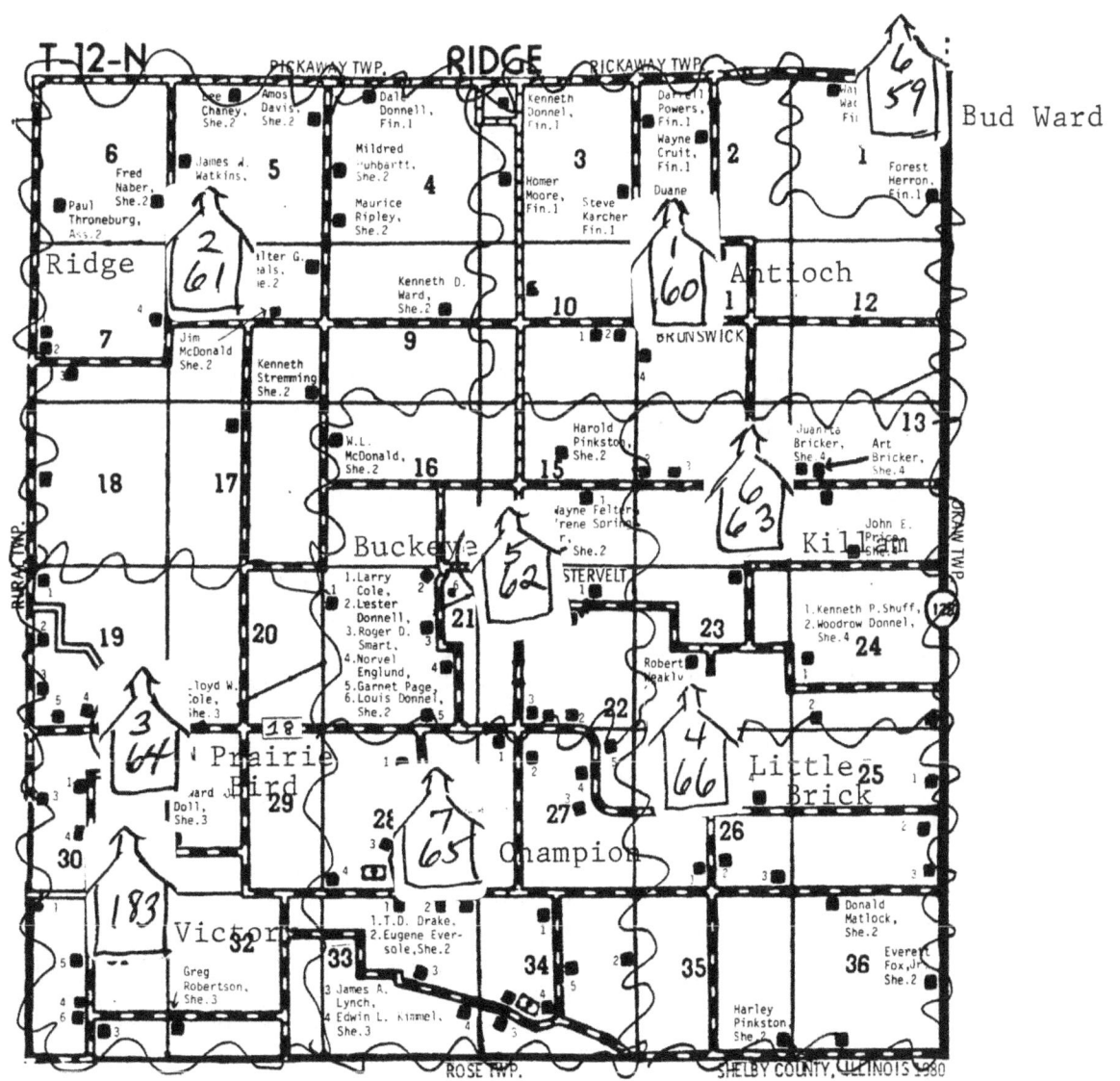

The wavy line indicates the 1903 school district.

RIDGE TOWNSHIP

The first school was taught in a house in section 23 near the old campground on Robinson Creek. Two schools--log cabins--were built in the same year, 1835; one was in the northwest quarter of section 33 on the west side of Robinson Creek; the second, Elm Spring, stood 80 yards from the springs in section 11.

In April 1849, the school districts of the township were created by a vote of the people at the Willis Whitfield's school house. Six districts were created beginning with number one, each three miles square, in the upper northeast, two in upper northwest, three on west, and so on. Trustees were Charles E. Woodward, Charles Hart, and C. P. Miller.

ANTIOCH OR BRUNSWICK
District 1 or 60

Antioch school was located in the northwest quarter of section 11 of Ridge township. School was held in this area as early as 1835. The earliest existant record was a schedule of a common school kept by William T. Craig from January to April 1850. Directors then were Thomas Wilson and John Barrickman. The students in the schedule were residents of Pickaway township to the north--Daniel Redington, Obid Redington, Hiram Redington, Mary Redington, and James Durkee.

Taxes for district one were 20 cents per 100 in 1866, and directors were William Calvert and Samuel Killam. Three years later, taxes were 35 percent per 100, and directors were A.C. Busby and Samuel Weakly.

Directors of the 1880's were James Reichart, M. B. Debrun, John W. Killam, J.S. Barrickman, and Josiah Propeck. In 1888, John W. and Kate Boys sold the plot in section 12 for the school.

Some teachers at Antioch school were: Mary O'Connor, 1888; Viola Michael, 1889-90; S.B. Carr, 1892-93; G.F. Ledbetter, 1893-95; C.E. Hart, 1900; Frankie Clark, 1909; Paul Christman, 1917; Thomas E. Anderson, 1924; Rhoda G. Cain, 1926-27; Lawrence A. Smith, 1934-36; Isabell Hall, 1938-39; Gloyd Archey, 1940; Opal Perry, 1941-42; C.A. Smart, 1943; L.C. Francisco, 1944=45; Lois Lyon, 1946.

Lois Lyon was the last teacher with eleven pupils; directors were Eli Skidmore, Henry Biedert, and Russel Woolen.

In 1900, there were 64 pupils enrolled with an average daily attendance of 48. Students with perfect attendance during February were: Cora Donnel, Linnie Winchester, Sidney Calvert, Cora Calvert, Carlie Gardner, Homer Gardner, Arthur Reichart, Ray Weakly, Thad Winchester, Homer Weakly, Arel Barrickman, Elda Jenkins, Hazel Jenkins, Lota Jenkins, May

Calvert and Linnie Winchester.

LLOYD MILLER
Lloyd attended all his grade school classes at Brunswick and his two daughters attended also, Dorothy Ann Banks Wooters and Yvonne Banks Cartwright. His wife Ruby was director for two or three years.

Other teachers they remembered were Tom Anderson, Zelma Salmons, Ellis Simmons, and Ester Hoke.

EARL F. RAWLINGS
He attended Brunswick school from 1918 to 1926, and had teachers Ellis Simmons, Tom E. Anderson, Zelma Salmons, Florence Kern, Barbara Kensil, and Harry Jackson. Jackson was the teacher that built a slide for the children. It got a lot of use for several years except the children who were not allowed to use it for wearing out their clothes.

Earl's oldest sister also attended Brunswick before he started school. His sister was Leota Baptist. Other individuals that attended Brunwick at various times were Ross Burk, Sport Rodman, and so on.

Mary Agnes (Mamie) Yost taught school in Ridge township during the spring terms of 1897 and 1898. She was born 26 December 1877. They wouldn't hire her for the winter term because they didn't think she could handle the big boys that came to the school during the winter. She married Will Gladfelter and moved to Kansas.

MARY MARGARET MOORE SMITH
She attended Brunswick school and had teachers Easter Hoke, Lawrence Smith and Isabell Hall, all in the 1930's.

Mary was the daughter of Homer E. and Ruth M. Brewer Moore; granddaughter of Willis and Effie Harrell Moore, and Joshia and Ruth Claypool Brewer.

Brunswick school sold in 1949 to C. T. DeMonbun.

RIDGE OR
PLEASANT RIDGE
District 2 or 61

Ridge school was located in the northwest corner of section 8 in Ridge township. Taxes in 1866 were 40 cents per 100, and directors were H.C. Carpenter and Aaron Small. Three years later, for building, taxes were $1 per 100, and directors were Samuel J. Downs, Aaron Small and John Rawlings.

Directors of the 1880's were William A. Berryman, J.J. Fritz, John W. Beery, Anderson Hunter, and David M. Yost.

Some teachers of Ridge school were: J. M. Bruner, 1888; Lew Leighty, 1889; Silas Green, 1890; S.B. Carr, 1891; Lena

M. Klein, 1892; T.H. Hardy, 1893; Belle Elliott, 1892; Carrie D. Wilson, 1894; Minnie Gladfelter, 1901; Edna Middlesworth, 1909; Opal Knearem, 1924; Ruth I. Turney, 1926; Lillie Pritts, 1927; R. T. Rawlings, 1934-35; Betty Derrick, 1939; Ruth Weakly, 1940; Opal Potter, 1941-43; Faye Hodges, 1944-46.

Faye Hodges was the last teacher with 22 pupils; the directors were Roland McDonald, Daniel Grubb, and Harold Eversole.

Students in the June 1892 end of the year program were: Fred Carr, Emma McDonald, Fannie Miller, Bessie Eversole, Daisy Friesner, Emmma Berry, Harvey Eversole, Emma Smith, Lura Carr, Willie Friesner, Dosha Beery, Lorin Carpenter, Frank Smith, Minnie Small, Ralph Carpenter, Erma Small, Edith Smith, Nellie Smith, Pearlie Eversole, Walter McDonald, Iola Weakly, and Orpha Friesner.

Ridge school sold in 1950 to Dan A. Smith, Jr.

JOYCE WININGS COLLUM
She attended Ridge school for 9 years, and had teachers Daisy Wiggins, Ruby Turney, Opal Knearam, and Lillian Pritts.

"The trip we took in Raymond McDonald's truck to the Shelbyville Centennial in October 1927. A beautiful day when we left and a rain came up and it rained on us all the way home. What a bunch of wet kids. Mrs. Smith (Beulah's mother), Mrs. McDonald (Wilma's mother), Lillian Pritts and all! What a way to remember a day at school!"

Joyce was the daughter of Lewis and Florence Bandy Winings; and granddaughter of J. J. and Ella Tohill Winings, and Sherman and Anna Lorenson Bandy.

Ridge school in Raymond McDonald's truck in 1927, heading for the Shelbyville centennial. Photo courtesy of Joyce Collum

HARLEY EVERSOLE
He attended Ridge school for two years, 1910 and 1911, and had teacher Elson Corley.

"I was born on March 9, 1904--80 years. I can well remember my first day of school in September of 1910. I was walking down the road to school and was passsing my uncle and aunt's house, and my aunt was standing in the yard, waving to me. We moved to Vandalia in the spring of 1912."

Harley was the son of William and Bertha Wheatley Eversole; grandson of Jacob and Katherine Swartz Eversole, and great-grandson of David and Elizabeth Miller Eversole.

HAROLD EVERSOLE
He attended Ridge school, 1910 to 1912, and had teacher Elson Corley who lived in Westervelt, and had a daughter Lucille who attended the school also.

"Since I was young, I don't remember too many things that happened. I do remember that Gussie Small climbed over the school yard fence when he got to school, and tore the seat out of his pants, and the teacher pinned his pants together with a safety pin."

Harold was the son of William and Bertha Eversole; the grandson of Jacob and Katherine Eversole, and great-grandson of David and Elizabeth Miller Eversole. This Eversole family had attended Ridge school for three generations.

WILMA L. MCDONALD
She attended Ridge and had teacher Lillie Pritts; she attended for seven years.

Wilma was the daughter of Raymond and Edna Middleton McDonald; and granddaughter of Stephen and Lillie Himes McDonald, and William and Etta B. Hall Middleton.

LAWRENCE WININGS
He attended Ridge school from 1919 to 1926, and had teachers Floyd Trout, Daisy Wiggins, and Opal Knearem.

"When I was in about the third grade, several of the older boys had bicyles that they rode to school. One day at recess, they were riding the bikes around and around the schoolhouse like on a racetrack. One of the bigger boys who was quite a bit overweight had a new bicycle only a few days before kept going faster and faster around the schoolhouse when at one point where there was a slight incline on a turn that created a condition like a banked turn on a racetrack, he was going so fast on the turn that the wheels on his bike slowly but surely collapsed from his weight and the added stress of centrifugal force on the banked turn. It was quite comical to see the very surprised look on his face followed by a look of dismay when the bike gave way under him, and he realized what had happened."

Lawrence was the son of Lewis O. and Florence C. Bandy Winings; grandson of John Jackson and Cynthia Ellen Tohill Winings, and Sherman and Annie Catherine Lorenson Bandy; and great-grandson of John and Charlotte (Baka?) Winings, John and Martha Springer Tohill, John Perry and Keziah Burnett Bandy, and Jorgenson and Sarah Sweazy Lorenson.

Ridge school with teacher Lillian Pritts at top. Class of 1928 with back row, Lewis Winings, Earl Dewitt, Johnny Reider, Eula Carrol, Beulah Smith; middle row, ? Carrol, Wilma McDonald, Enid Winings, Roberta Dewitt, Joyce Winings; front row, two Carrol boys and David Winings.
Photo courtesy of Joyce Collum

PRAIRIE BIRD OR
HENTON
District 3 or 64

Prairie Bird school was located in the northeast quarter of section 30 of Ridge township. Taxes were 30 cents per 100, and directors were John L. Small and John R. Craig in 1869.

Directors of the 1880's were Joseph Hish, M.D. Lane, G.W. Roberts, Caleb Runkel and O.S. Carr.

Some teachers at Prairie Bird school were: Andrew Patton, 1890; Sherman Crook, 1891; Tina Miner, 1892; Morton Neil, 1893; Minnie Gladfelter, 1894; Gertie Herron, 1901; Paul Christman, 1909; Ervil C. Pierce, 1917; Wesley Haverstock, 1924-standard school; Ellis Simmons, 1926-standard school-1927; Virginia S. Stephens, 1934; Ruth Marshall, 1935; Betty Jenkins, 1937; Frank Foor, 1939; Oneita Phillips, 1940-44.

Oneita Phillips was the last teacher of the one room school with 25 pupils; directors were G.W. Downs, Maryl Willoughby, and Claude Mose.

The next year the Henton school was consolidated, and became a two teacher school.

In 1894, teacher Minnie Gladfelter had two students in the end-of-the-year program, Clara Miller and Walter Lane.

The school sold in 1950 to Earl M. Gray.

LITTLE BRICK OR BOYS OR JONES
District 4 or 66

Little Brick school was located in the middle of section 26 of Ridge township, then later in the southwest corner of section 25. Taxes in 1866 were $1 per 100, and directors were John Weakly and James Boys. Three years later, the taxes were the same and directors were James Boys, John Weakly and Allen Jones.

The directors of the 1880's were J.C. Brown, John Leach, William Weakly, William Hardy, and Edgar Allen.

Some teachers at Little Brick school were: Hiram Kensil, 1888; Lou Oliver, 1889-91; Isaac Wortman, 1892-93; Eliza Fisher, 1894; Rose Aichele, 1901; Wilkinson R. Boys, 1909; Ethel Roessler, 1917; L. Flora Sayers, 1924; Mildred Montgomery, 1926-27; Ruth E. Boys, 1934-38; Ava M. Pogue, 1939-41; Ora B. Kellett, 1942-43; Florence Hill, 1944-45.

Florence Hill was the last teacher with ten pupils; the directors were Glen Donnel, Orville Eversole and Robert Clausen.

Some students who attended the Little Brick school in 1892-1893 were: Carrie Boys, Cora Turney, Carrie Turney, Maud Hardy, Florence Hardy, Alex Boys, Homer Boys, Edgar Hashbarger, Charley Dannenberger, Norton Waggoner, Carlie Oman, Harry Dannenberger, and Florence Hord.

The school was sold in 1948.

LEONA MCNEESE

She attended Little Brick school for the seventh grade, and also attended Liberty school and Assumption school. At Little Brick, she had teacher Lena Thomas.

Little Brick school northwest of Shelbyville.
Photo courtesy of Shelby County Historical and Genealogical Soc.

..."We were in Obed district where attendance was about 60. My parents though a smaller school would give us a better chance so we attended at Liberty, west of Yantisville. Attendance was about 12. My parents did not send us to school until we were 7 years old. I took first and second under Ervil Pierce in one year....

My brother was high school age so mother took all of us to Assumption where we all attended high school. We lived in a non-high school district so could choose the high school we wanted to attend. Our transportation to grade school was riding ponies two and a half miles one way. One neighbor told my mother we rode like Indians.

Most impressive incident--spelling matches and ciphering matches after recess Friday afternoons. When a second grader can get to the head of the spelling line and win an unfinished wood pencil, one must realize that the teacher was giving the younger ones easy words. Gave me an incentive. At 7th grade level, I entered the county spelling contest at the Shelbyville Courthouse. To be eligible for the county, I had to win the local as well as township contests.

There was no competition or parental interest until I reached the court house. My father took me 18 miles one way to the county contest.

Most amusing--but not for me. I was sitting on the porch at school putting on my boots when a boy came by, grabbed my boot and ran, but he made the mistake of setting down his dinner bucket near by. I was most irritated so kicked the dinner bucket just as the teacher came to the door. She promptly took me inside and gave me a lecture without investigating the complete incident. I never explained; just took it because my parents had instructed me to not do anything to irritate the school board members' children because we were going out of our district...."

Leona was the daughter of William R. and Mary L. Smith Thomas; granddaughter of James and Melvina Casey Thomas, and Hence and Perlina Butts Smith; and great-granddaughter of Allen and Karen Robertson Smith.

KILLAM
District 6 or 63

Killam school in 1917 with teacher Barbara Kensil. In circle, Dan and Ruby Killam.

Photo courtesy of Ruby Wheat

Killam school was located in the southeast quarter of section 14 of Ridge township. Directors in 1889 were J.T. Killam, Reuben Motts, and J.W. Killam. The trustees had received land for the school in 1888 from John T. and Mollie E. Killam.

Some teachers at Killam school were: Carrie Wright, 1890; Ella Baxter, 1891-92; Lucy Duvall, 1893; James W. Meeds, 1894; Pearl Price, 1900; Edith Porter, 1901; Maude Middlesworth, 1909; Hazel Barnett, 1924-standard school; Clover Wortman, 1926-standard school; Charles Farmer, 1927;

Cora Pontius, 1934-35; Warren K. Jackson,1938; Laveda B. Dawdy, 1939-40; no school in 1941-43; Dorothy Forsythe, 1944.

Dorothy Forsythe was the last teacher with five pupils; the directors were Oran Donnel, Roy Killam and Noble Sands.

Students attending Killam school in 1892 were: Ada Killam, Mark Piety, Cora Bates, Cora Morehead, Maggie Bates, Edith Wilson, Edith Piety, Charley Sheumaker, Oran Gardner, Oscar Sheumaker, Ila Bradley, Will Adams, Stella Killam, Bertha Bates, Maud Killam, Arthur Bradley, Luther Killam, Lee Adams, John Bates, Clarence Bradley, Ora Wilson, Carl Gardner, Ella Baxter, teacher, Will Gardner, Charley Bradley, and Huston Adams.

Killam school sold in 1948.

Edith Porter, teacher at Killam school in 1901
Photo in author's collection

MARY KATHERINE FLESNER

She attended Killam school for seven years, and had teachers Martha Davis, Hazel Barnett, Harold Longenbaugh, Clover Wortman, Charles Farmer, Daisy Sands and Lucille Johnston.

Mary was the daughter of Isaac L. and Katherine Lane Killam; and granddaughter of Samuel and Eleanor Royce Killam, and Malcolm and Matilda Updegraff Lane.

DAN KILLAM

He attended Killam school from 1917 to 1924, and had teachers Barbara Kensil Huddleston, Irma Reed, Helen Seamen Shoemaker, and Martha Davis.

"I can't think of any (amusing or favorite memory.) ...John T. Killam donated the land for the school which was built in the early 1900's.

When the school was abandoned in favor of consolidation

in the early 1940's, Art Yakey bought the building and moved it to Shelbyville. It now sits crosswise on a lot across from Glenwood Cemetery, and was remodeled into a one and half story house. The land the school was on went back into the Killam estate."

Dan was the son of Luther L. and Fern Blackstone Killam; grandson of John T. and Mollie Worthman Killam, and Dan and Cassandra Lower Blackstone; great-grandson of Isaac and Nancy Smith Killam, and Hiram and Catherine Ellington Blackstone.

HELEN SEAMAN SHAFFER SANNER

She taught at Killam school in 1920 or 21, and two of her pupils also became teachers--Ruby Killam Wheat and Daisy Sands Rittgers.

She also taught at Liberty, west of Yantisville, Hale school, Chadwick, Obed...

Helen always enjoyed working with the students in the small school setting. She was also active in teaching classes at church.

Helen was the daughter of George Durbin and Alta Weakly Seaman; granddaughter of J.O. and Frances Durbin Seaman, and Alva Paul and Mary Ann Miller Weakly.

RUBY KILLAM WHEAT

"My grandfather John T. (Thomas) Killam had to take his children so far to a school, that in about 1887, he gave a piece of land for a school. It was built and opened in 1888, and named Killam school, district 63. There was always a Killam on the school board.

In addition...other Killam teachers...were Myrtle Stoddard, Electa Largent, Ethel Roessler, Irma Reed, Barbara Kensil, Martha Davis, Helen Seaman, Daisy Sands Rittgers, Vera Barnett, and Clover Wortman....

In 1946, 'school was out' forever--the building sold and moved to Shelbyville, East North Sixth Street. Its present house number is 315."

Ruby taught from 1929 to 1961, at Empire, West Salem, North Liberty, Cherry Grove, East Salem, and Clarksburg schools.

BUD WARD
District 6 union or 59

Bud Ward school was located in the northeast corner of section 1 of Ridge township. Residents of this area in 1866 had taxes of $1.25 per 100, and directors were J.W. Cullumber, J.W. Scott and H. Hendrick. Three years later, the taxes were $1.50 per 100, and directors were the same.

Directors in 1881 were W. L. Davis, Henry Crowl, and J.M. Pogue.

Some teachers at Bud Ward school were: M. M. Lane, 1888; F. H. Lane, 1891; Theodore Bayless, 1892; F. A. Fritter, 1893; C. H. Robinson, 1894; Bertha Braham, 1901; Vernon Williams, 1909; Clay Smith, 1917; Genevieve Smith, 1922; Lelar Wilhelm, 1924; Ava Pogue, 1926; Beulah W. Hoke, 1935; Ethel M. Wilson, 1938-39; Gertrude Mary Miller, 1940; no school 1941; Ava Pogue, 1942; Ava Burger, 1943-45; Hazel B. Weakly, Eliza Cooper Fry, and (Mary Ellen) Shoaff.

Ava Burger was the last teacher with nine pupils; the directors were Ray Heiland, Wayne Newman, and Roy Macklin.

In 1947 the school was sold back to J. A. Biedert; the building is still standing on the corner of Route 128 and the Findlay-Assumption crossroad.

BUCKEYE
District 5 or 62

Buckeye school was located in the northwest quarter of section 22 of Ridge township. Jacob and Elizabeth Brunner sold the land to trustees in 1888. Directors in 1889 were H. C. Courtright, Sylvester Wagner and J. Reeder.

Some of the teacher at Buckeye school were: Lizzie Dazey, 1889; Nora Barrickman, 1890; Anna Miner, 1891; J.P. Clay, 1892; S.B. Carr, 1893; George Lane, 1894; Laura Durkee, 1901; Elfletah Marxmiller, 1909.

Buckeye school was closed before 1917 when it became consolidated with Westervelt or became a two teacher school.

In 1893 there were 34 pupils enrolled with an average daily attendance of 27. Pupils who attended that year were: John Yost, Archer Courtright, Chance Yost, John Bowman, C. Wagner, Mary Gladfelter, John Sands, A. Wagner, Myrtle Courtright, Howard Bowman, George Sands, Amanda Yost, Elmer Wagner, Oscar Yost, Blanche Courtright, Clinton Gladfelter, Benjamin Bowman, Mary Yost, Rhoda Yost, J. Reeder, Lucinda Reeder, N. Gladfelter, S. Wagner, H.C. Courtright, S. Bowman, Mrs. Lewis Donnel, Clarence Wagner and Henry Small, and John Lantz.

CHAMPION
District 7 or 65

Champion school was located in the southeast quarter of section 28. John and Sarah E. Smith sold the land to the trustees in 1889. Directors for the 1880's were Daniel Stumpf, G.L. Brehm, E. K. Schwartz, J.C. Brown and Joseph Cross.

Some teachers at Champion school were: Lou Oliver, 1890; Pearl Warner, 1892; Isaac Wortman, 1893; F. H. Lane, 1894; C.A. Ruff, 1900-01; E. O. Corley, 1909; Charles E. Wheat, 1912; N.A. Waggoner, 1913; Lawrence Smith, 1914-17; Amelia Marxman, 1918; R.E. McClary and Helen Howe, 1919; Lawrence Smith, 1922; Lucille Corley, 1924-standard school; T.E. Anderson, 1926-standard school-27; Ava M. Pogue, 1934-

35; Lucille Mickey, 1939-40; Juanita Henderson, 1941-42; Viola Kennedy, 1943-44; Florence Wortman, 1945.

Florence Wortman was the last teacher with 14 pupils; the directors were Otis Weakly, Iva Kircher and Clarence Kull.

Marguerite Flaharty

In 1909, Marguerite Flaharty who attended Champion school took second place on the final examination with an average of 90½. O. C. Corley was her teacher, and she had an average of 85 to 94 on all her school work.

In 1894, there were 45 pupils enrolled with an average daily attendance of 40. Some of them were: May Smith, Orin Smith, Lawrence Smith, Dora Shannon, Ora Shannon, Lou Nolen, Ota Nolen, Donie Nolen, Jack Steidley, Carrie Steidley, Nina Boys, Dewitt Boys, Clarence Goodwin, Ed Clem Cross, William Cross, John Craig, Chandos Lappin, Effie Groves, and Edna Groves.

Six years later, there were 22 pupils enrolled with an average daily attendance of 18. Some of them were: Fabian Boys, Dewitt Boys, Roy Weakly, Nita Pfeiffer, Nettie Small, Eura Smith, Blanche Smith, Belle Love, Edna Smith, Sadie Weakly, Floy Boys, Wilkinson Boys, and Forrest Smith.

The school sold in 1948.

VICTORY
District 183

Victory school was located one mile south and one-fourth mile east of Henton in section 31 of Ridge township. Some of the teachers at Victory school were: Sara Anne Engel, 1922; Bernadine LeGrand, 1924; Purella Beckett, 1926; Lois Warner, 1927; Vesta Harris, 1934-35; Alta Lee, 1939-40; Sadie Price, 1941.

Sadie Price was the last teacher with 5 pupils; the directors were Mary Runkel, Ethel Lash, and Edna Brown.

The school and outbuildings were sold in 1945.

LEVERETT WEAKLY

He attended Champion school from 1920 to 1927, and had teachers Lucille Corley, Bud Smith and Edith Howe.

He was the son of Earl and Mattie Carnes Weakly; and grandson of John and Maggie Carnes, and Robert and ____ Hood Weakly.

Leverett's wife, Ruth Weakly, attended Stewardson

Grade school, and had teachers Mary Pinkston and W. Haverstock. She was the daughter of Ralph and Nellie Mae Munch Whitacre; and granddaughter of Johnson and Ida Whitacre.

HELEN WILLIAMSON

She attended Champion school for six years, and had teachers T.E. Anderson, Regis McClory, and Ava M. Pogue.

"I always liked to attend school and enjoyed the Christmas programs and gift exchanges. Most of the people in the district attended the programs even though they had no children attending school at that time.

I remember getting a check for 56 cents for 56 perfect spelling lessons, and how thrilled I was to go the bank and get it cashed."

Helen was the daughter of Andrew and Esther Martz Dagen; granddaughter of William T. and Caroline Pfeiffer Martz, and Jacob and Louise Heinz Dagen; and great-granddaugher of Henry and Margaret Singer Martz.

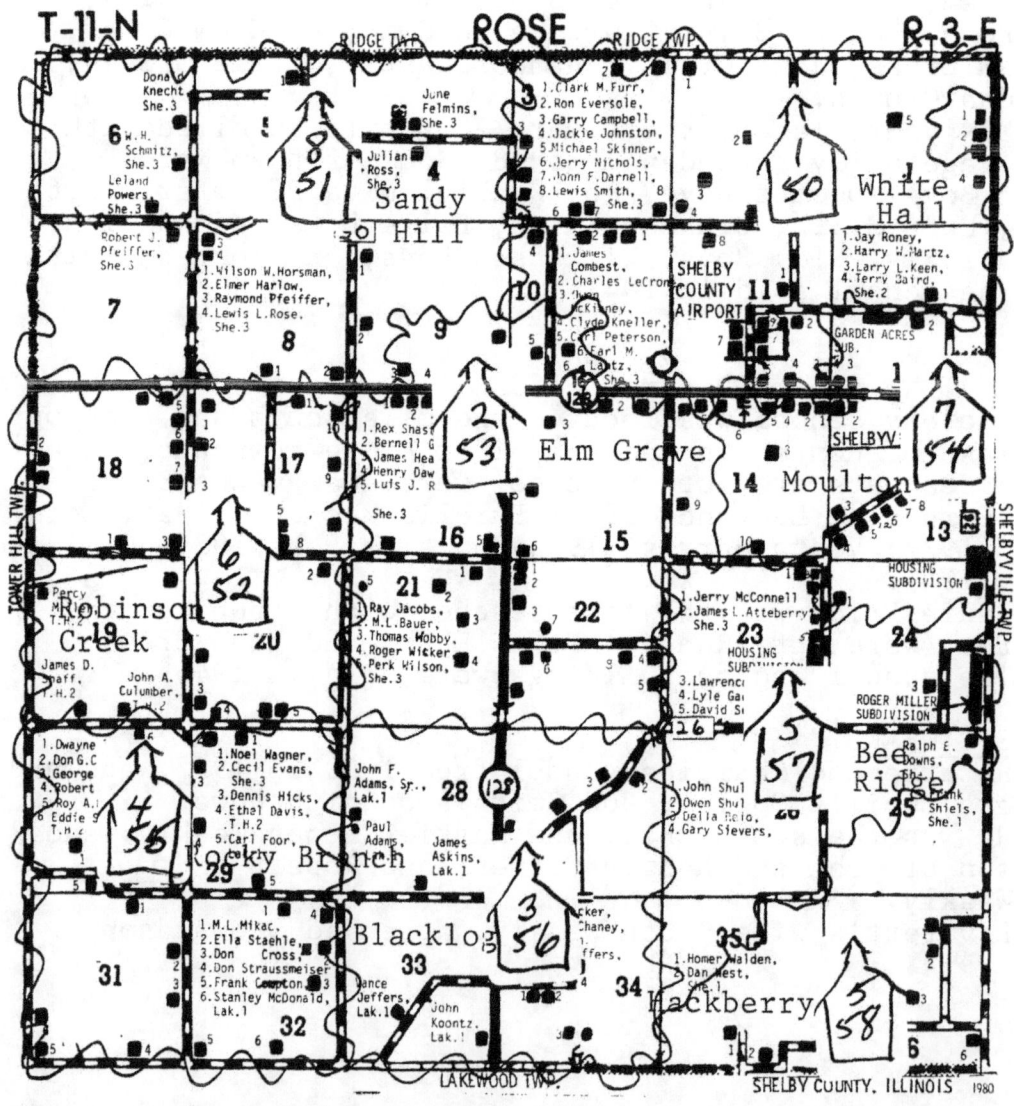

The wavy line indicates the 1903 school district.

ROSE TOWNSHIP

This township was settled as early as 1824. The first school was probably taught in the log church built on the Robinson Creek near the township line.

In 1845, the trustees of Rose township borrowed money from the county commissioner for the schools. Abram H. Dutton, Thomas Hardy, Senior, and Edwin J. Shallenberger promised to pay back the monies in semi-annual installments, with 8 per cent interest, until the full sum of $50 was repaid.

Again in 1854, for Rose township, D. Dawdy, John H. Dawdy and A. J. Dawdy promised to pay school trustees the sum of $55 with an interest of ten percent yearly.

The 1845 transaction had interest paid up to January 1856; the 1854, interest paid up till July 1856.

WHITE HALL
District 1 or 50

White Hall school was located in the southeast quarter of section 2 of Rose township. Residents had a tax of one percent per 100 in 1866, and directors were James Weakly, and Philip Roessler. Three years later, the taxes and directors were the same.

The directors of the 1880's were John H. Hoffman, W.S. Amlin, E. Roessler, Marion Beery, and John M. Camfield.

Some of the teachers at White Hall school were: John Warren, 1888; Pal Richardson, 1889; Laura York, 1890; Rose Worley, 1891; Vesta Carlisle, 1892; Emma Gerhard, 1893-94; Winnie Groves, 1898-99; Henry F. Roessler, 1899; Henry F. Roessler and Ada Lutz, 1900; Ada Lutz, 1901; Calvin Green and H.F. Roessler, 1902; Elza Smith, 1902; Ralph Roessler and George E. Braden, 1903; George E. Braden and Ralph Roessler, 1904; H.F. Roessler and Flora Allen, 1905; N.A. Waggoner and Ethel C. Van Reed, 1905; Margaret Mochel, 1906; Elma Middlesworth, 1907; Elma Middlesworth and Margaret Mochel, 1908; Maggie Mochel, 1909; Ruth Williams and G.C. Barnhart, 1910; Ada D. Auld, 1911-12; Pearl Winson and Rose Williams, 1913; Cleveland Peek, 1922-24 (brick); Zelma June Salmons, 1926; Irene Smith, 1927; Claudie M. Hatfield, 1934; Claudie M. Tull, 1935; U.L. Evans, 1939-40; Ruby Kelley, 1941; Agnes Willey, 1942-44; Maxine Mullins, 1945.

Maxine Mullins was the last teacher with 8 pupils; the directors were Roy Kimmel, C.E. Tice, and M.E. Shasteen.

White Hall school and all its property were sold in 1950 to Alexander Boys for $1250.

In 1892, the average daily attendance was 35, and a few students who attended that year were: Lottie Ruff, Clarence Tice, Susie Berry and Louise Berry.

Eight years later, the average attendence was 17, and some of them were: Gracie Wilson, Homer Schlack, Docie Mochel,

Walter Wilson, Harmon Ruff, Manda Wilson, Ira Roessler, Edith Kneller, and Lena Schlack.

ELM GROVE OR ROSE CENTER
District 2 or 53

Elm Grove school was located in the souteast corner of the northeast quarter of section 16 of Rose township. Taxes in 1866 were 80 cents per 100, and directors were George Stretch and Michael Wendling. Three years later, taxes were 60 cents per 100, and directors were George Stoneburner and Louis Mittendorf.

Directors of the 1880's were Marcus Mercer, John W. Forsyth, Harry Stilgebouer, Jacob Mauer, and Joseph Peek. Anna Fleming sold an acre to the trustees in 1895 that was located in the southeast quarter of section 16. The new brick school--called Rose Center--was finally completed in 1908. The brick structure was the third building built on the site from 1895 to 1908. It was built at the cost of $1,400.

Some teachers at Elm Grove or Rose Center school were: Rose Moutry, 1888-89; Laura York, 1890; Ella Cleary, 1891-92; L. P. Baker, 1893-94; Bertha Perryman, 1898-1900; Eva Barrett, 1901-03; Leota Mercer, 1904; J.T. Barr and Eva L. Renner, 1905; Eva Renner, 1906; Maggie Skidmore and Hazel Jackson, 1907; Edward Kimmel, 1908; Ella Finley, 1909; John Spracklin, 1910; Cleveland Peek, 1911-13; Wilma Klarman, 1924; Cleveland Peek, 1926; Olive Stockdale, 1927; Virginia K. Parr, 1934-35; Ruth E. Boys, 1939; Opal C. Kite, 1940-41; Neva King, 1942; Grace Hall, 1943; Nellie Hyland, 1944-45; Marilou Christman, 1946.

Marilou Christman was the last teacher with 8 pupils; directors were Arch Cresswell, Warren Peek and Rolla Carroll.

Students at the school in 1894 were: Pearl Augenstein, Belle Schintzer, Roy Forsyth, Grace Marxmiller, Charles Forsyth, J. P. Baker, Winifred Good, Louis Lipkey, Christina Bauer, Alice Albin, Mack Foster, Frank Albin, J. P. Parker, John Peek, Pearl Albin, Annie Lipkey, Sam Albin, Lola Miller, Arthur Augenstein, Elbert Goodman, Mable Good, Carl Kneller, Eddie Kimmel, Goldie Stilgebouer, Sam Albin, Bertha Kircher, Anna Kircher, Cora Peek, John Peek, and Clevie Peek.

The school was sold to John Steele in 1951 for $1825.

BLACK LOG
District 3 or 56

Black Log school was located in the northwest quarter of section 34 of Rose township. Taxes in 1866 were one percent per 100, and directors were Joseph Carter, T. B. Clinkenbeard, Josephus Reed, and G.W. Lock.

The directors of the 1880's were Joseph Basil, G.W. Stephens, William F. Reed, E.D. Hendley and Henry Carder.

Some of the teachers at Black Log school were: Calvin Green, 1889; Nora Brandon, 1890; Ella Perryman, 1892; R.J. Herron, 1893; J.L. Hart, 1894; Victoria Bauer, 1898-99; Lydia McKittrick, 1900; Victoria Bauer, 1901; Josephine Viseur and Arthur Williams, 1902; Rose Worley, 1903; Eva Barrett and Nettie Eckert, 1904; Nettie Eckert, 1905; Cleveland Peek, 1906-07; Ella Walker and Nettie Fox, 1908; Charlie Dush, 1909; Amy Phillips and Nettie Davis, 1910; Ruth Williams, 1911; Mary Cox, 1912; Franklin Foor, 1913; Clover Wortman, 1922; Roy Wakefield, 1924-26; Cleve Peek, 1927; Orletta Askins, 1934; Kathryn E. Cook, 1935; Virginia Parr, 1939-41; Ruby Carter, 1942; Mildred Thomas, 1943; Hattie Wakefield, 1944, and Nellie Hyland, 1945-46.

The last teacher was Nellie Hyland with 12 pupils; the directors were Dallas Jeffers, Victor Moore and Ed Matheny.

Black Log school was sold at public auction in 1950 to Floyd F. Yakey for $460.

BEN F. WHEELER
He attended Rose Center school for 8 years, and had teachers Ruth Boys, Ruth Parr, and Mr. Peek.
Ben was the son of Loral and Frank Wheeler.

ROCKY BRANCH
District 4 or 55

Rocky Branch school was located in the southeast quarter of section 30 of Rose township. Taxes for building in 1866 were $1 per 100, and the directors were Benjamin Tallman, Jacob Leighty and Benjamin C. Ward. Three years later, taxes were 3 percent per 100, and the directors were Lewis Perryman and Clark Thomas.

The directors of the 1880's were John Funk, Thomas Higgins, L. M. Martin, and Anthony Bauer.

Some of the teacher at Rocky Branch school were: Ed Graybill, 1888; Cora Featherstun, 1889; Ed Graybill, 1890; Clara Graybill, 1891; Hiram Kensil, 1892; Iva Grisso, 1893; Eva Barrett, 1894-99; Carrie Seitz, 1900; Elijah Jones and Lottie Williams, 1901; Victoria Bauer, 1902; Stella Christy and Mary Durkee, 1903; Mary Durkee and Bertha O. Baird, 1904; Anna Lane, 1905; John Spracklin, 1906; Edward Kimmel and Margaret Mochel, 1907; Cleveland Peek, 1908; Grace Scovil, 1909; Hesse Nance, 1910; Vivien Fletcher, 1911; Eunice Morgan, 1912; Leroy Hunter, 1922; Josephine Jenkins, 1924; Frank Foor, 1926-27; Harold O. Wakefield, 1934; Forrest Moore, 1935; W. Wayne Sherwood, 1939; Helen McDonald, 1940; Helen McDonald Thompson, 1941; no school 1942; Isabell McDonald, 1943-45; Ferne Boone, 1946, and Faye Hodges, 1948.

Faye Hodges was the last teacher with 19 pupils; the directors were Russel Williams, Bain Wetzel and Joe Christner.

The Rocky Branch school was sold to Kenneth Plowman in 1951 for $774.

BEE RIDGE
District 5 or 57

Bee Ridge school was located in the northeast quarter of section 26 of Rose township. Michael and Catherine Igo had deeded a parcel in 1874 to the trustees. Taxes in 1866 were $1 per 100, and the directors were John S. Igo and William M. Cones. For a new schoolhouse in 1869; taxes were $3 per 100, and directors were S. P. Swallow, Samuel Igo and Moses Flanders.

The directors of the 1880's were M. Flanders, James Davis, Lewis C. Beem, Z. Spannagel and William Hamer.

Some of the teachers at Bee Ridge school were: T.B. Wortman, 1889; Minnie Fleming, 1890; Nora Barrickman, 1892; Maggie Cleary, 1893; Homer Peters, 1894; Lizzie Coplin, 1898; Bertha Wilson, 1899-00; Frank Voiles, 1901; Henry Roessler and Lydia McKittrick, 1902; Ida McKittrick, 1903; N.A. Wagner, 1904-05; Stella Christy, 1906-07; Grace Barrett, 1908;

Marie Stillwell, 1909; Okla Sturgis, 1910; Florence Hickman, 1911; G.E. Moore and Florence Hickman, 1912; Pearl LeGrande, 1913; Alleva Nance, 1917; Edna Britton, 1924; Thelma Cooper, 1926; Bernice Lance, 1927; Lucille M. Smith, 1934; Lucille M. Barbee, 1935; Ruth E. Thompson, 1939; Ellis Simmons, 1940; no school 1941 to 45; Florence Hill, 1946.

Florence Hill was the last teacher with 12 pupils; the directors were F. A. Warner, T. J. Parks and Clarence Shull.

EDWIN SCHROCK

He attended Bee Ridge school for seven years, and had teachers Edna Britton, C. Hatfield, D. James, J. Lewis, Bernice Lane and Ruby Battershell.

"One boy had been trapping and caught a skunk; he changed clothes and took a bath but still smelled so bad the teacher sent him home."

Edwin was the son of Dan and Anna Roth Schrock; grandson of Peter and Kathyrn Roshart Schrock and Peter and Barbara Springer Roth.

ROBINSON CREEK
District 6 or 52

Robinson Creek school was located in the northwest quarter of section 20 of Rose township. John and Margaret Foster had deeded an acre to the trustees in 1876. Residents in 1866 had taxes of three percent per 100, and the directors were E. Devore, James Grace, and Henry Williams. Taxes were still the same in 1869, and the directors were Elijah Devore and Michael Grace.

Robinson Creek school today. Photo courtesy of Thelma Burris

Some of the directors of the 1880's were Jacob Fringer, William Rockett, John Kimlel, and Nelson Neil.

Some of the teachers at Robinson Creek school were: J. M. Perryman, 1888; J.S. Pritchard, 1889; Hattie Watton, 1890; C. P. Middleton, 1891; Clarence Lane, 1892; C. P. Middleton, 1893; Fannie Davis, 1894; C.E. Hart, 1898; Hattie Reade, 1899; Jessie Mitchell, 1901; Agnes Barrett, 1902; J.F. Mitchell, 1903; Arthur Williams, 1904; Vere Frazier, 1905; Anna Lane, 1906; Fay Frazier, 1907; Will A. Steward, 1908; F. H. Lane, 1909; Cleveland Peek, 1910-11; Charles E. Wheat, 1912; J. T. Barr, 1913; Maude Tucker, 1917; Frank White, 1924; Opal Knearem, 1926; Zelma Salmons, 1927; Mattie Dugan, 1934-35; Lois Bair, 1939-40; Ellis Simmons, 1941-32; Silver B. Horsman, 1943; W. K. Rose, 1944-45; Juanita Henderson, 1946.

Juanita Henderson was the last teacher with 16 pupils; the directors were Roy Furr, Wilbur Lupton and Lester Gaton.

Robinson Creek school was sold to Wilbur Lupton in 1950 for $225.

A few students who attended Robinson Creek in 1899 were Leland Voiles, Gracie Voiles and Mattie Kimlel.

VERNIE RAY BECKETT

She attended Robinson Creek school from 1900 to 1910, and had teachers Jess Mitchell, Faye Frazier, Vera Frazier, Cleve Peek, Anna Lane, Frank Lane and Joe Bauer.

"Vera Frazier was up at the blackboard writing. There was a boy (he was an orphan). He snapped his fingers and the teacher turned around. She saw paper wads flying everywhere. The next day the board of directors was on hand. They were told if they ever found out who started it, they would be expelled."

Vernie was the daughter of Arthur and Burrilla Read Beckett; and granddaughter of Robert F. and Georgetta Read.

THELMA M. SYFERT BURRIS

She attended Robinson Creek school for three years, and had teachers Frank White and Olive Hampton Stockdale.

"I visited Frank Foor of Pana. He taught Robinson Creek school around 1915-16. He began teaching as soon as he graduated. Paid $40 a month. Played with the children outside. Some of the boys were taller than he was.

The most I remember were the high top laced shoes, black bloomers and the scratchy long underwear."

Thelma was the daughter of Tony and Mary Stockdale Syfert; granddaughter of George and Margaret Martin Syfert, and Solomon and Caroline Fletcher Stockdale; and great-granddaughter of Michael and Mary Mars Syfert, who married second Eliza Thomason.

Frank White, teacher at Robinson Creek school in 1924-25. Later became county superintendent

Photo courtesy of Thelma Burris

Frances Syfert, Celestine Schmitz and Pauline Smiley at Robinson Creek school in 1924

Photo courtesy of Thelma Burris

MOULTON
District 7 or 54

Moulton school was located in lots 1 and 2, block 39 in town of Moulton, later Shelbyville, northeast quarter of section 13 of Rose township. M.D. Gregory had leased land to the trustees in 1863. Taxes in 1866 were $1 per 100, and the directors were Henry F. Murdock, Fred Pauschert and Barnam Brooker. Taxes were the same in 1869, and the directors were J.B. Reeve and John Cutler.

Some of the directors in the 1880's were J. H. White, Aaron Cutler, F.A. Pauschert and Henry Spears. William and Leah James leased land to the trustees for Moulton in 1894 on the same location as previously cited.

Some of the teachers at Moulton school were: Hattie Walton, 1888-89; Lena Klein, 1890; Lizzie Campfield, 1891; Irving M. Douthith, 1892; Della Sheley, 1894; Effie Briggs, 1898; Grace Carr, 1899-00; Ella Walker, 1901; Daisy Reed, 1902; Ralph E. Roessler and Cora Domas, 1903; Flora Allen and Cora Domas, 1904; Myrtle Gregory, 1904; Roy Fleming, 1905; Hilda Reiss, 1906; Glapha Bechtel, 1907-08; Nellie Fox, 1909; Mae Kull and Rachel Giles, 1910; Pearl Winson, 1911; John Spracklin, 1912-13; W.F. White, 1922; Thelma Cooper, 1924; Gertrude Cooper, 1926-27; Roy Strohl, 1934; Opal C. Kite, 1935-39; Opal Runkel, 1940; Mona Anderson, 1941-45; Maurine Kantner, 1946.

Maurine Kantner was the last teacher with 12 pupils; the directors were Albert Mochel, Louis Lieb and Frank Reider.

Moulton school was sold in 1950.

Some students who attended Moulton school under Nora Barrickman in 1894 were: Della Munson, Anna Augustein, Vida Downs, Amelia Pauschert, Albert Mochel, Carrie Pauschert, Frank Kidwell, Georgia Downs, Harry Pauschert, Bertha Pauschert, Julia Pauschert, Albert Pauschert and Anna Mochel.

SANDY HILL
District 8 or 51

Sandy Hill school was located in the southeast quarter of section 5 of Rose township. Taxes in 1866 were one and a quarter percent per 100, and the directors were A.T. Friesner and J. Kercher. For building purposes in 1869, taxes were $2 per 100, and directors were G.F. Walker and John Pfeiffer.

Some directors in the 1880's were J. P. Heinz, W.P. Ruff, and Jacob Pfeiffer.

Some teaches at the Sandy Hill school were: Lottie Lane, 1888; Walter Neil, 1889; Emma Auld, 1890; Grace Carr, 1892; S.S. Crook, 1893; B.W. Travis, 1894; Henry Clausen, 1898; Ella Walker, 1899; Hettie Reade and Ella Walker, 1900; Walter Howard, 1901; Ida Middleton, 1902; Walter Howard,

Moulton school as it looked in later years as a residence. Structure is now completely gone.
Photo courtesy of Shelby County Historical and Genealogical Society

1903; Grace Douthit, 1904; Ralph Roessler and Cleveland Peek, 1904; Mable Good and Cora Domas, 1905; Ella Walker, 1906; Nellie Fox, 1907; Ella Walker, 1908; John Spracklin, 1909; C.E. Trout, 1910; Reuel M. Good, 1911; Lillian Tressler, 1912; G.C. Barnhart and Clee Barnhart, 1913; E.C. Corley and Sadie Price, 1913; Ruby I. Myers, 1922; Daisy Wiggins, 1924-26; Juanita Moore, 1927; Mildred Hudson, 1934; Lyle R. Specht, 1935; Nellie G. Hamilton, 1939; Alfred Dye, 1940-41; Frank Foor, 1942-43; Mary Hampton, 1944-46.

The last teacher at Sandy Hill school was Mary Hampton with a school of 20 pupils; the directors were Walter Pfeiffer, Paul Roessler and Arthur Pfeiffer.

The school was sold to Julius Pfeiffer in 1950 for $650.

Some students who attended school in 1900 were: Tillie Kull, Katie Luck, Julie Luck, May Pfeiffer, Arthur Faderer, Clinton Faderer, Elmer Harlow, Arthur Grant, Neta Heinz, Stella Ruff, Lee Jackson, Georgie Heinz, Roy Kull, Angie

Walker, Edwin Sturgeon, Elzie Heinz, and Mae Kull.

RUTH BEERY ALWARD

She attended Sandy Hill school and had teachers Frank White, Vern Wallace, and Opal Ledbetter. She also attended Pin Hook school in Richland township, and Prairie in Windsor township.

Ruth was the daughter of Theodore Fredrick and Cora Isabel Ruff Beery, and granddaughter of George and Sophia Stumpf Ruff, and Christian and ____Strohl Beery.

HACKBERRY
District 5 union or 58

Hackberry school was located in the southwest quarter of section 36 of Rose township on the township line.

A new frame school house was built in 1877 on the northwest corner of C.T. Reber's farm. Directors that year were Frank Wortman, John Hawthorne and Joseph Waits. John Reinohl built the school "with hewed logs two rounds to be oak 20 x 24 ft. in the clear, two windows 10 x 14 on each side, one window in one end, door in the other end, eight stone peers sufficient in size and depth for a building of this kind. Ceiling to be 10 feet high. Lath and plastered over head, painted with lime and sand."

Directors in 1881 were A. H. Perryman and W. T. Wortman.

Some teachers at Hackberry school were: Alfred Perryman, 1868-had 13 students; James Groves, 1869; Matt Florence Young, 1870; Isaac Patton, 1871; John Percy, 1873; Allie Yost, 1876; Alfred Perryman, 1877; W. F. Critchfield, 1878; John W. Creekmur, 1879; Jennie Worley, 1882; Lou E. Worley, 1883; Elsie Penwell, 1884; C. E. Springstun, 1885; Emma Wilson, 1886; James P. Clay, 1887; Emma Wilson, 1888; Thomas Wortman, 1889-90; Holley Price, 1891; Josie Jones, 1892; Mollie Fenton, 1892; Mollie Fenton, 1892; Viola Barrett, 1893-94; Loula Berry and Isaac Wortman, 1894; Isaac Wortman, 1895; Harriett E. Dean and L. R. Forsyth, 1895; Charles Pugh and Byron Travis, 1896; Byron Travis, Olin McCulough, and Myrtle Taylor, 1897; J. P. Clay, 1898; Charles Pugh, 1899; Robert Pugh, 1900; Jim Clay, 1901; Stella Christy, 1902; Grace Strohl, 1903; W. C. Green, 1904; Samuel Strohl and William Steele, 1905; Mabel Good, 1906; Anetta Eckert, 1907; Wallace Carnes, 1908; Lillie Fox, 1909; Willie Cihak, 1910; Fern Biggs, 1910-11; Rose Williams and Roy Strohl, 1912; Leota Cox and Nile Hickman, 1913; Ruth Huber, 1915; J. M.Yakey, 1916; Fern Dihel, 1917; Isaac Wortman, 1918; James Yakey, 1919; T.E. Anderson, 1920; Aneita Hill, 1921; Florence E. Smith, 1922; Mary Davis, 1923; Gertrude E. Cooper, 1924-25; Mabel Hall, and Mary Davis, 1926-27; Opal C. Kite, 1934; Leland Maxedon, 1935; Lorna Stephens, 1939; Ruth

Greenlee, 1940; Helen Stephens, 1941-45; Wayne Argenbright, 1946.

Wayne Argenbright was the last teacher with 18 pupils; the directors were C.C. Hamilton, Fay Atteberry, and C. L. Furr.

M. J. and Bethel Mars bought the school in 1951 for $675.

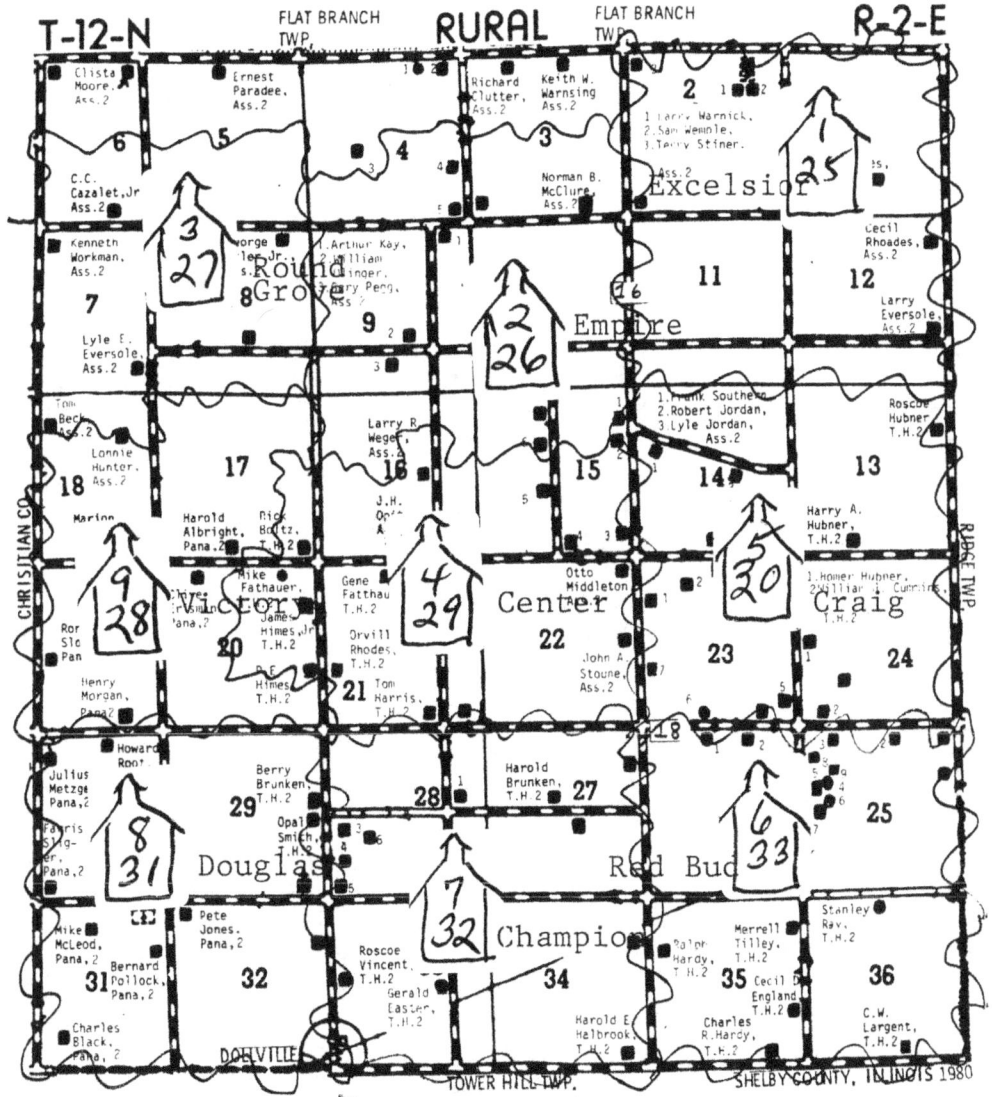

RURAL TOWNSHIP

This township was settled in 1830 on the head of Mud Creek in section 14. Through this section ran the old Shelbyville-Springfield road. A stage stand near a spring on the creek provided the needed water for such a stage stop.

In 1845 the first log school house was built in section 27. The building was also used as a church in the early days.

There were seven school districts in 1866, and 9 by 1875.

EXCELSIOR
District 1 or 25

Excelsior school was located in the southwest quarter of section 1 of Rural township. Taxes in 1866 were 30 cents per 100, and directors were J. L. Jenkins and William Oller. Three years later, the taxes were 35 cents per 100, and directors were Daniel Smith, Joseph Morrow and J. L. Jenkins.

Some of the directors of the 1880's were M. V. Pierce, H. M. Wemple, A. J. Foltz and S. H. Brownback. Martin V. Miller had deeded land to the trustees in 1877.

Some teachers at Excelsior school were: Sallie Longenbaugh, 1890; Ellen Page, 1892; Nella Carr, 1893; Emma Perryman, 1894; Grace Carr, 1901; Odell Breckenridge, 1909; Mabel Anderson, 1924; Estella Robertson, 1926-27; Enid E. McKinley, 1934; Zelma R. Smith, 1935; Josephine V. Jenkins, 1939; Enid Winings, 1940-42; Maxine Tucker, 1943, and Isaac Hoffman.

Maxine Tucker was the last teacher with 5 pupils; the directors were Samuel M. Wemple, D.C. Davidson, and S.G. Potter.

Students who attended in 1934 were: Ruth Wemple, Wayne Wemple, Maxine Wemple, Raymond Wemple, Mary Wemple, Marjorie Weakly, Irene Fried, Betty Fried, and Betty Sloan, Genevieve Wemple, Paul Kroenlein, Virginia Weakly, Helen Figgins, Helen Fried, Jean Behl, and Paulien Wemple.

Other teachers at Excelsior were: Inabelle Sturgeon, 1922; Cora B. Lane, 1929; and Zelma S. Breeding, 1938.

HELEN MARJORIE DAVIS

She attended Excelsior school for eight years, and had teachers Mabel Anderson, Florence Biedert, Cora Lane, Beulah Maloney, and Enid McKinley.

"I remember mostly the Christmas programs that were held at night, when all the parents came and the kerosene lamps with reflectors were lit. Also on the last day of school, the parents would come with well filled baskets of food for a picnic dinner that was spread on tables outside.

One lasting lesson that stayed with me all my life was in front of the school. We had large boxes that contained maps and charts. In physiology, we had a map that showed the liver and lungs of a smoker and a non-smoker. This is not really a funny or heartwarming memory, but it made such an impression on me that I have never smoked."

Helen was a daughter of Edward Otto and Hannah Tabbert Figgins; granddaughter of Henry and Emma Boldt Figgins, and Charles and Caroline Heideman Tabbert; and great-granddaughter of Fielden Figgins, Adolphus Boldt, and Carl Fred and Caroline Bugenhagan Tabbert.

EMPIRE
District 2 or 26

Empire school was located in the southwest quarter of section 10 of Rural township. Isaac and Elizabeth Cartmell had deeded land to the trustees in 1877.

Some of the directors of the 1880's were: William Porter, T. W. Cartmell, T. P. Lowe, D.A. Ray and Just Wright.

Some teachers at Empire school were: Mary Leighty, 1890; Purella Reed, 1891; Louis Metsker, 1892; Nella Carr, 1894; Fred Metsker, 1901; Cecil Mae Clegg, 1909; A. W. Thompson, 1921-22; Elsie B. Tabor, 1924; Neta Tucker Guthrie, 1925-26; Hal Guthrie, 1930; R. T. Rawlings, 1931-33; S.R. Stephens, 1934-35; Irene Cranmer, 1936-37; Nancy Margaret Heim, 1938; Purella Beckett, 1927; Ruby Killam, 1929; Elmer E. Smith, 1935; Deloris Mowry, 1939-40; no school 1941-42; Lola McClure, 1943-44.

Lola McClure was the last teacher with 9 pupils; the directors were Emmett Heiter, Tillie Lupton and Bert Davis.

Some students who attended Empire school in 1894 were: Mabel Loser, Claude Loser, Ernest Alkire, Oscar Alkire, Etta Burk, Addie Burk, Clarence Lowe, Charley Lowe, Bert DeBaun, Mollie Cartmel, Jennie Cartmel, Ike Cartmel, Amy Mose, Lizzie Mose, Lorena Alkire, Lizzie Alkire, Annie Moltz, and Fred Moltz.

ROUND GROVE
District 3 or 27

Round Grove school was located in the northwest quarter of section 8 of Rural township. Taxes in 1866 were 30 cents per 100, and the directors were D.E. Russell and Daniel A. Downs. Three years later, the taxes were 3 and ¼ percent per 100, and the directors were C.D. Pitzer, S.C. Myers, and William C. Moore.

The directors of the 1880's were W. Brimley, N.B. McClure, J. W. Padgett and H. M. Gregory. Nathial and Malinda McClure deeded land to the trustees in 1891.

Some teachers at Round Grove school were: Jessie Elmore, 1890; Lillie Cannon, 1891; Minnie Gladfelter, 1893; Maude Reading, 1894; C.W. Wallace, 1901; Roxana Whipple, 1909; Mabel M. Buchanan, 1917; Lucille Schahrer, 1924; Gladys Harper, 1926-27; Carl Tankersley, 1931-32; Ruby Hiler, 1933-34; Enid E. McKinley, 1935; Dora Lee Myers, 1939-40; Lyla Smith, 1941-42; Ruby Kelley, 1944; and Opal Olive Potter, 1945.

Opal Olive Potter was the last teacher with 11 pupils; the directors were Oscar Workman, Harold Hart and S.B. McClure.

Empire school in 1929-30. Teacher Ruby Killam Wheat. Back row, Warren Cartmell, Wade Lupton, Richard Breeding, James Breeding, Wayne Rowley, Wayne Breeding, teacher; front, John Lamb, Anna Bolin, Mabel Bolin and Wendell Cartmell. Absent that day: Orval Bolin, LaVene McConnell and LaVeta McConnell.   Photo courtesy of Ruby Wheat

---

CENTER
District 4 or 29

Center school was located in the northeast quarter of section 21 of Rural township. Taxes were $1.15 per 100 in 1869, and directors were Joseph Chesshire and A. McClaren.

Some directors of the 1880's were Samuel Harper, J.H. Mose, Jacob Hebel and William M. Myers. John A. Fanson had deeded land to the trustees in 1892.

Some teachers at Center school were: John M. Forsythe, 1888-90; W. H. Sands, 1891; J.C. Lane, 1893; L.R. Forsythe, 1894; Arthur Bryson, 1901; Clemie Warnick, 1909; A.W. Thompson, 1917; George W. Whaley, 1922; Ella Singer, 1923; Homer Stilgebouer, 1924; Elsie B. Tabor, 1925; Rose Jewel Pattengale, 1926; Velma Cooper, 1927; Mildred Pontius, 1930; Esther Frankenfeld, 1931; A.W. Thompson, 1934; Pearl Seiber, 1935-38; Eula Reed, 1939-42; Eula Brunken, 1943; Esther Gerhold,

1944; Elsie Hosto, 1945-46.

Elsie Hosto was the last teacher with 19 pupils; the directors were C.G. Auer, J. F. Himes and Otto Middleton.

CRAIG
District 5 or 30

Craig school was located in the northeast quarter of section 23 of Rural township. Taxes in 1869 were two and a quarter percent, and directors were Casper Ernst and Robert Harper.

Some of the directors in the 1880's were Sylvester Wagner, Daniel Fakner, G.B. Hill, and A. H. Fulton. Daniel and Sarah Smith deeded land to the trustees in 1896.

Some teachers at Craig school were: Minnie Vanderpool, 1888; Morton H. Neil, 1891; Nella Carr, 1892; Nell Fitzgerald, 1893; Ella Perryman, 1894; H.W. Hawley, 1901; Margaret W. Muller, 1917; Purella Beckett, 1923-24; Evelyn Moffett, 1925; Dorothy Perryman, 1927; Esther A. Hoke, 1927-28; Cleta H. Smith, 1929-32; Zelma R. Smith, 1933; Velma D. Schahrer, 1934-36; Dorothy E. McMillen, 1939; A. W. Thompson, 1940-43; Josephine Jenkins, 1944; and Mary Mathias, 1945-46.

Mary Mathias was the last teacher with 11 pupils; the directors were Paul Warner, A. J. Hubner and Fred Metzger.

RED BUD
District 6 or 33

Red Bud school was located in the southeast quarter of section 26 of Rural township. Jasper and Naoma Armstrong deeded land to the trustees in 1880.

Taxes in 1869 were 35 cents per 100, and the directors were J.W. Vermillion, Jacob Hebel and Jacob T. Maurer. Some directors of the 1880's were F. Maurer, Charles B. Hart, Henry Behler and Daniel S. Tripp.

Some teachers at Red Bud school were: Ollie Brown, 1888; Emma Speiser, 1889; John Sweeney, 1890; Wesley N. Neil, 1892; Mary S. Leighty, 1893; F.W. Metsker, 1894; Mattie Thomas, 1901; Martella Hart, 1909; Nora Brandon, 1923; Etta C. Culp, 1924; Forest Fowler, 1926-28; A.W. Thompson, 1929-30; Forest Moore, 1931; Josephine Jenkins, 1932; Mathilda Greensavage, 1934; Helen J. Conlee, 1939; Harold E. McMillan, 1940; Enid McKinley, 1941-44; Enid McElroy, 1945-46.

Enid McElroy was the last teacher with 9 pupils; the directors were Sam Miller, Burrell Roberts and Merrell Tilley.

Red Bud school was sold to Mary Elizabeth Roberts in 1954.

CHAMPION
District 7 or 32

Champion school was located in the northeast quarter of section 33 of Rural township. Nelson and Emma Neil deeded land to the trustees in 1883.

Some directors of the 1880's were Tilman Neil, John Jenkins, Jacob Galster, J. W. Jenkins and C. L. Smith.

Some of the teachers at Champion school were: Newt Fluckey, 1888; E.F. Karle, 1890-92; Wesley N. Neil, 1893; Blanche Connelly, 1894; E.F. Karle, 1901; Leone Wirey, 1909; H. W. Stilgebauer, 1922; Clara Marshall, 1924; H. W. Stilgebauer, 1925-27; Lola Knoop, 1931-32; Perry E. Pritts, 1934-42; Mary Kantner, 1943; Verla Daughterly, 1944-45; and Isabelle McDonald, 1946.

Isabell Mc Donald was the last teacher with 13 pupils; the directors were William Brunken, G. E. McClure and Gerald Morrow.

Champion school in 1942 with teacher Perry Pritts. Shown are Evelyn Weber, Ruth Doll Crabtree, Frederick Brunken and Frederick Killam.

Photo courtesy of Daily Union

FRANK W. KILLAM
He attended Champion school as did his father. The school was only ¼ mile from his home. There at Champion he had teachers Glen Stilgebauer, Lola Mc Clure, Carl Tankersley, and Perry Pritts.

DOUGLAS OR RAGWEED?
District 8 or 31

Douglas school was located in the southeast quarter of section 30 of Rural township. Taxes in 1866 were 90 cents per 100, and the directors were James L. Lupton, Henry Mose and Christian Eberspacher.

Some of the directors at Douglas school in 1880's were John Heberlein, Adam Metzger, John F. Mautz, F.G. Weber, and John E. Metzger. John E. and Caroline Metzger deeded land to the trustees in 1879.

Some of the teachers at Douglas school were: Jennie O'Brien, 1888; M. E. Killam, 1889; Jennie O'Brien, 1890; Etta McLin, 1891; Ella Perryman, 1893; Carrie Hoxey, 1894; C.W. Wallace, 1900; Marie Shempf, 1901; Norma Rhodes, 1909; Freda E. Metzger, 1917; Pauline Miller, 1921; Verna B. Hines, 1922; Mary L. Keelan, Ginla Mae Casner, 1925-27; Elvera A. Rau, 1928-30; Ruth E. Alverson, 1934; H.W. Stilgebauer, 1934; Audrey N. Simmons, 1939; Rosalyn M. Hauten, 1938; Nannie Ellis, 1940-41; Wilma Ann Vincent, 1942; H.W. Stilgebauer, 1943-44; Betty Parr, 1945, and Verla Daughtery, 1946.

Verla Daughtery was the last teacher with 11 pupils; the directors were Edward P. Metzger, Edward C. Eberspacher, and Collins Burgener.

Students who attended Douglas school in 1900 were: Fred Weber, Orval Metzger, Rosa Metzger, Bertha McDaniel, Hollie Chaney, Bertha Weber, Harry McDaniel, Alma Weber, Carl Metzger, Gertie Frankenfield, Otto Frankenfield, Robert Metzger, Florence Chaney, George Metzger, John Weber, Albert Frankenfield, Mollie Weber, Harry Weber, George Siegfried, Emma Frankenfield, Lulu Mautz and Jacob Weber.

VICTOR
District 9 or 28

Victor school was located in the northeast quarter of section 19 of Rural township. Mercy and Rebecca Lupton leased land to the trustees in 1885.

Some directors of the 1880's were S. N. Lupton, William Himes and Joseph Chesshire.

Some of the teachers at Victor school were: Lucy Lupton, 1888; Anna Shempf, 1889; Edward Syfert, 1891; Isaac Baker, 1892; Maggie Cronin, 1893; Maggie McKee, 1894; Mollie Cartmell, 1901; Ethel Fanson, 1909; Bernice Sturgeon, 1922; Kathleen Cisna, 1924; Pauline Tucker, 1926-30; Bernice Cvengros, 1933; Gladys Harper, 1934-35; Opal Olive Potter, 1939; and Edna

Cochran, 1940.

Edna Cochran was the last teacher with 6 pupils; the directors were James Swanson, Edna Cockran and Mace Cockran.

Victor school was sold to Edna Cockran in 1954.

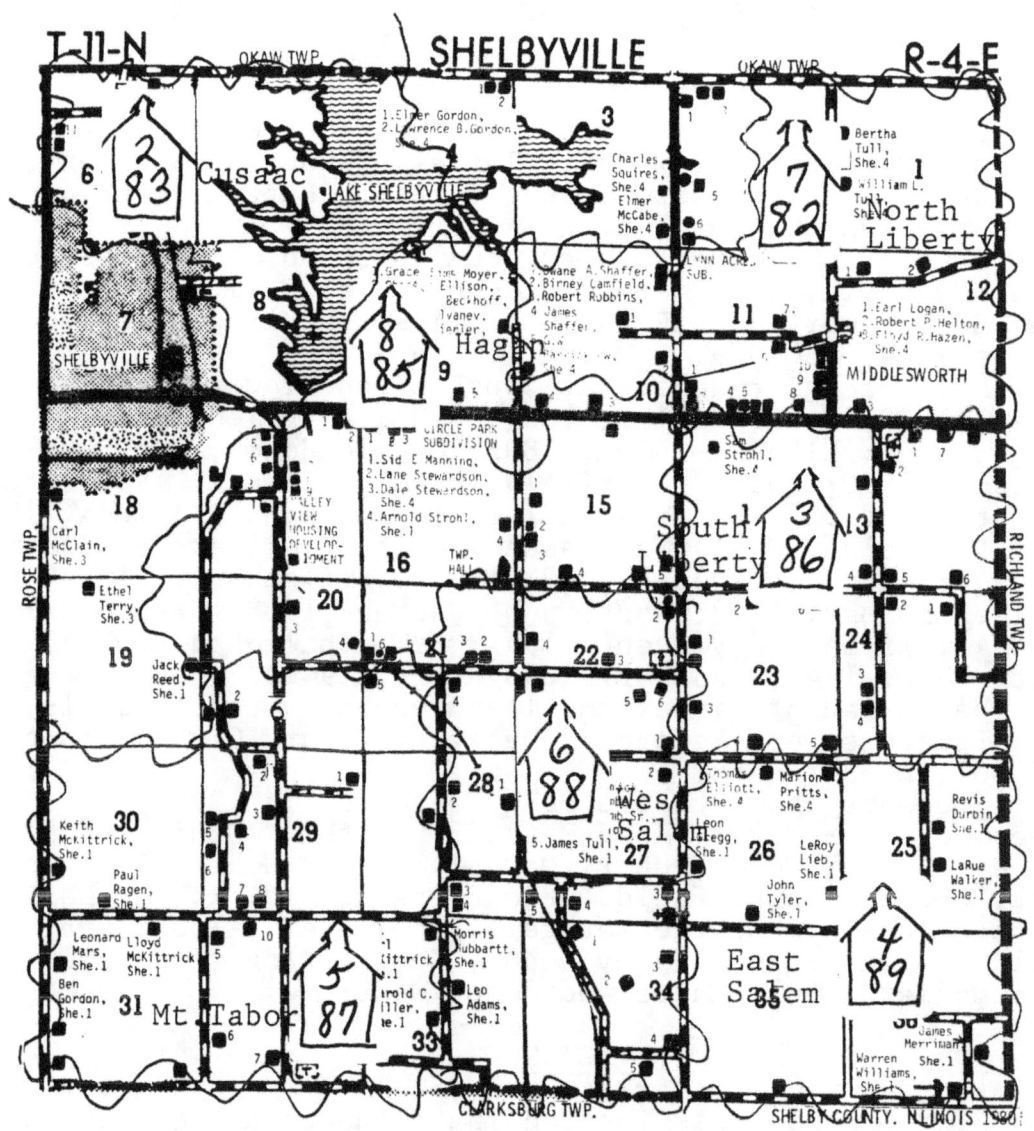

SHELBYVILLE TOWNSHIP

This township had the second school of the county--the first at Cold Springs with Moses Storey as the first teacher, and the second here with Joseph Oliver as the first teacher. The first early school built after the log courthouse was called the Prentice school, and a record from it appears on page 27.

The following map was created circa 1855, and shows the school districts of Shelbyville township as well as the roads, marked prairies or ponds and the A & T R.R.

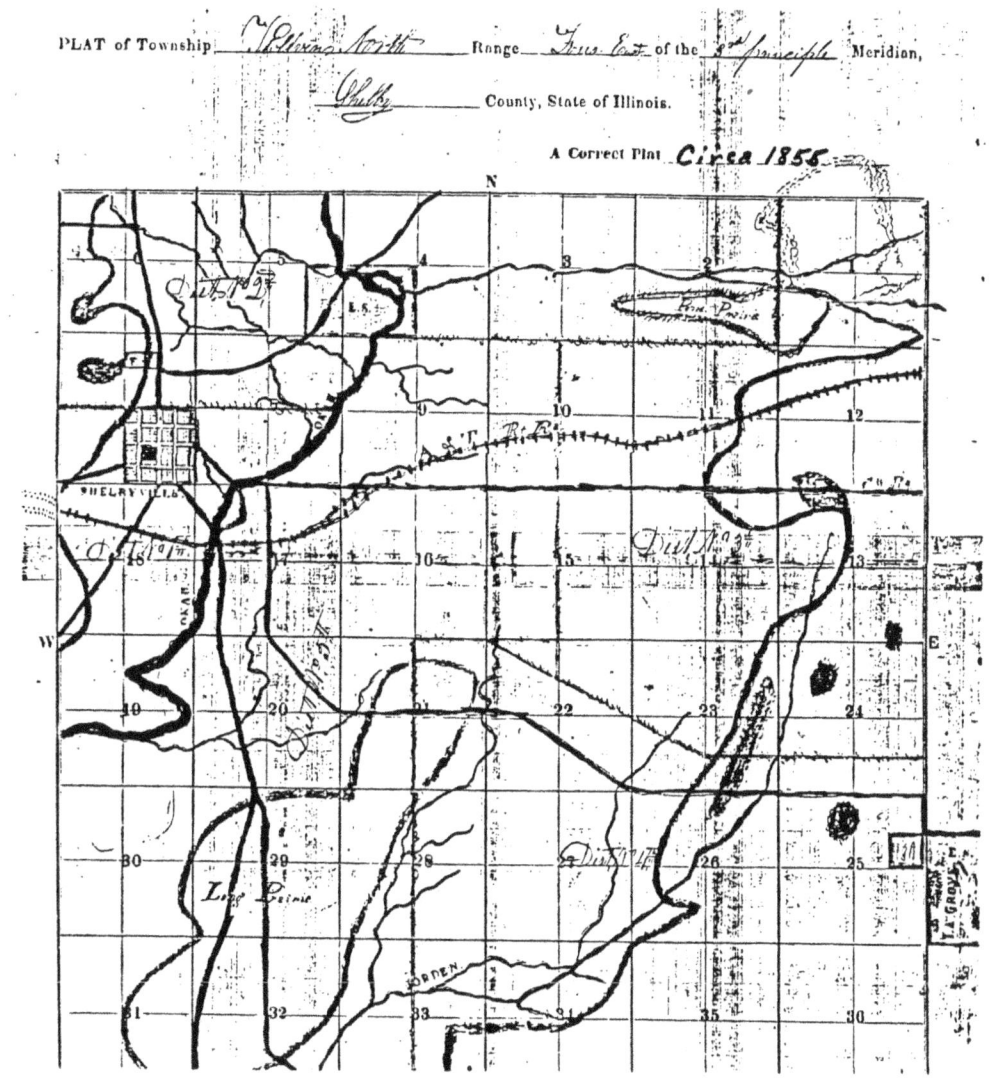

CUSAAC
District 2 or 83

Cusaac school was located in the northeast quarter of section 6 of Shelbyville township. Taxes in 1866 were one and half percent per 100, and the directors were Samuel Strohl and J. J. Page. For building purposes three years later, the taxes were $2 per 100, and directors were Samuel Strohl and J. J. Page.

Some of the directors of the 1880's were L. B. Dittoe, Jacob Coplin, J. W. Scott and Stephen Lumpp.

Some teachers at Cusaac school were: Rose Richardson, 1888; Francis Davis, 1892; Josie Aurand, 1893; Norton Waggoner, 1894; Flora Allen, 1901; Mary Burnett, 1909; Helen Lindsay, 1922-25-standard school (school called Ward); Oscar Fred Storm, 1926-standard school, redecorated; 34; Robert Gill, 1935; Ruth Greenlee, 1939; June Boys, 1940-41; Opal F. Kite, 1942; Arvetta Lewellyn, 1943; Nannie Ellis, 1944.

Nannie Ellis was the last teacher with 23 pupils; the directors were J. T. Kensil, Floyd Waggoner and Glen Barker.

CLYDE REYNOLDS
He attended Cusaac school for eight years and had teachers Mrs. Wydick, Miss Nance, Mrs. Anderson, Charles Henning, Fred Grab, and Jess Gill.

"There is not much to tell, only the pie suppers and box lunches they had. On Easter Sunday some of us boys would take eggs and go to the timber and boil them. Some would take water cans, salt and pepper. One boy who lived on a farm would bring the eggs."

Clyde was the son of T.J. and Lina Winson Reynolds; grandson of Frank and Mary Winson.

LIBERTY OR
SOUTH LIBERTY
District 3 or 86

South Liberty was located in the southwest quarter of section 14 of Shelbyville township. Taxes in 1866 were 75¢ per 100, and the directors were A. E. Douthit, D. L. Thompson and William Wilhelm who were elected in August that year. Isaac Helton was the fourth candidate who did not make director that year. Three years later, the taxes were 50¢ per 100, and directors were A.E. Douthit and Thomas Rice.

Some of the directors of the 1880's were Samuel Huffer, L. N. Douthit, W. H. Douthit, Jesse Overpoch, John Kessel and F. M. Douthit. Thomas and Sarah Stewardson deeded land for the school in 1888.

Some teachers of South Liberty school were: Gust. Reiss, 1886; Thomas Baker, 1888-90; F. J. Snapp, 1891; Hollie Price, 1892; Ella Cleary, 1893; S.S. Crook, 1894; Ada Burke, 1901; Norma James, 1909; Julia Fay McVay, 1917; Oscar Storm, 1922; Robert Zimmer, 1924-standard school; Irene Luce, 1926-standard school; Florence Juhkne, 1927; Ulmont Evans, 1934-35; Ruth Weakly, 1939; Enid Durst, 1940-43; Lillian Goddard, 1944; Sylvia Strohl, 1945-46.

Sylvia Strohl was the last teacher with 17 pupils; the directors were C. H. Gritzmacher, Herbert Barker and Earl Helton.

South Liberty was sold in 1950 to Herbert Barker.

Some students who attended Liberty school in 1892 were: Estella Huffer, Ella Thomas, Pearl Douthit, Julia Reed, Anna Wiggens, Eva Fox, Dora Douthit, Effie Douthit, Samuel Huffer, Mary Cihak, Elmer Douthit, Harlie Douthit, John Cihak, Burke Huffer, Irving Douthit, Goldie Douthit, Frank Cihak, Jennie Rexroad, May Douthit, Pearl Marsh, Charles Stewardson, Lizzie Fox, Daisy Wiggens, N. Miller, Nellie Bean, Lawrence Huffer, Eva Miller, Arthur Huffer and Harlie Stewardson.

SALEM OR EAST SALEM
District 4 or 89

East Salem school was located in the northwest quarter of section 36 of Shelbyville township. An election was held at the Salem school house in 1849, directors elected were John S. Thomas, William Green and Samuel Herod. During that time, there were 81 children under the age of 21 living in the district. By household, Emily Green had 6 children under 21; William Green, 3; John Fleming, 15; Jacob Sitler, 4; Samuel Herod, 4; James W. Herod, 7; Andrew Anderson, 4; Francis Davidson, 6; John Thomas, 7; John Igo, 5; Bethel Humphreys, 6; Titus Davidson, 8; David Venters, 6; Lewit Venters, 1; George Venters, 8, and Abraham Miller, 1.

Taxes in 1866 were 50 cents per 100, and directors were Uriah Bryant, James Henry and George Himes. Taxes were the same three years later, and the directors were Jacob Sitler and James B. Reed.

Some directors of the 1880's were Thomas Sittler, D.Y. Milligan, John F. Fleming, T. J. Gollogher, and S.W. Fleming. John and Bridget Rice deeded an acre to the trustees in 1883.

Some of the teachers at Salem or East Salem were: J.E. Reynolds, 1888; F. M. Green, 1890; Nora Barrickman, 1890; V. B. Cruitt, 1891; M. F. Walters and Sofa Smith, 1892; A.B. Storm and Mrs. C. H. Klump, 1893; G.W. Chisenhall, 1894; Ales Beck, 1901; Verne Kern, 1909; Clara Fox, 1917; Beatrice Jones, 1922; Charlotte Timperley, 1924-standard school; Arloa Knight, 1926-27; Gloyd Archey, 1934-35; Enid O. Durst, 1939; Agnes Willey, 1941; Naomi Ripley, 1942; Robert Gill, 1943-44; Margaret Stephens, 1945; Vera Everett, 1946.

Vera Everett was the last teacher with 22 pupils; the directors were Jesse R. Durbin, Ray Westenhaver, and William Carsell.

Enrollment was 41 students in 1892, and some students who attended that year were: May Rice, Stella Amlin, Effie Amlin, Bruce Amlin, Mary Thomas, Isaac Thomas, Rhodes Green, Carl Green, Roy Green, Thomas Alday, and Roscoe Markland.

In 1893, enrollment was 43 students, and a few of the students who attended were: Herbert Green, Corda McGilligan, Bertha Dittoe, Carl Green, Warren Green, Albert Alday, Tom Alday, Jacob Milligan, Anson Milligan, Effie Amlin, Estella Amlin, Bruce Amlin, and Ira Elliott.

The school was sold in 1951 to W. A. and Lois Gordon for $660.

MT. TABOR
District 5 or 87

Mt. Tabor school was located in the E½ of the northwest quarter of section 32 of Shelbyvile township. Three directors were elected in 1850 to superintend the district. Elected were Isaac P. Johnson, Joshua Guilford, and Peter

Fleming. Residents of the district that year were Peter Fleming, Joshua Guilford, James M. Owens, William Henry, Charles H. Guilford, Benjamin Radcliff, Alexander Johnson, Anthony Knox, Adam A. Owens, Samuel A. Clesson, John Couch, John J. Owens, and Isaac P. Johnson.

Taxes in 1866 were 50 cents per 100, and directors were A. H. Patton and H. H. Davis. Three years later, the taxes were 30 cents per 100, and the directors were Isaac Patton, Thomas Carnes and Abraham Coplin.

Some of the directors of the 1880's were: S.W. Wilson, Joseph Sappin, J. M. Harvy, Jr., John M. Bean, John H. Yencer and Wiliam Henry, Jr. J. Paul Grove had leased land to the trustees in 1875.

Some teachers at Mt. Tabor school were: F. J. Snapp, 1892; Leslie Stiarwalt, 1893; Calvin Green, 1894; James Wright, 1901; William Huffer, 1909; Robert Gill, 1917; Retha Bullington, 1924-27; L. D. Williams, 1934-35; Oneita Mills Phillips, 1939; Frank Foor, 1940-41; Aster Derry, 1942; Dorothy Forsythe, 1943; Willis Rawlings, 1944; Harry D. Steck, 1945, and Willis Rawlings, 1946.

Willis Rawlings was the last teacher with 30 pupils; the directors were Paul McKittrick, Gerald Smith and Joe Christner.

Mt. Tabor school was sold in 1950 at public auction.

WEST SALEM
District 6 or 88

West Salem school was located in the southwest corner of the southwest quarter of the northwest quarter of section 27 of Shelbyville township. Taxes in 1869 were a half percent per 100, and the directors were Uriah Bryant and John B. Hickman.

Some directors of the 1880's were Ryan Gowdy, John Kensil, Daniel Venters, George K. Venters, Thomas Sittler, and John F. Miller. Malcolm C. Andrews had leased land to the trustees in 1882.

Some of the teachers at West Salem school were: Oscar Read, 1886; Silas Green, 1889; J. P. Clay and Mr. Baker, 1890; Lee Frazer, 1891; Calvin Green, 1892-93; T. H. Cramer, 1894; Warren Green, 1900-01; Raymond Goddard, 1909; Perry E. Fletcher, 1917; Robert Gill, 1924-26; Enid Olmstead, 1927; Maurine Elder, 1934; O. O. Barker, 1935; Carolyn Specht, 1939; Kathleen Weakly, 1940; Cora Pontius, 1941; Mary Hampton, 1942; Nannie I. Ellis, 1943 and Mary Kantner, 1944-46.

Mary Kantner was the last teacher with 16 pupils; the directors were William Kensil, Earl Thomas and D. J. Kensil.

The school was rebuilt of brick in 1903, and torn down in 1947.

Thirty-three pupils were enrolled in 1893, and a few of them were: Alice Corley, Lizzie Corley, Mollie Fraker, Oliver

Thomas, Nora Thomas, Amanda Green, Jacob Sittler, Maud Fleming, Willie Fleming and Linder Fleming.

In 1900, there were 30 pupils enrolled and some of them were: Bertha Kensil, Grace Kensil, Ruby Rice, Vera Rice, Letha Rice, Jennie Bainbridge, Thomas Bainbridge, Johnnie Kensil, Elza Stewardson, Perry Venters, Roy Venters, Guy Bivins, Ross Henry, Harland Dickinson, Bruce Stewardson, Verdie Hughes, George Reed, and Iva Wells.

EULA MILLER DURST

She attended West Salem school, and had teachers W.A. Storm, C.R. Goddard, T.H. Stewardson, Fern Biggs Fox, Lily Fox Carnes, P. E. Fletcher and Myrtle Stewardson.

Eula was the daughter of Jesse and Katherine Ellis Miller; and granddaughter of Jesse and Mary Frances Welton Miller and John and Fannie Fraker Ellis.

JOHN W. MCNEESE

He attended West Salem, Center in Dry Point, Sylvan school, and so on.

"The first Illinois school that I attended was Center school located just north of Cowden. The teacher's name was Lester Barton. The following year I attended Bee Ridge located southwest of Shelbyville, and the teacher's name was Pearl LeGrande Schwenker.

I attended West Salem school, southeast of Shelbyville, for the next three years. P. E. Fletcher was the teacher. Nellie Fox Carnes taught there prior to Mr. Fletcher. The next year I in Sylvan district but schools were closed due to the flu. That was also the year we moved to a farm north of Westervelt. I did not attend school. I was 15 that year so Dad kept me very busy with farm chores, moving, etc. When you are the oldest boy in a family of ten children, someone has to work to support the younger children in the family.

The year following moving, I was permitted to attend Brunswick school and finished the eighth grade by going when there was no farm work to do. Sometime after that, I attended two winter terms at Sparks Business College, again going when there was no farm work to do. I started operating the garage (Westervelt) when I was 23, 1927. I sold out in 1969, built a small shop at home while continuing to farm until my stroke in 1982.

Amusing incident: I liked to catch bumble bees-drones--put them in my ink well and listened to them buzz. When I came in after recess, I caught a grasshopper and put it down the back of some girl's dress. She screamed, told the teach and he said, 'John McNeese, did you put a bumble bee down her collar?' I replied, 'No, it was a grasshopper'. The teacher turned facing the blackboard and said no more. That of course was not amusing to the girl. Mr. Fletcher was a good teacher and helped me when I needed extra help during recess period.

Impressive incident: During the first week of school under Mr. Fletcher there was no discipline so we thought we were going to have a wonderful year. The next week he announced that we had done as we pleased for the first week and now it was his turn. He carried through on that statement."

John was the son of William L. and Laura B. DeWeese McNeese; grandson of George and Delilah Holt McNeese, and Hiram and ? Evans DeWeese; and great-grandson of Sam McNeese and Isaac Holt.

West Salem school in 1934 with teacher Ruby Killam Wheat. At least half of her pupils were Mennonite--"wonderful, beautiful children. They could speak two languages when they entered school." The families consisted of the Elliotts, Hostetlers, Rebers, Kropfs, Eash, McCabes, St. Johns, and Stewardson.   Photo courtesy of Ruby K. Wheat

North Liberty
District 7 or 82

North Liberty school was located in the southeast quarter of section 2 of Shelbyville township. Taxes in 1869 were $1.25 per 100 for building purposes, and the directors were H. H. Davis, J. M. Biggs and B.A. Mansfield.

Some directors of the 1880's were S. J. Ditzler, Thomas Dobbins, William Wilhelm, and J. A. Patterson. William and

Rhoda Douthit had deeded land to the trustees in 1876.

Some of the teachers at North Liberty school were: Mollie Rice, 1888; Edward Reynolds, 1889; Carrie Douthit, 1890; Emma Auld, 1891; Eugene Markland, 1892; Nora Barrickman, 1893; J. M. Douthit, 1894; Otto O. Barbee, 1901; Ora Bodine, 1909; Ethel Hazen, 1917; Jesse Gill, 1922; Roy Strohl, 1924-27; Ruby Killam, 1934-35; Opal K. Runkel, 1939; Doyle Whitacre, 1940; Paul Christman, 1941-42; Opal Kite, 1943-44; Wayne Arganbright, 1945, and Opal Kite, 1946.

Opal Kite was the last teacher with 8 pupils; the directors were Joe Barker, Bertha Tull and Ester Mc Coy.

North Liberty school was sold to Emma E. Clay in 1950 for $400.

JAMES C. HAYES, JR.

He attended North Liberty for one year, and had teacher Opal Kite.

James was the son of James C. and Margaret Hulick Hayes, and grandson of Dr. and Mrs. C. H. Hulick.

North Liberty school circa late 19th century or early 20th.
Photo courtesy of Nadine McCabe,
Shelby County Historical and
Genealogical Society

HAGAN, WEST LIBERTY,
THORNTON, BRUSTER
District 8 or 85

Hagan school was located in the southwest quarter of section 9 of Shelbyville township. Some directors of the 1880's were W. W. Thornton, Thomas J. Bruster, Robert Biggs, and Thomas Hagan.

The school in 1894, called Bruster at that time, burned. David F. and Belle Richardson deeded a half acre for the school later that year.

Some teachers at Hagan school were: Ida Hagan, 1888; Hiram Kensil, 1889; Lis Hagan, 1890; Maggie Cleary, 1891-92; Minnie F. Rainey, 1893; Robert Parrish, 1894; W. F. Herron, 1900; George M. Hudson, 1901; William A. Steward, 1909 (now called West Liberty); Otis Kruzan, 1924; Ruby Rose Walden, 1926-27; Paul Christman, 1934; Roy Strohl, 1935; Monica Mickey, 1939-40; Cora Pontius, 1941; Monica Mickey, 1942; Georgia Summers, 1943-44; and Mary K. Kellett, 1945-46.

Mary K. Kellett was the last teacher with 10 pupils; the directors were Albert Huffer, Lee Heckert and J. E. Douthit.

In 1900, there were 33 pupils enrolled, and some of them were: Fern Giles, Rachel Giles, Mettie Ackart, Dessie Downs, Fred Clesson, Hary Downs, Loyd Downs, and Eber Manning.

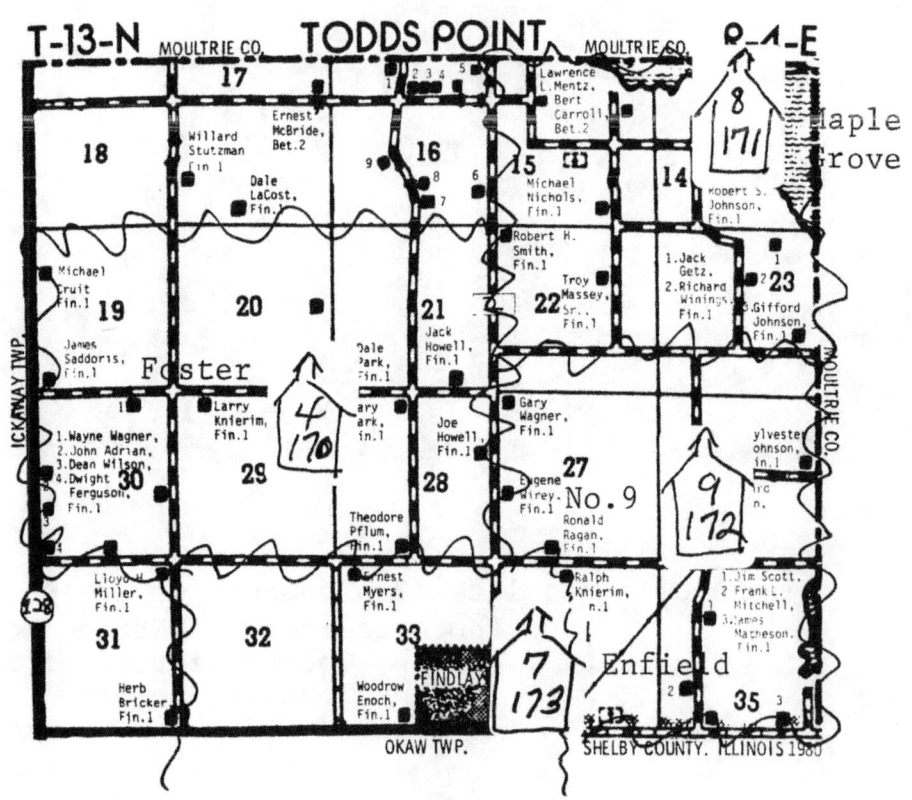

Foster school, Todds Point township. Taken circa early 1900's.   Photo courtesy of Lois Cruitt

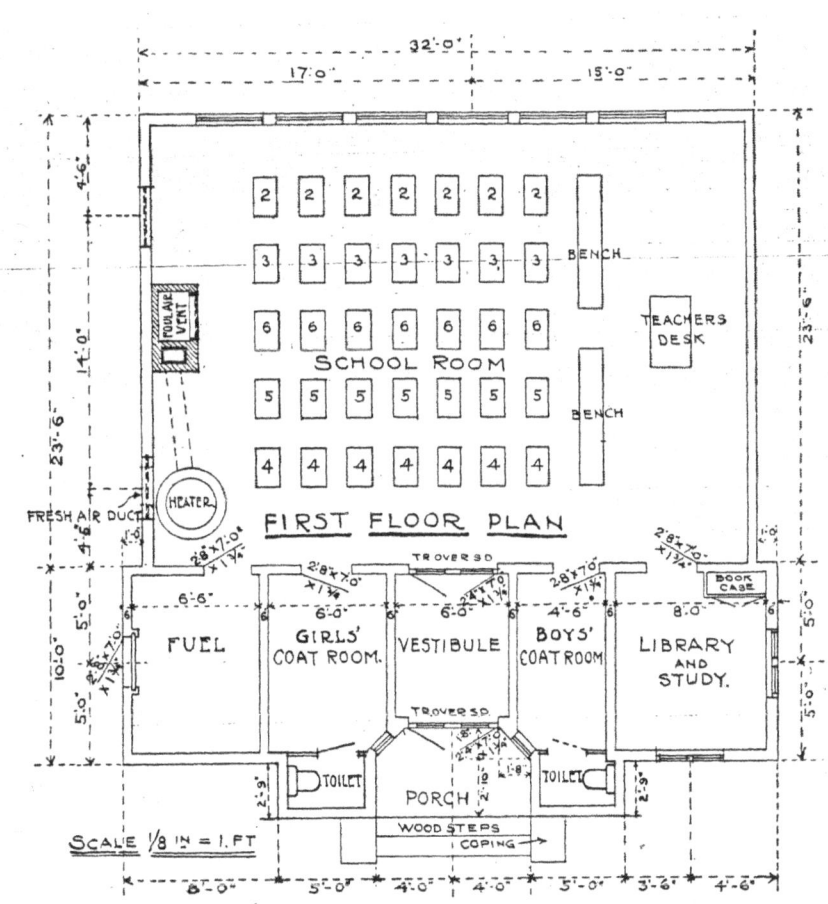

Floor Plan—Without Basement.

TODDS POINT TOWNSHIP

Todds Point township was settled in 1835 near its northern edge in section 16, and by 1856 began the town Todds Point. It probably near there that the first school was taught in a deserted log cabin.

FOSTER
District 4 or 170

Foster school was located in the northeast quarter of section 29 of Todds Point township. Taxes in 1866 were 75¢ per 100, and directors were Jordan French and J. Foster. Three years later, the taxes were 3/4 cents per 100, and directors were Thomas Hadwin, James Foster, and Frank Blasdell.

Some of the directors in the 1880's were A.G. Fox, E.D. Mast, Samuel H. Wright, and Thomas Robertson.

Some of the teachers at Foster school were: Ella Smith, 1888; Vinnie Tabor, 1889; H. W. Wright, 1891; George M. Barbee, 1892; E.A.Crowl, 1893-94; W.D. Herron, 1901; R. J. Herron, 1909; Lillie Tressler, 1910; Bart L. Herron, 1924-standard school-27; Robert Gill, 1934; Edith H. Hoke, 1935; Ruth Davis, 1939-41; no school 1942; Essie Mowry, 1943-44; and Pauline Allen , 1945.

Pauline Allen was the last teacher with 11 pupils; the directors were Nellie Stewardson, Gertrude M. Beyers, and John Park, Jr.

Some students who attended Foster school in 1910 were: Ruth Newby, Ada Little, John Park, Ruth Berry, Gladys Park, and Wayne Park.

DUDLEY D. WRIGHT

He attended Foster school from 1891 to 1892, and had teacher Hubert Wright.

"When I attended Foster school, a favorite game at recess was a form of baseball. Also 'Ante Over' in which a ball was thrown over the school building to be caught."

Dudley was the son of Samuel H. and Nancy Shouse Wright; grandson of William and Martha Dawdy Wright; and great-grandson of Robert and Elizabeth Roney Wright.

ENFIELD
District 7 or 73

Enfield school was located in the southwest quarter of section 34 of Todds Point township. There was a special tax in 1866 of three percent, and directors were Charles C. Dosh, John Carder and S. Sappenfield.

William and Mary E. Wright deeded land to the trustees in 1884.

Some of the teachers at Enfield were: Walter Woodrow, 1890; J. H. Baxter, 1891; L. E. Camfield, 1892; F.A. Fritter,

1893; and V.B. Cruitt, 1894.

By 1901, Enfield became consolidated with the schools of Findlay.

MAPLE GROVE
District 8 or 171

Maple Grove school was located in the E½ of section 14 of Todds Point township. Samuel S.B. and Hannah L. Johnson deeded land to the trustees in 1883.

Some directors of the 1880's were J. W. Pearce, S.S.B. Johnson, and Oscar Cavender.

Some teachers at Maple Grove were: Hiram Pogue, 1888; E. K. Jackson, 1889-90; W. Woodrow, 1891; Nannie Wright, 1892; Clara Lehman, 1893; G. M. Barbee, 1894; L.C. Francisco, 1899; Lola M. Tull, 1901; Lucy Schlobolm, 1909; Bart L. Herron, 1917; Essie Banks, 1922; Hazel Wortman, 1924; Dora Freeman, 1926-27; Ruth Merryman, 1934-35; Dorothy Totten, 1939-40; Alta Lee, 1941; C.A. Garst, 1942; Marie Stevens, 1943-44; and Marjorie Enoch, 1945.

Marjorie Enoch was the last teacher with 8 pupils; the directors were Frank Williams, Gilbert Uphoff, and Leonard Bolin.

There were 29 pupils enrolled in 1899, and some of them were: Earnest Johnson, Truman Webb, Ray Bland, Verna Harmison, Edna Harmison, Oka Harmison, Walter Henderson, Ethel Henderson, Nellie McKinney, Nettie McKinney, Edward McKinney, Jacob Perry, Edna Perry, Nellie Perry, Vira Perry, Earl Harmison, Elpha Harmison and Fay Harmison.

For a time in the early 1900's, Maple Grove was consolidated with district 191 of Moultrie county. In 1928, the residents petitioned and made Maple Grove once again into a common school district in Shelby county.

BERTHA HALL
She attended Maple Grove school for eight years, and had teachers Cora B. Lane and Bart L. Herron.
Bertha was the daughter of George and Martha Marlow Mayberry; and granddaughter of Rebecca Marlow and Pink Mayberry.

DORA FREEMAN PERRY
She attended Maple Grove school for four years, and had teachers Bart Herron, Olive Rose Pogue, and Essie Banks Mowry.
Dora was the daughter of David Walker and Effie Dora Mann Freeman; and granddaughter of Anderson and Mary Martin Freeman, and Robert and Margaret Brooks Mann.

IRENE GOODWIN WOOD
She attended Maple Grove school from 1912 to 1917, and had teachers Owen Thomas, D.A. Mays and Daisy Wiggens.
"The Charlie Hines family had several girls in school. When the roads were real muddy, their older brother Paul took them and all the neighbor children to and from school in the wagon."
Irene was the daughter of John and Minnie Mathew Goodwin; and granddaughter of Mr. and Mrs. George Matthew, Sr., and Thomas and Martha Goodwin.

NUMBER 9
District 9 or 172

Number 9 school was located in the southwest quarter of section 26 of Todds Point township.
In 1889, directors were W. H. Monroe and D.A. Dunham.
Some of the teachers at Number 9 were: William Tabor, 1889; Walter Woodrow, 1890; E. K. Jackson, 1891; W. F. Miner, 1892; W.D. Herron, 1893-94; Lola M. Tull, 1899; R.J. Herron, 1901; Bessie Farmer, 1909; Hester Gaddis, 1924; Charles N. Farmer, 1926; Opal Alice Banks, 1927; Dora Freeman, 1934; Clover Hall, 1935; Betty Coventry, 1939; Laveda Dawdy, 1944-46.
Laveda Dawdy was the last teacher with 7 pupils; the directors were Harry Burkhead, Frank Mitchell and Etta Coleclasure.
There were 51 students enrolled in 1899 with an average daily attendance of 36. Some of them were: James Robinson, Ethel Robinson, Lloyd Robinson, Beulah Robinson, Wayne Francisco, Katie Woods, Mollie Woods, Arthur Davis, Alma Trigg, Willie Shaffer, and Trela Shaffer.

RUBY BRADLEY YOUNGER
She attended Number 9 school for 8 years, and had teachers Maud Spicer, Bart Herron, Velma Wilson, and Hester

Gaddis Gaston.

Ruby was the daughter of Hollis and Maude Kelly Bradley; and granddaughter of W.R. and Emma Musson Kelly, and S.L. and Emma Siebert Bradley.

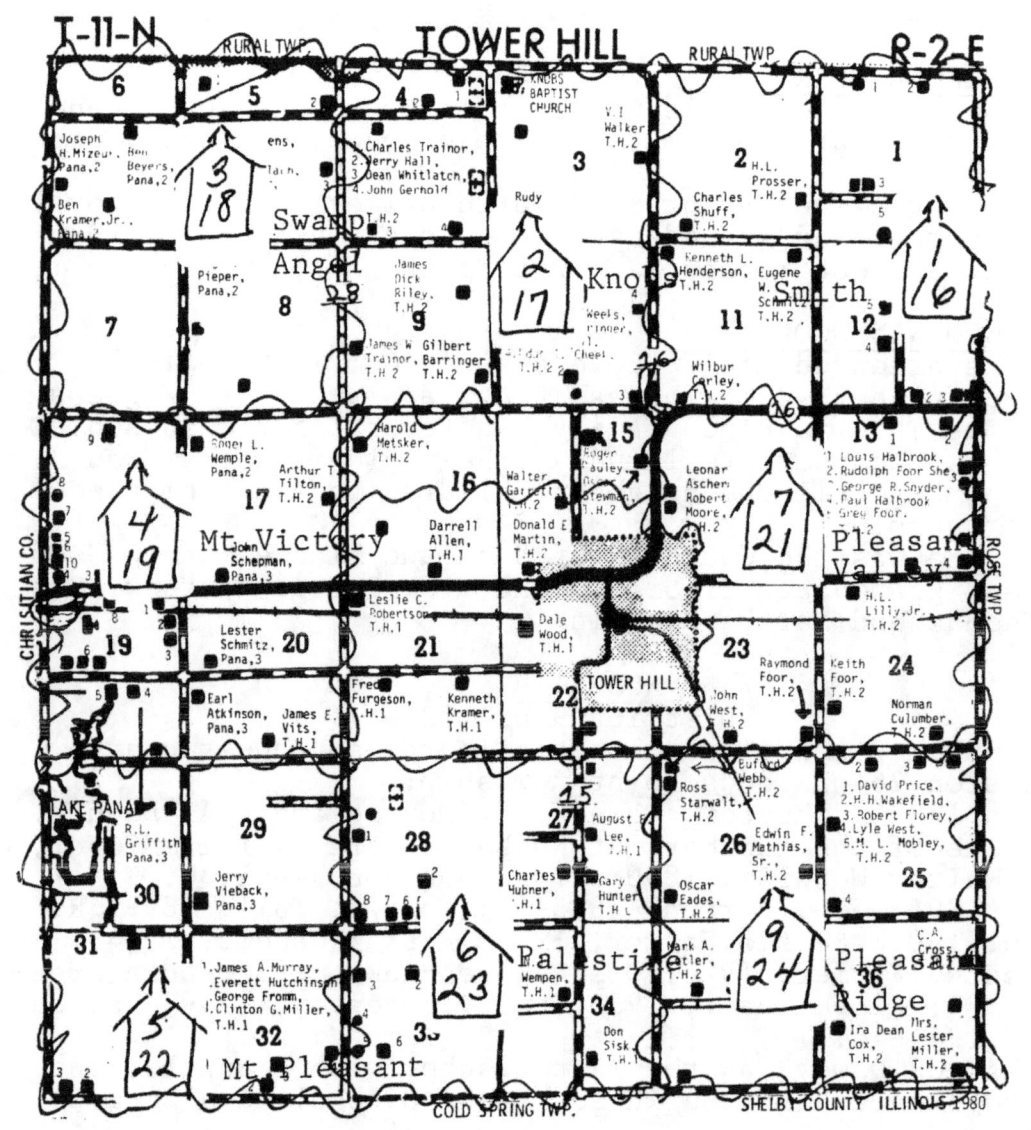

TOWER HILL TOWNSHIP

This township was settled early. At a meeting in Aug. 1849, the township was divided into two districts--district 1, the northern half with sections 1 to 15, and district 2, the remainder. Trustees then were Adam Hart and Washburn Wade.

By 1855, there were four school districts. For district 4, a new school was built that year with a tax of 50 cents per 100, and it was probably near the later day Pleasant

Ridge school in the northeast quarter of section 35 of Tower Hill township. School directors that year for district 4 were William Wirey, William C. Liston and Nathan Puckett. Residents of that district were: William H. Riley, Mary A. Liston, Eli Sprinkel, Daniel Lockwood, John Maddock, John Sharrock, Henry Brownback, John R. Warren, Henry Evey, James Sharrock, Barnet V. Y. Jester, Margrett Shanks, James Branding, Jane Neil, Thomas W. Craddick, John Wirey, William C. Liston, William Wirey, Luther Puckett, Judy Puckett, Nathan Puckett, John Dutton, David Young, John Jones, Zebedee Smith, Sr., and Zebedee Smith, Jr.

In 1863, there were five school districts and by 1876, there nine school districts which remained until school consolidation.

SMITH OR PLEASANT HILL
District 1 or 16

Smith school was located in the northeast quarter of section 16 of Tower Hill township. For building purposes in 1866, taxes were $1.50 per 100, and directors were Samuel Smith and James M. Selby. Three years later, taxes were one percent per 100, and directors were Samuel Smith and Richard Peek.

Some directors of the 1880's were Joseph Smith, A. Simons, G.W. Grisso, and S.S. Dove.

Some of the teachers at Smith school were: Ella Leighty, 1888; Ollie Brown, 1889; W.J. Richardson, 1890; Morton Neil, 1892; Iva Grisso, 1893; Mary Durkee, 1901; Ella Hubner, 1909; Jesse L. Cullumber, 1917; Frank Foor, 1922-24-standard school; Otto Neatherly, 1926-standard school; Edward Jackson, 1927; Rhoda Cain, 1934-35; H.W. Stilgebauer, 1939-42; no school 1943; Rhoda Cain, 1945-46, and Ruth Foor, 1948.

Ruth Foor was the last teacher with 6 pupils; the directors were Burl Shuff, Carrol Smith and Frank Largent.

In 1908 there were 18 boys and 16 girls enrolled in the month of October. They were: Elza Moore, Frank Moore, Alva Thompson, Roy Hudson, Andrew Elliss, John Bassett, Floyd Moore, George Gingery, Abe Elliss, Walter Elliss, Harlie Poteet, Lewie Poteet, Elmer smith, Floyd Smith, John Stockdale, Ross Gingery, Homer Poteet, Elsie Gingery, Hazel Moore, Edna Eliss, Gertrude Lockard, Alta Smith, and Frieda Kerr.

KNOBS
District 2 or 17

Knobs school was located in the northeast quarter of section 10 of Tower Hill township. During the 1860's the school house stood near the Knobs cemetery in section 4 in the southeast quarter. Taxes in 1866 were 50 cents per 100, and directors were J. M. Bowman, and William Read. Three years later, the directors were John M. Bowman, Thomas Walker and John Frank.

Some directors of the 1880's were J.W. Rhodes, L. Warren, T.C. Eiler and J. S. Tilley. A school was built in 1884 south in section 10, and materials cost $400 for the building.

Some of the teachers at Knobs school were: Homer Eiler, 1889; James W. Tolly, 1890; Blanche Connelly, 1891; L.R. Connelly, 1892; Ellen Page, 1893; Otis W. Warren, 1894; Ricka Shoch Kroh, 1901; Ida Leighty, 1908; J. Roy Struble, 1909-11; Pauline Miller, 1922; A.W. Thompson, 1924-standard school-26; Hazel Tilley Christman, 1927; Eula Reed, 1934; E.E. Briggs, 1939-40; Frieda Christman, 1941; Myrtle C. Galbreath, 1942; Amy Angleton, 1943-45; Hattie Glick, 1946; Fred Metzger, Ralph Hayward, Mary Cruitt, Minnie Galster Wallace, Ella Walker, Frank Lane, Elizabeth Whaley, Ida Leighty Graves, Jim Tolly, Nettie Dutton, Arthur Culumber, James Linder, Enid McKinley McElroy, Opal McKinley Potter, Eva Schaehrer Wright and Mary Mathias.

Hattie Glick was the last teacher with 7 pupils; the directors were H. S. Barringer, Ed C. Schoch, and Truman Tilley.

There were 27 students enrolled in 1891. Some of them were: Martha Tolly, Charlie Eiler, John Rhodes, Sallie Callender, Nelse Dutton, Martha Dutton, Olive Eiler, Ida Rhodes, Rosa Aichle, Dwight Eiler and Willie Aichle.

ROY STRUBLE

He wrote the following in 1971 in a letter Mrs. Schoch. He had taught at the Knobs school from 1909 to 1911.

"The first year the school was heated by a large 'pot-bellied' stove that stood in the center of the room. It provided intense heat for those who were close to it; but farther away the rooom was sometimes uncomfortable in cold weather. During the summer of 1910, the school board bought a Smith System heating and ventilating unit. By the way, Smith Systems are still manufactured and sold in neighboring Minneapolis.

The new heater provided for fresh air from the outside; there was a humidifier. I recall how frequently I had to carry water to fill the reservoir that provided for moisture in the air. The entire room was very comfortable. Coal had to be carried from the coal shed that stood just south of the school house and next to the road. I think we burned about 2½ tons of coal each year. The ashes had to be carried out too. As I remember it, the second year we burned about half a ton less of coal.

There was no electricity. I remember some wall kerosene lights around the wall, but they were never used. I've been trying to remember whether there was a clock. There must have been for I don't remember that I wore a watch in those days.

There was a hall (cloakroom) just inside the front door. There were shelves for lunch pails; in cold weather, lunch pails were brought inside. I remember a water cooler. I don't recall that individual cups had been invented then; I know I tried to get a 'bubbling' drinking fountain, but I don't remember that we ever got that far along.

There was a belfry at the front of the building. The bell was rung promptly at 8:30 every morning; tardy bell at 9. I have a very faint recollection that we also rang the bell at 12:30 every day and again at one o'clock.

The windows were covered with very large screen--about 1 inch mesh--to avoid breakage and to deter persons wanting to enter the school illegally.

The floor had to be swept daily. I never heard of sweeping compound I went to college, so I just let the dust rise. I always tied a damp handkerchief over my nose to keep from breathing the dust and I tied another handkerchief over my head to keep my hair from getting dusty.

There were large maple trees on all four sides of the school. They made the school building cooler in the hot weather. At each of the back corners were toilets--boys at the southeast corner, girls at the northeast. Screens weren't known then. The door was right in front, but I can't recall that any problems arose because of a seeming lack of privacy.

We didn't have anything in the way of physical education equipment. No one ever thought of providing balls and bats; we brought those from home. There were no other playground pieces of equipment such as are standard today.

There were a few books in the case, but I don't recall that anyone ever used any of them. Measured by today's standards the school was very poorly equipped, but I'm sure that in the days before my time and afterwards, the Knobs school did a better job of educating the students than they do today with all their extra equipment."

SWAMP ANGEL
District 3 or 18

Swamp Angel school was located in the southwest quarter of section 5 of Tower Hill township. Some directors of the 1880's were David Rau, David Boepple, E. Grogan, and J. H. Kirkpatrick. Edward and Julia A. Grogan deeded land to the trustees in 1889.

Some of the teachers at Swamp Angel school were: T. J. Conner, Rosina Mautz, J.S. Tilley, E.F. Warren, M.S. Andes, John Warren, Gust Reiss, D. H. Evey, S.A. Moon, C. O. Farrell, 1888; C.E. Springstun, E.T. Karls, 1891; Nelson Warren, 1892-93; Emma Fleming, 1892; Lucy Davis, 1894; Lee W. Frazier, Lena Klein, T. H. Cramer, A. L. Leighty, Lydia McKittrick, Rosa Aichele, F. H. Lane, 1901; Fritts Simpson, Fred Evey, 1909; V. N. Barr, 1922; Jewell Pattengale, 1924; Florence

Knobs school taken May 1, 1905. Note the older students among the younger.   Photo courtesy of Shelby County Historical and Genealogical Society

Hall, 1926-27; Mary M. Augellis, 1934; Wilma A. Miller, 1935; Helen L. Borton, 1939-40; Mabel Stockdale, 1941-43.
    Mabel Stockdale was the last teacher with 6 pupils; the directors were Earnest Jones, Charles W. Rau and Clarence Sisk.
    The directors in 1873 were George Truscott, S. Tilley and Dexter Corley.
    Some students who attended Swamp Angel school in 1892 were: Bertha Kirk, Mattie Kirk, Charlie Kirk, Charley Schempf, Harry Barth, Mollie Galster, Carl Leyh, Lizzie Doll, Emma Stewart, Grace Mautz, Rosa Barth, Minnie Galster, Mollie Kirk, Jane Kirk, Lydia Doll, Willie Stewart, Louis Barth, Sue Tilley, Katie Schempf, Ellen Singer, Emma Dinig and Morris Kirk.
    Alonzo Frailey bought the school in 1949. Anna Doll, a resident of Pana in 1982, attended the school before 1900. When she was in the first grade there, there were 34 students enrolled.

MT. VICTORY
District 4 or 19

Mt. Victory school was located in the southeast quarter of section 18 of Tower Hill township. Taxes in 1866 were 60 cents per 100, and the directors were J. R. Warren, A.J. Harwood and John Sharrock. Three years later, taxes were 40 cents per 100, and directors were John R. Warren, and John Sharrock. A new school was built in the year 1870-71.

Some directors of the school in the 1880's were W.C. Farrell, R. H. Read, A.Moon, and Aaron Bonser. Logan and Mary Seitz deeded land to the trustees in 1891.

Some of the teacher at Mt.Victory school were: John Leighty, 1871; Samuel Brown, 1872; Samuel Hanson, John Andes, William Eiler, Gilbert Sallee, John Brown, Ed Lyford, Dexter Corley, John L. Hall, Kate Rayhill, Etta Neil, Ella Powers, Silas Moon, Connie Vincent, Sarah Howard, Lewis Leighty, Alice Metsker, Jesse Mount, Charles Miller, John Warren, Frank J. Snapp, J. D. Peiffer, Charles Faught, G.F. Ledbetter, 1892; Nettie Dutton, Abe Leighty, Nora Brandon, Thomas Higgins, 1893-94; Mr. Hendricks, Mary Leighty, 1891; Harry Bonser, Mr. ? Danielly, Goldie Tressler, Anna Lane Sibbitt, Clemintine Warnick, Thomas Park, Mary Simpson, May O'Farrell, Glapha Seitz, Amy Fry, John Spracklin, Ms. Weakly, Mrs. Tucker, Puella Bonser, Cecil Clegg Evey, Purella Read Beckett, Cora Lane, 1922; Ada Spidle, Ms. Freitag, Bernice Sturgeon, 1924; Gladys Moore, 1927; Noel Nance, 1926; Florence Hall, 1929; Eva Busby, 1901; Jettie Tressler, 1909; H.W. Stilgebauer, 1934; Juanita Moore, 1935; Kathleen Weakly, 1939; Rhoda Cain, 1940; Bertha Howell, 1941; Norma G. Jones, 1942-44; and Ruth Nance, 1945-46.

Ruth Nance was the last teacher with 10 pupils; the directors were Carl Hearn, Everett Laughlin and Perry Metsker.

Ronnie Sweeney bought the school in 1951.

Students who attended Mt. Victory school in 1892 were: Harry Bonser, Glapha Seitz, John Hearn, Rosa Seitz, Bertha Fluckey, Elmer Hanson, Archie O'Farrell, Carlos Seitz, Carrie Seitz, Stella Bonser, Bert and Jed Durst, Luella Bonser, Hettie Reed, Minnie Reed, Anna Watterson, Jesse Phipps, and Vick O'Farrell.

A reunion was held of the school in 1940 in the home of Mrs. Jessee Phipps. Mrs. George Brownback was the oldest student there. Mrs. Charles Sibbitt and Bertha Mc Lane gave an old school dialogue.

MT. PLEASANT
District 5 or 22

Mt. Pleasant school was located in the southeast quarter of section 31 of Tower Hill township. The district was created in 1876.

Some directors of the 1880's were A. J. Foltz, S. M.

Jester, William Osborn and John Weller.

Some teacher at Mt. Pleasant school were: Lou Myrick, 1892; H.S. Fairchild, 1894; Thomas E. Morrison, 1901; Isabel Casey, 1909; Florence Hall, 1924; Nyle Funk, 1926; Hattie Graham, 1927; Juanita Moore, 1934; Hal Guthrie, 1935; T. S. Washburn, 1939; George Weaver, 1940-41; Amy Angleton, 1942; Glenna Dildine, 1943; Ruth Nance, 1944; Beatrice Warren, 1945; and Norma Lee Watson, 1946.

Norma Lee Watson was the lsat teacher with 6 pupils; the directors were James Sellers, Homer Pinkston and Omer McBride.

The trustees sold the school to Harvey O. and Leone F. Walter in 1951.

PALESTINE
District 6 or 23

Palestine school was located in the northeast quarter of section 33 of Tower Hill township. District 6 existed by 1876.

Some directors of the 1880's were: W. R. Liston, A. Gillaspie, Nathan Puckett, B. G. Miller, and George Elben. Benjamine and Sabina Miller leased the land to the trustees in 1898.

Some of the teachers at Palestine school were: Newt Fluckey, 1889; Nettie Miller, 1890; Nellie Fitzgerald, 1891; Lizzie McCormick, 1892; George Lane, 1893; Mary Simpson, 1894; Jesse Fry, 1901; Sarah Finly, 1909; George Tressler, 1917; Selma D. Funk, 1924-standard school-26; Ruby Marie Hiler, 1927; S. Vera Conlee, 1934-35; Hattie Wakefield, 1939-40; Kathleen Cullen, 1941-42; Anetta Jones, 1943-45; Beatrice Warren, 1946.

Beatrice Warren was the last teacher with 6 pupils; the directors were Acle Sisk, William Rueff and Bert Weller.

In Feb. 1938, music was being taught at the school under the direction of Mrs. Ervin Foor in both vocal and instrumental.

Harry Lewey bought the school in 1951.

AUGUST E. LEE

He attended Palestine school from 1920 to 25, and 1927-29, and had teachers Nellie Stretch, Guy Henderson, Selma Funk, Ruby Hiler, and Gertrude Miller.

August was the son of Ward B. and Aletha Flo Osborn Lee; and grandson of John B. and Betty Wheeler Lee, and William and Lucy Wade Osborn.

PLEASANT VALLEY OR FROG POND
District 7 or 21

Pleasant Valley school was located in the southeast quarter of section 14 of Tower Hill township. The school was built in 1871 and opened that same fall. Jacob and John J. Leighty of Tower Hill were the builders.

Some directors of the 1880's were G.W. Grisso, W.J. Pugh, R. T. Hall, E. McCormick, Daniel Sweney, and George Gingery.

Some of the teachers at Pleasant Valley were: Elias Torrence, 1871; George Corley, 1872; Isaih Bryant, 1875; Sanford Tilley, 1875; I.L.Brant, 1876; Cora Lane, 1877; Will E.McCormick, 1877; John Mc Cormick, 1878; Josie Lane, 1879; John McCormick, 1880; Mary O'Brien, 1881; Hattie Milliken, 1882; Alice Metsker, 1882; W.E. McCormick, 1883; Mack M. Lane, 1884; W.E. McCormick, 1884; Ella Leighty, 1885; W.E. McCormick, 1885; A.L. Leighty, 1888; William Richardson, 1889; J.A. McCormick, 1890; C.F. Evey, 1894; Mary E. Cruitt, 1894; Ottis Warren, 1895; Thomas Parks, Jr., 1896; Oma Brant, 1897; Frank Lane, 1898; Retta Park, 1900; Mary A. Weber, 1901; Cora Lane, 1902; FRitts Simpson, 1904; EFfie M. Rueff, 1905; Mary E. Durkee, 1906; Cynthia McKittrick, 1906; Home Stilgebauer, 1908; Purella Beckett, 1917; Howard J. Neil, 1922; Pauline Miller, 1924; Cora B. Lane, 1926-27; Minnie G. Strain, 1934-35; A. W. Thompson, 1939; Emmett W. Culumber, 1940; Rhoda Cain, 1941-42; Faye HOdges, 1943; Marie Kackley, 1944; Nadene Lynch, 1945; and Lois Lilly Himes, 1946.

Lois Himes was the last teacher with 7 pupils; the directors were Raymond Foor, Virgil Urfer, and Nettie Scharher.

PUCKETT OR SHEEPSHANKS OR PLEASANT RIDGE
District 9 or 24

Pleasant Ridge school was located in the northeast corner of section 35 of Tower Hill township. Taxes in 1866 were $1 per 100, and the directors were William Smith and H. M. M. Dowell. Three years later, the taxes were 50 cents per 100, and the directors were William Wirey and John Dutton.

Some directors of the 1880's were James McKittrick, Peter Specht, and D. O. Miller. James and Julia A. McKittrick leased land to the trustees in 1882.

Some of the teachers at Pleasant Ridge were: Lizzie Hall, 1883; Belle Rosenberry, and J.C. Wallace, 1885; Hattie Milliken, 1887; William McCormick, 1888; J.A. McCormick and Maude Tilley, 1889; A. L. Leighty, 1890-91; J. N. Fluckey, 1892; J. H. Sweeney, 1893; Maggie Cleary, 1894; E.B. Christman, 1895; A. M. Cannon, 1896-97; Oliver McCullough, 1898; A.L. Leighty, 1899; Gus Metsker, and H.S. Fairchild, 1900; Augusta McKittrick, 1901; May O. Farrell, 1902; W. A. Baker, 1903; Lois Weeks, 1909; Nellie M. Stretch, 1917; Cora B. Lane, 1924-standard school; John Stockdale, 1927; Nellie Morrow, 1934-35; Rhoda Cain, 1939;

Florence Jones, 1940-41; Hattie Wakefield, 1942; Mary Baumgarte, 1943; no school 1945-46; Bernice Lilly, 1946.
   Bernice Lilly was the last teacher with 2 pupils; the directors were Harve Wakefield, D.E. Bilyeu and Leslie McKittrick.
   The school sold to the American Legion in 1951.

Pleasant Prairie, 1940-41 with teacher Florence H. Jones. Pictured are: back, Arlene ?, Margaret Wicker, teacher, Russell Baumgarte, Virginia Wicker, Nellie Lou Babb; front, Mary Ann Wicker, Rosalie McKittrick, Rosemary Babb, Nancy Wicker, Louis McKittrick and Joan Babb.
                    Photo in author's collection

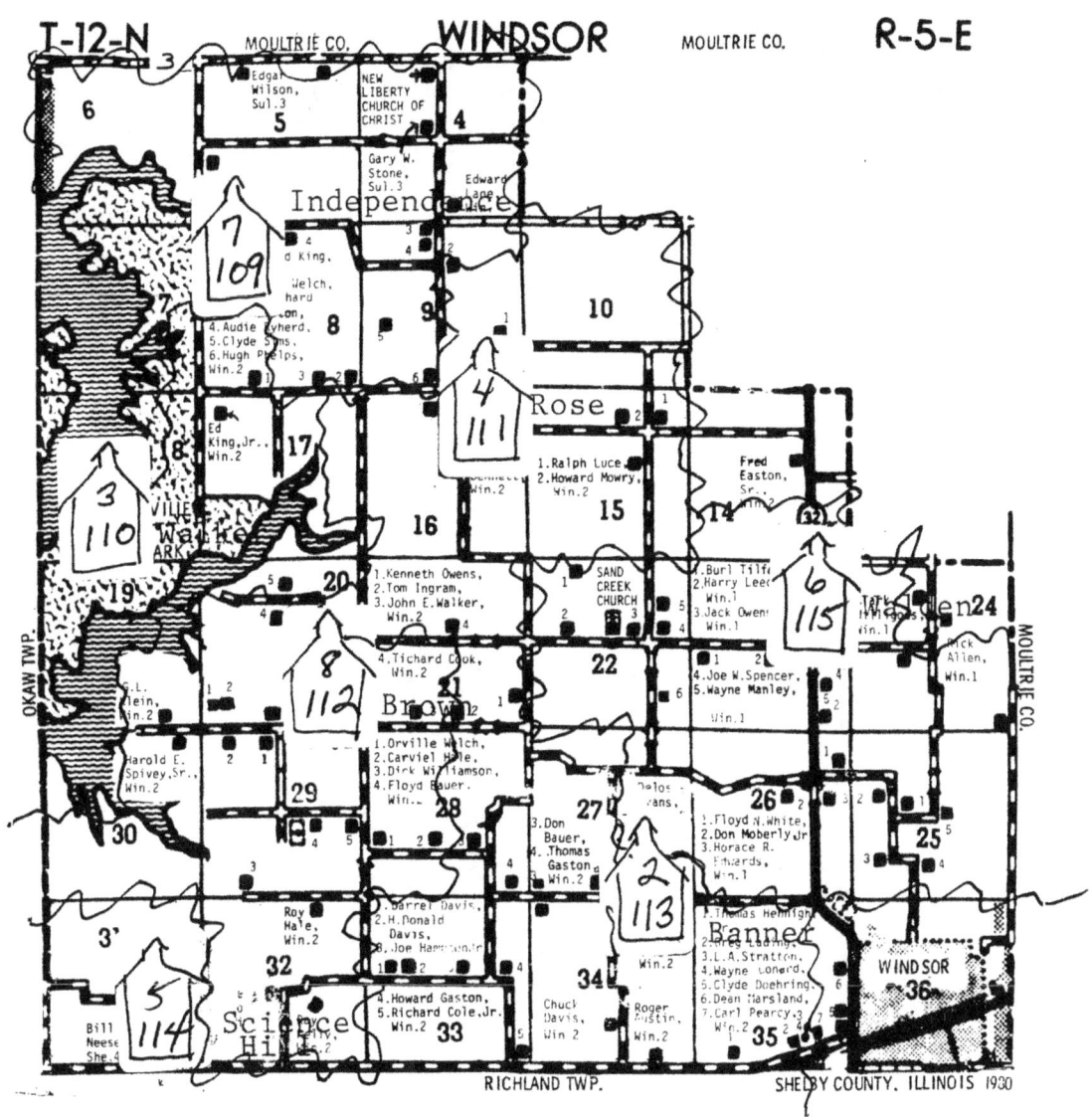

WINDSOR TOWNSHIP

Windsor township had the first school house in 1835 in the Upper Sand Creek area. The teacher the first year was S.R. Davis.

BANNER
District 2 or 113

Banner school was located in the southeast quarter of section 27 of Windsor township. Taxes in 1866 were 3/4 ¢ per 100, and the directors were E.A. Robison and Benjamin Wallis. Three years later, taxes were 50 cents per 100, and the directors were William Davis and Edwin A. Robison.

Some directors of the 1880's were John Walden, John Weger, J.M. Wallis, J.B. Gorrell, and H.T. Walker.

Some of the teachers at Banner school were: Fannie Garrett, 1892; Delia Warren, 1893; Viola Griffith, 1894; E.A. Crowl, 1901; C.C. Guinn, 1909; Ellis Simmons, 1924; Corwin Hamilton, 1926-standard school; Elizabeth Rose Jackson,

1927; Inez Storm, 1934-35; Grace Camfield, 1939; Nora DuHamel, 1940-41; Georgia Summers, 1942; Doris Hampton, 1943; Ethel Dietz, 1944, and Ruth Davis, 1945.

Ruth Davis was the last teacher in 1945 with four pupils; the directors were John Moffett, Horace Doty and Floyd Williamson.

A public sale was held in 1947; items sold included the school site, building, two toilets, one book case, one lot of books, 9 desks, 5 slate blackboards, one piano, one 5 burner oil stove, one furnace and one pump. Horace and Lucille Doty bought the land.

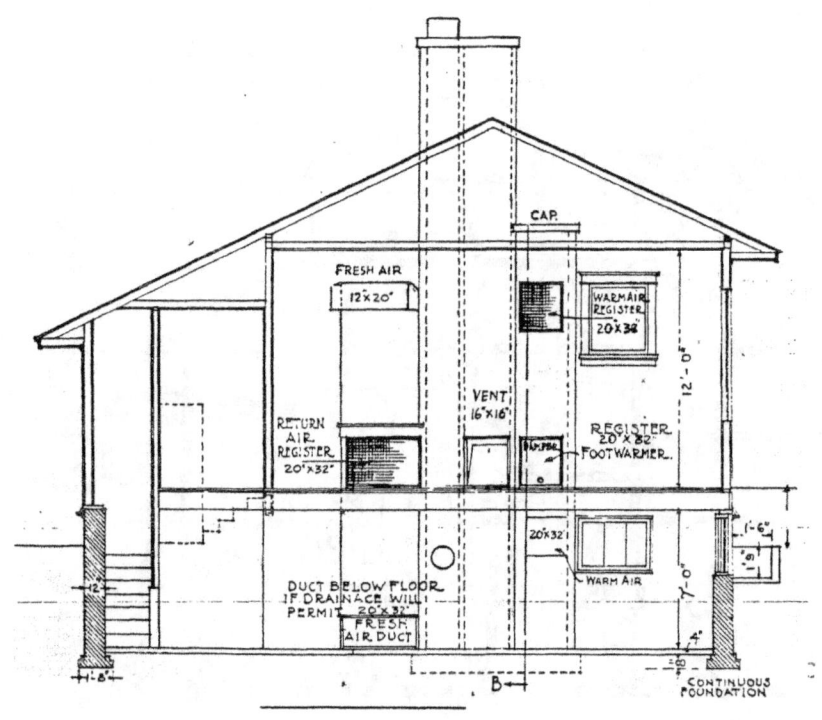

ROBERT O. ROSS

He attended Banner school for five years, and had teachers Gladys Jackson, William Herron, Edna Farrell, and Wilma Rose.

Robert was the son of Amon L. and Myrtle E. Blue Ross; and grandson of L.P. and Katherine Curry Ross, and W. M. and Alice Wade Blue.

WALKER OR SANDCREEK OR RED FOX
District 3 or 110

Walker school was located in the southwest quarter of section 18 of Windsor township. The school was first built in 1866 with three percent per 100 for construction, and the directors were M.V. Quigley, John Shuck, and E. Simpson. Taxes three years later were $1.50 per 100, and directors were W.D. Walker, M.V. Quigley, and Daniel Minor.

The school was appraised at $300 in 1879, and some of the directors in the 1880's were W.D. Walker, Monroe Miner, William Cain and Thomas Miner. Eugene and Mary Quigley deeded land to the trustees in 1885 in the southeast quarter of section 18; by 1894, the school was in the southwest quarter of section 18 on land deeded by G.W. and Mary E. Richardson.

Some of the teachers at Walker school were: E.E. Herron, 1888-89; James Miner, 1890; E.N. Herron, 1891; Della Warren, 1892; E.E. Herron, 1893; Frank White, 1894; William Baker, 1901; Frank White, 1909; Harry M. Robb, 1917; Hester Gaddis, 1922; Mrs. Ava Thompson, 1924; Hester G. Gaston, 1926; Deana Swinford, 1927; T.E. Anderson, 1934-35; Ethel Williamson, 1939; Carolee Herron, 1940; Juanita Graven, 1945-46.

Juanita Graven was the last teacher with 11 pupils; the directors were Ralph Graven, Dexter Mahoney and Joe Dunn.

John O. and Hester G. Gaston bought the property in 1948.

LUZETTA GASTON FERGUSON

She attended Walker school from 1932 to 1937, and had teachers Loy Francisco Herron, Tom E. Anderson, and Mona Chisonol Andrerson.

"Mona Anderson was an outstanding teacher. When I was in the 7th grade, she brought her typewriter from home for me to tinker with. (Can't imagine a teacher today doing that.) She also taught us to appreciate nature, taking us on tours through the woods and pointing out various wild flowers and plants. One day we found a flying squirrel and we had it in a cage inside the school building. Then in time, it died and we had a funeral for it and buried it on the schoolground."

Luzetta was the daughter of John O. and Hester Gaddis Gaston; granddaughter of Ludlow and Sophrona Skidmore Gaston, and Thomas and Melpha West Gaddis; and great-granddaughter of Oliver Burns and Elizabeth Taylor Gaston, John L. and Serinda Mallony Skidmore, George W. and Hester Burns Gaddis, and John and Clarinda Stevens West.

ROSE
District 4 or 111

Rose school was located in the northeast quarter of section 16 of Windsor township. Taxes in 1866 were $2.80 per 100 for repairs to the school, and the directors were John Rose, James Walker and William Goddard. Three years later, taxes were $1.25 per 100, and the directors were William Goddard, James W. Walker and Daniel Shaw.

In June 1879, the school was appraised at $275. Some directors of the 1880's were J. P. Rose, Daniel Shaw, E.C. Clark, T.V. Rose, T. M. Goddard, and John H. Baker. James K.P. and Clarinda Rose leased land for the school in 1896.

Some teachers at Rose school were: T. L. Hilsabeck,

Walker school or Red Fox in 1935-36. Front row, Maurice Herron, Morris Tull, Clara Bell LeCrone, Betty Gaston, Ruth Reynolds, Billie Gaston. 2nd row, Kenneth Reynolds, Don Gaston, Luzetta Gaston, Vada Mae Tull, Thomas Gaston. 3rd row, Evelyn Jordan, Dale Tull, Dale Jordan, Pauline Reynolds, and teacher Mona Anderson.
Photo courtesy of Luzetta Ferguson

1885; W. W. Shoeberger, 1887-88; E.E. Herron, 1890-92; E.P. Chapman, 1893-94; Roy Rose, 1901; Ray Reynolds, 1909; Byron Wilson, 1917; Cecil Hamilton, 1922; Ina E. Rose, 1924-standard school, brick; Juanita Rose, 1926-standard school, brick-27; Margaret Robison, 1934-40; Thelma Collins, 1941-43; Nadene Steele, 1944, and Thelma Gannaway, 1945.

Thelma Gannaway was the last teacher with 11 pupils; the directors were Charles A. Walker, Lloyd E. Lofland, and Fred Walker, Jr.

At Rose school in 1885, students were Willie Guin, age 7; John Guin, age 15; Charley Guin, age 10, and Frank White, age 11. Both Charles Guin and Frank White later became teachers and county superintendents.

Rose school with 12 desks and seats, 6 benches, one

teacher's desk, two chairs, one book case, four pictures, one clock, one furnace, and six slate blackboards were sold in 1947.

RALPH CECIL BAKER

He attended Rose school from 1900 to 1908, and had teachers Webb Rose, and Roy Rose.

"The most memorable event for me was my first day at school. Mother had laid out clean clothes which included what I was used to wearing around home, a dress. I was uneasy as I trotted along the road with my older brothers, Harvey and Rudolph. Sure enough, I was the only boy wearing a dress. Such a razzing I had to take. When the teacher dismissed her pupils for the noon lunch and no one was watching me, I hurried home and announced that I wasn't 'goin' back to that ol' school.' Mother said nothing, but next morning, she had laid out pants, so I dressed properly and began my education the second day of school.

Of the twelve to fifteen pupils usually in attendance at Rose school, I remember best Harley Price, who was about my age, tough as nails, and a real friend in need. My parents often warned their boys, 'If you get a whipping at school, you'll get another at home.' As a first grader, I was an awful coward, so I tried to be as unnoticeable as possible. One day as we pupils were settling in after an exciting noon hour game of baseball, I still had the ball in my hand, and unthinkingly tossed it high in the air. It landed plop on my desk; total silence fell on the room. The teacher was coming, whip in hand, toward me when Harley Price stood up and said, 'Mr. Rose, I threw that ball.' I tried to say no, but my mouth was so dry and stiff only a faint squeak came out. So Harley took my whipping, and winked at me as he returned to his seat. That day I was spared two whippings and became Harley's most loyal buddy."

Ralph was the son of John Harvey and Mary Jane Banks Baker; grandson of William K. and Lucinda Virginia Carter Baker, and Adam and Sarah A. Pope Banks; and great-grandson of John Ashley and Elizabeth Dillard Baker, James S. and Lydia Druisilla Fugate Carter, Chilton and Eliza Shafer Banks, and Peter and Judish Pope.

WALDEN
District 5 or 114

Walden school was located in the southwest quarter of section 23 of Windsor township. Taxes in 1866 were 25 cents per 100, and $1.50 per 100 for building, and the directors were Jacob Grider and James Davis.

Some directors of the 1880's were James Reynolds, Charles Walden, Sam Baxter, Jr., H. N. Walden. Levi P. and Elizabeth Jackson leased land to the trustees in 1896.

Some of the teachers at Walden school were: Belle Record, 1888; Hiram Kensil, 1890; Lolo Tull, 1893; Mellis C.Ellis, 1894; William Huffer, 1901; Grace Douthit, 1904; L.D. Henneigh, 1909; Sadie Morgan, 1922; Lois Grider, 1924; Doris Finley, 1926; Corwin Hamilton, 1927; Laveda C. Dawdy, 1934; Mary A. Furr, 1935; Roscoe A. Hash, 1939-43; Thelma Gannaway, 1944; Lois Jean Bartley, 1945, and Lois Jean Minor, 1946.

Lois Jean Minor was the last teacher with 8 pupils; the directors were Fred Helton, Jake Anderson, and Bruce Hudson.

Students who attended Walden in 1904 were: Florence Anderson, Orva Reynolds, Guy Reynolds, Gertie Lane, Charles Sexson, Albert Cox, Leota Robison, Oda Walden, Gertie Cox, Viola Robison, Marie Walden, Grace Walden, Esther Robison, Claude Waltrip, George Anderson, Hugh Robison, Ollie Cox, Ralph Anderson, Dewey Walden, Edna Cox, Glenn Reynolds, Phynea Sherroll, and Ethel Sherroll.

THEODA WALDEN BAKER
She attended Walden school from 1899 to 1906, and had teachers as cited.

Theoda was the daughter of Harlin and Minnie Walden Walden; granddaughter of Hugh Nelson and Mariah Linton Davis Walden, and William Thomas and Susan Margaret Burns Walden; and great-granddaughter of Hugh and Mary Montgomery Walden, William N. and Nancy Linton Davis, John and Nancy Grider Walden, and Nicholas and Susanna Cann Burns.

YVONNE MAYNARD
"The land for the school was donated by Hugh Nelson Walden, probably in the 1860's. There were at least two different buildings on the site...By 1913, this building was replaced with a larger one, boasting a front porch and cloak rooms on either side of the central entrance way. The teacher's desk stood on a platform, perhaps 8 inches above the main floor. Sometime during the World War II years, the old oiled floor and platform was replaced with a fine hardwood floor. Joy (Hennigh) Caspary recalls that the new floor was a lot of trouble because shoe soles and heels left black marks that the pupils had to scour off with steel wool. By 1950 Walden was closed and the district's children were bused into Windsor. The hardwood floor was sold and removed, but the rest of the building still stands, broken and weather-stained."

SCIENCE HILL
District 6 or 115

Science Hill school was located in the southeast quarter of section 31 of Windsor township. Taxes in 1869 were 50 cents per 100, and directors were B.H. Lovins and James S. Davis.

Some directors of the 1880's were Pat Barry, R.E.

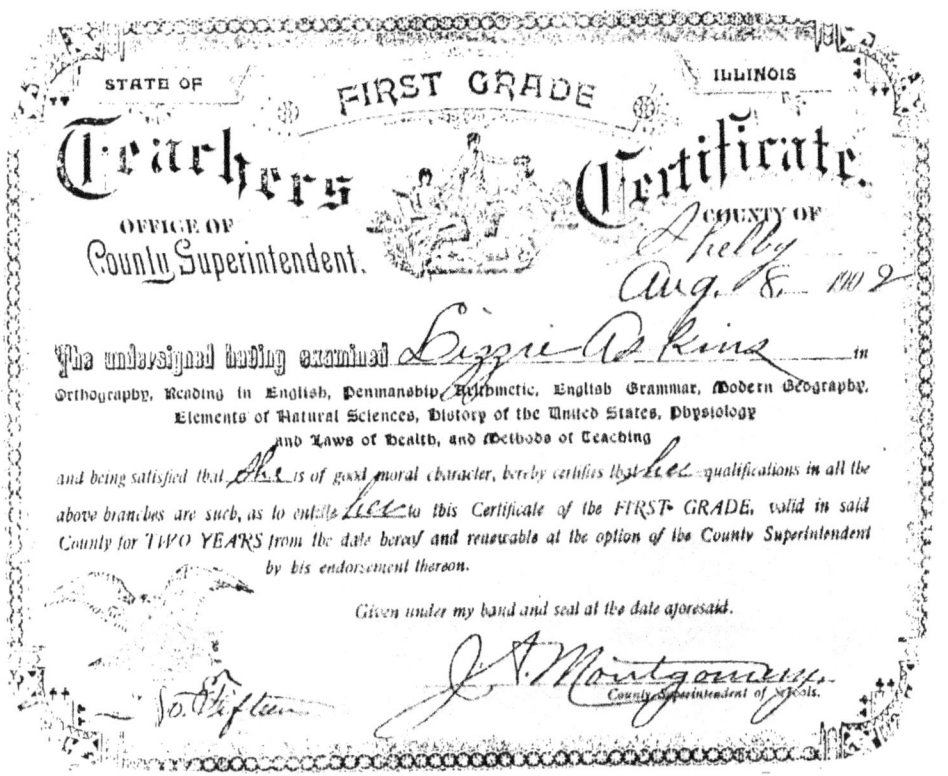

Walker, James S. Davis, William Wallace and Jacob Grider.
Some of the teachers at Science Hill school were: J. M. Tull, 1890; W. Hilligoss, 1891; Hettie Ensey, 1893; Minnie Neary, 1894; J.E. Crockett, 1901; Hugh Hilsabeck, Sr., 1909; Sarah Simmons, 1917; Iva M. Robb, 1922; Thelma Theola Ross, 1924-standard school; Alma Nichols, 1926-standard school-27; Grace Whitacre, 1934-35; Bertha Howell, 1939-40; E.E. Briggs, 1941; Grace Goddard, 1942; Inez Riney, 1943-44; and Ruth Maxedon, 1945.
Ruth Maxedon was the last teacher with 12 pupils; the directors were Harold Curry, Horace Edwards, and William E. Kull.
Science Hill school and all its fixtures--book case, one lot of books, 15 desks, two teachers desks, set of maps, ten slateblackboards, two pictures, pump and flag-- were sold in 1947. H. E. and Hazel Spencer bought the school site.

INDEPENDENCE
District 7 or 109 or 139

Independence school was located in the northwest quarter of section 8 of Windsor township.
Some directors of the 1880's were J. H. Richardson, William T. Neill, G.W. Gaddis, and F. P. Neill. Monroe and Margaret Miner leased land to the trustees in 1895.
Some teachers at Independence school were: H.B. Stine, 1890; Lisa Ellis, 1891; Dora Baugher, 1892-93; Nannie Wilhelm, 1894; Harry Barnhart, 1901; Alma Davis, 1909; Wilna Rose, 1924; Florence Biedert, 1926; Mary Elizabeth Gilbert, 1927; Juanita R. Williamson, 1934-35; Hester G. Gaston, 1937-41; Warren Williams, 1942-43; Juanita Graven,

Science Hill in summer of 1909 with teacher Nellie Gladville. Back row, Elizabeth Lovins, Leta Swiney, Howard Hilligoss, Susie English, Earl Hamilton, Lois Barnhart, and Ferne Wallace. 2nd row, Morris Hilligoss, Delmar Williamson, and Forest Lovins. Front row, Cecil Hamilton and Elmer Williamson.   Photo courtesy of Verna Hilligoss

---

1944; Alta Davis, 1945, and Ruth Martin, 1946.

Ruth Martin was the last teacher with 14 pupils; the directors were Lowell Reese, D.A. Shuck, and Willis Allen.

The school was sold to T.H. Carter of Charleston in 1947.

In 1912, 43 students were enrolled with an average daily attendance of 37. Some of them were: Lola Williamson, Edith Williamson, Blanche Johnson, Bertha Francisco, Minnie Harvey, Margaret Yoakum, Mary Gaddis, Linda Gaddis, Nellie Walker, Bessie Tull, Nora Johnson, Hester Gaddis, Leah Baker, Esther Johnson, Rolla Francisco, Raymond Getz, Walter Walker, Orville Walker, Charles Johnson, Everett Sealock, Johnnie Tull, and John Gaddis.

INA B. CAIN STROHL

She attended Independence school for 8 years, and had teachers Hugh Hilsabeck, Paul Christman, Alma Davis Turrentine.

"I was bashful little girl, and I chewed gum at the school house. My teacher made me stand up and chew before the school."

Ina was the daughter of William and Violet Morris Cain; and granddaughter of E.C. and Elizabeth Morris, and William and Sally Tull Cain.

A reunion of Independence school was held in September, 1937 with 283 present. A basket dinner was held in the grove across from the school. The highlights of the group gathering were talks given by Clarence Tull, and Homer and Murphy Herron.

BROWN OR EUREKA
District 8 or 112

Brown school was located in the southeast quarter of section 20 of Windsor township. Taxes in 1866 were a half percent per 100, and directors were W. H. Brown and Peter P. Warren. Three years later, taxes were $1.30 for a new building, and directors were James Chrisenhall and Peter P. Warren.

Some of the directors of the 1880's were H.W. Brown, W. W. Warren, Peter Robison, and J.T. Warren.

Some teachers at Brown school were: Thomas H. Tull, 1888; S.H. Wallace, 1890; W.W. Griffith, 1892; Will Inman, 1893; Minnie Neary, 1894; Thomas L. Griffith, 1901; Elsie Rose, 1909 (school now called Eureka); Marguerite Edwards, 1924-standard school; Bernice Lane, 1926-standard school; Edna Farrell, 1927; Mabel B. Smith, 1934-35; Inez Storm, 1939; Warren Jackson, 1940; Florence Biedert, 1941; Hester Gaston, 1942-45, and Nadene Fugate, 1946.

Nadene Fugate was the last teacher with 8 pupils; the directors were Ward Warren, Alva Reynolds, and Medford Neatherly.

The school was sold to Edna and Lavena Ferrell in 1949.

Some residents of the school district in 1894 were: Layfayette Baldwin, C.D. Baker, C. M. Brown, Charlotte Chase, Henry Cox, Sam Chrisenhall, W.B. Ellis, James Florey, T.J. Guinn, H. K. Harris, D. M. Hudson, J.W. Harris, J.H. Johnson, A.E. Lovins, P.H. McVey, William J. Mahoney, James A. Moberly, J.L. Nance, W.S. Proctor, J.W. Roberts, Peter Robison, W.H. Rose, Sarah Robison, W.S. Steed, J.B. Tull, B.D. Tull, J.W. Tull, P.P. Warren, W.W. Warren, John Weger, W.L. Wood, R. M. Walker, and P.T. Warren.

Brown school in 1894-95. Photo courtesy of Margaret Bruns. Class shown with teacher Minnie Neary.

Eureka school 1941-42. Back row, Hester Gaston, teacher, Polly Neatherly, Jr. Goddard, Mack Davis, Frank Warren. Front, Annette Spencer, Kay Reynolds, Earl Stevens, Betty Jewel Neal, Paul Mummel, Joe Spencer.
Photo courtesy of Luzetta Ferguson

OTHA LEE MILLS

Otha attended Center school in Big Spring township for 8½ years from 1910 to 1919, and had teachers Mable Coons, Sylvia Beals, Zelma Haskett, Wade Steel, Jimmie Lucas, Vesta Carlisle, and Sadie Morgan.

"Only incident I remember in my early years of school. I was rather small. One of my early teachers had to answer nature's call. In those days that meant a trip out back, and some of the older students locked her out. She couldn't get back in the school house. She, being one of the first year teacherss, was young and timid. I remember she went out back of the school building and cried."

Otha was the daughter or son of William Benjamin and Blanche May Shumard Mills; grandchild of Gilbert Terrel and Mary Shelby Baker Mills, and Amos Oliver and Malissa Alice Harper Shumard; and great-grandchild of Benjamin Bentley and Catherine Figgins Mills, William and Nancy Davis Baker, and Lige Harper.

TEACHERS AND MISCELLANEOUS
Chapter Five

The oldest list existant which identifies people as teachers was the document petition to the Shelby County Board of Supervisers dated Aug. 22, 1876. The names are or were in alphabetical order but their particular school for that year was not given.

Those individual teachers were: A.F. Allen, J.L. Andes, M. Barbee, J. Barton, M.M. Barnhart, F. Burns, B. Campbell, J. Christman, J.O. Chisenhall, S.F. Corley, C. Cutler, Lizzie Cobb, Mary Cobb, G.W. Durand, Carrie Deery, Mary Eddy, E.A. Fritter, Louisa J. Fry, Jennie L. Foster, B.H. Gain, G.F. Gratton, J.A. Goodan, J.A. Hilsabeck, T. Hilsabeck, W.S. Hogeland, J.H. Hill, O.A. Hott, Anthia D. Harper, Mary Humphrey, Lizzie Jolly, J.T. Jones, J.F. Kull, Joanna Kinney, F. Lindley, G. Lindley, Mary C. Longenbaugh, Josie Lane, Georgie McIntosh, W.W. McVay, J.E. McTaggart, C.J. Miner, J.A. Montgomery, S. Moon, Mollie Myers, Mary E. Myres, Ella C. Neff, Kittie Oller, Dora Oller, Laura Patton, W.H. Ragan, E.A. Richardson, A. Roberts, T.L. Rose, J.S. Tull, Laura E. Roessler, Emma Steidley, Lizzie Springston, Belle Stephenson, C.W. Tallman, B.W. Travis, W.H. Turner, Netta Woods, Rachel Woods, Hattie Whittington, K. Garvin, Emma Oliver, Mary Hannaman, Anna B. Huffer, Lucinda Wilson, S. Carrie Wilkins, J.B. Walker, J. Wallace, W.O. Wallace, R. Small, E.F. Warren, N.C. Robinson, Mary Payne, Mary Chapman, Amanda Gallagher, Josie McClosky, Maude Flowers, Barbara Stilgebower, Mollie Caldwell, Allie J. Yost, W.C. Graybill, J.W. Sharrock, J.T. Knox, W.T. Reed, W. McKittrick, J.H. Hagan, M. Fitch, C.W. Steward, M. Rose, L.M. Padget, G.R. Graybill, P.C. Buchannon, J.A. Patton, J. Stufflebeam, C.F. Toby, T.N. Robinson, F. Leathers, J.C. Woods, C.J.

Brown, D.T. Knowles, and G. Cooper.

During the year 1885, the typical examination for state certification of teaching had the following: reading, 2 hours, including etymology, phonetics, etc.; English grammar, 2 hours; geography, 2 hours; U.S. history, 2 hours; school law, 2 hours; civil government, 2 hours--included an essay on Illinois; astronomy, and geometry, 2 hours.

A typical program for early Shelby county institutes for teachers would be something like this: 6 March 1886, Professor John C. Cook of Northern Illinois Normal will give a lecture in Shelbyville on Friday evening. All teachers of the county are expected to attend. The program for the next day included a reading circle led by J.F. Christman; a discussion led by Z.P. Ferguson; a talk by C.W. Tallman on the sociability of teachers; a talk by Miss Ida Hogeland on relations between teachers and directors, etc. This particular program was organized by Lee W. Frazer, R. M. Herron and W.B. Marshutz.

Fifth Annual
Rural School Music Festival
Shelbyville, Illinois, October 12, 1935
AUSPICIES MUSIC DEPARTMENT OF WOMAN'S CLUB

Mrs. Douglas Shoaff, Chairman.

HIGH SCHOOL AUDITORIUM

PART I

Rural School Contests, 9-12 A. M.

EVENTS

I. Onward Christian Soldiers: (School Song) to be sung from memory. M. M. quarter note, 108-112. The LeBosquet silver cup is awarded to the winner of this event.

II. Any group number chosen by the teacher, including harmonica—time limit four minutes.

III. Individual performance, vocal or instrumental. This class is divided into two groups—first to fourth grades and fifth to eighth grades. Each selection to be performed from memory, time limit two minutes.

IV. Hymn playing from the following: "Joy to the World," "O, Come All Ye Faithful," "Keller's American Hymn," "Onward Christian Soldiers" or any such hymn.

V. Duets—vocal of instrumental. These numbers must be two part compositions, time limit two minutes.

VI. Original composition.

VII. Posters to be displayed at the Festival.

VIII. Story of Johann Sebastian Bach.

IX. A prize will be given to the school entering the most events and making the best score in the opinion of the judges, according to quality of work.

PART II.

Group of sacred songs—to be selected.

St. Paul's Children's Chorus of Strasburg (45 voices) William A. Kramer, Director.

Walther's Prize Song from Die Meister Singer—Wagner. Arr. by A. Wilhelmy—Dean Christman (Mrs. Mildred Holloway McConnell, accompanist).

Folk Dance—Carolyn and Bruce Penwell—Beecher City.

Solos—John Norman, Decatur, Illinois, Supervisor of Music, Shelbyville Schools (Mrs. McConnell, Accompanist).

Greetings from Dr. D. E. Lindstrom—University of Illinois, Department of Agriculture, Extension Service.

Tap Dance—Jean Chihak—Cowden (John Hawk at the Piano).

O Sole Mio—Neopolitan Street Song—Eduardo Di Capera. Serenade—Schubert—Robert Stiarwalt (baritone).

Violin Selections—Madelyn Pygman—Graduate of Millikin University, Decatur, Illinois.

"School Days Dance" by "Cowden Caperers"—Jean Beaumont, Delmar Lockart, Rosemary Moore, Betty Pat Fry, Norma Perryman, Carolyn Penwell and Bruce Penwell.

Announcement of Winners and Awarding of Prizes—Mrs. F. C. Bolinger

Rural School Choruses: Keller's American Hymn, Joy to the World, O' Come All Ye Faithful.

The Festival has been arranged by Mrs. Dudley Chaffee, Chairman of Music in Rural Schools, National Federation of Music Clubs; Assisted by Mrs. C. E. Walker, Local Chairman, Mrs. D. L. Shoaff, Chairman of the Music Club, Mrs. Kenneth F. Kelly, Sec. and Treas. and Chairman of Registration, Mrs. Frank C. Bolinger, Chairman of Prizes, Mr. John Hawk, Chairman of Judges, Mr. Lewis Craig, Chairman of Poster Judges, Miss Martha Wright, Chairman of Publicity, Miss June Boys, Pres. of Schubert-Cottlow Junior Music Club, Chairman of General Arrangements, Mr. John Hawk Chairman of Exhibitions, Mrs. Mona Anderson, Chairman of Teachers Committee and Miss Barbara Downs, Chairman of Merry Melodiers Helpers.

Since the beginning of the Rural School Music Movement in the Shelby County Festival of 1932, the idea has been taken up by 20 of the 46 musically organized States in this Country with much success and enthusiasm. Because of the interest and influence of the County Superintendent of Schools, Franklin County, Kentucky, that couty is to have a Music Supervisor for the Rural Schools to prepare them for the Festival which will be a county wide event at first, later to extend to the whole State. The latest calls for help and advice have come from Loup City, Nebraska in the drouth area and Clarksdale, Miss. Illinois has to its credit: Victrola Chorus in Will County; Musical Training at the Teacher's Institute in Peoria County; Traveling Library in Sangamon County which is routed through the County Superintendent's Office; and a Supervisor of Music in several rural schools in Macon County. Shelby will have to improve if it is to maintain its leadership. In the five years of special musical activiity new pianos have been placed in a number of Rural Schools in this County and many old instruments put in usable condition. Some fine musical talent has been recognized, some remarkable talent discovered and given an opportunity for development. Do you consider this worth while and are you willing to help more in the future than you have in the past to get the most out of these opportunities which will not last always? TEACHERS AND PATRONS ARE URGED TO COME TO THE REGISTRATION ROOM IMMEDIATELY AFTER THE PROGRAM FOR A SHORT CONFERENCE. SHALL WE HAVE THE FESTIVAL AFTER THE DISTRICT INSTITUTE IN 1936?

A BIG THANKYOU

To all who responded to the questionnaire in one way or another. The following individuals returned the form but did not attend the rural schools. Thanks also to them.

Unidentified teacher of
 Roley school, 1920-21
Mary E. Alton
Charles Sherman Anderson
Norma Jones Barber
William F. Barkhurst
George Wilson Bauer

Gertrude Mickey Beyers
Violet McArdle Bieber
M&M Charles Bolyard
Paul N. Bremen
Helen Bilyeu Bright
Isabel and Marie Bruns
M&M Robert Campbell

Wanda Compton	M&M John Kilhoffer
Ginny Crum	Mary Jones Maze
M&M Lewis Dugan	Mrs. Clarence Neeley
Edna Fickes Fisher	Henry A. Peterson
June Frede	Rodell Radcliff
M&M Kenneth Funk	Frances N. Richardson
George Glasscock, Sr.	M. Rohlf
M&M George B. Gray	Delia Lape
M&M Gilbert Grinnell	Katie Sarver
Grace Hartwig	Annetta M. Smith
Lucy Heady	M&M Charles Stockman
M&M Earl Hopkins	Jerry D. Storm
M&M Kenneth Hunter	Elvira A. Tefft
Robert Jackson	Helen McDonald Thompson
Edith Rickett Johns	Frances Wall Tipton
Robert L. Jones	Evelyn E. Wilkins
Juanita Hartman Kepley	M&M Gladys Wise

Herbert Witbart

Late additions to the work:

Opal Brownlee attended Summitt school in Cold Spring and had teachers Gloyd Duncan and Victoria Peifer. She attended for three years. She was the daughter of Lewis and Rhoda Bechtel Banning; granddaughter of Andrew and Belle Hopkins Bechtel, and great-granddaughter of Melinda Hopkins.

Jessie Landers attended Pleasant Union or Dog Prairie and had teachers Flora Moore, Orthal Tate, Burl Moon, Dorothy Corley, Genevieve Rogers Corley. She attended for 8 years. She was the daughter of Rachel Rogers Syfert and Simon Syfert; granddaughter of David and Armenda Myers Rogers, and Noah and Catherine Friesner Syfert.

Lewis D. Howe attended Center school in Lakewood township and had teachers Del Banning, Hazel Howe, Ray Hudson, Gleason Cosart, Naomi Kirk, Nellie McConnell and Bertha Baird. He was the son of Berlin and Tracy Moore Howe; grandson of S.A.D. and Grace Roland Howe, and John L. and Melcena Cosart Moore.

A SPECIAL THANK YOU to Carolyn Christman Hart for the loan of her copy of RURAL SCHOOLS OF ILLINOIS, a 1929 publication of the state of Illinois.

Please check all spelling variations of the surname.

INDEX

Note: Names may be given with first initial or first name whole. Women teachers may be listed under maiden or married name.

Abbott family,11; Louisa,84.
Abercrombie, Bernice,38;Ella, 38;R.F.,37.
Abraham, Harley,127;Lola,127; Noma,125;Ross,127.
Ackart, Mettie,186.
Adams, C.C.,138;Lee,156;Huston,156;Noma,112;Pearl,79; Reginald,119;Thomas,113;W. J.,102;William,136,156.
Adamson,Ephraim,101.
Affleck, Mary, 8.
Agney, Robert,115.
Ahl, Clara,130.
Aichele, George,109;Rose,153; 192,193;Willie,192.
Akers, H.H.,36;Joshua,40;M.J., 36;Mary,40;Thornton,40.
Akins, John H.,71;Samuel,25; William H.,71.
Albin, Alice,163;Frank,163; Pearl,163;Sam,163.
Alday,Robert, 181;Tom,181.
Aldridge,Myrtle,73.
Alkire,Elizabeth,120;Ernest, 173;Lizzie,173;Lorena,173; Oscar,173.
Allen,?,142;Belle,92;Charles, 106;E.B.,95;Edna,144;Elgar, 112,153;Flora,161,168,179; Florence,21,90,147;Glenna, 55;Henry,86;Jean,94;Jedediah,86,96,144;Joe,94;John, 144;Kathryn,94;Letta,96; Louise,106;Lucy,106;Mariah, 17;Mary,94;Meletta,97;Mr., 114;Pauline,123,187;Richard,94;Ruth,94;Sarah,96; Thomas,60;Violet,60;Willis, 206.
Allied Gun & Rod Club,138.
Allison,J.S.,36.
Alsop,Ethel,100;J.J.,99.
Altag,Chris,133;Haman,133;Sophia,144.
Alverson,C.H.,126;Ruth,119, 177.
Alward,Howard,126;Ruth,170.
American Legion,62,198.
Amlin,Bruce,181;Effie,181;Estella,181;W.S.,161.
Anderson,Agnes,133,136;Albert, 43;Andrew,181;Catherine,45, 133,135;Charles,136;Florence,204;Frank,136;Fred,45; George,38,204;Hans,45;Jake, 204;Mabel,172;Mary,73,84, 138;Mathias,45;Mrs.,180; Mona,96,112,168,201,202;Nettie,99;Ralph,204;Rita,48, 133;Thomas,96,113,116,148, 149,158,160,170,201;Ruth, 136.
Andes,John,195;Lenore,126;M. S.,193.
Andrew(s),?,142;Charley,106; David,106;Grace,139;Lucille,139;Lulu,106;Malcolm, 182;Marie,139.
Christy,Andrick,125.
Angel,Willie,74.
Angell,Robert,40.
Angleton,Amy,192,196.
Anion, Anna,144.
Antioch school,148.
Archey, Clem,70;Gloyd,116,148, 181;J.W.,54;Maude,52;Virgil,70.
Arganbright,Cora,86;Sylvester,85;Wayne,87,171,185.

Arledge,Charles,28;James,28; John,28.
Armstrong,Beverly,118;Jasper, 175;John,118;Naoma,175;William,101.
Arnold,Frank,100;Nathan,45.
Ash,David,54.
Ashbrook,Grant,113,146;Lizzie,37,127;Minnie,37.
Ash Grove school,32.
Ash Grove township,29.
Askins, Addie,56,58;Burl,68; Cleve,65;Clyde,67;Elbert, 67;Ina,59;J.J.,67,74;J.L., 66;James,64;Lizzie,64;Onie, 65;Orletta,163;Reuben,64; Ruby,65;Walter,66;Willie, 129.
Assumption school,153.
Atkins,Elizabeth,25;Lemuel, 25.
Atkinson,Don,127;John,123; Opal,119;Thomas,123;William,123.
Atteberry,Fay,171;Seripta, 124.
Auer,C.G.,175.
Augellis, Mary,194.
Augenstein,Anna,168;Arthur, 163;Daniel,137;Pearl,163; Raymond,136.
Auld,Ada,161;Clara,68;Emma, 168,185.
Aurand,Josie,179.
Austin College,21.
Austin, Alexander,27;Henry, 27;Honoria,119,120;Lucinda, 27;Minerva,136;William,71.
Ayers,Hattie,128;Musa,74.

Babb,Joan,198;Nellie,198; Rosemary,198;T.H.,54;W.N., 53,54.
Baber,John,92.
Bailey,A.W.,136;J.W.,95,100; O.C.,19;Samuel,138.
Bailey school,138.
Bain, Frank J.,51,52.
Bainbridge,Jennie,183;Thomas,183.
Bair, Lois,166.
Baird,Bertha,67,68,71,73,90, 99,164;Claire,120;DeForest,120;John,71,114,145; Mary,121.
Baker,C.D.,207;Charles,46; Clarinda,20;Elizabeth,134; Evan,42;Fannie,77;Faraba, 45;George,119;Harvey,203; Isaac,120,177;J.P.,163; John,201,203;Leah,206;Leroy,95,136,137,138,163;Marie,38,47,146;Mary,209;Mr., 182;Ralph,203;Ray,85;Renaldo,46;Rudolph,203;Samuel,47;Theoda,204;Thomas, 92,142,143,180;W.A.,197; William,201,203,209.
Baker school,42.
Balch,Felix,26;Jane,26;John, 26;Monroe,26;Silvester,26.
Baldwin,Arnold,65;Harley,65; Lafayette,207;Uriah,137.
Bales,Raymond,53.
Bandy,Florence,150,152;John, 152;Sherman,150,152.
Banks,Adam,203;Chilton,203; Mary,203;Essie,113,188; Opal,189;Verna,114,123.
Banner school,20,31,199,200.

Banning,Alexander,68;Angie, 68;Arwilda,68;Bessie,74; Charles,68;Charlotte,68; Clark,66;Delbert,74,78,88, 96;Eddie,67;Fred,68;H.D., 71;John,68;Joseph,68;Lorenza,66;M.L.,67;Maria,108; Myrtle,68;Noel,66;Rayburn, 67,68;Susannah,66;Thomas, 66;Walter,108.
Bantner,Marilyn,123.
Baptist,Leota,149.
Barbee,Blanche,90;Clifford, 90;Eddie,108;G.M.,85,188; George,187;Hazel,16;John, 126;Lois,90,128;Lucille, 165;Mary,126;Maxine,114; Milton,5,15,16,17,18,84; Myrtle,126;Otto,185;William,126.
Barber,A.D.,73;Charles,102; Edna,103;Nellie,102.
Barden,Ebenezer,64.
Barker,?,142;Bertha,20;Callie,20;Daniel,24;Elizabeth,24;Ethel,136,146;Ferne,20;Glen,180;Herbert, 180;Hiram,24;Irma,20;J.R., 20;Jay,20;Joe,185;O.O.,5, 20,21,108,142,182.
Barlow,John,108;Louie,108.
Barnes,Henry,138;Laura,134.
Barnhart,G.C.,161,169;Harry, 205;Lois,206;M.,91,95,115.
Barnett,Elizabeth,86;Hazel, 155,156;Vera,157.
Barr,Joe,84,85,90,95,134, 135,137,163,166;V.N.,193; Valette,112;William,113, 114.
Barrett,Agnes,74,166;Earl, 47;Ethel,58,59,53;Eva,65, 71,163,164;Grace,164;John, 38,44,46,95;Leah,26;Mary, 26;Viola,66,74,170;Rachel, 26;Samuel,26.
Barrickman,Arel,148;J.S., 148;John,148;Maria,16; Nora,158,164,168,181,185.
Barringer,H.S.,192.
Barrow,James,67;P.L.,67.
Barry,Edward,36;Pat,204.
Bartels,Lucille,81;102.
Bartha,Harry,194;Louis,194; Rosa,194.
Bartholmey,Conrad,135.
Barthrick,Daniel,6;Eliza, 6.
Bartimus,Clifford,123;George,48;Grace,48;William, 48.
Bartlett,John,99.
Bartley,Fern,145;Lois,40, 204.
Barton,Charley,65;David, 64;Edna,79;Harley,65;James,64,65;Lester,65,183; Lizzie,64;William,64.
Bartow,Lucille,52,53.
Bartscht,Sara,99,101,102; Wenzel,99.
Basil,Joseph,163.
Bass,Alva,128;Lyda,95;Vida, 76.
Bassett,John,191.
Bassler,Pauline,80,81.
Basye,M.M.,6.
Bateman,Opal,130.
Bates,Bertha,156;Cora,156; John,156;Maggie,156.

NOTE: Chapter Five is not included in the index.

213

Battershell,Ruby,165.
Batton,Harold,107.
Batty,Homer,128;Jesse,128;
　Maude,128;Minnie,128;Myrl,128.
Bauer,Anthony,164;Christian,146,163;Floyd,142;
　Joe,166;John,146;Orval,
　136;Otto,146;Ralph,37;
　Victoria,163,164.
Baugher,Dora,205;Nina,47.
Baumgarten,Conea,146;Emma,
　81;Lewis,134,146;Mary,
　198;Orta,133;Rachel,146;
　Russell,198.
Baxter,Ella,113,114A,114,
　155,156;Fred,86,115;James,
　38,114,115,116,187;Newton,
　114,115;Sam,203;Theodore,
　117,158;W.C.,46;William,
　114,115.
Beal,Samuel,94.
Beals,Archibald,45;Eliza,45;
　Goldys,137;John,45;Maud,
　45,137;Ora,45,136;Ruby,47;
　Sylvia,209;Walter,71.
Beaman,Mary,116.
Bean,John,182;Nellie,180.
Beasley,Bertha,135.
Beattie,Isabella,27;Mary,27;
　Sarah,27.
Bechtel,George,55;Glapha,168;
　Rosella,52,55,56,58,59.
Beck,Ales,136,181;Benton,110;
　Cecelia,146;Claude,42,133;
　Effa,84,133,138;George,109;
　James,24;Joseph,119;Nancy,
　24;Roxana,138;Thomas,24;
　William,24,119.
Becker,Arnold,45;Fred,78,79;
　Omer,79;William,79.
Beckett,Arthur,109,166;Elgel,
　108;J.A.,54;Jessie,76;John,
　108;Pearlie,76;Purella,159,
　173,175,195,197;Sam,109;
　Tressia,76;Vernie,166;Willie,76.
Beecher City,137.
Beem,Lewis,164.
Bee Ridge school,164,165,183.
Beery,Christian,170;Dosha,
　150;Israel,77;John,149;
　Marvin,161;Mary,77;Susan,
　77;Theodore,170.
Beeson,Hannah,116;Henry,116.
Behl,Jean,172.
Behler, Henry,175.
Beitz,Freda,123.
Beldon,Beatrice,81,82;Burl,
　40;Dale,41,142;Dean,40;Grace,40.
Bell,Clara,58;George,40,58;
　Maria,58;Thomas,42.
Bemis,James,48.
Bender,Grace,73.
Bennett,Burl,31;E.P.,33;Emma,
　107;O.R.,35;Sarah,40;William,33,40;Willie,59.
Berkley, Shelly,115.
Berry,Emma,150;Louise,161;
　Loula,170;Ruth,187;Susie,
　161.
Berryman,William,149.
Besing,C.F.,137.
Bethel school,85,86,87,111,
　113.
Betts,Hattie,31;Mrs.William,
　31.
Beyers,Gertrude,187.
Bible,Bert,117;Lena,117.
Bickner,E.,80;William,80.
Biedert,Florence,99,115,172,
　205,207;Henry,148;J.A.,158.
Biehler,Louie,114.

Biggs,Fern,170;J.M.,184;Robert,186.
Bilyeu,D.E.,198;George,124;
　Nancy,124.
Bingamon,John,31,33,36,38,
　142;Robert,35,37,45,47;
　Rose,136.
Binion,W.F.,71.
Birdsell,Gertie Kingery,86.
Birkey,Mary,113A.
Bissen,Elias,64.
Bitner,Samuel,39.
Bivens,Guy,183.
Bjurstrom,Gertrude,40.
Black,Robert,144;Sadie,120;
　Thomas,144.
Blackerby,Helen,61;Roscoe,
　61;William,61.
Black Log school,68,163.
Blackstone,Dan,157;Fern,157;
　Hiram,114,157.
Blackwell,Edward,52;Mattie,
　52.
Blanchard,Carrie,81.
Bland,Austin,59;Lois,120;Ray,
　188;Thomas,34.
Blasdell,Frank,187.
Blauvelt,A.L.,135.
Blomquist,O.W.,46.
Blue,Erasmus,133,134;Myrtle,
　200.
Blystone,Anderson,42;Emma,36.
Blythe,Alfred,44;Ezra,44,133;
　Francis,44,106;G.W.,44;Hettie,44;Jon,34,37,135;Seth,
　44.
Boden,Mildred,38.
Bodine,Eva,52;George,84;Ora,
　185.
Boehm,Glenn,72.
Boepple,David,193.
Bohlen,Minnie,40;Peter,101;
　William,102.
Boilings Springs school,57,
　58,67,68.
Boise,Edna,84;Nanna,136.
Boldman,Rebecca,26;Ruhana,26;
　William,26.
Bolds,G.,133.
Boldt,Adolphus,172;James,48;
　Ray,48.
Bolen,Edna,138;Ruth,38.
Boles,Lydia,139.
Boley,Cecil,82;John,82.
Bolin,Anna,174;Leonard,188;
　Mabel,174;Orval,174.
Boling,Clem,31.
Bond,Hazel,105.
Bone,Camellia,123.
Bonser,Aaron,195;Harry,195;
　Luella,195;Puella,195;Stella,195.
Boon,W.J.,3.
Boon school,114,114A.
Boone,Ferne,55,164.
Borton,Helen,194.
Bowman,Addie,65;Benj.,158;
　C.S.,65;C.T.,51.66;Caleb,
　26;Caroline,26;Elizabeth,
　82;Gerald,70;Glen,70;Howard,158;Isem,26;John,158,
　191,192;S.,158.
Boyce,Lucille,45,81.
Boyer,Freda,123;G.K.,120.
Boys,Alexander,114,153,161;
　Carrie,153;Dewitt,159;
　Fabian,159;Floy,159;Homer,
　153;James,153;John,148;
　June,179;Kate,148;Nina,159;
　Ruth,114,153,163,164;Wilkinson,159;153.
Boys school,153.
Bowser,Ida,110;Roma,110;Rosa,
　110.

Brackin,J.H.,34.
Braden,Ezekiel,119;George,
　120,127,161.
Braden,Lora,115.
Bradley,Arthur,156;Charley,
　156;Clarence,156;Hollis,
　190;Ila,156;S.L.,190.
Brady,Juanita,100;H.D.,98.
Brahm,Bertha,158.
Branding,James,191.
Brandon,Mattie,72;Nora,54,
　56,163,175,195.
Brandson,Viola,86.
Brandt,Clarence,139.
Brant,A.M.,36;Neddie,30;
　Oma,197.
Breckenridge,Odell,172.
Brednow,August,133.
Breeding,Charles,77;Fay,77;
　James,174;Richard,174;
　Wayne,174;Zelma,172.
Brehm,G.L.,158.
Brehmer,Cho,133;H.J.,133.
Brewer,Joshia,149;Ruth,149.
Brewster,Jeff,14.
Bridges,Helen,38,46,47.127;
　Leota,38;Roy,38.
Bridgman,Geneva,77;Guy,77.
Bridgwater,Albert,102;Christian,102;Levi,102.
Brightman,James,112.
Briggs,Effie,168,192,205.
Brimley,W.,173.
Brinker,Adam,127.
Britton,Doris,86;Edna,165.
Brockmeier,Dorothea,144.
Brooker,Bannam,168;Fanny,
　54.
Brooks,J.P.,10;Margaret,189.
Brookshire,Bessie,81,82.
Broomfield, ?,142.
Brown school,207,208.
Brown,Ada,137;C.J.,53;C.M.,
　207;David,85,86;Edith,80;
　Edna,159;Elmer,91;Ethel,
　37;George,95;Herschel,42;
　J.C.,106,107,153,158;Jacob,55;James,61,84;Jeanne,
　55;John,52,195;J.F.,32;J.
　J.,31;Joseph,31;Lucy,52,
　53;Mildred,96,97;Ollie,51,
　175,191;Parson,114;Polly,
　52;Samuel,195;Violet,35;
　W.H.,207;W.A.,146.
Brownback,Mrs.George,195;
　Henry,191;S.H.,172.
Bruce,George,37.
Brule,Gladys,81;Norbert,81.
Brumfield,John,53.
Bruner,J.M.,149.
Brunken,Eula,174;Fred.176;
　William,176.
Brunner,Elizabeth,158;Jacob,
　158.
Bruns,Fred,137;John,107;
　Margaret,98,99,117,208;
　William,99.
Brunswick,149.
Brunswick school,148,183.
Bruster school,186.
Bruster, Thomas,186.
Bryant,Edgar,61;Ethel,131;
　Isiah,197;James,61;John,
　68;Morgan,56;Lydia,27;
　Malinda,27;Ruth,119;Sarah,
　27;Urana,56;Uriah,181,182;
　William,61,62.
Bryson,Arthur,174;Goldie,116;
　James,115;John,115;Nellie,
　116;P.R.,115;S.A.,77;W.D.,
　115;Zelma,113,113A,114A,
　115.
Buchanan,India,37;Lola,109;
　Mabel,173;Olive,37;Samuel,
　52,53,56,65.

Bucher,Joseph,66.
Buck,Lemuel,102.
Buckeye school,158.
Buckingham,B.F.,51.
Buckner,H.W.,60.
Bud Ward school,157,158.
Buell school,109.
Buesking,Carl,144;Curtis,
  144;Henry,144.
Bugenhagen,Caroline,172.
Buller,J.,52.
Bullerman,Ed,127;George,
  138;H.,98.
Bullington,Reatha,93,96,182.
Bullock,Lydia,103.
Bumgardner,Barbara,56;Ella,
  99,105;Frona,54,105.
Bunch,Felix,52.
Bunker,Elizabeth,86.
Burchfield,Ed,136.
Burdick,J.K.,65.
Burger,Ava,158.
Burgner,Alfred,77,177;Amy,
  77;Christopher,77;Fred,77.
Burk,Ada,92,98,138,173,180;
  Etta,173;Ross,149;Nettie,
  92.
Burke school,99.
Burkhead,Harry,189.
Burnett,Keziah,152;Mary,80,
  179.
Burns,B.F.,31,32;Hester,201;
  Nicholas,204;Susan,204.
Burrell,Roy,37;Sophia,96.
Burris,J.T.,60;J.S.,53;Thelma,165,166.
Burrows,George,120.
Busby,A.C.,148;Eva,195;Nettie,
  86.
Bush,Daniel,96.
Bushar,Ferne,130.
Butler,Bob,73;Elsie,73;Joseph,2,36;R.H.,19.
Butts,Perlina,155.
Byland,T.C.,95.

Cain,Rhoda,52,106,148,191,
  195,197;William,201,207.
Callender,Sallie,192.
Calvert,Cora,148;May,149;
  Sidney,148;William,148.
Calvin,L.G.,81.
Camac,William,102.
Camic,Ellen,142.
Camfield,Grace,32,200;John,
  161;L.E.,187.
Campbell,Edward,11;Edna,95;
  J.C.,37;J.F.,55;Jemina,78,
  90,95;Lide,36;Nathan,79;
  S.C.,91;William,81.
Campfield,Lizzie,168.
Cann,Susanna,204.
Cannon,A.M.,197;D.C.,35;Lillie,173.
Carder,Henry,163;John,116,
  187.
Carey,Isaac,45;J.H.,46.
Carlisle,Vesta,66,68,72,130,
  130,161,209;W.A.,65.
Carlyle,Emma,126.
Carnes,Cora,85;Frank,64;Joe,
  108;John,159;Lily,183;Maggie,159;Mattie,159;Thomas,
  182;Wallace,170.
Carney,Joshua,105.
Carpenter,Georgia,17;H.C.,
  149;Lorin,150;Ralph,150.
Carr,Fred,150;Grace,130,168,
  172;J.W.,135;Lura,150;Melba,130;Nella,172,173,175;
  O.S.,153;S.B.,148,149,158.
Carroll,?,152;Edith,62;Eula,
  152;Frank,119;Rolla,163;
  Roscoe,101,119;Roy,128.
Carruthers,Carl,37,42,43,46;
  Emma,35;G.R.,37;Gertie,37;
  John,33,35,37,38;Lulu,36,
  37,42;R.N.37,66;Stella,37.
Carsell,William,181.
Carter,James,203;Joseph,112,
  163;Ruby,92,100,163;T.H.,
  206;Virginia,203.
Cartmell,Eliz.,173;Ike,173;
  Isaac,173;Jennie,173;Mollie,173,177;T.W.,173;Warren,174;Wendell,174.
Cartwright,Yvonne,149.
Carey,John,46.
Cary school,46.
Casey,Chloe,131;Isabell,196;
  James,79;John,16;Melvina,
  155.
Cash,C.C.,31.
Caskey,George,56;Jesse,146;
  Lois,52,61.
Casner,Ginla,177.
Caspary,Joy,204.
Casstevens,E.N.,40;Edna,71;
  J.D.,71;J.M.,39;Julia,40;
  T.J.,40.
Cavender,Oscar,188.
Center school,45,54,64,67,
  108,109,123,174,175,183,
  209.
Certin,John,80.
Chadwick school,76,77,157.
Chadwick,William,76.
Chafee,George,11.
Chamberlain,A.L.,109;Barbara,110;D.W.,38;Egbert,109;
  Ernest,38;Pete,109;Wilmer,
  109;Zelpha,62,95,96.
Chambers,?,142.
Champion,J.R.,36.
Champion school,65,68,69,158,
  159,160,175,176,177.
Chaney,Florence,177;Hollie,
  177.
Chapman,Bessie,47;Earl,115;
  Ed,113A,114,115,202;Fanny,
  134;Raymond,115;S.R.,114.
Chapplear,Charles,45,46,47,
  135;Lola,46,137.
Charleston,206.
Chase,Charlotte,207.
Chatham,Louise,147.
Cheney,John,106.
Cherry,Andrew,57,58;Charles,
  56,57;Clara,57;Dr.T.E.,57;
  George,56,58,69,57;J.Harrison,56,57,58;James,57;Lillie,56;Marie,56,58;Pearl,
  56,58;Sarah,56;William,116.
Cherry Grove school,84,122,
  123,124,125,151.
Chesshire,Joseph,174,177.
Chisenhall,G.W.,84,91,181;J.
  O.,32,37.
Christenberry,J.J.,143.
Chrisenhall,James,207;Sam,
  207.
Christian county,81,124.
Christie,Tom,79.
Christman,Dollie,109;E.B.,
  197;Frieda,48,192;Hazel,
  192;Louis,115;Marilou,163;
  Paul,96,116,133,143,144,
  148,153,185,186,207.
Christner, Joe,164,182.
Christy,Ida,74,67;James,74;
  Stella,164,170.
Churchill,Edith,128,130.
Cihak,Bessie,68;Frank,180;
  John,135,180;Mary,180;Willis,135,170.
Cisna,Kathleen,177.
Civil War,2.
Clagett,N.W.,99.
Clara,Ella,84.
Clarage,Nathan,112;Wm.,112.
Clark,Effie,35;Eliz.,54,60,
  109,201;Frankie,148;George,109;Georgia,53;Mary,
  124;Osia,109;Rachel,109;
  William,109.
Clarksburg,69.
Clarksburg school,157.
Clarksburg township,84.
Clausen,Henry,71,87,168;
  Robert,153.
Clary,Ella,71.
Clawson,Calvin,24;Daniel,
  24;Dean,33;Fay,33,36;
  Frank,33,44,136;Henry,
  96,97;J.F.,35;Jack,33,37;
  James,24,37;John,24,47,
  42;Levi,24;Nancy,33,24;
  Nellie,35;Sarah,24;Sylvester,32,33,37,45;Wm.,
  33,24.
Clay,C.P.,112;Emma,116,
  185;James P.,85,120,158,
  170,182.
Claypool,Ruth,149.
Clayton,Phoebe,16.
Cleary,Ella,98,163,180;Maggie,65,67,164,186,197.
Cleason,Mary,108.
Clegg,Cecil,173.
Cleland,T.E.,16.
Clem,Inez,31,37.
Clements,America,27;Christiana,27.
Clesson,Fred,186;Samuel,
  182.
Cline,A.L.,135.
Clinkenbeard,T.B.,163.
Clipston,Joe,102.
Clucas,Blanche,109.
Cly,Lena,57.
Cobb,Mary,65.
Cochran,Agnes,76;James,24;
  Edna,178;Georgia,76;J.H.,
  32;Jefferson,24;Juna,76;
  Laura,82;Mace,178;Robert,
  76;W.C.,75.
Cohea,Frank,135;Orval,135.
Colbert,Charles,31,33,35,37,
  40,42,102;W.B.,45,78,79.
Coldspring settlement,1.
Cole, ?,142;C.E.,125;Ed,127;
  Ellen,142;George,127;Hanna,102;Hazel,128;May,127;
  Pearl,119;Ronald,128;Sammy,127.
Coleclasure,Etta,189.
Coleman,Clarence,60,108.
Coles county,8.
Coles,Gov.Edward,1.
Collins,Daniel,144;Edward,
  142,144;Genevieve,144;
  Ivel,62;Thelma,202;Virgil,
  144.
Collum,Gov.,15;Joyce,150.
Colson,William,39.
Colston,William,137.
Combest,Albert,106;Anna,
  106.
Compton,C.E.,91;Charles,96;
  Clara,88;Elva,93;George,68;
  Jonathon,86;June,93;Leverett,92;May,108;Mell,86;
  Rosemary,96;Royce,93;Russell,96;Verda,93,94.
Cones,William,164.
Conlee,Helen,175;S.Vera,196.
Conley,D.S.,125;Jennie,125;
  Roy,125.
Connelly,Blanche,176,192;L.
  R.,192.
Conner,Absolom,7;Charles,77,
  101,126;T.J.,193;W.W.,94.
Connor school,81.
Conrad,Opal,34.
Consolidation law,4.

Constitution,school law of 1870,3,4.
Cook,Carrie,144;H.,143;Kathryn,163;T.L.,92.
Coons,Jacob,45,46;Mabel,209.
Cooper,Ms.,126;Gertrude,168,170;Thelma,128,165,168;Velma,174.
Cope,Mattie,109.
Coplin,Abraham,182;Jacob,179;Lizzie,164.
Copperas school,46.
Cordray,Dorothy,130;Noble,130;Woodrow,130.
Corley,A.J.,53;Addie,61;Alice,182;B.B.,51,52,53,54;Billy,58;Bryant,26,27;C.,59;Caniel,62;D.C.,51,52,53;Daniel,62;Dexter,194,195;E.C.,169;E.O.,128,158;Edith,65,128;Elias,26,27;Eliz.,66;Ella,51;Elmer,61;Elson,130,151;Elvina,53;Etta,59;Frank,59;George,53,197;Jean,58;Jimmy,58;Levi,15,62,128,131;Lizzie,182;Louella,61;Lucille,128,129,158,159;Lydia,125;M.C.,56;Mabel,66;Mary,131;Nathaniel,131;Nelson,147;O.C.,159;Owen,59,62;S.F.,51,52;William,60,66;Willie,61;Willis,52.
Corley school,58,59,110.
Corneil,Harriett,51.
Corrington school,81,82.
Cosart,Ella,71;Franklin,71;Henry,71.
Cothern,Hazel,56,62.
Cotrel,Thomas,128;Zena E,128.
Couch,John,182.
Coulter,Charles,38;Katie,36;Nell,121.
County school report,9,10,12,13,19,21.
Courtesy,Agnes,65.
Courtright,Archer,158;Blanche,158;H.C.,158;Jesse,100;Myrtle,158.
Coventry, Betty,189.
Cowan,J.W.,105.
Cowden,57,58,64,110,183.
Cox,Albert,204;Edna,204;Ethel,126;Floyd,119,121;Gertie,204;Guy,123,121;Henry,207;Isiah,126;Leota,36,37,170;Mary,163;Minerva,57,58;Mora,126;Ollie,204;Opal,135;Pearl,51,52;Ralph,96,138;Ruby,119;Ruth,123;Walter,126.
Crabtree,Ruth,176.
Craddick,Thomas,191.
Craig,Jasper,52,53;John,152,159;William,148.
Craig school,175.
Crain,Betty,119;Fannie,119.
Cramer,T.H.,182,193.
Cranmer,Irene,173.
Craven,Laura,126.
Crawford,George,107.
Creekmur,John,51,54,170;Wm.,50.
Crenshaw,Mary,40.
Cresswell, Arch,163.
Critchfield,W.F.,170.
Crockett,Alma,36;Frank,33,36,37,42;J.E.,205;John,38.
Cronin,Ellen,80;Maggie,177.
Crook,S.S.,180;Sherman,153,168.
Crosby,George,106.

Cross,Edward,47,159;Everett,85;G.W.,35,42;J.D.,94;James,42;Joseph,158;Mamie,45;Stephen,40;Verna,85;Violet,44;William,159.
Crouch,Forrest,60;Nellie,54.
Crowder,Earl,56,105;Edith,147;John,147.
Crowl,E.A.,120,187,199;Henry,116,157.
Cruitt,Mary,192,197;V.B.,181,188.
Crumb,Eliz.,86.
Crume,Belle,37.
Cruthis,Darrell,47,115.
Culberson,H.L.,54;Eula,108;Maxine,127;Ora,119,125.
Cullen,Kathleen,196.
Culumber,Arthur,192;Emmett,197;J.W.,157;Jesse,191;William,127;Marion,100.
Culp,Etta,57,59,175;J.F.,56.
Culver,Donald,48;Edward,101;Joyce,48;Kathleen,48;Ruther,136.
Curlin,Clarence,65;Onie,65.
Curry,Bruce,51;Ed,40;Harold,205;I.J.,39;Jennie,37;John,31;Katherine,200;Lavina,40;Lois,40;Nora,33;Samuel,98,143;Walter,40;William,40.
Curry school,31.
Curtis,Fay,33,146.
Cusaac school,179,180.
Cutler,Aaron,168;Elmer,107;James,9;John,168;Margaret,9.
Cuttill,Ralph,112.
Cvengros,Bernice,177.

Dagen,Andrew,160;Jacob,160.
Daily Union,176.
Daisey,Lizzie,87.
Dalton,Bertha,120.
Danelin,Arthur,86.
Danhke,Elizabeth,137.
Daniel,Laura,108.
Danielly,Mr.,195.
Daniels,Amanda,88;J.B.,36;Marion,88;Nathan,134;Thomas,134;Tonia,134.
Danneberger, Charles,56,153;Harry,153.
Dappert,Dwight,48;Frances,137;Jacob,138;Otto,47,48;Ward,47,136,138.
Darst,Leela,52.
Daugherty,Deloris,43;John,42;George,43;H.B.,72.
Daughtery school,47.
Daughterly,Verla,176,177.
Dautenhahn,Dorothy,47,133.
Davis,Alma,205;Alta,206;Arthur,189;Bert,173;C.M.,59,61;Charles,96;Eva,52;Fannie,166;Francis,115,179;James,203,204,205;H.H.,182,184;Harlan,89;Harry,90;Helen,172;Howard,96;Hugh,66;James,164;Jeff,124;John,53;Lucy,193;Mack,208;Mariah,204;Martha,156,157;Mary,100,120,170;Nancy,209;Nellie,90,163;Ruth,187;S.R.,84;Rollin,91;Rosemary,93;Ruth,115,116,200;S.R.,199;Samuel,96;Velma,58;W.L.,157;William,96,199,204.
Davidson,D.C.,172;Francis,181;Titus,181.
Davlin,Art,58.

Dawdy,A.J.,161;D.J.,112,161;John,161;Laveda,112,156,189,204;Martha,187.
Dayhuff,Alverda,95.
Dazey,James,112;Jennie,172;Joseph,112;Lizzie,112,113,158;William,112.
Deal,E.,137;John,58;Lamora,58;Lucinda,58;Washington,58.
Dean,Chester,82;Harriet,170.
Dearing,Dr. W.P.,21.
Dearman,Kenneth,36.
DeBaun,Bert,173;E.S.,106,
Debrun,M.B.,148.
Decatur,124,144.
DeGarmo,Carrie,122;Prof,13.
Deitz, ?,142.
Demoss,C.H.,80.
Demonbun,C.T.,149.
Denton,F.O.,71;Margaret,68;S.,77.
Derrick,Betty,150.
Derry,Aster,182.
Devore,David,72;Eleanor,137;Elijah,165.
Dewar,Wayne,31.
Deweese,Hiram,184;Laura,184.
Dewitt,Earl,152;Roberta,152.
Dickey,Harry,53.
Dickinson,Harland,143,183.
Dickman,Elsie,78,79.
Dickson,Isaac,34;Isabel,40;Joseph,172.
Diefenthaler, Lois,107,110;Sarah,110.
Diehl,Celia,95;Ellia,85;James,92;Fern,170;Mary,40,
Dietz,Ethel,38,200.
Dildine,Geneva,87;Glenna,138,196.
Dill,Alleva,67,71,72.
Dillard,Eliz.,203.
Dillon,Mary,82.
Dinig,Emma,194.
Dittoe,Bertha,181;L.B.,179.
Ditzler,S.J.,184.
Dixon,George,112.
Dixie or Tennessee school,110.
Dobbins,Thomas,148.
Dobbs,Molly,54;Thomas,60.
Doding,F.,133.
Dodson,Evelyn,108;Ichabod,7,112;Louisa,62.
Doehring,Clarence,33;Elmer,146.
Dog Prairie school,61.
Doll,Anna,194;Codfrcy,35;Lizzie,194;Lulu,37;Lydia,194;Shirley,42,46.
Dollerhide,Abs.,6.
Domas,Cora,168,169;Darvin,76.
Donahue, John,45.
Doner, Henry,51,54,56.
Donnel,Ben,113A;Cora,148;Eliz,131;Glen,153;J.H.,102;Mrs. Lewis,158;Oran,156;William,8.
Doser,Charles,116.
Dosh,Charles,187.
Doty,Horace,200;Lucille,200.
Douglas school,177.
Douthit,A.E.,180;Bertha,143;Carrie,142,143,185;Dora,143,180;Effie,120,180;Elmer,180;Francis,28,180;George,28;Goldie,180;Grace,169,204;Harlie,180;Irving,168,180;J.E.,186;J.M.,185;Jasper,14;L.N.,180;May,180;Pearl,180,185;Rhoda,185;William,28,180,185.

Dove,E.F.,100;S.S.,191.
Dow,Benjamin,126;Mary,54,59.
Dowell,H.M.,197;Helen,65;
  Myra,56,65,67;Simon,64,66.
Downey,Richard,46.
Downs,Daniel,7,173;Dessie,
  186;G.W.,153;Georgia,168;
  Hary,186;Loyd,186;Samuel,
  149;Vida,168.
Doyld,William,133.
Doyle,B.F.,102;C.A.,108,106.
Drain,May,106;R.S.,106.
Drake,Edna,40;Ethel,40;Rachel,40;Ralph,40.
Drenen,Cyram,26;James W.,26;
  John,26;Joseph,26;Luvena,
  26;Robert,26;William,26.
Drenning,Hiram,27;Robert,
  27.
Duckett,Levi,65.
Duddleston,Nelson,135.
Duduit,Kathryn,110;Mildred,
  108.
Duever,Lena,48.
Duffy,Alfred,37;Mae L.,37;
  Susan,37.
Dugan,Belva,42;Dugan,Mattie,
  66,166.
Dugout school,115,116,117.
DuHamel,Nora,200.
Dumont,William,100.
Dunaway,Carl,73;James F.,55;
  James R.,73;Thomas,99;Richard,73.
Duncan,Clair,79;John,79;John
  G.,55,56,66;Joseph,1;Susanne,79.
Dunham,D.A.,189.
Dunkel,Anna,131.
Dunlap,Claude,108,138;Jesse,
  99;Walter,138.
Dunn,Joe,201.
Durand,A.M.,84.
Durbin,Frances,157;Jesse,181.
Durham,Mrs.W.T.,103.
Durkee,G.R.,127;James,148;
  Laura,7,158;Lizzie,122;
  Mary,164,191,197.
Durst,Bert,195;Enid,180,181;
  Eula,183;Jacob,91;Jed,195.
Dush,Charlie,72,74,163;Lizzie,65,71;Willie,71.
Dutton,Abram,161;John,191,
  197;Martha,192;Nellie,195;
  Nelse,192;Nettie,192;T.R.,
  100.
Duvall,Edward,47;Lucy,114,
  155.
Dye,Alfred,169.

Eads,Eston,53;Rhea,53.
Eaglin,Earla,106.
Earp,James,112.
Eash, ?,184.
East Center school,118,119,
  120,121.
Easton,Marjorie,40;William,
  26.
East Salem school,18,157,
  181.
Eberspacher,Christian,177;
  Edward,177.
Eby,Jacob E.,114,115;John,
  114A,Sally,114A,115.
Eckard,Nona,106,110.
Eckart,Anetta,55,163,170;
  Nellie,52,85;Sallie,58,68,
  72,74.
Eddy,William, 65.
Edgar,Nelle,115.
Edmiston,Fannie,120.
Edwards,Hazel,35;Horace,205;
  Marguerite,207;Niniah,2.
Egbert,Samuel,7.

Eiler,Charles,192;Dwight,192;
  Homer,192;Olive,192;T.C.,
  192;William,195.
Ekiss,Cora,120.
Elam,Dora,136;Joel,135,136;
  L.D.,45;Robert,136;T.L.,45.
Elben,George,196.
Elbert,Florence,91;Max,85;
  Victor,91.
Elder,Maurine,182.
Ellington,Catherine,157.
Elliott, ?,184;Bell,91,133,
  150;Florence,138;Ira,181;
  William,84.
Ellis,Abe,191;Andrew,191;
  Bernice,72;C.R.,31;Dorothy,
  35,143;Edna,191;J.,36;Jessey,24;John,183;Katherine,
  183;Lillie,100,101,32,143;
  Lissa,31,205;Mella,84,120,
  204;Nannie,177,179,180,182;
  W.B.,207;W.F.,84;Walter,
  191;Z.B.,142.
Ellison,Kenneth,80.
Elm Flat school,31,33.
Elm Grove school,126,133,163,
  162.
Elmers,Noble,118.
Elmore,Jessie,173.
Elm Spring school.
Elson,Lloyd,33.
Elwell, Maggie,54.
Emery,John,105.
Empire school,157,173,174.
Emrich,Jacob,92.
Endsley,Maynard,67.
Enfield school,187,188.
Engel,Frieda,147;Sara,159.
English,Susie,206.
Enoch,Marjorie,188.
Ensey,Hettie,47,205.
Ensminger,Andrew,143.
Erisman,Nellie,80.
Ernst,Casper,175.
Ethridge,Edward,73;Sarah,73.
Ernest,Nathaniel,122;Sarah,
  122.
Eureka school,207,208.
Evalt,Henry,116.
Evans,Burl,73;John,80;L.D.,
  79,80,81;Ulmont L.,66,161,
  180.
Evens,Julia,24;Nancy,24;Robert,24.
Everett,Vera,134,138,181.
Eversole,Bessie,150;David,
  151;Harley,78,151;Harold,
  150,151;Harvey,150;Jacob,
  151;Orville,153;Pearlie,
  150;William,151.
Evey,Allis,7;Captolia,59;C.
  F.,64,197;Cecil,195;D.H.,
  193;Drucilla,7;Edward,2,5,
  7,8;Fred,193;Henry,7,191.
Ewing,Harry,42.
Excelsior school,172.

Faderer,Arthur,169;Clinton,
  169.
Fairchild,H.,65,196,197;H.R,
  50;Homer L.,51.
Fakner,Daniel,175.
Falk,Elizabeth,147;John,136.
Fame school,80.
Fancher,69,91,96.
Fancher,John,94.
Fanson,Ethel,177;John,174.
Farley,Jeff,40.
Farmer,Alta,127,120;Bessie,
  189;Charles,112,125,127,
  155,156,189.
Farr,Inez,38.
Farrell,C.O.,193;Edna,200,
  207;Lavena,207;May,197;
  W.C.,195.

Farrier,Ruth,59.
Faucett,C.T.,136.
Faught,Charles,195.
Faulkner, ?,58.
Faust,Sylvester,85.
Fayette County,105.
Fear,Fannie,123.
Fearman,J.A.,113;Sally,6.
Featherstun,Cora,164.
Federman,Harold,79.
Feery,Alice,79.
Fellers,H.W.,51;Supvr.,60;
  William G.,52;William M.,
  51,52,54,55,59,61.
Feltringer,Margaret,138.
Fenton,Mollie,46,138,170.
Ferguson,Anderson,40;C.H.,
  31;Fayette,133;John,33,
  37,38;Florence,40;Luzetta,
  201,208;Ruth,37;Westwood,
  37;Zachariah,32,37,40,142.
Ferrell,Edna,32;Irene,35,37;
  May,51.
Fickes,Chris,79;Don,80.
Field,Arloa,90,93,94,98.
Figenbaum,Harriett,47;Henry,
  36.
Figgins,Catherine,209;Edward,172;Fielden,44,172;
  Gaylord,133;Helen,172;
  Henry,172;John,44.
Findlay,188.
Findlay-Assumption blacktop,
  158.
Fink,Ben,109;Glenda,109;
  John,109.
Finkbine,Ann,65.
Finks,Arthur,65;Cleo,65;
  Isaac,65;Lonnie,65.
Finley,Doris,115,204;Ella,
  54,56,163;Sarah,196.
Fischer,Olivia,110.
Fisher,Anna,145;Edna,80;
  Eliza,153;Forest,86;
  Isabella,54;James,26;
  Jessie,108;John,26;Nancy,
  26;William,26.
Fitzgerald,Nellie,47,175,196.
Flaharty,Marguerite,159.
Flanders,Moses,164.
Flat Branch school,36.
Flat Branch township,75.
Fleming,Allie,120;Anna,162;
  Carrie,84;Charles,5,18,19;
  Fleming,Edna,87;Emma,84,
  85,193;Homer,18;Jean,87;
  John,84,181;Joseph,18;
  Linder,183;Mary,18;Maud,
  183;Minnie,92,114,138,164;
  Orville,81;Peter,182;Roy,
  18,80,168;Samuel,18,181;
  Willie,183.
Flenner,Charles,87,92.
Flenniken,Clarissa,136.
Flesner,Mary,156.
Fletcher,Caroline,166;John,
  25,72;M.G.,72,73;Perry,92,
  182,183;Ruby,73;U.G.,61,73;
  Vivien,51,52,59,164.
Fling,?,142.
Florey,James,207;Ruth,99.
Flowers,J.W.,86.
Fluckey,Bertha,195;Gladys,
  64;J.N.,51,197;Marie,98;
  Newt,176,196.
Flugar,Mary,91.
Fogle,Clara,67,74.
Foltz,A.J.,172,195;W.B.,79.
Foor,Floy,76;Frank,153,163,
  164,169,182,191;Jessie,76;
  M.,76;Mrs.Ervin,196;Molly,
  80;Raymond,197;Ruth,191;
  W.C.,50.
Forbes,William,28.
Ford,Ethel,113,115.

Forest school,48.
Forsyth,Charles,163;Dorothy,
   156,182;John,19,162,174;L.,
   R.,170,174;Roy,163.
Fosley,R.J.,40.
Foster,Alex,51,52;Anna,54;
   Calvin,24;Floy,52,54,70;
   J.,187;James,187;Jennie,
   120;John,24,123,165;Mack,
   163;Margaret,165;Susan,
   24;William,52,59.
Foster school,113,186A,187.
Fought,C.A.,120;Frank,113.
Four Mile school, 39.
Fowler,Cynthia,86;Forrest,
   64,69,71,73,175;John,67.
Fox,A.G.,187;Clara,86,134,
   181;Eva,180;Fern,183;Kit-
   tie,85;Lillie,170;Lizzie,
   180;Nellie,163,168.
Frailey,Alonzo,194.
Fraker,Fannie,183;Helen,80;
   Mary,18;Mollie,182.
Francisco,Alfred,112;Allen,
   112;Cecil,115;Eli,112;
   Bertha,206;Howard,112;
   Isari,112;L.C.,148,188;
   Peter,112;Rolla,206;Way-
   ne,189.
Frank,John,192.
Frankenfield,Albert,177;Cla-
   ra,107;Emma,177;Gertie,
   177;Otto,177.
Franklin,Annie,51.
Fraser,Helen,27;John,27;Tho-
   mas,27.
Fraught,Sadie,53.
Fraizer,A.B.,53;Fay,166;Lee,
   5,19,20,32,44,143,182,193;
   Lewis A.,19;Vere,166.
Freeman,Anderson,189;David,
   189;Dora,188,189;Frances,
   103;James,102,103.
Freeland,Miss,120.
Free school bills,1,2.
Freitag,Miss,195.
Fremont school,31,34,35.
French,Augustus,2;E.S.,127;
   Earl,47,137;Jordan,187.
Freshwater,Dianna,122.
Freybarger,Michael,113.
Fridley,John,101,102;Julia,
   102.
Fried,Helen,172;Irene,172.
Friendship school,119,125.
Friese,Irvin,136;Isaac,135;
   Walter,134.
Friesner,A.T.,168;Daisy,150;
   Orpha,150;Willie,150.
Fringer,Jacob,166.
Fritter,Enoch,86;F.A.,158,
   187.
Fritts,Thomas,11,13.
Fritz,Beulah,45,136;J.J.,149;
   Ora,47.
Frizzell,Jane,145;John,53.
Frog Pond school,57,196.
Fromme,Ray,46.
Frost,Clara,57,58;Clyde,56.
Fry,Aimee,54,59,195;Bell,123;
   C.W.,105;Carrie,123;Edgar,
   65;Eliza,158;Eva,123;Jasper,
   105;Jennie,53;Jesse,196;Liz,
   51;Vera,74.
Fugate,Lydia,203;Nadene,207.
Fuhrman,Mary,91.
Full Gospel church,66.
Fuller,Margaret,99.
Fulton,A.H.,175.
Fulte,Letha,87.
Fultz,Andrew,70.
Funk,Daniel,122;John,164;Mary,
   134;Nyle,70,196;Selma,81,
   196.
Furguson,D.L.,112.

Furr,C.L.,171;Mary,130,204;
   Roy,166.
Gabhart,John,114A;Gaddis,Geo-
   rge,205;Hester,189,201,206;
   John,206;Linda,206;Mary,206;
   Thomas,201.
Galbreath,Myrtle,192.
Galster,Jacob,176;Minnie,194;
   Mollie,194.
Gannaway,Thelma,202,204.
Gardner,Carl,156;Carlie,148;
   Homer,148;Oran,156;Will,156.
Garrett,Fannie,199.
Garst,C.A.,188.
Gaston,Betty,202;Billie,202;
   Don,202;Gaston,Hester,190,
   201,205,207,208;John,201;
   Ludlow,201;Luzetta,202;
   Oliver,201;Thomas,202.
Gain,B.H.,122.
Gale,Lottie,109.
Gallagher,A.,84;Amanda,95;
   Daniel,84,91;Delia,86;Eli-
   za,86;Ersel,91;Florence,
   91;Guy,91;H.C.,86;Jacob,93,
   96,97;Lucretia,91;Mary,94,
   95;Mattie,94,95;Minerva,85;
   Newton,96,97;Ray,96,97;
   Sarah,96;Simon,86,91;Steph-
   en,96.
Gammill,Ruth,40.
Ganaway,D.C.,36;Eliz.,32;J.
   C.,36;Richard,31,32;Robert-
   son,32;Russell,32;Thelma,95;
   Sam,32.
Garber,Alma,107;Belle,107;
   Bill,107;Catherine,107;
   Frederick,106;Ferdinand,
   107;Henry,107.
Gardner,Harry,37,40;S.D.,37,
   40.
Garner,F.O.,27;James,27;Let-
   ith,27;Narcissus,27;Nathan,
   27.
Garrett,Otto,139;Pearl,57,
   105,106.
Garretson,Jessie,110.
Garrison,Sybil,201.
Garvin,Clara,31,32,40;Liz-
   zie,35,36.
Gaskill,Aaron,35;Jacob,109.
Gaskill school,31,36,37.
Gaton,Lester,166.
Gatons,George,54;Jessie,53;
   Nellie,51,54;Ruth,54.
Gebhart,Mart,114A;Maude,114A;
   Pearl,114A.
Geer,Albert,86;Anna,86;T.R.,
   85.
Gehm,Cleo,80.
Gentry,Oscar,46,47.
Gerhard,Emma,87,92,161.
Gerhold,Esther,174.
Getz,John,77;Mary,123;Minnie,
   77,82;Peter,82;Raymond,206.
Gharrett,Carrie,37.
Gibbons,J.R.,48.
Gibson,Maude,120;Oliver,101.
Giesler,Glen,45,47,135,136;
   William,38.
Gilbert,Mary,205;Neil,127.
Giles,Fern,186;Rachel,168,
   186;W.S.,100.
Gilford,Debbie,50.
Gill,Jesse,100,116,180,185;
   Robert,38,47,60,91,96,116,
   179,181,182,187.
Gillapsie,A.,196.
Gilmore,Ruby,64,133.
Gilpin,Albert,33,36;J.W.,36.
Gingery,Elsie,191;George,191,
   197;Jacob,80;Ross,191.
Gladfelter,Clinton,158;Mary,
   158;Minnie,130,150,153,173;
   N.,158;Will,149.

Gladman,Hazel,53,133,138.
Gladville,Nellie,206.
Glenwood Cemetery,157.
Glick,Albin,85;C.M.,51;Ed,
   50;Hattie,54,59,192;John,
   52;Victor,54.
Goad,Edgar,74.
Goddard,C.R.,183;Grace,205;
   Jr.,208;Lillian,115,180;
   Raymond,182;Rose,32;T.M.,
   201;William,201.
Goff,Hanna,134.
Gollagher,John,85;T.J.,181.
Gonterman,Bertha,80.
Good,Carrie,36,46;Flora,46;
   Jennie,36,38;John,48;Mabel,
   128,163,169,170;Minnie,36;
   Nellie,36,38,47;Renel,169;
   Winifred,163.
Goodman,Elbert,163.
Goodrich,Clara,68,97;Sarah,
   96.
Goodwill school,102,103.
Goodwin,Clarence,159;George,
   118;John,189;Martha,189;
   Thomas,189.
Gordon,A.,77;Ben,116;George,
   116;Lois,181;Mabel,92;
   W.A.,181.
Gorman,Emma,121;Grace,121;
   John,119;Mary,121.
Gorrell,J.B.,199.
Gottman,Ralph,87.
Gould,Ada,115.
Gowan,Marie,100.
Gowdy,Ryan,182.
Gower,Allis,53;Anna,60;Jen-
   nie,53,60.
Grabb,Fred,90,93,138,139,180.
Grace,James,165;Michael,165.
Graden,Milton,87.
Graham,Hattie,196;Martha,54.
Grant,Albert,36;Arthur,169.
Grathwell,Samuel,21.
Graven,Cecil,115;Fern,113A;
   John,117;Juanita,115,200,
   205;Lola,113A;Maurine,115;
   Ralph,201.
Graves,Ida,96,192;Mrs.R.A.,
   95.
Gray,Bertha,36;Cena,108;Earl,
   153;J.H.,38;Jehu,39;Pearl,
   33,47;Laurence,120.
Graybill,B.W.E.,86;Beatrice,
   115;Burt,95;Clara,87,114,
   164;E.C.,55;Ed,164;Fay,120;
   Harry,85;Hiram,84,91;J.T.,
   99;John,94;Laura,99;Mary,
   73;Thomas,73,84,91,92,85,
   99,133.
Green,Amanda,85,134,183;Bas-
   il,27,107,110;Calvin,85,87,
   161,163,182;Carl,181;Ella,
   138;Emily,181;F.M.,181;Her-
   bert,181;Mayme,134;Rhodes,
   181;Roy,181;Silas,85,87,95,
   149,182;Warren,85,86,170,
   180,182;William,27,181;You-
   ger,30.
Greenleaf school,64,66,69.
Greenlee,Ruth,171,179.
Greensavage,Mathilda,175.
Green Valley school,106,107.
Gregg,E.A.,80;John,65;Leon,
   87;Pauline,87;Sadie,66.
Gregory,Aldyth,101;Alta,126;
   Carl,126;Deborah,103;Ed-
   ward,125;Frank,126;Glen,
   126;H.M.,173;James,125;
   John,52,53;Lizzie,84;M.D.,
   168;Myrtle,168;Walter,125.
Grider,Herman,31;Jacob,203,
   205;Lois,109,204;Nancy,204.
Griffin,James,146.

Griffith,Joseph,28;M.S.,38;
  Mahala,28;Naoma,28;T.L.,
  142;Thomas,207;Viola,199;
  Violet,36,38;W.W.,103,207.
Grisso,G.W.,191,197;Iva,
  164,191.
Gritzmacher,C.H.,180.
Grogan,Edward,193;Julie,193.
Groom,R.H.,79.
Gross,John,77.
Grove,Abraham,140;Alice,139;
  Aubrey,95,139;Clarence,
  139;Durward,139,140;Edna,
  159;Edwin,139,140;Effie,
  159;Elza,139,140;I.E.,100;
  J.Paul,182;James,91,92,170;
  Samuel,127;Thomas,139,140;
  Vera,137,139;Winnie,161.
Grove school,19,90,91.
Grubb,Cleta,80;Daniel,150.
Gruenwald,Rosa,92.
Gruntman,Fred,136.
Grupe,Charles,135;Lena,135.
Guilford,Charles,182;Joshua,
  181.
Guin,Charles B.,5,20,199,202;
  Ervin,20;T.J.,207;Willie,
  20,202.
Gunterman,Mildred,144.
Guthrie,Hal,61,68,72,73,76,
  173,196;Ned,55,115,173;Wm.,
  106.

Hackberry school,170.
Hacker,Anna,91;Henry,91.
Hackle,Vienna,107.
Hadley,W.T.,60.
Hadwin,Thomas,187.
Hagan,H.M.,68,85,119;Ida,91,
  186;John,84,134;Lis,186;
  Oka,140;Thomas,186;William,
  140.
Hagan school, 186.
Hagerman,Zepha,136.
Hahn,Delia,86;Elmer,86;Roscoe,
  134.
Halbrook,Lucretia,106.
Hale,John,112.
Hale school,127,157.
Hall,Agnes,66;Anna,54,128;
  Anson,26;Anthony,3,4,5,10,
  11;Asbury,26;Bird,25;Clover,
  189;Etta,151;Florence,55,194,
  195,196;Grace,56,67,70,163;
  Isaac,26;Isabell,148,149;
  Iva,67,74;John,195;Jonathon,
  24;Joseph,68;Liza,51,65,197;
  Mabel,138,139,170;Mary,24;
  Mattie,71;Orson,55;Pernetta,
  24;R.T.,197;T.N.,64;W.Wesley,
  12,26;William,6.
Hallman,F.W.,133.
Hamblen,Agnes,102;Elsie,110;
  Helen,101.
Hamer,William,164.
Hamilton,C.C.,171;Cecil,202,
  206;Corwin,199,204;Earl,206;
  Nellie,59,61,169;Ocla,106;
  Stella,54;Vera,146;W.,105.
Hampton,Doris,200;Mary,55,169,
  182;Olive,116.
Hancock,?,142;Fannie,133;
  Nell,147;Rose,84.
Hand,James,54.
Hankins,Blanche,133;Martha,
  135.
Hanks,A.J.,45.
Hannaman,Carl,90;George,85;
  Mary,86.
Hanson,Elmer,195;Samuel,195.
Harbert,Elizabeth,127.
Hardy,Florence,153;H.H.,122;
  Maud,153;T.H.,150;Thomas,
  161;William,153.

Harley,Carl,127.
Harlow,Elmer,169;Wintress,
  88,90.
Harmison,Earl,188;Edna,188;
  Elpha,188;Fay,188;Oka,188;
  Verna,188.
Harmon,Adaline,27;Adolph,48;
  Charles,48;Emma,47,48,139;
  John,70;Mary,27;Mevil,69,
  70;Mollie,137;Rose,47,48,
  137,138;Walmsley,70.
Harmon school,69,70.
Harper,Beth,100;Carrie,76,81;
  E.W.,102;Frances,102;Gladys,
  103,173,177;Lige,209;Malissa,209;Robert,175;Samuel,
  174.
Harrell,Effie,149;Ruth,77.
Harrington,A.E.,137.
Harris family,111;Grace,80;
  H.K.,207;J.W.,207;Lurie,
  135;Malinda,99;Rose,120;
  Vesta,134,159;Wm.,19,20,
  80.
Harrison,E.,91.
Harrol,J.T.,65.
Hart,Adam,190;Alice,20;Charles,99,148,166,175;Clem,
  33;Ed,127;Harold,173;Henry,
  6;J.Louie,120,163;Martella,
  175;Martha,130;Mary,36.
Hartman,F.,80;Sara,79.
Hartsell,Vernon,33;Wm.,33,37.
Hartwick,E.,68.
Harves,Benj.,146.
Harvey,Minnie,206;J.M.Jr.,
  182.
Harwood,A.J.,195;Louetta,108.
Hash,Fred,44;Mildred,146;Roscoe,32,134,143,204;Ruby,146.
Hashbarger,Edgar,153.
Haskett,Zelma,209.
Haslam,J.T.,103.
Hasler,Alma,91.
Hastings,Jennie,46.
Hatfield,Claudie,161,165.
Hatke,Delores,48;Erma,48.
Hatten,Delilah,67;John Wm.,
  67;Nora,66.
Hauten,Rosalyn,177.
Haverfield,J.T.,80.
Haverstock,Fred,45;John,136;
  Nina,44,47;Wesley,153.
Hawbecker,Daisy,85;John,84;
  Otta,85.
Hawk,Michael,141;William,
  141.
Hawley,H.W.,175.
Hawthorne,John,170.
Hawyer,?,58.
Haydon,Louisa,99;Wm.,99.
Hayes,Andy,82;James,185;Ruth,
  131;Wayne,80.
Hayward,Nettie,85;Ralph,85,
  192.
Haze,Charles,133.
Hazen,Ethel,185.
Headen,G.E.,128.
Hearn,Carl,195;John,195.
Hebel, Jacob,174,175.
Heberlein,John,177.
Heckert,Lee,186.
Hedges,Faye,164;Mary,118.
Hedrick,John,71.
Hege,Mary,86,96,144.
Heideman,Carl,138;Caroline,
  115.
Heiland,Coleen,115;Ray,158.
Heim,Nancy,173.
Heinz,Elzie,170;Georgia,169;
  J.P.,168;Louise,160;Neta,
  169.
Heiter,Emmett,173.
Heitmeyer,?,82;Mary,118.

Hellman,Bertha,106;Dean,43.
Helton,Earl,180;Fred,204;
  Isaac,180;P.B.,105.
Hemer,Carl,126;Gertrude,101;
  Henry,102;Thomas,102.
Henderson,Calvin,100;Emery,
  59;Ethel,188;Ezra,59;George,58;Guy,52,54,55,59,196;
  J.W.,52,59;Jane,62;John,
  47,112,120,115;Juanita,56,
  66,68,159,166;Leland,127;
  Maggie,59;Nancy,52;Neva,
  100;Tony,59;Walter,188;
  Willie,76.
Hendley,E.D.,163.
Hendrick,H.,157.
Hendricks,John,114;Luther,
  117;Mary,105;Mr.,195;Robert,102;Samuel,114;Thomas,
  105;W.Edward,114,137;Walter,
  114A,Wilbur,106;Zimary,112.
Hendricks school,116,117.
Hennigh,L.D.,204.
Henning,Charles,180.
Hennon,Margaret,76.
Henry,Bushrod,111;James,181;
  Ross,183;Stella,84;Wm.,182.
Henson,David,27;John,27;Sarah,
  27.
Henton,123,159.
Henton,Lelah,77.
Henton school,152,153.
Herborn school,136.
Heriot,Clara,125.
Herndon,Margaret,113.
Herod,James,181;Samuel,181.
Herrick,110.
Herrick school,69.
Herrick township act,60,61.
Herron,Bart,112,115,116,187,
  188,189;Carolle,115,201;
  Charles,113,114;Claire,115;
  Cleo,115;Dan,115;E.E.,95,
  201,202;Edward,114,137;F.P.,
  113,116;George,153;Homer,7;
  John,114;Lester,115;Loy,115,
  201;M.L.,95,112;Marie,113A;
  Mart,114;Maude,112;Morris,
  202;Murphy,207;Ollie,114;
  R.J.,187,189;Robert,114,54,
  163;W.D.,33,142,187,189;W.F.,
  77,186;Walter,27;William,200.
Hettiger,Mathias,106.
Hiatt,Clark,44;George,44;Glen,
  44;Hannah,44;Lyman,44/
Hiatt school,44,69.
Hickey,Crawford,114.
Hickman,Alta,85;Florence,68,86,
  88,91,165;John,182;Lowell,87;
  Mab,86;Neda,86;Niles,68,88,92,
  93,96,95,134,170;Wanita,84.
Hickory school,106.
Higgenbotham,Charles,76;Earl,
  76;Florence,80.
Higgins,Clem,35;Jack,84;Thomas,
  164,195.
Hight,Robert,101;W.W.,101.
Hiler,Liller,143;Ruby,173,196.
Hill,A.R.,37;Alice,76,128,120;
  Andrew,116;Aneita,170;David,
  77;Elsie,77;Florence,153,165;
  G.B.,175;James,115,116;Leon,
  77;Louisa,77;Lydia,128;Martha,
  116;Myrtle,77;Oscar,77;R.S.,
  16;Ruth,128;William,126,116.
Hillard,Charles,122,126.
Hilligoss,Howard,206;Morris,
  206;Verna,206;W.,205.
Hillyard,Martha,88.
Hilsabeck,H.A.,32;Hugh,95,205,
  207;J.A.,32,65;Lora,138;
  Travis,20,33,35,40,137,142,
  201;Will,114.
Hilvety,V.F.,102.

219

Himes,Alta,130;George,
 181;J.F.,175;Lillie,
 151;Lois,197;Martha,
 68;Rachel,68;William,
 68,177.
Hines,Charles,189;Margaret,80,119;Mayme,102,119;
 Paul,119,189;Verna,177.
Hinton,Ethel,106;Felix,
 54;Katherine,119;Lela,
 109;Lloyd,58;Lois,109;
 Martin,59;Paschal,12.
Hipes,Charles,103.
Hish,Joseph,153.
Hitchcock,Bertie,106;Charlie,106.
Hobbs,Austin,67;Henson,67;
 Lola,67;Mary,67.
Hobson,Dollie,127;John,106.
Hodges,Faye,150,197.
Hodson,Emma,87;James,65;
 Nelly,65.
Hoene,Alphone,48.
Hoese, Bertha,136.
Hoewing,George,78,80.
Hoffman,Fern,69,88;Francis,
 46,55,143;Golda,79;Grace,
 80;Isaac,172;John,47,161;
 Josie,37;Lawrence,85.
Hogeland,Ida,86,95;J.W.,84;
 Kit,91.
Hogge,Doy,67,73.
Hoke,Beulah,54,158;Edith,
 187;Ester,149,175;Francis,
 128.
Holiday,74.
Holland school,69,92,93.
Holland township,84.
Hollaway,Cora,44.
Holliday,Clarence,74.
Holloway,R.T.,11.
Holman,E.L.,74.
Holmes,Joan,68.
Holt,Delilah,184;Isaac,51,53,
 54,66,184;J.G.,65;T.J.,51.
Homer,Iven,134.
Homrighouse,John W.,135.
Hoodlet,Peter,51.
Hopkins,Robert,33.
Hord,Florence,153.
Horn,Ruby,123.
Hornbeck,Claris,50,53;M.D.,
 53;Mary,53;Ruby,74.
Hornbeck school,50.
Horsley, Berry,40;Dora,40.
Horsman,?,58;C.J.,53;Silver,
 61,166.
Hostetler,?,184;Arch,114.
Hosto,Elsie,175.
Hott,George,122;O.A.,122.
Houchin,Ewing,44.
Houser,Grace,85;Maude,85.
Housh,Jane,81,103;John,77;
 P.B.,77.
Howard,Prof.,75;Sarah,175;
 Walter,168.
Howe,Carl,90;Clyde,64;E.M.,
 92;Edith,89,88,90,159;
 Eliakim,89;Frances,91;Hazel,96;Helen,67,124,158;J.
 Calvin,89;Louise,90;M.M.,
 84,87;Marinda,68,91,88,90;
 Mark,91;Mary,89;Myra,71;
 Roy,89;S.A.D.,67;Tom,89;
 Wendell,89;William,84.
Howell,Bertha,106,195,205;
 R.B.,35;Vashti,105.
Howse,Greta,113,126;Laura,77.
Hoxey,Carrie,177.
Hoy,Daniel,122.
Hubbard,Ella,32;Myrtle,69.
Hubbartt,A.L.,99;C.W.,99;
 Emma,71,74,100;F.M.,100;
 Ira,99;J.H.,98;Myrtle,92;
 Pauline,86,87.

Hubbs,Louis,115.
Huber,Bessie,108;David,88;
 Eliz.,88;Harold,89,90;
 Helen,90;Henry,88;Lydia,
 88;Marvin,89;Opal,88,91;
 Ralph,90;Robert,84,87,108;
 Ruth,59,91,87,89,108,103,
 123,170;Wintress,90.
Hubner,A.J.,175;Ella,191.
Huddleston,Barbara,156.
Hudson,Berte,144;Bruce,204;
 D.M.,207;Garnet,116;George,186;Mildred,169;Pearl,
 56;Ray,57,67,71;Roy,191.
Huff,Agnes,44,45,46;Helen,
 43,44;Mabel,43,47;Mary E.,
 131.
Huffer,Albert,186;Amanda,92,
 136;Annie, 51;Arthur,180;
 Burke,180;Ellen,91;Estella,
 180;J.D.,64;Josiah,135;
 Lawrence,180;Samuel,180;
 William,85,182,204.
Huffman,Clint,42;Cora,116;John,
 116;Josie,46.
Huffmaster,Clara,108.
Hugaway school,100.
Hughes,Verdie,183.
Hulick,C.H.,185;Margaret,185.
Hull,John,84,134.
Humphrey,Bethel,181;Mary,92,95;
 Rose,53,54,118;Ruth,79;Walter,
 102.
Hunk,John,46;Mary,47.
Hunt,G.H.,100.
Hunter,A.M.,105;Ada,76;Anderson,149;Daisy,74;Edna,76;
 Ella,15;Ethel,100;James,15;
 Leroy,55,66,69,164;Robert,
 128;Roy,76.
Huntington,Susie,32.
Hurst,Floyd,85.
Hust,Albert,36.
Hutchison,T.G.,81.
Hutton,Josye,35;Wayne,35.
Hyde,J.B.,119.
Hyatt school,44,69.
Hyland,?,142;Nellie,163;Nettie,163;Theresa,66.

Igo,Catherine,164;John,164,
 181;Michael,164;Samuel,
 164.
Illinois Power LightCo.,124.
Independence school,75,205,
 206,207.
Indiana,144.
Ingle,John,109.
Ingram,Naomi,118.
Inman,Henry,62;Thomas,54,95;
 William,65,207.
Ireland,Roy,108.
Isley,Cloren,95.
Iveson,Ann,57,58;Spence,52.

Jackson,?,32;E.K.,188,189;
 Edward,191;Eliz.,199,203;
 Gladys,200;Harry,149;Hazel,
 163;Lee,169;Levi,203;Martha
 Parr,55,66;Mathew,50;Myrtle,
 76;Pauline,117;Solon,98;Warren,98,116,117,156,207.
Jackson school,141.
Jacobs,Harry,81;Luther,84;Russell,130;Ruth,81;Wayne,81.
James,D.,165;Gertie,66;Leah,
 168;Norma,114,115,180;Thebe,69.
Janes,Evelyn,110;William,168.
Jarvis,Inez,40.
Jeffers,Dallas,163.
Jenkins,A.,77;Betty,153;Clark,
 60;Elda,148;George,130;Hazel,148;John,176;Josephine,
 53,66,64,70,164,172,175;Lota,
 148;Maxine,54,70.

Jensen,Alice,44;Blanche,44,76;
 C.,44;Grover,44.
Jesse,Clyde,77.
Jester,Barnet,191;S.M.,196.
Jimmason,O.C.,46.
Joachim,Harry,135.
Johnson,Albert,51,56,67;Alex.,
 182;Blanche,206;C.O.,44;C.W.,
 71;Charles,206;Earnest,188;
 Eliz.,53;Ella,53,71,105;Erma,
 102;Esther,206;Frank,53;Grant,71;Hannah,188;Isaac,181,
 182;J.E.,135;J.H.,207;Jacob,
 61;Jessie,55;Lura,109;Mary,
 79;Nella,138;Nora,206;Samuel,
 188;Velma,46.
Johnston,J.Wilson,54;Jacob,51,
 54;James,94;Lourene,51;Lucille,156.
Johnston school,54,55.
Jolly,C.W.,44,107;Lizzie,120.
Jones,Alton,153;Anetta,52,59,
 196;Barbara,57,58;Beatrice,
 181;Charles,134;Delbert,66,68,
 69,72,92,93,94,88,120,135;
 Earnest,194;Edith,134,138;
 Elijah,68,164;Florence,198;
 Forrest,147;Guy,135;Harry,
 147;Hazel,96;Jennie,77;John,
 61,86,191;Joseph,134;Josie,
 170;M.C.,64;Martha,25;Nancy,
 25;Nathan,25;Nelson,134;Norma,52,195;Orville,52;R.R.,71;
 Richard,25;Samuel,25;Sarah,
 25;Stella,72;W.A.,99;Wm.,147.
Jones school,153.
Jordan,?,111;Aileen,101;Dale,
 202;Eddie,77;Edyth,77;Eileen,
 78;Evelyn,202;Horace,77;Lloyd,127;Lucile,126;Ross,127.
Juhkne,Florence,180;Wm.,32.

Kackley,Marie,47,197.
Kail,Henry,35.
Kaiser,John,109.
Kansas,149.
Kantner,Mary,176,182;Maurine,
 168.
Karch,George,92.
Karle,E.F.,176.
Karls,E.T.,193.
Kauf,Philip,141.
Kauffman,D.J.,109.
Kay,Claude,109;John,109;Velma,
 109.
Kearney,A.W.,134;Flora,143.
Keck,Anna,47;George,42;Joseph,
 47;Regina,46,137.
Keelen,Helen,102.
Keelan,Mary,177.
Keirn,Bernadine,108.
Keller,David,133;Jesse,137;Naomi,102,103;Nora,100;Opal,
 145;Ora,125.
Kellett,Mary,186;Ora,136,153.
Kelley,Mary,51;R.A.,107;Ruby,
 161,173.
Kelly,Alvin,107;Joseph,54,55;
 Mamie,145;Maude,190;Ruby,
 80;W.R.,190;Wm.,26.
Kennedy,D.T.,42;Emily,147;
 Frank,43;P.S.,46;Viola,159;
 Wm.,38.
Kenney,Joanna,37;John,37.
Kensil,Barbara,149,155,157;
 Bertha,183;D.J.,182;Grace,
 183;Hiram,84,95,157,164,186,
 204;J.T.,180;John,182,183;
 Wm.,182.
Kercher,J.,168.
Kern,Helen,40,138;Florence,149;
 Verne,181.
Kerr,Frieda,191.
Kershner,Zenobia,9.

Kesler,Charles,74;H.O.,74;
　Lois,73;Moody,73.
Kessel,Albert,143;John,180.
Kessler,Elmer,100;Harold,135;
　Harry,73;Irvin,135;John,100;
　Lloyd,100;Mary,100;Oscar,
　138;Rosella,135;Samuel,72.
Keys,F.H.,92.
Keystone school,69,138.
Kidwell,Frank,168.
Killam,Ada,156;Dan,155,156;
　Frank,177;Fred,176;Isaac,
　156,157;JohnT.,155,157,156;
　John W.,148,155;Luther,156,
　157;M.E.,177;Maud,156;Mollie,155;Roy,156;Ruby,155,
　173,174,185;Samuel,148,155,
　156;Stella,156.
Kilpatrick family,125.
Kimbrough,Artie,36.
Kimmel,Eddie,163,164;John,166;
　Mattie,166;Roy,161.
Kinder,Margaret,96.
King,Albert,53;Irene,99;Nelson,53;Neva,163;Permelia,54,
　56;Samuel,2,5,9,10,27,28.
Kingston,Ray,116.
Kircher,Anna,163;Bertha,163;
　Florence,146;Iva,159.
Kirk,Ada,40;Bertha,194;Beulah,
　65;Charley,194;Charlotte,54,
　55;Jane,194;Mattie,194;Molly,194;Morris,194.
Kirkpatrick,Harriett,51;J.H.,
　193.
Kitch,Sam,114.
Kite,Opal,163,168,170,179,185;
　Vera,85,137,140.
Kiwanis Club,22.
Klarman,Dorothy,138;Emma,137;
　Grace,45;Wilma,138,163.
Klauser,Frances,91.
Kleeman & Goldstein,15.
Klein,Lena M.,76,150,168,193.
Klepzig,Joe,64.
Klitzke,August,136.
Klump,Ada,91;John,133;Mrs.C.H.
　181.
Knapp,Lilly,146;Ethel,135,138.
Knearem,Opal,77,117,128,150,
　151,166.
Kneller,Carl,163;Edith,162;
　Hannah,144,147.
Knight,Arloa,98,138,181.
Knobs school,191,192,193,194.
Knoop,Lola,76,176.
Kroh,Ricka,192.
Kropf,?,184.
Knox,Anthony,182;J.T.,137;
　James,85;John,84,91;Rob,112.
Kocher,Eveline,144.
Koester,Carolena,138;Wm.,138.
Koons,Lee,53;Lucille,53.
Koontz,Elverna,134,138;Jake,
　98;Louise,141;Wilson,141.
Kopp,Elsie,119,125.
Kost,Elias,52.
Krietemeier,Joyce,67,146.
Kroenlein,Paul,172.
Kruger,Chris,136;Ernest,135,
　136.
Kruzan,Otis,186.
Kuhle,F.Herman,81;Lewis,81.
Kull,Adam,144,147;Christ.,
　147;Clara,136,144;Clarence,159;Esther,33;James,143;
　Lawrence,36;Mae,168,170;
　Maria,33;Maurine,145;Roy,
　169;Tillie,169;Wm.,147,
　205.
Kuster,Mildred,136.

Lake Shelbyville,111.
Lakewood,64,69.
Lamb,John,101,174;W.O.D.,101.
Lambain,Clarence,119.
Lambert,A.Y.,42.
Lambing,Laura,84.
Lancaster Co.,Pa.,131.
Landers,Bennie,55.
Landes,Hiram,37.
Lane,A.L.,71;Anna,164,168;
　Bernice,165,207;Charles,
　102,107,120;Clyde,42;Cora,
　172,189,195,197;Frank,158,
　166,192,193,197;George,158,
　196;Gertie,204;J.C.,174;
　Josie,197;Katherine,156;
　Lottie,168;M.D.,11,153;M.
　M.,158;Mack,197;Malcolm,
　156;Paul,88;Walter,153.
Lankford,Grace,61,109;John,
　94;Lorene,72.
Lansden,Grace,126.
Lanson,A.,80;Sarah,80.
Lantz,Bessie,91;Harvey,91;
　John,158;Julia,91;W.B.,
　86.
Lape,Delbert,91;Johnnie,91;
　Margaret,106;Ralph,71.
Lappin,Chandos,159.
Lapsley,James,37.
Largent,Electa,98,136,157;
　Frank,191.
Larrimore,Benjamin,53.
Lash,Ethel,159;Irene,123.
Latch,Orval,43.
Latimer,Mildred,42.
Laue,Mabel,100.
Laughlin,Ettie,120;Everett,
　195;F.L.,133;James,123;P.
　P.,123,127.
Laver,Adie,135;Sadie,44,47.
Lawrence,Abraham,124;Hannah,
　124;Raymond,42.
Leach,John,153.
Leathers,John B.,84,138,135;
　Mamie,91;Mary,65;Mollie,
　91;S.S.,91.
LeCrone,Clara,202.
Ledbetter,G.F.,148,195;Opal,
　170.
Lee,Alta,116,127,159,188;Anna,113;August,196;J.P.,66;
　John,196;Jonanthon,105;
　Ward,196.
Lees,Edward,109;James,109.
Leffler,Maurice,42.
Legrand,Bernadine,159;Pearl,
　165.
Lehman,Clara,188.
Leighty,A.L.,54,193,197;Abe,
　195;Edith,71;Ella,55,56,54,
　59,191,197;G.W.,52;Ida,192;
　Jacob,164,197;John,195,197;
　Lewis,95,149,195;Mary,52,53,
　71,99,173,175,195.
Lemen,J.M.,114.
Lemhan,Emily,73.
Lenox,J.L.,142,143.
Levering,Dora,87.
Lewellyn,Arvetta,179.
Lewey,Harry,196.
Lewis,Burt,71;Charles,71,85,
　92,95;Frank,91;Jemima,90,
　165;W.B.,87,91,95.
Leyh,Carl,194.
Liberty school,129,130,131,
　153,157,180.
Libotte,Ruth,31.
Lichenwalter,Gayle,114.
Lieb,Louis,168.
Light,Alma,100.
Lilly,Bernice,198.
Linder,James,192.
Lindley,Curney,84;Dorothy,
　46;Frank,120.
Lindsay,Helen,179.

Lines,Charles,87.
Linn,Eva,59;Hazel,60;Nona,59,
　106;W.T.,59.
Linton,Nancy,204.
Lipkey,Annie,163;Louis,163.
Liston,Mary,191;Nannie,50;
　W.R.,196;Wm.,191.
Little,Ada,187.
Little Brick school,147,153,
　154.
Lively,Florence,99.
Livers,Rebecca,7.
Loar,George,95.
Lock,G.W.,163.
Lockard,Gertrude,191;Mont,76.
Lockart,Bessie,73;Carolyn,69;
　Corda,79;Flossie,36;Glennie,
　73;Harley,73;Harry,73;Jacob,
　79;Jennie,73;Lenora,43;Leo,
　79;Logan,73;Lura,74;Mabel,
　33;Mamie,73;Otto,62,73;Pearl,
　64,99,100;Quincy,73;Susie,
　54.
Lockmiller,Raymond,123,130,131.
Lockwood,Daniel,51,191;Lorene,
　106.
Lockwood school,51,55.
Locust Grove school,127.
Lodge school,31,38.
Lofland,?,121;Dora,121;Lloyd,
　202;Theodore,127.
Lohr,Lela,52.
Lone Elm school,43.
Long Grove school,101.
Long,Jacob,76;Joseph,71.
Longenbach,B.A.,122;Ed,130;
　Eliad,125;Ellie,127;George,
　126,127;Harold,156;J.E.,79,
　127;S.J.,122;Sallie,128,172.
Lorenson,Annie,150,152;Jorgenson,152.
Lorton,H.G.,72;Lucy,73,110;
　Mamie,73;Mary,100;Thomas,73.
Loser,Claude,173;Mabel,173.
Love,Belle,159;Justin,101,120.
Lovelass,Mescal,40.
Lovell,Minnie,65.
Lovins,A.E.,207;B.H.,204;Eliz.,
　206;Forest,206.
Lowe,Charles,173;Clarence,173;
　Ella,37;T.P.,173.
Lowell,Margaret,138.
Lower,Cassandra,157.
Lowery,Harvey,143.
Lucas,Jimmie,209;Millie,91;
　Roy,91.
Luce,Grace,145;Irene,180.
Luck,Julie,169;Katie,169.
Lucy,Charles,80;Eliza,80.
Lucy school,80.
Ludwig,Otto,80;P.G.,81.
Lugar,Fannie,47,137;Giles,45;
　Leon,136.
Lumpp,Stephen,179.
Lupton,James,177;Lucy,177;Mercy,
　177;Rebecca,177;S.B.,177;
　Tillie,173;Wade,174;Wilbur,
　166.
Lutz,Ada,31,37,38,133,136,161;
　Mary,136.
Lyford,Ed,195.
Lyle,A.F.,19.
Lynch,Nadene,197;Verla,54.
Lyon,Lois,148;Marjorie,40;Oneta,
　130.

McAllister,Emma,143;Lillie,38;
　Lydia,36;Maude,45.
McAndrew,Jane,35;Jennie,38;Maggie,35.
McBride,Omer,196.
McCabe,?,184.
McCain,Golda,52.
McCaleb,Melvin,110.

McCartney,John,28.
McCarty,Charley,89;Eva,123; Victor,123.
McClain,Amos,28;Edmund,28; Joseph,28;Margaret,28; Martha,28;Wm.,28.
McClanahan,C.H.,68;Ed,69; J.A.,8.
McClaren,A,174.
McClellan,Silas,124.
McClory,Guy,47;Joseph,46; Mary,47,48;P.H.,37;Regis, 42,46,47,96,115,158,160.
McClosky,David,90;Josephine, 85,86.
McClure,G.E.,176;Lola,173,177; Lois,80;Nathial,173;Malinda,173;N.B.,173;S.B.,173.
McConnell,Jesse,106;LaVene, 174;LaVeta,174;Nellie,67.
McCormick,Clinton,137;E.,197; Ferdinand,137;J.A.,197; John,197;Lizzie,196;Prof. 13,14;William,197.
McCoy,Alice,59;B.,109;Ester, 185.
McCracken,Ephraim,53;Onie, 123.
McCulley,Phidellia,143.
McCullough,Olin,170;Oliver, 197.
McCurdy,C.H.,92;John,108; Stella,108.
McDaniel,Bertha,177;Harry, 177;Mary,34;William,34.
McDermith,Harry,73;J.G.,68; James,53,54,87;S.E.,95.
McDonald,Charles,131;Helen, 55,164;Herman,127;Isabelle, 164,176;John,131;Lettie,95; Raymond,150,151;Roland,150; Stephen,151;Thomas,131;Walter,150;Wilma,151,152.
McElroy,Enid,175,192.
McGee,Milford,68.
McGilligan,Corda,181;Mildred, 116;Standley,79,80.
McGinley,Ebner,81;William,80.
McGlennen,Geraldine,87.
McGrail,Cora,71.
McGranahan,Albert,35;Cora,135.
McGrath,J.H.,77;Margaret,47, 101,102,118.
McGrew,Enoch,5,11,12,14,122.
McIntosh,Georgia,40;Wm.,31,37.
McIntyre,Albert,108;Josephine, 108.
McKay,Charles,24;John,46.
McKee,Maggie,177;Unity,62.
McKinley,Enid,81,172,173,175.
McKinney,Edna,35,56,42,47;Ed, 188;Nellie,188;Inez,33;Missouri,62;Nettie,188.
McKinsey,Jane,24.
McKittrick,Ada,76;Albert,76; Augusta,197;Cynthia,54,197; Ellis,130;Emery,76;Ida,164; James,197;Julia,197;Leslie, 198;Louise,198;Lydia,163, 164,193;Margaret,84,86;Mark, 91;Mils,84;Paul,182;Ray,76; Rosalie,198;Samuel,51;Thomas,50.
McLane,Bertha,195.
McLaughlin,D.,65.
McLin,Etta,177.
McMahan,B.W.,54,56;John,55.
McManmie,Edna,109.
McMillan,Dorothy,46,175;Harold,32,112,175;Mary,73;Kelsey,67.
McNeely,Juanita,143.
McNeese,George,184;Jo,108; John,183;Leona,153,154,155;

Sam,184;William,184.
McNutt,J.W.,60;John,59,61,62; Merle,106;N.P.,12,105;Wade, 105.
McQueen,Elisha,77.
McTaggart,A.C.,106;H.C.,51.
McVay,Ada,145;Alice,36;Fay,59; Julia,180;Maggie,38,48;Mollie,31,42;P.H.,207;W.W.,32.

Macklin,Anna,121;Clara,125; Dessie,125;Elda,130;Joseph, 125;Leroy,128;Loren,130; Ross,121;Roy,128,158.
Mackrell,Joseph,115.
Maddock,John,191.
Mahan,Clara,119.
Mahoney,Dexter,201;Lewis,114; William,207.
Mahoney school,113A,114,114A, 115.
Major,Nellie,40;Seneca,40.
Malhoit,Nora,80.
Maloney,Beulah,172;Mae,78; Serinda,201.
Manhart,John,136;Ruth,45,139, 140;S.B.,136.
Manley,Robert,81;William,110.
Mann,Effie,199;Robert,189.
Manning,Eber,186.
Mansfield,B.A.,184;Grace,79.
Manual,George,58;Joseph,58; Loren,110;Sarah,58;Wm.Fred, 58.
Maple Grove school,102,118,119, 188,189.
March,Louisa,110.
Markland,Eugene,86,87,125,185; Montie,100;Roscoe,181.
Marlow,Martha,189;Rebecca,189.
Marks,Ida,56.
Mars,Bethel,171;Clara,84,87,91, 92,89,85,95;Dista,92;Lysta, 87;M.J.,171;Mary,166.
Marsh,Pearl,180;William,97.
Marshall,?,125;Clara,119, 176;Elmer,123,124;James, 124;Nellie,126;Nettie,123; Ruth,153;William,124.
Marshutz,William,5,15,16.
Martin,Bertha,123;J.,143;L.M., 164;Margaret,166;Mary,189; Minnie,48;Ruth,206.
Martz,Esther,160;Henry,160; William T.,160.
Marvell,Ed,40.
Marxmen,Amelia,158.
Marxmiller,Elfletah,158;Grace,163.
Masonic Hall Lodge No.595,38.
Massey,Sarah Jane,73.
Mast,E.D.,187.
Matheny,Colonel,112;Ed,163; James,20.
Mathews,George,189;J.H.,123; John,120;Minnie,189;Serepta,73.
Mathias,Belinda,27;Brinton, 126;Charles,125;D.M.,128; Dessa,126;Emerson,126;Hoy, 125;Lannie,126;Levi,27;Louise,126;Mary,27,130,175, 192;Ollie,126,127;Samuel, 125,126;Winnie,126.
Mathis,D.M.,113.
Matlock,Clarence,80;Frank, 76.
Matson,Fern,98.
Mattox,Carl,86;Catherine,62, 113;E.Della,47;Gladys,99.
Maurer,F.,175;Jacob,162,175.
Mausey,Charles,80.
Mautz,Grace,194;John,177;Lulu,177;Rosina,193.

Maxedon,Leland,170;Ruth,205.
May,D.H.,53.
Mayberry,Belle,121;Bertha,188, 189;Ed,121;George,189;Ira, 121;Manford,121;Pink,189.
Mayflower school,37.
Mayhew,Amanda,32;Calvin,36.
Mayhill,Parentha,77.
Maynard,Yvonne,204.
Mays,D.A.,189.
Mead,T.W.B.,122.
Mears,L.E.,116.
Mechlen,Levi,84,86,92.
Meeds,James,155.
Meek,Rita,48.
Meers,Elnora,137.
Mehl,Walter,46.
Mercer,James,122;Leota,163; Marcus,162.
Merrick,Isaac,96;Mary,96.
Merryman,Ruth,115,188.
Metzger,Adam,177;Alice,195,197; Carl,177;Caroline,177;Edward,177;F.W.,175;Fred,173,175, 192;Freda,177;George,177;Gus, 197;John,177;Louis,173;Orval, 177;Perry,195;Robert,177;Rosa,177.
Meyers,Harry,98;S.C.,173.
Michael,Viola,148.
Mickey,Lucille,159;Monica,186.
Middlesworth,C.J.,94;Edna,150; Elma,128;Grace,67;Hardin, 71,85;Jacob,64,96;Mamie,87, 96;Mary,91;Maude,155;Roe,73, 110;Sarah,96,97;Sylvia,128.
Middleton,Anthony,65,76;C.P., 128,143,166;C.W.,71;Charles, 67,68,91,96,87,92,95,97;Christ,67;Edna,151;Gertrude, 96,97;Hanson,24;Ida,168;Jennie,65,66,67,68,71,74,87,99; Katie,76;Otto,175;Robert,68, 96,97;Russel,68;Wayne,76;Wm., 151.
Miers,Peter,6.
Mietzner,Eda,137;Noah,138;Wm., 98,138.
Miles,Bertha,135,144;Luther, 107;Terra,107.
Miller,Abraham,181;Anna,51; B.G.,196;Benedict,59;Benjamin,196;Bessie,126;Charles, 195;Clara,153;D.O.,197;Edna, 108;Eliz.,151;Ella,59;Ellen, 113;Enola,92;Eva,180;F.M., 92;Fannie,150;Gertrude,76, 158,196;Glen,90;Harold,55, 56;Irene,81;Jesse,183;John, 112,182;Joseph,112;Lloyd,149; Lola,163;Wilma,194;Lorenxi, 28;Lucy,60;Lulu,84,85;Margaret,102;Martin,172;Mary,26, 157;Mathew,134;Mattie,76;N., 180;Nettie,51,196;Noah,61; Ona,108;Opal,89,112;P.T.,92; Pauline,57,177,197;Roy,112; Ruby,89,149;Salina,196;Samuel,100,103,175;Sarah,57,58; T.P.,52,53;Tobias,112;Vivian,94;W.A.,84;W.T.,99;Wm., 137.
Milligan,Anson,181;D.Y.,181; Jacob,181.
Milliken,Bessie,123;C.S.,50,51, 53;Etta,123;Hattie,197;Jannie,123;Jim,123;Lizzie,51; M.E.,51;May,123.
Mills,Benjamin,46;Gilbert,209; Helen,53,78;Jesse,46;Oneita, 105;Otha,209;W.W.k46;Wm.,209.
Milton,Grace,128.
Miner,A.O.,127,128;Anna,158; Charles,84,86,114;Daniel,

99,200;G.F.,92;Harriet,99;
   James,31,32,201;Margaret,
   205;Monroe,201,205;Robert,
   114,95;Scott,114;Thomas P.,
   85,116,120,201;Tina,153;
   W.F.,189;Will,127.
Minor,Arloa,66;C.J.,120;Lois,
   204;Lucian,6.
Mitchell,?,67;Edgar,40;Frank,
   189;Jessie,166;Ora,40;Oscar,
   40;Stella,40.
Mittendorf,Louis,162.
Mixon,Nellie,136.
Moberly,E.,143;James,207.
Mochel,Albert,168;Anna,168;
   Docie,161;Maggie,161;Margaret,161,164.
Mode school,95,96.
Moffett,Evelyn,175;John,200.
Mohler,Maggie,59.
Moll,Daniel,127;E.A.,122;Zadie,127.
Moltz,Annie,173;Fred,173.
Monroe,Florence,55;W.H.,189.
Montgomery,Cora,36;George,36;
   James A.,5,17,31;John,17;
   Mary,204;Mildred,153.
Montooth,May,55.
Moon,A.R.,60,195;Burl,61;
   Ethel,127;F.F.,60;James,60,
   62;Jesse,61;Margaret,62;Silas,195;Spencer,51,52,53,
   193.
Moonshine school,62.
Moore,Elza,191;Ethel,119;Flora,76,107;Floy,35;Floyd,
   191;Forrest,108,119,164,
   175;Frank,191;G.E.,165;
   G.W.,71;Garnet,96;George,
   23,33,35,64;Gertie,66,72;
   Gladys,195;Hazel,191;Helen,57;Homer,149;J.L.,51;
   James,51,66,68,71;John,
   65;Juanita,64,169,195,196;
   Luella,71;Milton,85;Minnie,91;Verlea,68;Victor,
   163;William,173;Willis,
   149.
Moran,Cleo,134;Emma,46;George,46;Maggie,68;Thomas,
   46.
Morefield,Charles,106.
Morehead,Cora,156.
Morehouse,Aaron,67.
Morgan,Ava,60;Beatrice,80;
   Clara,105;Eunice,164;George,24;Gladys,109;Harry,
   51;James,108;Mabel,32,56;
   Mamie,37,43;Mattie,109;
   Sadie,33,204,209;William,
   24.
Morris,E.C.,207;Eliza.,207;
   Lucille,114,126,128;Ruth,
   116;Violet,207.
Morrison,A.J.,51,52;A.N.,51;
   Chattie,56;Ella,106;J.W.,
   54;John,7;Lizzie,60;Lucy,
   36;Mary,106;Paul,110;Thomas,54,59,196.
Morrow,Gerald,176;Joseph,172;
   Nellie,67,197.
Morse,Earl,113A,115;Foy,54;
   Frank,115;Henry,114;Kenneth,115;Lora,115;Maxine,
   115.
Mose,Amy,173;B.F.,143;Claude,
   153;Florence,147;Henry,177;
   J.H.,174;Lizzie,173.
Moser,J.,48.
Moss,Mildred,81,101;Mollie,
   79;Vera,79.
Motts,Reuben,155.
Moulton,Samuel W.,2,5,8,9.
Moulton school,168,169.
Moultrie county,123,188.

Mound school,137.
Mount,Anne,105;Jesse,52,53,
   195;Mathias,105.
Mt. Pleasant school,105,195.
Mt. Tabor school,69,181,182.
Mt. Victory school,195.
Mounts,Nellie,76;Wm.,76.
Mouser, Homer,5,11,14.
Moutry,Rose,163.
Moweaqua,78,124.
Moweaqua township,101.
Mowel,Abraham,35,42.
Mowry,Delores,80,173;Dorothy,76;Essie,127,187,189.
Moyer,Anna,114A;Ray,114A,
   Tarcy,114A.
Muchow,Minnie,110,138.
Mud Creek,171.
Mud Run school,68,69,71.
Mueller,Albert,134;Samuel,
   137;Thelma,44.
Muller,Margaret,175.
Mullins,Maxine,161.
Mulverhill,Simon,67.
Mummel,George,92;Paul,208.
Munch,Nellie,160.
Munn,Hannah,89.
Munson,Beulah,51;Della,168;
   Jessie,81;Johanna,45;Myrtle,81.
Murdock,Henry,14,168.
Murphy,Josephine,58.
Murray,Jane,68.
Murry,Nona,61,62,52,54,73;
   Wade,61.
Musser,Ella,74;Josie,74;
   Kathryn,100;Orville,74.
Musson,Alvin,99;Emma,190;
   Marjorie,88.
Myers,Dora,102,173;Hattie,
   52,53,56;Mary,51,52,53,56;
   Peter,60;Ruby,88,169;W.L.,
   54,56;William,174.
Myrick,Lou,196.

Nance,?,57;Aleoa,56;Alleva,
   72,165;Hesse,56,58,72,164;
   Irvil,54,67;J.L.,207;M.,79;
   Maurice,68;Miles,73,95;Miss,
   180;Noel,55,195;Ruth,195,
   196;Wm.,71;Winnie,74.
Nantz,John,37.
Neal,Betty,208;L.P.,56.
Neary,Mary,205,207,208.
Neatherly,Medford,207;Otto,
   191;Polly,208.
Neber,Andrew,146.
Neece,Dale,106;Henrietta,60.
Neel,George,109;J.C.,67.
Nehil,Fred,74.
Nehring,Wm.,133.
Neighbor,H.W.,36;L.B.,30.
Neihls,Carl,96;Maria,96.
Neil,Emma,175;Etta,195;F.P.,
   205;Howard,77,197;James,
   123;Jane,191;Morton,153,
   175,191;Nelson,166,175;
   S.G.,122;Tilman,176;Walter,168;Wesley,175,176;Wm.,
   205.
Nelms,Hugh,40.
Newberry,Meda,73,110.
Newby,Ruth,187.
Newcomb,Mildred,126.
New Harmony school,52.
Newkirk,H.M.,66;Henry,53;
   Norris,51;W.W.,50,51,54,
   56.
Newlan,Harry,134;Jacob,134;
   Marion,134;Mark,134.
Newman,Wayne,158.
Ney,F.W.,79;Frederick,80.
Nichols,Alma,33,34,128,205;
   Charles,107;Florence,110;
   Opal,127;Sarah,106.

Niles,Alice,96;Elisha,112.
Nippe,Fred,134;Joe,134;Ruth,
   36,133,146.
Nirkam,Henry,81.
Nicewanger,Ruth,134.
Niswonger,Estella,138.
Noaks,Sarah,102.
Noble,M.C.,34.
Nohren,Ethel,55;Merrell,55;
   Theodore,55.
Noland,Freda,126.
Nolen,Donie,159;Lou,159;
   Malinda,24;Mary,24;Ota,159.
Noon,Edith,128;James,123.
Normal school bill,2,8.
Normal University,2,11,13,18.
North Liberty school,157;
   184,185.
Northwest Ordinance,1.
Noyes,Thelma,47.
Number Four school,53.
Number Seven school,100.
Number Six school,57,68,69,
   108.
Number Nine school,189,190.
Nutter,John,118.

Oakes,Cora,76;Eula,76;Louis,
   76.
Oakland school,71.
Oakley school,47.
Obed,124,154.
Obed school,157.
O'Brien,Alice,80;Jennie,177;
   Mary,81,82,197.
Oconee township,105.
O'Conner,Mary,148.
Odem,?,111.
O'Farrell,Archie,195;May,195;
   Vick,195.
Okaw school,74.
Okaw township,111.
O'Kelley,John,67;Jurella,109.
Old Mode,94.
Old Union school,30,31.
Olehy,?,70.
Olinger,B.S.,99;Harley,73.
Oliver,Benjamin,6;Capt.,6;
   Eliza,6;Joseph,1,2,5,6,7,
   178;Lou,32,153,158;Margery,6;Mary,6;William,6.
Oller,Clara,90;Eliza,68;
   Henry,68;M.Wm.,68;Wm.,68,
   172.
Olmstead,Delbert,113A;Enid,
   182;Ethel,74;Faye,114.
Olshakie,Cornelia,107.
Oman,Carlie,153.
Opossum Creek,105.
Orris,Fred,119.
Osborn,A.L.,80;Aletta,196;
   Alice,81;Effie,77,80,81;
   Eva,81;James,81;Ruth,110;
   Susie,74;William,196.
Otta,A.,101.
Our Best Words,14,15.
Overpoch,Jesse,180.
Overton,Benjamin,7.
Owens,Adam,182;James,182;
   John,182.
Owing,Thomas,74.

Packer,Wm.,33,42.
Paczak,John,110.
Padgett,J.W.,173;Roy,76.
Page,Ellen,172,192;J.J.,179;
   Nicholas,26;William,26,27.
Paine,Grace,126;Mrs.,130.
Paisley,Lillie,123.
Palestine school,196.
Palmer,Grace,119;Harry,119;
   John,61;Ray,119;W.J.,125.
Pana,194.
Parish,Amanda,27.

Park,Gladys,187;John,187;
   Retta,197;Thomas,195,197;
   Wayne,187.
Parker,Charles,103;J.P.,163;
   Lemuel,102;Linden,46;W.G.,
   113.
Parkhurst,E.K.,99.
Parks,Minnie,130;Samuel,24;
   T.J.,165;W.,118.
Parr,Arlene,51;Betty,177;
   George,35;Guy,35;Guy R.,
   35;Lonnie,F.,Jr.,64,69;
   Ruth,164;Virginia,163.
Parrish,Robert,186.
Parsons,Lesa,40.
Pasley,Vivian,123.
Patient,Pearl,113A.
Patrick,Della,85.
Pattengale,Jewell,193;Morrill,109;Rose,174.
Patterson,Alva,47;Ben,47;
   Clarence,68;Ethel,92,100;
   James,28,184;Norton,90;
   Pearl,90;Rhoda,28;S.B.,33;
   Sarah,28.
Patton,A.H.,182;Andrew,153;
   Isaac,91,92,170;James,51;
   Isaac,182;Laura,65;Mary,
   85;Samuel,65;Warren,124;
   Willie,123.
Paulk,Amanda,7.
Pauschert,Albert,168;Amelia,
   168;Bertha,168;Carrie,168;
   Fred,168;Harry,168;Julia,
   168.
Payne,Ruth,119,120.
Pea,Jonathon,54.
Pearce,J.W.,188.
Pearson,Jesse,123;Nancy,40.
Pease,Everett,90;Glen,90;
   Grace,90;Hobart,90;John,
   52;Marie,90;Paul,90.
Peber,E.A.,146.
Pee,J.,52.
Peek,Carrie,65;Cleveland,161,
   163,164,166,169;Cora,163;
   James,26;John,163;Joseph,
   162;Margaret,26;Mary,26;
   Thomas,26;Warren,163;Richard,191.
Peer,Omer,51.
Peifer,Celestine,45;Edgar,71;
   J.D.,71;S.D.,95;W.H.,71.
Penn township,118.
Penwell,Elsie,170.
People Spring school,50.
Percy, John,170;Samuel,
   91.
Perkins,Helen,73,108.
Perry,Edna,188;Jacob,188;
   Mary,127;Nellie,188;Opal,
   148;Rozin,105;Vira,188;
   Dora,189.
Perryman,A.,65;A.H.,51,114,
   170;A.V.,25;Alfred,92,170;
   Anna M.,85;Bertha,163;C.
   C.,51;Dorothy,175;Ella,91,
   163,175,177;Emma,71,172;
   Friese,65;J.B.,53;J.M.,
   166;James,24,120;Julia,
   24;Lewis,164;Lucie,92;
   Margaret,56;Mr.,114;S.Henry,24,25;Silas,24.
Person,Ali,112.
Peters,Adolph,91,135;Ella,
   74;Homer,84,164;J.Russel,
   47;Kit,33;R.A.,136.
Petty,Earl,107;H.D.,72.
Pettyjohn,Curtis,67;David,
   67;Leverett,67;Nettie,68.
Pfeiffer,Arthur,169;Caroline,
   160;J.D.,195;John,168;
   Julius,169;May,169;Nita,
   159;Victoria,55;Walter,169.

Pfingsten,A.W.,138;Henry,136;
   Mary,138.
Pfluger,Mary,137,138.
Phegley,Edward,64;Ocla,65.
Phelps,George,33,35,36,37,38.
Phillips,Amy,163;Bailey,6;
   John,67,74;L.H.,100;Mary,
   68,91,99;Oneita,153,182;
   Ruby,96;Sue,36,40.
Phipps,Jesse,195;Lucille,
   108;Mrs. Jesse,195.
Piatt,Mary,122.
Pickaway township,122.
Pierce,A.G.,75;Clark,119;
   Doris,87;Ervil,131,153,154;
   Frances,87;Leon,87;Leslie,
   76;M.V.,172.
Piety,Edith,156;Mark,156.
Pikesh,Mary,144.
Pilchard,Edwin,144.
Pin Hook school,142,143,170.
Pinkard,Fern,133.
Pinkley,N.T.,72.
Pinkston,A.F.,78;Harley,126;
   Homer,196;Jesse,126;Mary,
   160.
Pinney,G.W.,59.
Piper,Maude,76.
Pitzer,C.D.,173.
Pleak school,77,78,79.
Pleasant Flower school,81,
   82.
Pleasant Grove school,69,72,
   73,110.
Pleasant Hill school,50,51,
   191.
Pleasant Plains school,100.
Pleasant Ridge school,149,190,
   197,198.
Pleasant Union school,61,69.
Pleasant Valley school,196,
   197.
Ploughman,Charles,24.
Plowman,Kenneth,164.
Poe,Abner,23;Hannah,147;J.F.,
   141;James,32.
Pogue,Ava,153,158,160;Helen,
   130;Hiram,127,188;James,
   116,157;Mamie,128;Olive,
   189.
Polley,Everett,71.
Ponsler,Clarence,92,95,98,99,
   100,135,138;Edith,84,100,
   138;Mary,85,96,100,115,119;
   Prudence,86,98,125.
Pontius,Agnes,81;Cora,135;
   B.F.,122;Cora,156,182,186;
   Mildred,80,92,143;Stanley,
   84,126;W.H.,126.
Poole,Adith,101.
Pope,Clarence,106;Judith,203;
   Peter,203;Sarah,203;Wm.,
   12.
Porter,Edith,155,156;Esther,
   107;Hazel,107;Herbert,107;
   Lenora,110;Lola,107;Newton,
   107;William,173.
Poteet,Harlie,191;Homer,191;
   Lewie,191;Mary,26.
Potter,Grace,80;Opal,130,150,
   173,177,192;S.G.,172.
Potts,M.R.,62;Merle,105.
Pound,J.R.,126;James F.,75.
Powel,N.E.Mrs.,94.
Powers,Ella,195;Grace,84.
Prairie Bird school,152,153.
Prairie Hall school,133.
Prairie Home school,124.
Prairie school,31,35,36,170,
   141,142.
Prairie township,133.
Prairieton township,81,124.
Prairie Union school,99.
Prater,Gordon,72;Ursula,143.

Preihs,Bess,105.
Prentice,O.H.,52;William,8.
Prentice school,27,178.
Prescott,H.Agnes,53,54,55.
Price,Charles,46,54,55,106;
   Crowin,109;Dona,56;Eva,54;
   Fanny,106,109;George,32;
   H.B.,59,60;Holly,119,170,
   180;Imogene,54;J.B.,59;
   J.E.,66;J.Henry,32;Jesse,51;
   John,30;Lenora,60,76;Lucy,
   106;N.C.,105;Pearl,109,155;
   Perry,66;Phyllis,109;R.H.,
   52;Sadie,47,127,159,169;
   William,51;Wm.H.,36.
Primmer,Barbara,119,125;M.
   H.,125;Simon P.,119,125.
Pritchard,Edward,138;S.J.,
   101,118,166.
Pritchett,B.J.,105.
Pritts,Lillian,116,117,150,
   152;Perry,64,71,73,116,176.
Procter,W.S.,207.
Propeck,Josiah,148.
Prosser,June,140;Sara,97;
   Sylvia,134.
Protsman,Claude,121;John,131;
   Laura,121,128,131;Mary,121,
   128.
Puckett,Judy,191;Luther,191;
   Nathan,191,196.
Puckett school,197,198.
Pugh,Charles,170;Robert,91,
   170;W.J.,197.
Purkiser,Elsie,40,120;Russell,
   40.
Puyear,Bill,126;Don,125.
Quackenbush,C.A.,107.
Quaker school,46.
Quicksall,Charles,127;Florence,
   137;Grace,136;J.A.,134,136;
   J.H.,45,48;John,135;Matilda,
   136;Minor,44,45;Ora,45;
   Thelma,31.
Quigle,Frances,136.
Quigley,Eugene,201;M.V.,200;
   Mary,201;Phoebe,115.
Quinn,Anna,136;Ed,45,48,137;
   John,45;Margaret,47;Sarah,
   35;Sylena,45,46,136.

Radcliff,Benjamin,182.
Ragan,Alberta,87;Dorothy,87;
   E.C.,88;Frances,93;Freda,
   87;Gleason,87;H.P.,91;Norma,
   93;Silas,86,92,95,134;Wm.,
   85,86,114.
Ragweed school,177.
Rainey,Minnie,186.
Ralston,Oma,124.
Ramsey,Dorothy,130;Michael,
   23,24.
Rand,Garnet,91.
Randall,M.A.,100.
Randle,G.P.,20.
Rankin,?,142;Eliz.,44;Emilie,
   44;Nadine,143;Rebecca,19;
   Samuel,37.
Ransford,Edward,76;Lula,76.
Rarick,Beryl,102.
Rau,Charles,194;David,193;
   Elvera,177.
Rawlings,Adrian,128;Arthur,
   130;C.J.,128;Earl,149;Ed,
   128;Gretta,130;John,130,
   149;L.M.,128;Mabel,38;R.T.,
   150,173;Tracey,126;Verne,
   130;Willis,100,143,182.
Ray,D.A.,173;Dorothy,47.
Rayhill,Kate,195.
Read,Georgetta,166;Hattie,
   166,168;Oscar,182;Purella,
   130,166;R.H.,195;Robert,166;
   Wm.,191.

Reading,Maude,173.
Reber,?,184;C.T.,170.
Record,Belle,204.
Rector,M.Loyd,123.
Red Bud school,175.
Redfern,Ottis,120.
Red Fox school,200.
Redington,David,148;Hiram, 148;Mary,148;Obid,148.
Reed,A.S.,110;Allen,29; Andrew,28;Anna,92;Daisy, 168;Elisia,28;Eliza,28; Ethel,130;Eula,174,192; George,183;Hettie,195; Homer,128;Irma,156,157; J.M.,31;J.W.,75;James, 28,181;John,28;Josephus, 163;Julia,180;Lavina, 28;Lella,120;Marion,28; Mary,28;Minnie,195;Newton,56;Nina,143;Perry, 28;Purella,173;Sarah,28; T.H.B.,122;Wm.,28,163.
Reeder,Josephine,22,158;Lucinda,158;Olive,136,138.
Reel,Ed,143;Ervin,143.
Reese,Lowell,206;Wm.,53.
Reeve,J.B.,168.
Reeves,Charles,51;S.W.,85.
Reichart,Arthur,148;James, 148.
Reichel,H.R.,96.
Reid,Gerald,67.
Reider,Frank,168;Johnny,152.
Reinohl,John,170.
Reiss,Gust.,180,193;Hilda, 168.
Renner,Antoni,44; Edna,114,115; Eva,163;Nancy,134;Wilson, 44,134.
Renshaw,Bryan,145;Caroline, 27;Charles,145;Everett,145; James,145;John,23,145;Wm., 145.
Rentfro,Della,40;Ellen,135; James,101;Morris,143;Sinia, 101;Velma,90.
Ressler,Bess,22.
Rexroad,Jennie,180.
Reynolds,Alta,80,81;Alva,207; Benjamin,67;Clyde,180;Edward,185;Glenn,204;Guy,204; J.E.,181;J.M.,77,92,101, 118;James,203;Jerry,40,68, 99,114;Kay,208;Kenneth,202; Louisa,86;Maude,116;Orva, 204;Pauline,202;Ray,202; Ruth,202;T.J.,39,180.
Rhap,Eliza,28;Henry,28.
Rhodes,Alice,54,60;Charles, Effie,59;Ida,192;John,192; Mattie,51,60;Norma,177;Roy, 60,72;Ruth,52,62.
Rice,Bridget,181;Calvin,98; Emma,47,84;F.May,87;Fannie, 84;John,181;Letha,183;May, 181,95,133;Mollie,87,91,185; Ruby,183;Thomas,180;Vera, 183.
Richard,W.W.,143.
Richards,Edna,145;Elmer,146; Everett,145;Florence,133; Letta,67;Mattie,74;Salla, 54;Wm.,143.
Richardson,Belle,186;David, 186;E.A.,114;J.H.,205;G.W., 201;Mary,201;Maude,52;Palmira,114,161;Rose,33,179; W.J.,191;Wm.,197.
Richart,R.A.,77.
Richland school,145,147.
Richland township,141.
Richman,Clyde,32,38;Kizie, 114;D.A.,143.

Rider,Aaron,92.
Ridge school,149,150,151,152.
Ridge township,148.
Ridlen,George,67.
Riebold,Anna,112;John,113.
Riefsteck,Walter,69.
Riggins,Eunice,20.
Riggs,Jessie,71,73,74.
Righter,L.H.,31;Thomas,92.
Riley,Grace,74;Harry,74; James,102;Wm.,191.
Rincker,C.F.,136;Melinda, 48;Thomas,136.
Riney,Henry,45;Inez,36,205.
Ripley,Dwane,86,87;Naomi,181.
Rittgers,Carl,92;Daisy,105, 157;Flo,109.
Roane,Sarah,124.
Robb,Harry,201;Iva,146,205.
Roberts,Alonzo,53;Betty,52, 62,106,109;Burrel,9,10, 175;Colmady,65;Ellie,33,36; Ethel,108;Frank,52,96;G.M., 153;George,99,117;J.W.,207; Jessie,56,58;John,51,64, 109,99;Lorenzo,42;Mary,42, 175;Warde,98;Wm.,113.
Robertson,?,58;Amelia,95; Effie,51;Estella,61,71,172; Isaac,58,61;Karen,155;Mary, 128;Mollie,55,71,122;Orville,56;Thomas,187;Wm.,51;W. S.,113.
Robinson,Beulah,189;C.H.,117, 158;Daisy,76;Ethel,189;Grace,123;Lloyd,189;Lucy,76;N. C.,31;Samuel,31;Wm.,141.
Robinson Creek,148,161.
Robinson Creek school,165, 166,167.
Robison,Edwin,199;Esther,204; Hugh,204;Leota,204;Margaret, 138,142,202;Peter,207;Sam, 112,114;Thomas,143;Viola, 204.
Roby,Harry,40;Frank,124;Ralph, 40.
Rockett,Wm.,166.
Rochkes,John,107.
Rockford school,134.
Rocky Branch school,164.
Rodman,James,75;Lloyd,128,130; Sidney,130;Sport,149.
Roellig,G.A.,134;Paul,134; Ruth,133,146.
Roessler,Ethel,147,153,157; Henry,161,164;Ira,162;Paul, 169;Phillip,161;Ralph,161, 168,169.
Rogers,Anna,96,97;Donna,127; Joseph,110;Margaret,96; Samuel,109;Sarah,73.
Roland,Jennie,51,92.
Roley,Dean,139;Harold,138; Samuel,134,138;Wilma,139.
Roley school,138,139,140.
Rolland,Annie,95;Emma,94.
Roller,Joseph,123.
Rominger,M.,36.
Roney,Elizabeth,187;J.Kenneth,5,22;John,22.
Rose,Alexander,26;Clarinda, 201;Elsie,207;F.H.,73;Ina, 202;Ivy,20;J.P.,201;J.R.P., 20;James,112,201;John,201; Juanita,202;Otto,76;Rebecca,103;Roy,202,203;Trua, 114;T.V.,201;W.H.,207;W.K., 37,136,134,144,166;Webb, 203;Wilma,200,205.
Rose Center school,162,164.
Rose school,20,32,201,202.
Rose township,161.

Rosenberry,Belle,197.
Rosenburg,O.H.T.,52.
Roshart,Kathyrn,165.
Ross,Amon,200;L.P.,200;Robert,200;Thelma,32,38,205.
Roth,Anna,165;Emma,107; Peter,165.
Roudybush,Etta,53,54;Grace, 59.
Round Grove school,102,173.
Round Prairie school,105,106, 110.
Rouse,E.W.,31,38;James,141.
Row,?,142;Alice,106;Bessie, 147;Ella,107.
Rowley,Wayne,174.
Roy,Ellen,33,47;J.M.,36.
Royce,Eleanor,156.
Ruble,?,142.
Ruby,Grace,74.
Ruch,John,18.
Ruff,?,143;Effie,197;Wm.,196; C.A.,158;Fred,135;George, 170;Harman,162;Isabel,170; Lottie,161;Stella,169;W. P.,168.
Rumer,Jessie,109.
Runkel,Caleb,153;Lorraine, 124;Mary,159;Opal,115,168, 185.
Runnels,Barney,34.
Runyon,Catherine,109;James, 109;Mattie,109.
Ruot,Eugene,108.
Rural township,171.
Russell,Blanche,65;C.L.,70; D.E.,173;E.G.,103;George, 102.
Rutherford,Sylvia,79.
Ruwe,Herman,134.

Saddoris,Allen,123.
St. John,184.
St. Paul Lutheran,146.
St. Pierre,Earl,112,127.
Sallee,George,59;Gilbert, 195;Maud,62.
Salmons,Wendell,57;Zelma, 76,149,161,166.
Sand Creek school,199,200.
Sanders,F.M.,118;Helen,60; Pauline,54.
Sands,Daisy,156;George,158; John,158;Noble,156;W.H., 80,174.
Sandy Hill school,18,168, 169,170.
Sanford,James,25.
Sanks,Mary,120.
Sanner,Bob,121;Clarence,118; David,119;Etta,121;Harriet, 61;Helen,157;Ira,121;John, 61;Lawrence,121;Martha,121; Naomi,119;Nellie,121;Robert, 121.
Sapperfield,Stewart,116,187.
Sappin,Joseph,182.
Sargent,?,142;C.M.,141.
Sarver,Goldie,124,125;John, 61;Thomas,62,95,100.
Sawyer,Georgia,38.
Sayers,Flora,153.
Sayler,Elden,71.
Schabbing,Joe,42.
Schafer,Vesta,85.
Schahrer,Lucille,173;Nettie, 197;Velma,175.
Scheef,Anna,138,147;John,147.
Schempf,Charley,194;Katie,194.
Schintzer,Belle,163.
Schlack,Homer,161;Lena,162.
Schlobohm,Irma,125,126;Lucy, 188.

Schmidt,Caroline,33.
Schmitz,Celestine,167;Fred, 110.
Schneider,John,119.
Schoch,Ed,192.
School laws of 1869,3; of 1885,15.
Schrath,Hazel,138.
Schrock,Dan,165;Edwin,165; Peter,165.
Schroll,Caroline,102;Christopher,102.
Schroth,Flossie,146.
Schull,E.D.,106.
Schultz,Celia,147;Faith,48; Frieda,48;Grace,45.
Schum,Clara,20.
Schwarm,Marilyn,107,123.
Schwartz,E.K.,158.
Schwenker,Pearl,183.
Schwereman,Joseph,37.
Schyler,Irl,44.
Science Hill school,204,205.
Scott,Glen,113;J.W.,157,179; James,112;Owen,44;Ruth, 100.
Scovil,Grace,71,103,164.
Scribner,Bessie,124;Clem,124; Cynthia,116.
Scroggins,Nellie,125.
Sealock,Everett,206.
Seaman,George,157;J.O.,157.
Sears,Penelope,40;Pleasant, 40.
Section school,64,65.
Seeley,?,58;H.,61;Pearl,58.
Seibert,Pearl,53,80,118,125, 174.
Seitz,Carlos,195;Carrie,164, 195;Glapha,195;Logan,195; Mary,195;Rosa,195;Rossie, 81.
Selby,James,191.
Sellers,James,196;Thornton, 56.
Selock,Rosalee,87.
Seltzer,Katherine,115.
Seminary building,12,13.
Settles,Jesse,35;Mary,35; Pearl,118.
Severe,Alice,91;Arlena,89; Bell,89;Cemia,89;Cora, 90;Edna,89,90;Gilbert,89; Iva,90;Jessie,89;Martha, 89;Nita,90;Ollie,89;Orlan, 90;Otie,89,108;Rose,90; Stella,89;Vern,89.
Severns,S.,55,64.
Sexson,Charles,204;Edna,44; Green B.,34;Isaac,32;Morgan F.,33;Perry,32;W.A., 34;Wm.D.,115.
Shaddock,Paul,118.
Shadows,Glen,31.
Shafer,Eliza,203;George,44; Nio,35.
Shaff,Dwight,110.
Shaffer,Agnes,133;Helen,77, 127,131;Henry,138;Trela, 189;Willie,189.
Shallenberger,Edwin,161;Flora,44;H.C.,143.
Shanholtzer,Amos,143;Eliza., 145;Jefferson,145.
Shanks,Margaret,191;Mr.,114.
Shannon,Dora,159;Ora,159.
Shaw,Daniel,201.
Sharrock,James,191;John,191, 195.
Shasteen,M.E.,161.
Shaw,W.H.,143;Wilma,134.
Shay,John,146.
Sheaks,Beatrice,33,34.
Sheehan,Clem,46.

Sheep Shanks school,57,197, 198.
Sheffler,Myrtle,120;Wm.,119, 120,121.
Shelby County Leader,15.
Shelby County School News,18, 19.
Shelby,W.,80,81.
Shelbyville,95,115.
Shelbyville Centennial,150.
Shelbyville Courthouse,154.
Shelbyville-Springfield road, 171.
Shelbyville township,178.
Sheley,Della,168.
Shell,Harry,67;Jacob,67;Jesse,67.
Shempf,Anna,177;Marie,80,177.
Shepherd,Florence,128,129; Frank,50;J.C.,103;Mary,118; Thomas,118.
Sherburn,Ettie,67.
Sherroll,Ethel,204;Phynea,204.
Sherwood,Gertie,66;Irene,80; James,66;Lura,66;Wayne,69, 143,244.
Sheumaker,Charley,156;Oscar, 156.
Shewmaker,?,142.
Shippy,Kate,131.
Shirley,Faraba,45.
Shoaff,Mary,158.
Shoeberger,W.W.,202.
Shoemaker,Dora,38;Helen,156.
Shouse,Nancy,187.
Shrader,Carl,134.
Shride,Cora,127;Mora,128; Noah,128.
Shroll,George,103.
Shuck,D.A.,206;John,200.
Shuff,Arthur,87;Burl,191; Roy,95,97,135;Wm.,91.
Shull,Clara,110;Clarence, 165;Dede,76;W.R.,85,95.
Shumaker,E.M.,114;Joe,48.
Shumard,Amos,209;Blanche, 209;Earl,139;Nona,135.
Shumway, 135.
Shutt,Doris,114;John,86; Preston,86;Virginia,87.
Sibbett,Anna,195;Mrs.Charles,195.
Sickels,Wm.,72;Mary,100.
Siebert,Emma,190.
Siegfried,George,177.
Silknitter,Ethel,54.
Silvers,Ed,92.
Simmen,Mr.,144.
Simmon,Nellie,31,36.
Simmons,Audrey,177;Eber,73; Ellis,115,149,153,165,166; James,73;Lunly,73;Mary,73; Nellie,138;Perry,73;Sarah, 205;Steve,73;Wm.,73.
Simon,David,75.
Simons,A.,191.
Simonson,Augusta,46;Martin, 46.
Simpson,?,124;Alfred,51; Clara,58;Ellis,199,200;Fritts,193,197;James,57,58; John,61;Mary,71,195,196; O.P.,106;Russell,54;Tilda, 110.
Sims,Baldwin,128;Beverly,128; Clyde,130;Edward,130;Estel, 126;John,128;Marie,130;Mary, 130;Millard,128;Ralph,130; Vivian,126,130,131;W.H.,43.
Singer,Ella,174;Ellen,194; Margaret,160.
Sisk,Acle,196;Clarence,194; George,105.
Sitler,Austin,81,95;Jacob, 181,183;Thomas,181,182.

Skidmore,Eli,148;John,201; Maggie,163;Roy,114A;Soprona,201;Wilber,114A.
Slater,Sidney,110;W.T.,110.
Slifer,George,33;Roy,99.
Sloan,Bertha,127;Betty,172; Charley,127;Docie,110.
Small,Aaron,149;Erma,150; Gussie,151;Henry,119,158; John,152;Minnie,150;Nettie,159.
Smallsued,George,71.
Smart,A.T.,60;Agnes,109; Allen,62;Bessie,56,58,54, 60;C.A.,148;Celesta,56; Donald,57;F.L.,51;John, 109;Mary,110;Mattie,60; Orthel,58,56.
Smiley,Pauline,167.
Smith,Alice,65,92;Allen,155; Alta,191;Belle,32;Bessie, 81;Beulah,152;Blanche,159; Bona,89,90;Bud,159;C.L., 176;Carrol,191;Chester,108; Clarence,90;Clay,134,158; Cleta,175;Clyde,91;Dan A., Jr.,150;Daniel,172,175; Doris,77;Earl,90;Ed.,66,61, 92,95;Edith,128,150;Edna, 159;Ella,85,187;Elmer,54,55, 56,59,66,87,173,191;Elza, 114,161;Emma,150;Florence, 170;Floyd,191;Forrest,159; Frank,150;Fred,55;G.H.,118; Genevieve,158;Gerald,182; Gladys,89;Glen,126;H.B.,91; Harvey,91;Hence,155;Hugh, 46;Irene,88,90,161;Jesse, 106;John,158;Joseph,7,191; Juanita,87;Lawrence,120, 148,149,158,159;Lyla,101; Lloyd,55;Lucille,165;Lyla, 81,173;Mabel,127,143,207; Mary,42,45,149,155;Maude, 128;Maureen,87;May,109, 126,159;Michael,40;Moses, 106;Myrtie,128;Nancy,157; Nellie,56,100,150;Noah, 95;Nora,130;Norman,84,85, 86,94;Orin,159;Ruby,145; Ruby P.,68;Samuel,191;Sarah, 158,175;Sofa,84,85,133,181; Wm.,197;Winand,109;Z.B., 32;Zebedee,191;Zelma,172, 175.
Smith school, 191.
Smock,Onita,78,79,126.
Snapp,Frank,55,125,180,182, 195.
Snell,F.P.,80;W.H.,77,80.
Snow,Richard,61;Thomas,61.
Snyder,Blanchette,80;Carrie, 91;Grace,81;Lula,80;Sylvia, 59;W.J.,81.
Soliday,H.P.,42.
South,Frank,77,87.
Spain,John,42.
Spannagel,Chris,33;Henry,33; Z.,164.
Spare,Hart,99.
Sparks,Amaziah,99;H.D.,19; Harry R.,96.
Sparks college,183.
Spears,Emma,85;Henry,168; T.M.,143.
Specht,Carolyn,100,182;Lyle, 64,169;Peter,197.
Speiser,Emma,175.
Spence,A.W.,76;Annette,208; Arthur,76;Edna,76;M.,76; Wm.,122.
Spencer County, Ind.,131.
Spencer,Annette,208;Hazel,205; Joe,208;Stella,130.

Sphar,Dorothy,58;Herman,58;
 J.W.,52.
Spicer,Akillis,112;Alta,117;
 Maude,112;Philemon,112.
Spidle,Ada,195.
Spitler,Jeff,120.
Spockwell,Lucie,59.
Spracklin,Adaline,66;George,
 66;John,55,128,163,164,168,
 169,195;Stella,72.
Spring,Eliza.,58;Frederick,58.
Springer,Barbara,165;Martha,
 152.
Spring,Rachel,58.
Springs,Hazel,92,93.
Springstun,C.E.,170,193.
Sprinkel,Eli,191.
Spurgeon,James,54;Lloyd,59;
 Lowell,59.
Spurgin,F.M.,52.
Staehle,Florence,133.
Stairwalt,Effie,92;Leslie,
 85;Emma,92;Leslie,182.
Staley,J.T.,108.
Standard school guidelines,
 5.
Standley,Earl,127;Maud,127;
 Pearl,127.
Stanfield,Jo.,100,137.
Stapleton,John,3,5,12,13,14;
 Joseph,12;Nancy,12;Wm.,12.
Stark school,56,57,58.
Steagall,Minnie,74.
Steck,Harry,182.
Steed,W.S.,207.
Steele,John,163;Lloyd,65;
 Melvin,67,98;Nadene,31;
 202;Vernon,65,87,91;W.G.,
 115;Wade,209;Wm.,65,87,
 170.
Stegmeyer,Lillie,76.
Steidley,A.J.,77,126;Carrie,
 159.
Stephens,Dutch,109;G.W.,
 163;Helen,85,127,171;Lorna,
 136,170;Margaret,181;S.R.,
 173;Virginia,153.
Stephenson,Theodore,36.
Stevens,Clarinda,201;Earl,
 208;Edward,109;Marie,188;
 Oliver,135;Thomas,110.
Stevenson,John,95;Michael,
 51.
Steward,Will,166,186.
Stewardson,134,135,184.
Stewardson,Agnes,133;Bruce,
 183;Charles,180;Elza,183;
 G.S.,160;Harlie,180;Har-
 ry,127;James,28;John,28;
 Myrtle,183;Nellie,187;
 Sarah,180;T.H.,183;Thomas,
 28,29,180;Wm.,143.
Stewart,Belle,121;Edith,121;
 J.A.,119;James,102;Liz,
 194;M. Wayne,102;Mayetta,
 74;Samuel,118;Willie,194.
Stiene,Charles,133.
Stilebouer,?,177;Chester,145;
 Eliza.,143;Goldie,163;H.W.,
 191,195;Harry,162;Hester,
 145;Homer,174,176,177,197;
 O.H.,53.
Stillwell,Marie,165.
Stine,H.B.,205;Jemina,91;
 Vida,86;W.B.,45,47,112.
Stiner,Charles,81;Karl,81.
Stitt,Minnie,76.
Stockdale,Florence,54,76;John,
 71,99,191,197;Mabel,128,194;
 Mary,166;Olive,163,166;Sol-
 omon,166.
Stoddard,Myrtle,157.
Stokes,Diana,122.
Stombaugh,Bernice,81;Lynn,103.
Stone,Florence,108;Prof,16.

Stoneburner,Dorothy,58;Frank-
 lin,57;George,162;John,59;
 Lena,56,57;Linzie,59.
Storey,Moses,1,50,178.
Storm,Arthur,33,181;Bess,32,
 44;Charles,48,146;Clint,
 35;D.L.,32,33;David,40;
 Dean,40;Donnie,44;Edgar,
 44;Eliza.,44;Elza,47;Grace,
 44;Grover,44;Guy,34;Guy V.,
 44,45;George,32;Guy V.,33;
 H.J.,35;Hal,35;Harry,44;
 Hazel,31;Hiram,24,33;Inez,
 200,207;Isaac,33;J.O.,35;
 James,44;John,40,44;James
 L.,34;Jane,35;Lester,44;
 Lillie,31,32;Margaret,44,
 134;Marie,35,38;Nellie,44;
 Oscar,44,143,144,145,147,
 179,180;Otis,35;Re,44;Reta,
 35;S.B.,133;T.G.,32;Truman,
 40;Vincent,31,32;W.A.,85,86,
 92,183;W.L.,31;Wm.,44;Wm.A.,
 33,84;Wm.B.,44;Zach,40.
Story,A.A.,76;George,75.
Strader,Nel,38.
Stradly,John,24.
Strain,John,56,60,54,109;Min-
 nie,60,197;Virginia,59,62.
Streng,Eva,33.
Stretch,George,162;Nellie,
 196,197.
Stringtown,68.
Stripling,Fanny,25;Jackson,
 25;Melinda,25.
Strohl,Ervin,85,88,90,91,96,
 97;Grace,170;Ina,207;Noah,
 86,88,89,91,134;Roy,95,114,
 142,168,170,185,186;Sam,91,
 95,170,179;Sylvia,180.
Struble,Roy,192.
Stuart,James,6.
Stump,Carrie,103,130;Glen,
 127;Jacob,126;Leta,125,127;
 Rolla,127.
Stumpf,Daniel,158;Sophia,170.
Sturgeon,Bernice,177,195;Ed-
 win,170;Inabelle,172.
Sturgis,Okla,165.
Sudbrink,Agnes,131.
Sudkamp,Ben.,47.
Suey,Wm.,106.
Sullivan,George,68.
Summers,Bernadine,90;Free-
 man,89,90;Georgia,87,186,
 200;Grace,89,92;L.D.,92;
 Marie,90;Maureen,87;Mor-
 ris,87;Opal,68,88,89;Ray,
 91;Ruby,89.
Summitt school,55.
Sunnyside school,78,79,80.
Supranowski,Casamira,96;
 Charles,96;George,96;R.J.,
 99.
Sutton,Elias,26;L.H.,26;Sam-
 antha,26.
Swain,Ethel,142,146.
Swallow,Annie,50;S.P.,164.
Swamp Angel school,193,194.
Swander,Naries,50.
Swank,Fern,138.
Swanker,Mrs.,130.
Swanson,James,178;Jasper,
 46.
Swartz,Dessie,127;Katherine,
 151;Leda,128;Roy,127.
Sweazy,Sarah,152.
Sweeney,Daniel,197;J.N.,197;
 John,175;Ronnie,195.
Swengle,Jennie,32,33,36,133;
 John,38;Reuben,35.
Swiney,John,107;Leta,206.
Swinford,Deana,201.
Swope,Louisa,96.

Syfert,Blanche,130;Edward,177;
 Elmer,95;Frances,167;Fred,
 100;George,100,166;Greta,
 126;Hattie,108;John,131;Leah,
 28;Levi,28;Lillie,108;Mary,
 28;Michael,166;Milton,99;
 Rachel,28;Raymond,131;Tony,
 166;Wm.,131;Willie,86.
Sylvan school,68,69,86,87,88,
 89,90,108,110,183.

Tabbert,Beulah,133;Carl,172;
 Charles,172;Hannah,172;
 Walter,45.
Tabor,Elsie,173,174;Vinnie,
 187;Wm.,189.
Tallman,Benj.,164.
Taniges,Eliza.,109;Elma,62,
 109;John,109;Mary,109.
Tankersley,Carl,81,173,177;
 Warren,81.
Tanner,John,6;Stevanna,85.
Tate,Orthel,109.
Taylor,Clyde,74;Dorothy,130;
 Eliza.,201;George,76;Leav-
 itt,121;Lewis,125;Margery,
 119,120;May,121;Minerva,
 73;Myra,67;Myrtle,170;Ray,
 142;Wm.,71.
Teater,Wm.,45.
Teegardin,Abraham,86;Catherine,
 86.
Tefft,Mary,35.
Temman,Frank,110.
Templeton,George,31;Roy,32.
Terrell,Daniel,127.
Terry,Ed,84,85;George,114.
Texas,144.
Textbooks of 1877,14.
Thenor,Margaret,38.
Thom,W.R.,65,67.
Thomas,Alice,140;Calvin,75;
 Clark,164;Cordia,76;Earl,
 182;Ella,53,180;F.M.,76;
 Isaac,181;James,77,155;John,
 181;Lena,64,153;Leona,126;
 Louis,85,95;Mary,181;Mattie,
 175;Mildred,163;Nora,183;
 Oliver,183;Omer,32,38,133,
 189;Ruth,143;S.D.,84;Wm.,
 155.
Thomason,Eliza,166;Lucille,
 125.
Thompson,A.H.,67;A.W.,197;
 Adeline,126;Alva,45,52,
 112,173,174,175,191;Clara,
 71;D.L.,180;Helen,164;G.M.,
 123;G.R.,34;H.B.,123;Howard,
 126;J.C.,101;J.G.,125;Joseph,
 53;Leonard,146;Lucille,81;
 Mill,64;Mrs. Ava,201;Ruth,
 106,165;Sarah,86;Sheldon,50,
 54,53,56.
Thorn,R.W.,71,72.
Thornton,Anthony,10;R.C.,
 84;W.F.,6;W.W.,186.
Thornton school,186.
Throckmorton,Charles,143;Otto,
 144,145.
Tice,C.E.,161;Clarence,161;
 LaRue,143.
Tilley,Ada,81;Eliza,35;Mer-
 rell,175;James,51,54,192,193;
 Maude,197;S.,194;Sanford,197;
 Sue,194;Truman,192.
Timperley,Charlotte,95,181;
 Henry,137.
Tipsword family,111.
Todd,John,6;Wm.,6.
Todds Point township,187.
Tohill,Cynthia,152;Ella,150;
 John,152.
Tolly Cemetery,122.

Tolly,Charley,126;Cornelius, 125;George,76;James,192; John,124;Jonathon,125;Martha,192;Roy,126;Samuel,125.
Tolson,Mark,102;Richard,103; Wayne,80.
Torrence,Ann,91;Daniel,53; Elias,197;Ethel,74;F.C., 65;Lola,100;T.C.,71,73.
Totten,Dorothy,188.
Towell,Glenda,109.
Tower Hill,191.
Tower Hill township,190.
Townsend,Fern,77.
Trainor,Rosa,78.
Travis,Alva,85,91;Byron,85, 168,170;H.R.,85;James, 119.
Tressler,Catherine,32;George,115,196;Golda,66,120, 123,195;James,53;Jetty, 72,124,195;Lillian,55,59, 67,68,71,74,109,123,125, 169,187;Mary,56;Myrtle, 134;Samuel,56;V.,32.
Triece,Isaac,135;Nettie,108.
Trigg,Alma,189.
Tripp,David,175;Effie,108; Homer,90;John,95.
Trout,C.E.,169;Floyd,151.
Trowbridge school,47.
Truitt,A.C.,122;David,112, 114.
Trulock,Doris,78.
Truscott,George,194.
Tucker,Annabelle,96;Hadley, 73;Maude,166;Maxine,172; Mrs.,195;Nita,51;Pauline, 177.
Tull,Ada,138;Bertha,32,185; Bessie,206;Clarence,207; Claudie,161;Dale,202;Eliza, 21;J.B.,207;J.M.,205;J.W., 207;James,92;Jesse,37,84; John,86,87,114,135,143, 206;Lola,188,189,204;Morris,202;Nathan,128;Sally, 207;Thomas,207;Vada,202; Victoria,128.
Turner,?,142;Alsuma,33;Bertie, 99;F.C.,44;Frank,59,62; Gladys,107;Isaac,85;J.L.B., 141;M.,52;M.L.,108;Marion, 59,60,62;Mabel,100;N.C., 146.
Turney,B.F.,113;Carrie,153; Cora,153;Felix,112;Ruth, 112,150;Whitfield,113.
Turney school,111,112.
Turrentine,Alan,207;Alma,108.
Tyler,Maude,120.
Tym,Charles,120.

Uhl,Clara,128.
Ulmer,Alice,134;Andrew,34,37; Caroline,33;Gilbert,134; Jacob,33;Mathias,33;Nelle, 145;Ralph,143;Sophia,37.
Ulrich,A.J.,113.
Union school,47,128,129,130.
Updegraff,Matilda,156.
Uphoff,Gilbert,188.
Upper Lakey Bend,111.
Urfer,Virgil,197.
Utterback,Sarah,24.

Vail,Ella,99.
Valentine,Anna,64,65;Jarvis, 29;Mary,28.
Valley school,69,100.
Vandament,John,134;Martha,134.
Vanderen,J.M.,35,42;Stephen, 33,36,38.
Vanderpool,Carrie,65;Minnie, 65,175.

Van Hise,Martha,86,91.
Van Reed,Ethel,68,161.
Van Syckel,John,81.
Veech,Mary,37,43,46.
Veisure,Jean,64;Elsie, 73,74;Josephine,163.
Venters,Daniel,182;David,181; Elred,31;George,181,182; Levit,181;Perry,183;Roy,183.
Vermillion,J.W.,175.
Vert,J.T.,102.
Vest,F.P.,110.
Victor school,69,177,178.
Victory school,123,159.
Vincent,Connie,52,195;Wilma, 177.
Virden,John,79;Willis,79.
Vits,George,106.
Vogel,Albert,133;Nita,143; Titus,98.
Voiles,Frank,84,85,164;Gracie,166;Leland,166.
Von Behren,Elverna,138;Wm., 133.
Voorhees,John,109.
Voris,George,95;Sophia,95.
Vouderheide,?,42.
Vulmer,Magdalene,18.

Wabash railroad,146.
Wabash school,45.
Wackley,Mary,113.
Waddell,Alice,126.
Wade,Alice,200;Allie,67;Andrew,134;Carrie,106;Charles, 108;George,71;Grace,67; James,45;John,92;Lucy,196; Orrie,70;Washburn,190.
Wafford,Clarence,54.
Waggoner,Floyd,180;John,6; Laura,27;N.A.,158,161,164; Norton,128,153,179.
Wagner,A.,158;Clarence,158; Elmer,158;Jessie,126;J., 114;Sylvester,158,175;Sarah,27;Stephen,27.
Waits,Joseph,170.
Wakefields,?,58.
Wakefield settlement,1.
Wakefield,Allen,24,50;Andrew, 24;C.A.,56;Charles,24,66; David,66;Harold,66,67,164; Harve,198;Hattie,56,163, 196,198;John,66;Kelsey,73, 96;Lloyd,51;Mariah,24;Mary, 24;Maud,51,59;Miranda,24; Paul,58,59,66;Pernetta,50; Rachel,24;Roy,66,70,163; Sarah,24;Silas,64.
Wakeland,Margie,42.
Walden,Benjamin,26;Charles, 203;Dewey,204;Grace,204; Harlin,204;Hugh,26,203,204; John,26,199,204;Louisa,26; Marie,204;Minnie,204;Oda, 204;Ruby,186;Wm.,204.
Walden school,203,204.
Walk,Clarence,47;Flossie,36.
Walker,A.E.,143;Angie,170; Charles,202;Ella,163,168, 169,192;Fred,202;G.F.,168; Gideon,64;Walker,H.T.,199; Ida,67,87;J.B.,33,35;J.W., 120;Jim,42,201;M.M.,120; Nellie,136,137,206;Orville, 206;Ralph,120,205;R.M.,207; Rena,138;Thomas,192;W.D., 201,200;Walter,206;Wm.,106.
Walker school,200,201,202.
Wall,Albert,61,78.
Wallace,Anthony,31,32,143; Benj.,199;Berlin,95;C.,87; C.W.,81,95,173,177;Daisy, 32;Deby,85;Fern,206;H.L., 95;J.C.,31,35,36,37,197;

J.E.,101,143;Jacob,33,35,36; Jessie,32,199;Martha,140; Minnie,192;Mollie,80;S.H., 207;S.M.,78,81,82;Vern,170; W. Berlin,114;W.L.,31,118; W.O.,31,33,37;Wm.,86,205.
Walters,Dale,55;Eileen,66; Harvey,196;J.A.,91;John,112; Leone,196;M.F.,181;Wm.,112; W.P.,137.
Walton,Hattie,168,166;J.D., 53.
Waltrip,Claude,204.
Wamsley,Thomas,51.
Wangelin,Wm.,133.
Ward,Benj.,164;Franklin,77; James,127;Laverne,113;Martha,116.
Warner,Andrew,92;Charley,85; F.A.,165;Jacob,114;Lois, 143,159;Mary,122;Paul,175; Pearl,158;Rose,84;Wesley, 85;Wiley,48.
Warnick,Clemie,53,54,67,125, 174,195;Lucy,53.
Warren,Beatrice,196;Cora,57; Della,47,199,201;E.F.,193; Florence,99,117;Frank,208; Ida,85;J.R.,195;J.T.,207; John,161,191,193,195;L.,192; Otis,192,197;Nelson,193; P.P.,207;P.T.,207;Pearl A., 70;Peter,207;Samuel,99; Sarah,99,W.W.,207;Ward,207.
Warthman,Walter,114A.
Washburn,T.S.,196.
Washer,Danny,139;Ervin,139, 140;Nathan,139,140.
Washington school,69,135.
Water Oak school,42.
Watkins,Raymond,40.
Watson,Clara,42,110;David, 31;J.W.,81;Lenora,59,108; Mr.,108;Norma,196;Opal,110; T.T.,80.
Watterson,Anna,195.
Watts,Goldie,85;Mabel,85.
Waymire,Harriet,27;James,27; Jane,27.
Weakly,Altie,128,157;Alva,157; Bessie,127;Earl,159;Erma, 128;Hazel,158;Homer,148; Howard,130;Iola,150;James, 161;John,153;Kathleen,182, 195;Leverett,159;Marjorie, 172;Ms.,195;Otis,159;Ray, 148;Roy,159;Robert,159; Ruth,150,159,160;Sadie,159; Samuel,148;Virginia,172; Wm.,153.
Wear,Barbara,140.
Weatherspoon,Samuel,42.
Weaver,George,56,60,108,196; Grace,107;Hazel,107;Mildred, 107;Myrtle,107;S.R.,106.
Webb,?,142;Amy,48.137;Everett, 40;Raymond,40;Stella,40; Truman,188.
Weber,Alma,177;Bertha,177; Evelyn,176;F.G.,177;Fred, 177;George,134;Harry,177; Helen,33;Jacob,177;John, 177;Lester,36;Mary,197;Michael,136;Mollie,177;W.H.,133.
Weeks,Lois,197.
Weger,John,199,207.
Weidner,Johanna,147.
Weir,Cora,128;Ella,128;Enos, 128.
Welch,Amadell,91;Charles,107; Gertrude,54.
Weller,John,196.
Wells,Bert,196;Iva,183.
Welsh,Paul,110.

Welton,Emma,87;Francis,85,
    134;John,134;Mary,183;
    Walter,85.
Wempen,Mildred,76;Ralph,76;
    Rose,76.
Wemple,Genevieve,172;H.M.,
    172;Mary,172;Maxine,172;
    Pauline,172;Raymond,172;
    Ruth,172;Samuel,172;Wayne,172.
Wendling,F.B.,95;Michael,
    162.
West Center school,118,119.
West,John,201;Melpha,201.
Westenhaver,Ezra,86;Jean,
    87;Joseph,86;Pauline,
    87;Ray,181;Tour,86.
Westervelt,158,183.
West Liberty school,186.
West Salem school,21,157,
    182,183,184.
Wetzel,Bain,164;Benj.,79;
    Nellie,79;Rheem,79.
Whaley,Eliza.,192;George,
    174.
Whately,Charles,99.
Wheat,Charley,85,134,138,158,
    166;Emogene,87;Everett,87;
    Fern,87;Kenneth,87;Margaret,85;Ruby,155,157,184;Stanley,85.
Wheatley,Bertha,151;Ralph,80.
Wheeler,Ben,164;Betty,196;
    Frank,164;Loral,164;Paul,
    87.
Whipple,Rosana,80,173.
Whitacre,Clyde,85;Doyle,85;
    Grace,205;Ralph,160.
Whitan,Prestley,100.
White,?,112;A.F.,98;Clytheria,
    21;Frank,201,202;George,40,
    133;James,98,168;Mildred,
    98;Norma,73;Ulysses,21,114;
    W.D.,36;W.Frank,5,21,22,33,
    143,146,166,167,168,170.
White Hall school,161.
White Oak school,59,60.
White school,97,98,99.
Whitehead,L.C.,103.
Whitfield,Silas,64;Willis,148.
Whitlatch,Joshua,143;Nancy,
    143;W.W.,143.
Whitlatch school,143,144,145.
Whitmer,Catherine,140;Henry,
    140;Mary,146.
Whitnerhouse,Thomas,106.
Whittington,H.C.,60;Norma,110.
Wicker,Margaret,198;Mary,198;
    Nancy,198;Virginia,198.
Widdersheim,Henry,47;Wm.,44.
Wiersum,Henry,43.
Wiggens,Anna,180;Daisy,102,125,
    134,150,151,169,180,189.
Wildcat school,37.
Wildermuth,Eli,90.
Wilhelm,Lelah,80,158;Nannie,
    37,40,105,205;Wm.,180,184.
Will,Rose,47.
Willard,Ella,115.
Willey,Agnes,99,161,181.
Willhelm,John,146.
Williams,Alma,135;Arlyn,136;
    Arthur,163,166;Baylis,50;
    Dee,96;Dick,96;Dow,96,135;
    Eliza.,24;Floyd,200;Frank,
    188;G.W.,84;Gladys,85;Helen,139;Henry,165;Iola,47;
    J.D.,136;J.F.,80,117;J.M.,
    95,135,134,137;J.P.,55;
    James,24,85;L.Dow,73,84,92,
    85,86,93,95,182;L.P.,56;
    Lottie,164;Lura,21;M.B.,
    133,136;Marie,124,133;
    Monroe,135,136;Morris,92,
    91,100;N.,11;Nevad,97;Owen,
    84;Pearl,84,85;Rose,161,170;
    Russel,164;Ruth,87,161,163;
    S.M.,84;Stella,138;Vernon,
    87,92,134,135,158;Warren,54,
    61,21,64,71,84,93,91,96,95,
    133,134,135,138,205.
Williamsburg,50.
Williamson, ?,142;Delmar,206;
    Edith,206;Elmer,143,206;
    Ethel,201;Helen,160;Juanita,
    205;Lola,206.
Williford,J.V.,118.
Willit,John,112.
Willoughby,Maryl,153.
Wills,John,99.
Wilmer,Anna,110.
Wilson,Anna,84;B.F.,84;Bertha,
    164;Byron,202;C.W.,47,138;
    Carrie,150;Charles,95;Clara,
    95;Claude,37;Cliff,143;E.F.,
    40,44,45;Edith,156;Edna,46;
    Emma,92,170;Ethel,117,158;
    Frank,85,91;Gracie,161;Ida,
    86;James,113;Laura,137,139;
    Lucille,37,43,47;Mauda,162;
    May,85;Minnie,85,87,95;Ora,
    156;Ruth,35;S.W.,86,182;
    Thomas,85,91,95,148;Velma,
    189;Walter,162;Wm.,38.
Wimberly,S.,106.
Winchester,Linnie,148,149;
    Thad,148.
Windsor township,199.
Winnings,David,152;Enid,152,
    172;J.J.,150;John,152;Joyce,80,123,152;Kenneth,38;
    Lawrence,151,152;Lewis,150,
    152;Morris,40.
Winson,Frank,180;Helen,116;
    Lina,180;Mary,180;Pearl,
    161,168.
Wireck,Minnie,91.
Wirey,John,191;Leone,176;
    Wm.,191,197.
Wirth,Dewey,133.
Wise,Leah,121;Solomon,119.
Wittenberg,Albert,138;Edward,
    138;Henry,138;Winnogean,
    135.
Wolf,Ann,122;Chloe,77;Michael,
    77;Ralph,95.
Wolfely,George,51.
Wollard,Joel,109.
Wolverton,Jessie,136.
Womack,John,31.
Wonus,Jacob,68;Rose,67.
Wood,Irene,189;W.L.,207.
Woodard,Elouise,55;Lyle,55.
Woodrow,Walter,187,188,189.
Woods,Clarabel,107;John,11;
    Katie,189;Ralph,116.
Woodward,Charles,148;Laura,
    129,131.
Woolard,Bernice,109;Celestine,55,60,109;Oran,109.
Woolen,Russel,148.
Wooters,Carl,77;Dorothy,
    149;Glen,78;Lawrence,125;
    Mary,77;W.F.,80.
Workman,Beulah,126;Eliza.,
    124;Will,81;Oscar,173;
    Raymond,114.
Worland,Hugh,46;S.F.,42.
Worley,Amanda,38;H.B.,36,38;
    Jennie,53,170;John,35,36;
    Lou,170;Rose,161,163.
Worley school,38.
Worthman,Mollie,157.
Wortman,Clover,88,90,156,155,
    157,163;Emma,65,85,92;Florence,159;Frank.170;Hazel,
    130,188;Henry,90;Isaac,
    68,87,88,95,153,158,170;
    James,112;M.,92;Thomas,164,
    170,85;W.F.,51;W.T.,170.
Wright,Carl,76;Carrie,155;
    Cloyd,71;Dudley,187;Effie,
    84;Eva,192;George,123,127;
    H.W.,113;Hubert,187;James,
    76,112,182;Just,80,173;
    Kathryn,101;Lela,77;Lena,
    123,125,127;Levi,116;Lucille,38;Mary,187;Minerva,
    134;Nannie,188;Robert,187;
    Samuel,187;Sarah,76;W.D.,
    84;W.P.,137;Wm.,187;Znobia,
    109.
Wright school,76.
Wyatt,Roy,119.
Wychoff,Charles,79;Ina,103.
Wydick,Mrs.,180.

Yakey,Art,157;Floyd,163;
    Jacob,137;James,170;Wm.,
    91.
Yantis,Cyrus,112;Daniel,130,
    126;Harley,128;Leroy,128;
    Melvin,113;Portia,125,128,
    130;Ralph,128;Solomon,128;
    Winnie,131.
Yantis school,122.
Yantisville,122,128,130.
Yarbrough,Edna,134;Jack,134.
Yates,Zora,110.
Yencer,John,182.
Yoakum,Margaret,206.
York,Charles,84,137;Laura,
    137,161,163;M.H.,136;Mary,
    95;Mildred,146.
Yost,Allie,170;Amanda,158;
    Chance,158;David,149;
    John,158;Mamie,149;Mary,
    158;Oscar,158;Rhoda,158.
Young,Abe,142;B.J.,53,65,
    91;Brigam,85;David,191;
    Florence,51;Gorden,110;
    Lulu,136;Matt,170;P.W.,
    53;Samuel,46.
Younger,Rachel,124;Ruby,
    189,190.
Younker,Virgil,81.

Zalman,Henry,135.
Zalman school,135,136.
Zanders,Mary,123.
Ziegler,Jacob,99.
Zimmer,Ernest,31,36,43;Jacob,
    35,36;Jennie,36,38;Nellie,
    33,36,134;Nelson,38;Philip,
    38;R.H.,44,45;Robert,31,36,
    37,133,180;Will,35,36.

www.ingramcontent.com/pod-product-compliance
Lightning Source LLC
Chambersburg PA
CBHW080547230426
43663CB00015B/2746